Trading Freedom

Trading Freedom

HOW TRADE WITH CHINA DEFINED EARLY AMERICA

Dael A. Norwood

The University of Chicago Press

CHICAGO AND LONDON

PUBLICATION OF THIS BOOK HAS BEEN AIDED BY A GRANT FROM THE BEVINGTON FUND.

The University of Chicago Press, Chicago 60637
The University of Chicago Press, Ltd., London
© 2022 by The University of Chicago
Published 2022
Printed in the United States of America

31 30 29 28 27 26 25 24 23 22   1 2 3 4 5

ISBN-13: 978-0-226-81558-9 (cloth)
ISBN-13: 978-0-226-81559-6 (e-book)
DOI: https://doi.org/10.7208/chicago/9780226815596.001.0001

Library of Congress Cataloging-in-Publication Data

Names: Norwood, Dael A., author.
Title: Trading freedom : how trade with China defined early America / Dael A. Norwood.
Other titles: American beginnings, 1500–1900.
Description: Chicago : University of Chicago Press, 2022. | Series: American beginnings, 1500–1900 | Includes bibliographical references and index.
Identifiers: LCCN 2021019314 | ISBN 9780226815589 (cloth) | ISBN 9780226815596 (ebook)
Subjects: LCSH: United States—Commerce—China. | China—Commerce—United States. | United States—Relations—China. | China—Relations—United States.
Classification: LCC HF3128 .N67 2022 | DDC 382.0973/051—dc23
LC record available at https://lccn.loc.gov/2021019314

♾ This paper meets the requirements of ANSI/NISO Z39.48-1992 (Permanence of Paper).

IN MEMORY OF MY FATHER, DAN NORWOOD.
IN HONOR OF MY MOTHER, PHYLLIS HUMPHREY NORWOOD.
AND FOR MICHELLE, ALWAYS.

Contents

America's Business with China

FIGURE 1. An early nineteenth-century view of the "Floating City" on the Pearl River (Zhujiang) at Canton (Guangzhou), with the foreign factories in the background. William Daniell, *The European Factories, Canton*, 1806, oil on canvas, https:// collections.britishart.yale.edu/catalog/tms:720, Yale Center for British Art, Paul Mellon Collection, B1981.25.210.

Fifty-seven years after he visited Canton (Guangzhou), Thomas Handasyd Perkins remembered the riverboats vividly. Craft "of all sizes, from a canoe" to vessels holding "fifty persons or more" crowded the waterways of the busy cosmopolitan city on the Pearl River, impressing and disorienting the young Boston merchant. Just twenty-five when he visited Canton, Perkins had spent nearly his entire life in the port cities of the Atlantic world, where harbors forested with masts were a familiar sight. But Canton's junks, barges, and sampans he pronounced beyond reckoning. "These boats of all descriptions," he told his children, "may be termed Legion—such is their number."[1]

Perkins never again visited China after that first trip, which he made as the supercargo for the Salem ship *Astrea* in 1789–90, but it makes sense that it was a river view that stuck with him in his later years. For foreign merchants like him, a visit to China was primarily an experience of navigating the curves, customs, and regulations of the Pearl River. Screened from the open ocean by sixty miles of inland navigation, Canton was the only Qing port open to foreign traders, who could access it only during the annual trading season (late summer to early winter), and only if they successfully negotiated the physical and bureaucratic hurdles that interrupted the river's course. The "Canton system"—foreigners' name for the way the Qing Empire organized and regulated foreign trade—produced a peculiarly riparian perspective on China, at least among Americans.

Although citizens of the new republic first encountered the Canton system near its high tide, it had emerged piecemeal over the early eighteenth century, the result of negotiations between the employees of European East India companies, local Chinese merchants, and Qing imperial officials. Never perfect or complete in execution or design, it functioned flexibly for nearly a century and a half before the conflagration of the First Opium War (1839–42) destroyed it, replacing it with the "Treaty Port" system, named for the treaties that Western powers forced on the Chinese "opening" dozens of ports to foreign traders. Although later in life Perkins played a role in destroying the Canton system, when he arrived in 1789 it was still in full operation.

Foreign trading ships like Perkins's *Astrea* entered the system at Macao, the Portuguese colony perched at the southwestern edge of the mouth of the Pearl River Delta. After procuring a pilot and completing the paperwork necessary to enter Qing territory proper, vessels proceeded upriver to Whampoa, Canton's anchorage for large foreign ships. Sailors were generally restricted to this area except when on leave, but merchants and ship captains continued on, traveling another dozen miles upriver to the "factories," the small foreign quarter southwest of Canton's walls, hard on the banks of the Pearl River. Combining warehouse space with offices and apartments for "factors" (merchants), the rented factories, or hongs, were where the business of the China trade got done. They were also, not incidentally, the cramped terminus of the commercial bureaucracy that surveilled and supplied visiting traders. A variety of Chinese-manned riverboats connected these points—offering different travel speeds

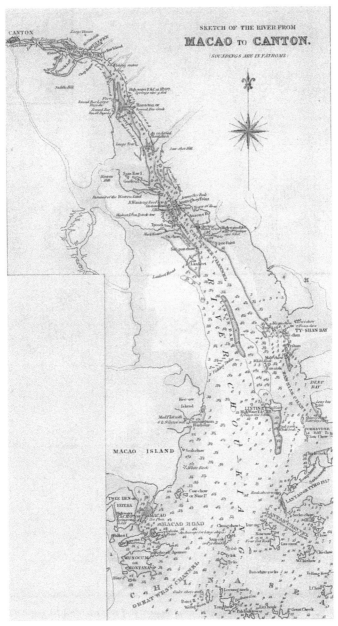

FIGURE 2. A detailed sketch of the Pearl River Delta, with key points in the China trade marked, including Macao, Lintin Island, Whampoa, and Canton. Edward Belcher and John Walker, *Canton and Its Approaches, Macao and Hong Kong*, 1856, https://purl.stanford.edu/sw365qv6908, courtesy of David Rumsey Map Collection, David Rumsey Map Center, Stanford Libraries.

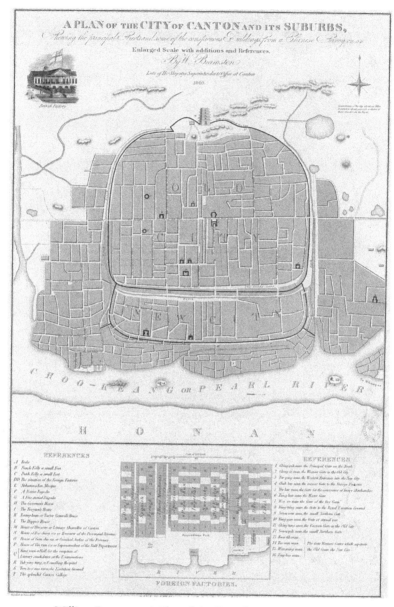

FIGURE 3. William Bramston, *A Plan of the City of Canton and Its Suburbs*, 1840.
https://gallica.bnf.fr/ark:/12148/btv1b531192710, Bibliothèque nationale de France.

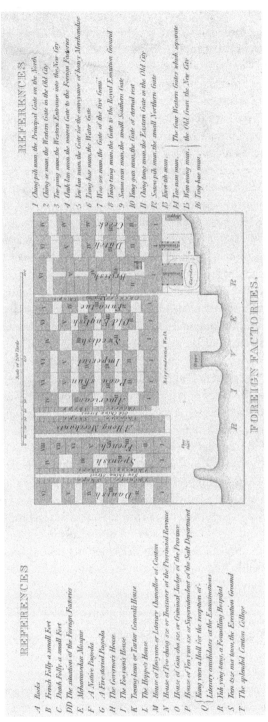

FIGURE 4. The neighborhood of the "foreign factories," the small suburban zone to which foreign merchants were restricted under the Canton system. William Bramston, *A Plan of the City of Canton and Its Suburbs*, 1840, https://gallica.bnf.fr/ark:/12148/btv1b53119271o. Bibliothèque nationale de France.

at different prices—and a chain of fortresses and customs houses staffed by officials working for Guangdong's provincial governor-general and Canton's customs superintendent (the Hoppo) oversaw travel between Macao, Whampoa, and Canton using patrols, checkpoints, and a system of sealed and stamped documents (chops).[2]

Designed to simultaneously foster and control international trade, the Canton system restricted foreigners to specific zones and compelled them to rely on a suite of licensed commercial professionals. Pilots guided ships to anchor, linguists mediated with customs authorities, and compradors provided provisions. Most important were hong merchants, members of the merchant guild, the Cohong, deputized by the government to guarantee foreign traders' tax payments. Large-scale traders, they mediated between traders and the Hoppo, rented out factory and wharf space, and bought and sold cargoes. Hong merchants were foreign traders' closest associates, at once their customers, suppliers, and peers—and sometimes men they regarded as friends, at least when it was to their advantage.

When Perkins became a temporary resident of the "Floating City" in 1789, the Canton system enabled him to conduct his business, providing contacts, context, and commodities.[3] Later he exploited the system's complexity to profit from smuggling schemes, in partnership with local Chinese traders. Here, too, topography mattered. As an American consul explained, the Pearl River Delta offered "numberless streams and canals that intersect each other, as do the fibers of the spider's web." The porousness and density of the "crowded river" meant that Chinese markets could be "approached from almost any quarter" to bypass the customs house, provided "cunning adventurers" outfitted themselves with the right-sized vessels and some well-placed bribes.[4] The Canton system may have limited entrepreneurs like Perkins to fleeting glimpses of the Qing Empire past the shore, but it also offered a temptation—as well as a means—to evade Qing revenue laws through smuggling. A man whose watchword was "il faut en profiter" ("you should take advantage"), Perkins later found success in exploiting these openings, which only confirmed and deepened his condescending view of Chinese law and Qing officialdom, a durable mentality widely shared among the foreign mercantile community in the factories.[5] Like the teas, silks, and porcelains he brought home, Perkins's perspective on China and the Chinese was a product of the trade.

Of course, factors beyond the Pearl River shaped Perkins's experience. Like many of the first generation of US merchants venturing to China, Perkins approached the sixteen-month trip on the *Astrea* as an extension of his previous employment—one of a series of efforts he made to gather first-hand intelligence about distant markets, expand his commercial network, and grow his capital. As a teenager he had apprenticed as a clerk in a Boston countinghouse, then he joined his older brother James at the bustling French Caribbean port of Cap-Français, Saint Domingue (present-day Cap-Haïtien), to coordinate shipments of flour, sugar, and slaves to other Atlantic destinations. His appointment as the *Astrea*'s supercargo—an agent for the cargo owners, who managed the commercial affairs on a voyage— was proof of his growing reputation and knack for using his social connections to advantage. When veteran shipmaster James Magee signed on to command the *Astrea*, he brought on Perkins, his niece's husband, to book freights and manage the ship's business.[6] Perkins later reminisced that his 1788 marriage, by connecting him to Magee, "determined the future course of my Mercantile Life," just as the ratification of the US Constitution that same year determined the life course of the nation.[7]

Though methodologically he approached it as he had other ventures, the China trade meant something more to Perkins—and to his country—than other branches of commerce. The 360-ton *Astrea* was the property of Salem shipping magnate Elias Hasket Derby, who since the end of the Revolutionary War had been seeking to profit from independence by sending American vessels to places where British regulations had never before let them (legally) go.[8] Voyages to what contemporaries called the "East Indies"—an expansive term encompassing all the maritime destinations east of the Cape of Good Hope—were among the most celebrated of the new adventures Americans attempted in the late eighteenth century. The distance and difficulties involved were extraordinary compared with the familiar routes of the Atlantic, but the potential rewards seemed greater to the same degree. Voyages to China, in particular, attracted official attention and public comment because they connected the infant republic to what was widely recognized as the oldest and wealthiest empire on earth. China was also the source of tea, a commodity that had a special place in the new nation's political imagination for its ties to the performance of gentility and its role in mobilizing resistance to British imperial authority.[9]

In the Enlightenment-influenced culture of the early republic, ships returning from the other side of the world were also valued for the knowledge they brought back. Often this knowledge was imagined to inhere in the commodities they carried. Upon his return from Canton, for example, the *Astrea*'s captain was lauded for a donation of Chinese goods to the "Museum of the University at Cambridge." One newspaper writer mused that the items would allow those "who love to trace the operations of nature" to "observe the progress of human ingenuity and industry in every part of the world."[10]

In contrast to the novelty of some of the items in the returning cargo, initial preparations for the *Astrea*'s voyage proceeded conventionally. As American merchant adventurers commonly did in the late eighteenth century, Perkins, Magee, and Derby had organized an ad hoc consortium of investors to pool capital and share risk for the voyage. When the ship cleared Salem's harbor in February 1789, it carried cargoes for twenty individuals or small concerns. In effect, the principals had mobilized their extended kin and social networks to assemble a floating capital. Despite the diversity of investors, the ship's cargo consisted primarily of two commodities, both well established among American merchants as salable in China: 88,674 pounds of ginseng, a wild-growing root popular in Asia for its medicinal properties; and $30,710 in Spanish silver dollars (pesos), a form of money that had served as the common currency in East-West trade for centuries.[11]

In plans for the voyage itself, the *Astrea* followed the pattern of earlier American China voyages, which in turn closely tracked precedents set by European (and particularly English) East Indies merchants. The ship was to sail around the Cape of Good Hope to the Dutch colonial port of Batavia (present-day Jakarta). After selling what would be in Derby's best "interest" there (what would earn the most profit), they were to fill up on sugar, coffee, and spices and continue to Canton to exchange their ginseng and silver for teas, silks, cottons, and porcelains before returning to home markets.[12] With little to do between ports, Perkins kept a detailed log of the voyage, judging the *Astrea*'s progress by comparing it with the route prescribed by sailing directions compiled by English East India Company captains and published as a handbook in London. And just as European mariners guided the ship's route and European trading practices helped determine its cargo, European printers structured Perkins's own writing: he fitted his notes on the peoples, landscapes, and commodities of the Indian Ocean and the China seas into the blank spaces of standardized forms meant to make distant weather patterns and shipping speeds more legible to metropolitan hydrographers.[13]

Given the long history of Atlantic traders in Asia, it is not surprising that Perkins found the mercantile cultures he encountered familiar. At the ports he visited there were many tools and rituals that made these spaces more navigable, from the construction of foreigners-only neighborhoods, to the wide use of pidgin English as a lingua franca, to the regular hosting of banquets as venues to build relationships and smooth transactions. Both Canton and Batavia were ports adapted for Western maritime trade, imperial outposts where central authorities had delegated power to merchant groups in exchange for steady revenues: at Batavia the directors and employees of the Dutch East India Company; at Canton the Cohong. While visiting traders everywhere rarely failed to complain about the various exactions the

commercial bureaucracy imposed, these were rarely heavy enough to prevent business altogether; negotiation was almost always possible, because
these places were designed to facilitate exchange.[14]

If he did not think so before he ventured to Asia, events after the *Astrea's*
return to the United States in late May 1790 would have convinced Perkins that his own new government now worked the same way.[15] As long
as revenue seemed forthcoming—eventually—merchants could, and did,
negotiate the payments they owed to the US government, to mutual advantage. The *Astrea* sailed back to a domestic market as overstocked with tea
as Canton's had been with ginseng. A new constitutional order had been
installed in its absence, and with it a new federal tariff that bit particularly
hard into tea profits. On behalf of himself and his fellow investors, the well-
connected Derby petitioned Congress for relief. Explaining that he had,
"not through any plan," found "nearly all his capital" invested in tea at a time
when the market was overstocked with an amount "more than sufficient for
the consumption for the United States for three years," Derby asked the national legislature for "such relief in your wisdom shall seem best." Though
he dressed his request in the floridly submissive language of a meek peti-
tioner, Derby was direct about exactly how he wanted the "guardians of the
liberty and trade of the citizens of this rising empire" to relieve him of the
"grievous burden" of paying his taxes on time: he should be allowed to pay
his import duties as he was able to sell his tea instead of at the moment he
imported it. That would preserve his credit, get the Treasury what it was
owed—someday—and not unduly strain the specie reserves of either merchant or nation.[16]

Derby got his wish. Revised customs laws in 1790 and 1791 allowed im-
porters of "all teas imported from China" to warehouse their goods for extended periods—eventually up to two years past the original importation—
and pay prorated customs duties as they made sales, in return for posting
bonds securing tax payments.[17] Like the officials managing international
trade at Batavia and Canton, the architects of the US government's fledgling
customs service, though wary of providing acts of "particular indulgence"
to individuals, were quite willing to accommodate merchants' needs.[18] This
was not a one-time affair. Providing short-term flexibility on trade duties
in order to encourage growth (and larger revenues) in the long term was a
defining feature of the early United States' federal administration—as was
offering unique protections to merchants trading directly with China.[19]

Like American customs officials, the material and political realities of the
China trade trained Perkins to adopt a broader outlook on his affairs. While
at Canton he met other traders, from whom he learned "many particulars
of the No[rth] West trade," the traffic in marine animal furs gathered in

the Pacific basin.[20] This intelligence convinced Perkins of the profitability of sending a ship to gather sea otter skins for sale on the Canton market. After a few false starts, this business would cement Perkins's commercial connection to China, becoming the first of a series of ventures that built the globe-spanning trading network that defined his career—as well as laying the foundation for the largest, longest-lived, and most successful American business in China during the nineteenth century: Russell and Company. The trip to Canton transformed Perkins's approach to commerce: expanding from managing routes connecting the North American mainland to the West Indies, he and his associates shifted to a grander sort of international arbitrage, operating global circuits of exchange by placing trusted associates at key ports to coordinate movements of Pacific furs, Chinese tea, Turkish opium, Mexican silver, and West Indian sugar, among dozens of other commodities. Visiting Canton, and participating in the China trade—construed broadly as marketing Chinese commodities to the rest of the world and bringing the world's products to China—produced Perkins's global perspective.

From the beginning of their republic, Americans have made China their business. They have done so in a number of ways—as diplomats and missionaries, mercenaries and educators—but for the most part they connected with China the way Perkins did, through commerce. It was rarely a simple relationship. Bereft of salable goods at home and credit abroad, the demands of the China trade took Americans around the world in search of silver specie and rare commodities, in complex circuits that ran from Boston to Batavia, London to Lima, Shanghai to San Francisco, and nearly everywhere in between. This trade was not independent of politics; it depended as much on the navigation of credit networks and international diplomacy as it did on the management of ships and sail. The China trade put American merchants and sailors into direct contact with a vast array of new peoples and places, and at critical moments it inspired policymakers and politicians to consider national projects and domestic disputes in global perspective. Because of the extent of the goods, capital, and people it involved, trade with China has profoundly shaped Americans' perceptions of themselves, their government, and their nation's place in the world. And in turn, the trade has shaped American institutions and politics.

This book examines the first century of this commercial contact in order to understand how Americans' commerce with China required, produced, and continually revised a global perspective on political economy. Its core contention is that the conflicts that defined eighteenth- and nineteenth-century American politics and statecraft—over sovereignty and slavery, free labor and immigration, industrial development and imperial expansion—were all profoundly affected by Americans' commerce with China. As it did for Perkins as an individual, Americans' participation in the China trade changed how US policymakers and publics understood their nation in the world and saw the possibilities open to it. The book begins with the first US trading voyage to Canton in 1784 and draws to a close a century later with the passage of the Chinese Exclusion Act and the death of major US China merchant firms, using these events to mark the opening and closing of the free passage of goods and people between the American republic and the Qing Empire, as well as the rise and fall of the "China trade" (as opposed to the "China market") as a potent part of Americans' political imaginary.

Before detailing the payoffs of this approach, it is perhaps worth stating clearly what this book is *not*. It is not a study of bilateral diplomatic relations between the United States and China, nor is it a business history of the China trade or any particular merchants or merchant firms engaged in it. While this book is in dialogue with works in these well-studied areas, it is at heart a study of US political economy: a detailed consideration of the links between governments, markets, and societies, and the individuals who comprise them. Like the lead weights that China-bound mariners threw overboard to sound out the water's hidden depths and plot the topography of the seafloor, *Trading Freedom*'s investigation of the American China trade functions as an instrument to map and measure the global aspects of US political economy.

Tracking how Americans have approached their commercial connection to China provides fresh insights into several ongoing scholarly conversations. By revealing Americans' intense and lasting focus on their China commerce as a contributing component of international relations, economic growth, and domestic statecraft, *Trading Freedom* reorients conversations about the interplay between national identity and political culture. It offers a new periodization—the long nineteenth century—for considering how and why Americans' varied understandings of global political economy affected the theory and practice of national power, as projected abroad and organized at home. An interest in growing the federal state to promote access to global trade flows, especially in China, was a key feature of statecraft in the early republic, for example, just as in the Civil War era the politics of slavery drove a deepening concern about how to separate the flow of Chinese goods from the movement of Chinese people. The growing conviction in the Gilded Age that China was primarily important as a vent for US exports was connected to the inflows of investment that developed the factories, farms, and mines of the continental United States as well as the death of all the major American merchant houses in China.

Attention to US-China commercial relations reveals critical developments in Americans' approaches to globalization and shows the deep ties between "domestic" political debates and Americans' commercial adventures abroad. The China trade extends our understanding of how Anglo-American relations proceeded in the global marketplace as well as through diplomatic channels. In Asia as elsewhere, Americans cooperated closely with British capital to advance the British imperial project, while at home opposition to these same projects commonly drove policy. Similarly, as a driver of monetary flows, the China trade had a significant role in the material realities of the financial panics and banking controversies that marked the nineteenth century, as well as in shaping how Americans understood—and attempted to address—their effects. Finally, in outlining how the free commerce in Chinese goods informed the exclusion of Chinese people, and vice versa, *Trading Freedom* contributes to an ongoing shift in how historians study capitalism, an approach that seeks to more fully explain how politics and economics intersected as much in exchange—commerce—as they did in production or consumption. Global commerce profoundly shaped how the United States developed as a culture, as an economy, and as a nation-state. The goods, people, and ideas involved in US trade with China offer a potent way to trace how Americans were embedded in the world, and the world in the United States.

Trading Freedom proceeds chronologically. In the course of a century, from the Confederation era to the Gilded Age, free commerce with China shifted from something Americans embraced as part of their national project, and sought to promote and expand, to something they feared would harm their nation, and thus sought to control and restrict. I characterize this change as the transition from Americans' interest in the "China trade" to their focus on the "China market," a conceptual shift from understanding US-China commercial relations as a mode of accessing a wider system of global commerce to figuring them as discrete sources of new consumers, labor, or commodities. My guiding principle has been to investigate a broad range of materials generated by businesses, governments, and media and to center my analysis on those characters, institutions, and incidents that did the most to establish or change the politics and political economy of US-China commercial relations.

Chapter 1 tracks how a trade that at first seemed to exemplify the promise and profit of independence instead revealed the weakness of the federal union and the limits of revolutionary change. Facing large state-backed joint-stock companies with greater resources and expertise, American China merchants asked policymakers for protection and support—and found sympathy and allies among the group of nationalists pushing for a

strong centralized federal government. This connection led to special protections for the China trade being built into the new nation's core commercial policies. Chapter 2 examines how this "pacific commercial policy"
played out during the era of rising partisan competition and global war
between Great Britain and France. Protection for US neutral commerce in
China attracted broad support among Federalists and Jeffersonian Republicans alike—but as the pressures on neutral trade rose, the costs of protecting US traders abroad led Americans to reconceptualize the role of the
China trade within US political economy, emphasizing the trade's dangers
over its potential benefits.

Chapter 3 investigates how Americans tried to put these new ideas into
practice, with ironic results. In their efforts to adapt to the new global economic order that peace in Europe produced, American statesmen tried to
preserve their independence by weaning the US from a reliance on trade,
while US China traders struggled to reorganize their businesses profitably.
Surprising their architects, these efforts drew Americans more tightly into
a London-centered global capitalist system that depended on slavery, dispossession, and smuggling to function. Chapter 4 tracks how the Opium
War, one of the violent episodes that emerged out of this volatile system,
brought the China trade back within the circle of US politics in a new way.
Britain's invasion of the China coast became an object of intense interest
across the United States not because the US public understood the deep
involvement of American merchants in opium smuggling—traders downplayed it—but because of the *political* problems it involved, both foreign
and domestic. The parallels between Britain's coercive enforcement of liberal trading policy and the threats liberal market ideas posed to property in
human beings alarmed slaveholders and emboldened abolitionists, drawing sustained attention to the war in American newspapers. This relevance
activated congressional concern and, unusually, funding for the diplomatic
effort needed to establish formal ties with China, a feat accomplished in
1844 by the Treaty of Wangxia.

New diplomatic connections informed new expectations for US-China
trade and created new circuits of information, migration, and capital. One
shift that came out of these connections involved rising expectations for the
volume and accessibility of trade with the Qing Empire. Chapter 5 examines
how firm plans for a transcontinental railroad emerged out of this moment.
Global commerce, hinging on China, was not just an expansionary issue
but a solution to the problem of an expanding, imperial union. Chapter 6
examines another side of new US-China connections: the growing involvement of US merchants in the "coolie" trade, and the creation of a consensus
among US policymakers that the traffic in bound Chinese migrants posed

a threat to both slavery and free labor. US slaveholders became convinced that the "importation" of indentured Asian laborers, begun as a way of supplying cheap labor to plantation societies, was part of a plot to halt the expansion of the slave system. Their advocacy shifted public opinion, persuading even antislavery activists to support a ban on American participation in this human traffic. This debate also cemented the connection between "coolies" and "slaves," mixing national and racial categories in law and in ideology. Chapter 7 looks at the Burlingame mission and finds in its rhetoric an expression of Reconstruction Republicans' vision for the United States—and in its failure, a geopolitical corollary to Reconstruction's failure to craft an enduring multiracial democracy, with the violence of Chinese Exclusion and Jim Crow the result.

The book's final chapter reckons with this collapse, examining how the "China trade" died—as a business and as an idea—and was replaced in Americans' political imaginary by the "China market." Beginning in the 1870s, the new infrastructures of globalization and the new dynamics of industrialization led to the decline of major US-China firms and helped shift how Americans understood their relationship with China. Whereas China's ports had once been understood as critical points of access to global trade, during the Gilded Age American financiers and policymakers became convinced that China was primarily useful as an outlet for American surplus or a zone for demonstrating great power status—but of low short-term importance either way. When the China trade died, ironically a victim of the first era of globalization, Americans' political investment in the free movement of goods and people died with it.

The United States has never existed in a vacuum. From the republic's earliest years, Americans rarely saw themselves as engaged solely in a North American realm, or even an Atlantic or a Pacific one; their frame of reference encompassed the entire globe. One of the core ways many early Americans defined themselves, and their nation, was through their commercial relations—the traffic in goods and people and ideas whose flows bound them to the rest of the world as well as marking them apart. The alleged novelty of our current era of "late" capitalism and global interconnectedness sometimes obscures the fact that the world inhabited by Abigail Adams, Frederick Douglass, and Rutherford B. Hayes was no less whole, no less round, and no less known to be so than our own. This book argues that understanding the role of global commerce, as illustrated by American trade with China, provides a way back to early Americans' mode of seeing—and with that vision, a deeper understanding of the context and motivations that moved them, and what the world had to do with it.

CHAPTER ONE

Founding a Free, Trading Republic

In Paris, John Adams worried for the future. In mid-July 1783 Adams was in the French capital to negotiate a final peace settlement with Great Britain, work he found frustrating and difficult. A fortnight before, Britain had issued a proclamation that reemphasized the empire's commitment to reserving trade with the British West Indies to their own subjects. Though he thought this a piece of "Refugee Politicks"—the result of lobbying by expatriate loyalists—Adams fretted that without access to the traditional outlets for American produce and charters for American ships, any plans for the "happiness and prosperity" of the new nation would be "straitened and shackled." The best way to respond, Adams advised the Continental Congress, was to retaliate in kind. Each state, he wrote, should lay the same punitive impost on British imports in order to convince London of the wisdom of freer trade policy.

Doubting, however, that even this "common danger . . . will induce a perfect unanimity among the States," Adams also ruminated on other ways of "making impressions upon the English." Some of his recommendations would be familiar to any student of early American political economy: growing West Indian products within the United States would help, he thought, as would encouraging domestic manufacturing. But Adams's advice reached beyond the Atlantic world, revealing a revolutionary geopolitics less familiar to historians. "Send Ships immediately to China," he told Congress, because "this trade is as open to us as to any nation." Putting competitive pressure on Britain in Asia, his logic ran, would force open markets in the Atlantic or, failing that, help compensate for their absence. Like many of his fellow revolutionaries, Adams saw overseas commerce as a continuation of international politics by other means—and China's trade as a key part of any political calculation made for the United States.[1]

As the Revolutionary War wound down and the problems of peace emerged, American elites turned to Chinese commerce as an important component of the republic's political economy. What they termed "the China trade," or "trade with the East Indies," was not simple, direct trade but access to a complex set of exchanges linking the ports of Asia—above all the hub of Canton—to the Americas, Africa, Europe, and the Pacific islands. Among an influential group of American leaders, the China trade seemed to offer a particularly useful instrument for expanding economic power and buttressing the infant republic's independence within a republican ideological framework. As the problems of peace became manifest, an interest in the China trade informed the way American leaders explained the need for a more consolidated nation-state, as well as how they shaped the core institutions that defined and animated it—notably the federal government's key source of revenue, the tariff, which singled out for special protection the traffic in goods imported "from China or India." These movements were made in dialogue with the evolving realities of Americans' trade in China, a practice that by the turn of the nineteenth century had revealed the limits of American statecraft. American policymakers looked to the China trade to slake their thirst for tea and nourish their revolutionary nation's political economy; the difficulties involved in seeking China's commerce led them to develop new ideas about what capabilities their new nation needed in order to survive in a competitive world.

Adams did not have to wait long for American ships to be sent out; trade with China launched with the nation's formal independence. In February 1784, just over a month after the Continental Congress had ratified the Treaty of Paris and proclaimed the end of the War of Independence, the ice damming New York's harbor receded, and in its wake came the *Empress of China*, a small, square-sterned ship bound for Canton.[2] The novelty of the ship's destination loaded the vessel with more than just ginseng and Spanish dollars as it sailed down the East River.[3] Backed by a group of prominent Philadelphia and New York merchants (including the Continental Congress's superintendent of finance, Robert Morris), and managed by several respected veterans of the Revolutionary War, the *Empress* bore Americans' hopes for a new era of prosperity.[4]

The *Empress* left a country in increasingly desperate straits. Independence had cost Americans dearly. The war had destroyed lives and property, and put state governments and the Continental Congress deeply in debt. The national government organized under the Articles of Confederation was too weak to improve matters, lacking mechanisms to tax, regulate trade, or normalize relations with other nations. Worse, by early 1784 Americans were beginning to realize what separation from the British Empire meant in economic terms. In the peace, they were cut off from the West Indian ports that had been the lifeblood of the colonial economy—but British and Continental merchants retained easy access to US ports and flooded them with goods, suffocating domestic producers and merchants. With no friendly outlets for their wares, few profitable routes for shipping, and no government capable of organizing a coherent response, the situation at the time of the *Empress*'s departure was grim indeed.[5]

The *Empress*'s voyage launched as part of a larger push to overcome these economic and political problems by expanding commerce. Proposals for exploring new branches of trade were common after the war—merchants gambled their ships and capital on new markets in the Mediterranean and the Baltic, in South America as well as in Asia. But while voyages like the *Empress*'s were unremarkable in their motivations, ventures to China were something more than just another kind of investment. During the first decades of the China trade American merchants from ports up and down the East Coast sailed the world over to accumulate the commodities, credit, and coin required for purchases in China. They gathered ginseng root from Appalachian forests, marine furs from the Pacific Northwest and southern South America, sandalwood from Hawaii, opium from Smyrna and Bengal, and, crucially in the early years, Spanish silver dollars, the favored currency of East-West trade, from commerce with Mexico, the Caribbean, South America, and Europe. Moreover, Americans conducted a carrying trade between these areas, sometimes finding it more effective to tramp around the globe on multiyear voyages than to simply go to China directly.

The necessity of global engagement helps explains why trading to Canton was seen as an entrée into a whole new world—and a prestigious endeavor. Americans were familiar with the giant chartered monopoly corporations that Europeans organized to meet the trade's challenges. The wealth and power that East India Companies amassed, and the military and maritime technology they deployed, gave the eighteenth-century "East Indies" trade a cachet similar to that of the twentieth-century aerospace industry. But the products of trade with China were important too. As its moment as an object of counterimperial protest helped to prove, Chinese tea remained a key article of consumption in early America. In addition to its restorative properties, tea was a crucial marker of gentility and status—as were Chinese textiles, porcelains, and furniture. Americans also valued the idea of a connection to China for its own sake. If the problem of "oriental despotism" was forgotten (as it sometimes was in moments of physiocratic excitement) Americans could imagine that the populous superpower, fueled by the world's most productive agriculture and sophisticated internal

FIGURE 5. A Spanish silver dollar, the key currency of the China trade, and the most important—and valuable—commodity American traders carried to Asia. 8 Reales, Mexico, 1805, http://n2t.net/ark:/65665/ng49ca746a9-9b61-704b-e053-15f76fa0b4fa, Division of Work and Industry, National Museum of American History, Smithsonian Institution.

transportation systems, was a model for what they hoped their new republic would become.[6] Americans' desire to participate in the China trade was overdetermined: it would prove Americans' mettle as traders, satisfy existing consumer demand, and put the nation in contact with one of the most sophisticated and powerful societies on the planet—all without exposing the republic to further encroachment from other Atlantic states.

For all these reasons, contemporary commentary on the *Empress*'s endeavor and other early voyages cast these ventures in terms of what historian James Fichter has usefully characterized as "public economy"—an enterprise aimed at generating both national glory and private profit.[7] In the case of the *Empress*, investors and a wide range of observers saw its voyage as a harbinger of a national commercial movement. Robert Morris, US superintendent of finance and part owner of the *Empress*, told John Jay, secretary of foreign affairs, that he was "sending some ships to China" not only for his own profit, but also "to encourage others in the adventurous pursuits of commerce."[8] Philadelphia's newspapers reported that this desire to serve the national interest extended even to the captain and his crew, who were allegedly "elated on being considered the first instruments, in the hands of Providence . . . to extend the commerce of the United States of America, to that distant, and to us unexplored country."[9]

The *Empress*'s successful return on May 11, 1785, with a cargo of teas, silks, cottons, and porcelain generated celebratory commentary.[10] This praise was motivated in part by how closely Americans identified the expansion of trade with escape from the "shackles of British mercantilism."[11] The pres-

FIGURE 6. A tea crate, similar in form to those that returned as part of the cargo of the *Empress of China*. *A man writes on sealed crates of tea, ready for export.* Painting by a Chinese artist, ca. 1850, https://wellcomecollection.org/works/dj3vse2z, Wellcome Collection. Attribution 4.0 International (CC BY 4.0).

ident of Congress, Richard Henry Lee, filled his letters that spring with news of the *Empress*'s arrival, gleefully describing it as "a proof of American enterprise," that "will probably mortify, as much as it will injure our old Oppressors, the British."[12] Editor and poet Philip Freneau later celebrated the voyage in verse as a demonstration of Americans' liberation from the mercantilist confines of the British Empire.[13] The congressional delegation from South Carolina expanded on this point in a report home, explaining that trade to the East Indies was noteworthy because it was "free from an inconvenience to which European connexions"—trade and politics—"expose us, that is, an interference in our Governments."[14] Even those less sanguine were still excited at the possibilities: William Grayson grumbled to his fellow Virginian James Madison about the apparent "Asiatic hauteur" shown by the Chinese, but he nonetheless declared that he "could heartily wish to see the merchts. of our State engaged in this business"—especially if they could find a way to smuggle Chinese goods into the West Indies.[15] Congress, as a body, congratulated the mariners, expressing "peculiar satisfaction" in "this first effort of the citizens of America to establish a direct trade with China."[16]

The apparent success of the *Empress* led to imitators—a handful at first, then a steady stream of voyages each year.[17] American merchants' approach to the business, dictated by their comparatively disadvantaged circumstances, differed markedly from their European competitors'. Instead of being managed by large joint-stock companies with deep pools of capital, American ventures to China were organized the same way shorter voyages were: as small one-off adventures by groups of local merchants, who minimized principal-agent problems by working with family members and by assigning shares in the venture to the ship's master, and in some cases also to a supercargo, an agent who traveled aboard the ship to oversee the venture's transactions abroad. Though they were traveling much farther, American China traders sailed with the same small crews in the sub-three hundred ton sloops, brigs, and ships they used for transatlantic or Caribbean voyages—not in the seasonal convoys of huge purpose-built "East Indiamen" their European rivals typically used.[18]

Some of these practices were the product of deliberation. When John Wingrove, a trader with experience in India, proposed creating official US trading posts ("factories") in Asia, the Continental Congress quickly killed his suggestion. Speaking for a congressional committee, Rufus King explained that they "were of Opinion that the commercial intercourse between the United States and India would be more prosperous if left unfettered in the hands of private adventurers, than if regulated by any system of a national complexion." This stated preference was convenient—the Continental Congress had no resources to support Wingrove's plan—but consistent with later practice. When it came to overseas commerce, early American leaders opposed corporate monopolies.[19]

In the late eighteenth century, some of the necessities that shaped Americans' China trade were also virtues. Using infrastructure, protocols, and contacts their rivals had developed, but operating with lower costs, American traders could take more risks and react more quickly to shifts in market prices as well as changes in winds. Their wandering routes exposed them to new opportunities for profitable freighting and arbitrage, growing the sphere of American commerce. In light of political decisions like the rejection of Wingrove's plan, Americans understood their successes in the China trade as proof of their mercantile prowess as well as their republican ideals.

The importance of going to China for securing Americans' place in the world was substantiated by reports coming back with the *Empress* itself. On his return to New York, Samuel Shaw, a respected Continental Army veteran who served as a supercargo on the voyage, moved quickly to deliver an official report on his experience to Congress.[20] Reflecting the widespread interest in the diplomatic import of the voyage, Shaw's account focused on how Americans were treated in China by European partners and rivals. He did not waste time explaining how business worked at Canton, declaring that "the situation is so well known as to render a detail unnecessary." Instead, Shaw reported that the American ship had received navigational and commercial aid "from our good allies the French," who had helped integrate the tyro American merchants into the port's foreign merchant community.[21] According to Shaw, even the English behaved cordially—a welcome surprising enough that it was elaborated on (and exaggerated) in the newspapers.[22] When he did find time to mention a meeting with Chinese merchants, Shaw focused primarily on Americans' image: "The Chinese were very indulgent towards us," he wrote, "they styled us the *New People.*"[23]

The *Empress*'s voyage and similar ventures further convinced John Adams of the political utility of private trade with China. He thought Americans should establish an official presence in Asia and use it to sell North American commodities and provide freight services for European traders who wished to move goods outside the monopoly restrictions imposed by various East India companies. Adams speculated that the knowledge the trade generated could be of strategic importance, serving as a bargaining chip that could help keep the nation safe and neutral during the next global conflagration set off by European rivalries.[24] As with so many other imagined enterprises in the new republic, private action would take the place of state capacity.

With further experience, however, the realities of commerce seemed to indicate the opposite conclusion: private trade needed public protection. Reporting from a later China trip in 1787, Samuel Shaw explained to Congress that Great Britain was trying to consolidate its commercial and political institutions in Asia in order to push out smaller private traders like him. Recalling the balance-of-power politics of the late American war, Shaw wondered if a "commercial confederation" of the nations who stood to lose the most if Britain consolidated its grip might serve "as the best means of checking and defeating such exorbitant pretensions."[25]

John Jay and other advocates for a stronger national government mobilized reports like Shaw's to promote their cause. Writing as Publius in the pro-Constitution *Federalist* essays, Jay argued that "the enterprise and address of our merchants and navigators" would lead Americans to capture a significant share of Western trade with China. This laudable success, Jay feared, could incite war with European powers—effectively an extension of Shaw's fears. This was a danger that Jay thought could be sensibly countered only by a more centralized union and a serious navy, institutions that would naturally be best organized by a more powerful federal government like the one envisioned by supporters of the new Constitution.[26]

That such arguments would appear in a pro-Constitution polemic is an indication of how the China trade's unique features linked it closely to the development of the American nation-state. For reformers who branded the Confederation system a dangerous anarchy, the threat to American commercial success in China posed by a cabal of European monopoly companies was useful—the extremity of Canton's competitive cockpit starkly illustrated the vulnerabilities of a decentralized federal system. It enabled "small *f*" federalists like Jay, Adams, and James Madison to frame their proposals for a strong national government as a realpolitik response to international trade, in contrast to the *doux commerce* ideals some of their opponents espoused.[27] This stance was not just rhetoric, either. Once the new federal government was in place, promoting trade with Asia became an immediate policy focus.

The first federal Congress convened under the new Constitution achieved a quorum on April 6, 1789. Two days later, debate on the tariff began. One of the most pressing agenda items for the new federal legislature was to frame a national commercial policy and provide the national government with a stable revenue, thereby addressing the problems that inspired the Constitutional Convention in Philadelphia.[28] Four months later the tariff, tonnage, and collection acts that passed created an American navigation system that fulfilled these goals. Collectively a legible framework for the political economy that nationalists had long wanted, this system's purpose was to provide the mechanisms needed to regulate and guide the nation's most

crucial economic activity—overseas trade—in order to secure the republic's future.[29] And at that system's heart were a series of measures intended
to protect and encourage American shipping—and to promote open and
direct trade between the United States and China.

The tariff was the most important of these measures, and the most complex.[30] Despite the heady rhetoric that accompanied the first meeting of the
federal Congress, debates in the House and Senate over revenue were largely
fights over details, with an eye to boosting regional economic specializa-
tions.[31] Massachusetts representatives, elected by rum distillers and fisher-
men, ardently pursued low duties on molasses but high duties on imported
cod; Pennsylvanians and Virginians wanted cheap hemp but protection for
steel forges; and South Carolinians, dedicated to cash crops grown by enslaved laborers, wanted a zero-duty trade in most everything. While most
congressmen crafted their arguments as appeals to principle, they quickly
got "in a flame when any articles were brought forward that were in any
considerable use" among their constituents.[32]

This narrow focus was contrary to what the tariff's originator, James
Madison, had intended. When he recommended the nation meet its needs
by taxing overseas commerce, Madison imagined a duty laid primarily for
revenue, with commercial discrimination against recalcitrant foreign powers a secondary objective. To that end he introduced a simple two-part
schedule of duties to the House, based on proposals first made to the Continental Congress. It suggested that most commodities be taxed ad valorem
("according to value"), meaning that the duty would be a set percentage of
the goods' price at the time of their purchase abroad, while a select set of
"enumerated" goods—luxury consumables like alcohol, sugar, tea, coffee,
cocoa, and pepper—should be taxed at a set rate per quantity, no matter
what the originating price (e.g., six cents per pound of tea). While Madison
left specific rates to be decided through debate, he also argued forcefully for
additional duties on goods imported by vessels from nations without commercial treaties with the United States.[33]

Madison's proposed discrimination between treaty and nontreaty imports was eventually lost, as was his similar effort on the tonnage act, which
taxed ships according to their carrying capacity. Both were rejected on the
grounds that such distinctions would trouble the country's diplomacy un-
necessarily. Instead, determining the schedule of tariff duties occupied the
House and Senate for the next few months. It was over the course of that
debate that another, much more important division between the members
began to emerge: whether the tariff should also attempt to "regulate"—that
is, promote—particular trades or industries by levying discriminating duties on certain foreign goods.

A question simultaneously of political philosophy and practical politics, disagreement about the ends of the tariff has been a perennial issue in American politics. Conflict between "free traders" who desired a revenue-only tariff and those "protectionists" who wanted to harness the customs for economic development made the tariff one of the main battlegrounds of American politics for the next century, until the income tax replaced it as the primary source of government revenue, and Congress shifted control over duty rates and trade regulations to the executive branch. Tariff debates also occasioned sharp conflict over slavery's role in the American economy, as Robin Einhorn has convincingly argued.[34] In contrast to later debates, however, those in the first federal Congress were less fraught on these subjects: legislators' visions of political economy had not yet reached the point of focusing on rival systems of domestic production—and on the slavery question Madison, among others, was quick to smooth over differences.[35]

Instead, the agreement on commerce that the delegates assembled in New York found reveals something important about the first Congress's concerns. Collectively, Congress's gaze was directed *outward*: most members were inclined to regard the state of the nation's commerce and navigation—the constitutive connections to the world beyond American shores—as among the most pressing concerns for the nation's economy and security. "Free trade," in this context, meant more than access to markets. It also signified freedom from Britain's grip on the US economy. The first Congress was thus in favor of measures for revenue, but also for some protection for the *industry* of American shipping (though theoretically only as would aid the nation as a whole). This was the middle ground occupied by key figures in the debate who declared themselves to be, as Madison did, friends "to free commerce" as well as "to such regulations as are calculated to promote our own interest, and this on national principles."[36]

Reflecting this vision of political economy and the realities of logrolling, the final tariff bill protected the American commercial sector as a whole, but its minor provisions were also constructed to address various local concerns. The goods on the expanded "enumerated" list—commodities like coffee, tea, or Madeira—were assigned specific rates of duty intended to benefit particular domestic interests. Meanwhile, the duty for "un-enumerated" goods, those that Congress saw no benefit in discriminating against (or allowing in more cheaply), paid a standard 5 percent ad valorem duty. In addition, the act offered a 10 percent discount on duties imported by vessels that were American-built and -owned, and a crucial "drawback" provision that allowed merchants to deposit goods in US ports for up to a year before reexporting them in exchange for a nominal tax of 1 percent of the original import duty. In this system almost all imports were taxed as simple commodities, with no regard to their point of origin or their mode of transport.

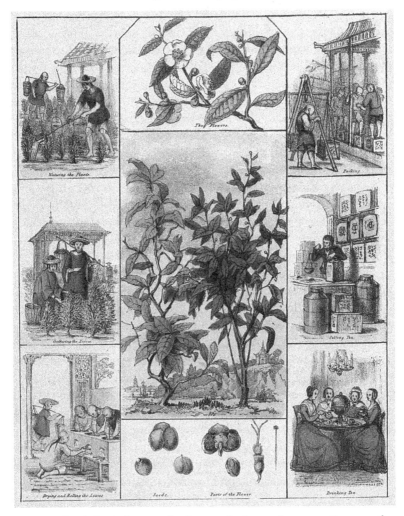

FIGURE 7. Depictions of tea production, marketing, and consumption were frequently used in advertising for Asian imports, as well as in explanations of the China trade. Absent from this depiction of the tea commodity chain is shipping—the economic activity related to tea that concerned early Americans most. *A tea plant [Camellia sinensis], its flowers and seeds, bordered by six scenes illustrating its use by man.* Lithograph, c. 1840, https://wellcomecollection.org/works/sd4au7qj, Wellcome Collection. Attribution 4.0 International (CC BY 4.0).

However, amid this uniformity, one branch of American commerce was singled out for special support: the traffic in goods imported "from China or India."[37] Unlike every other kind of commodity on the enumerated list, Congress took care to set different rates for Asian goods, distinguishing whether they had been brought directly from Asian ports or reexported from European markets, and whether American or foreign vessels carried them. Moreover, the act discriminated between varieties of tea, charging different duties according to their quality—distinctions no other commodity was granted.[38] Teas shipped directly from China by American merchants in American bottoms paid the lowest rates; teas shipped from Europe in American vessels paid slightly higher rates; and the highest taxes were on those teas brought to the US market by foreign merchants or in foreign ships.[39] The protection afforded American merchants trading directly with China was substantial: a pound of bohea tea (the cheapest grade) paid only six cents if it came from Canton, eight cents if it came via Europe, and fifteen cents if it was delivered via a foreign ship. More expensive grades of tea (souchong, hyson, and other green teas) saw a slightly lower, but still important, rise in duty cost. In addition to the difference in tea duties, the tariff also laid a blanket 12.5 percent duty on "all goods, wares and merchandises, other than teas, imported from China or India, in ships not built in the United States, and not wholly the property of a citizen or citizens thereof"— the highest percentage duty in the entire tariff schedule.[40]

These special features worked with other provisions in the tariff to ensure American dominance in the traffic in Asian goods to the United States and to give American merchants an edge in selling Asian goods in other markets. The drawback provision, in particular, was regarded by one of the chief architects of the legislation as "of the Utmost Importance" for "trade to the East," because it would allow Americans to reexport Asian goods to other Atlantic ports at a profit.[41] When taken together with the protections afforded by the tonnage law (which granted American-built and -owned vessels a significant discount on tonnage duties), the will of the first Congress is not hard to discern: they wanted Asian commerce to remain exclusively in American hands—and the United States to be linked directly to Asia.

These protections emerged out of debates in both the House and the Senate. To some extent they were motivated by "private" interests: the two most ardent promoters of commercial discrimination in the interest of Americans' Asian commerce, Thomas Fitzsimons in the House and Robert Morris in the Senate, were both merchants from Philadelphia active in the China trade. Their own pocketbooks, and those of their Quaker City colleagues, stood to benefit from discriminating duties.[42] But Fitzsimons and Morris did not act alone. Support for the measures transcended local or sectional interest, making the protection of Asian commerce into a contest over the role of commercial discriminations in American political economy.

An Irish merchant representing Philadelphia, Fitzsimons was the driving force behind most of the tariff's developmental sections, including those concerning Asian trade.[43] The graduated system of duties on tea, Fitzsimons explained when he first introduced the measure, was not meant "only as a revenue, but as a regulation of a commerce highly advantageous to the United States." American merchants, "finding their trade restrained and embarrassed," had since independence "been under the necessity of exploring channels to which they were heretofore unaccustomed," and in "the trade to China and the East Indies" they had at last "succeeded in discovering one that bids fair to increase our national importance and prosperity" as well as individual profits. The commerce with China was like other nascent industries, Fitzsimons argued: it required "some assistance in the beginning," particularly in this case "from the jealousy subsisting in Europe of this infant branch of commerce."[44] Fitzsimons was reiterating in Congress what had already become a familiar trinity of commentary on Americans' China trade: an emphasis on the trade's unique promise, its peculiar problems, and the "bogeyman of English competition and jealousy."[45]

When it came time to specify rates, Madison opposed protecting Americans' Asian commerce on the grounds that the purpose of trade should be to supply Americans with the cheapest possible goods. He was quickly argued down by a number of voices. Benjamin Goodhue, from the active Asia-trading port of Salem, Massachusetts, informed the House that the trade was a net bonus for the American economy as a whole because it allowed Americans to sell "very considerable quantities of ginseng, naval stores, lumber, and [naval] provisions" and other "superfluities" at "ports on this side of China, in order to procure the most suitable cargo" for Canton, in this way procuring "teas and nankeens" far more cheaply than from Europe.[46] In response, Madison shifted his position, arguing instead that the trade should not be protected because it brought only "luxuries" to the United States. This line of argument also failed. Elias Boudinot, a representative from New Jersey, quickly corrected Madison's error in supposing the trade was limited to luxuries, informing him that "our beef, pork, flour, and wheat, were shipped for this purpose, not to China, yet to ports where proper cargoes were taken in to answer the trade."[47] Americans' China trade, in other words, was a leading industry that would benefit the entire economy—not just a narrow interest. After a few days of debate, Madison conceded.[48] The victory was not an easy one; as Fitzsimons grumbled to a supporter, "[a] Great deal of pains" were taken to achieve the goal.[49] But arguments that emphasized the centrality of the China trade to American commerce convinced enough House members that the tariff bill was passed along to the Senate.

The upper house was more divided.[50] Some members were more radical in their proposals for the support of Asian commerce, while others were equally so in opposition to protection. At one extreme were those, like Tristram Dalton (from China trade–interested Newburyport, Massachusetts) and Charles Carroll (of Carrollton, Maryland), who proposed that foreign traders be banned entirely from the carriage and sale of Asian goods in American markets.[51] Opposition to protection was vocal, but more confused. Most curious was the partnership between staunch Connecticut Federalist Oliver Ellsworth and the antiadministration operator Richard Henry Lee, who had so excitedly informed his friends of the *Empress's* voyage a few years earlier. Though at one point they had both endorsed Dalton's proposal to grant Americans a complete monopoly on the trade, later they spoke out against a protected commerce.[52] More coherent, at least ideologically, were a group of Deep South senators: William Few of Georgia and South Carolina's Ralph Izard and Pierce Butler.[53] This bloc objected to using the tariff to encourage commerce in any capacity, seeing no "General Utility" in it for planters.[54]

In the end a moderate position aligned with the majority in the House carried the day. Pennsylvania's delegation again led the charge; in the Senate it was composed of Robert Morris and William Maclay. Morris was the former superintendent of finance and a major merchant involved in the China trade. Given his personal interest, Morris's support was perhaps predictable, but it was more restrained than that of some other senators, and he articulated it through speeches with econometric analyses of the costs and benefits of protection.[55] Maclay's support was more surprising. An acerbic, observant one-term senator, Maclay found promoting and protecting direct trade with China a blindingly obvious necessity and considered those opposing it frustratingly nonsensical. "Common prudence" dictated that a direct trade in tea was better than an indirect one, an assumption borne out, he told his colleagues, by the fact that "teas were now obtained vastly cheaper than before our merchants traded to China" and so "to talk of not protecting a trade sought after by all the world was a *phenomenon*" (he did not mean a happy one).[56] Maclay was persuaded that a tariff that encouraged key trades and industries together was needed to successfully resist English influence. Partly because of his efforts to push the bill through Congress, the tariff, with Asian trade provisions intact, cleared the Senate and finally became law on July 4, 1789.

On the rare occasions when they have stopped to examine it, historians have read the first tariff and its unusual discriminations in favor of direct American trade with China as a straightforward illustration of mercantile influence in Congress.[57] In this they follow publicist Mathew Carey's assessment of the first Congress's mercantile bias against protectionism, summarized most powerfully in his 1820 manifesto *The New Olive Branch*, which declared that the "revolting partiality that is displayed in this act" was a direct result of the mercantile interest's overrepresentation in Congress—especially in the persons of Thomas Fitzsimons and Robert Morris.[58]

Contemporaries in 1789 also saw the wrangling over the legislation's terms as the result of unseemly personal interest, but in a very different way. Arthur Lee, Richard Henry Lee's cousin, fumed to a correspondent that Fitzsimon's arrival in New York at the beginning of debate had "turnd Madison directly about & with him the House," away from passing a quick and temporary impost bill and toward framing a permanent piece of legislation, thereby causing "the loss of all the spring & East india imports—the distressing of the treasury & disgracing its Commissioners—& the throwing the government into the hands of the Philadelphia Bank," all to the benefit of greedy merchants.[59] Lee was not alone; others professed themselves "astonished" that Congress waited so long to promulgate an impost law and imagined that merchants' desire to avoid new taxes lay behind the delay.[60] Even William Maclay, though actively pushing for provisions protecting mercantile interests, was profoundly suspicious of his colleagues' motives—and never more so than when he felt the bill's passage was being delayed.[61] In 1789, those most suspicious of the tariff's passage were concerned with how the mercantile interest was using it to protect itself—but instead of focusing, like Carey, on how the particular terms of the bill might influence protection of domestic industries, they were worried about how its delay affected the government's revenues and the market's prices.

Once the tariff and related acts were secured, national policymakers' concern with the China trade shifted to focus on revenues. In part this change reflected the accretion of experience in tax collection, though Alexander Hamilton's increased role in shaping economic policy, after his appointment as treasury secretary in September 1789, also played a role.[62] Hamilton's reports to Congress made it clear that revenues were not yet sufficient to meet the nation's expenses—so pleas for policies that might reduce the Treasury's interest, like higher protective duties on foreign tea imports, fell on deaf ears. However, this same desire for the regular collection of customs also led policymakers to make significant efforts to accommodate merchants' requests for procedural changes, provided they would lead to fatter receipts. Merchants trading to China and the East Indies asked for, and received, generous customs payment terms as well as less onerous warehousing and reexport fees—but no higher trade barriers.[63]

After 1790 the nation's basic commercial policies were set, but the China trade continued to play an important role in American political thought. After a long day of disputation over how the Senate should provide "advice and consent" to the executive on appointments in the foreign service,

Maclay ruminated in his diary about the subtext of the debate, the substance of American foreign policy:

> China, geographically speaking, may be called the counterpart to our American world. Oh, that we could make her policy the political model of our conduct with respect to other nations—ready to dispose of her superfluities to all the world! She stands committed by no engagement to any foreign part of it; dealing with every comer, she seems to say, "We trade with you and you with us, while common interest sanctifies the connection; but, that dissolved, we know no other engagement."[64]

In Maclay's geopolitical vision—one he shared with most other nationalists of the era—commerce was more than a means to prosperity. It was also the ideal form of intercourse between nations, and the only one that would leave the United States free to prosper without also drawing the new republic into Old World intrigue. Echoing Maclay's notes, George Washington explained in his Farewell Address in 1796 that the "great rule of conduct for us in regard to foreign nations [was] in extending our commercial relations, [and] to have with them as little *political* connection as possible."[65] A stance of determined political isolation buttressed by strong commercial relations was, in the imagination of the architects of the American federal state, the situation to which all statesmen should aspire to guide the nation. As it happens, it was also a model that described Americans' relationship with China—at least as seen from the center of American power.

The perspective of merchants trading in Asia was rather different. They faced a number of obstacles in their pursuit of profit. The first problem was the most basic: how to pay for goods. Even before they had firsthand experience, Americans knew that the bulk of Europeans' purchases in China had for centuries been made with silver specie, in the form of Spanish milled dollars. American promoters of the China commerce were aware of the United States' relative dearth of hard currency or salable produce; but they argued that ginseng from the North American backcountry, or the marine furs, rare woods, and sea creatures of the western Pacific, would prove practical replacements for silver.

Things did not turn out that way. Although Appalachian ginseng, Oregonian sea otter pelts, Patagonian seal furs, Hawaiian sandalwood, Pacific bêche-de-mer, and other luxury consumables were at times important components of American ships' China-bound cargoes, none of these commodities dominated American trade the way kegs of silver coins did. As a business matter, Americans' reliance on silver specie was a mixed blessing:

it limited the trade's growth, but the requirement for coin up front also sta-
bilized the commerce by sharply limiting the availability of credit for speculation—at least until Americans were well enough established in the trade to
receive credit from their Chinese or European partners.[66] Also, the annual
export of millions of dollars in Spanish silver dollars—legal currency in the
United States—was a liability in public discussions of the trade.[67]

The "how" of making purchases presented other problems: bringing
transactions to a successful close in Canton could be as arduous as the
journey to the port. Navigating the Canton system required deft management of piloting, registration and taxation rituals, continuous negotiation
with the employees of the Hoppo, or customs superintendent, and the establishment of multiple dependent relationships with quasi-public agents
like hong merchants, linguists, and compradors. These restrictions, and the
expensive bureaucracy they entailed, left neophyte American traders bewil-
dered and turned old hands bitter.[68]

Trade in other parts of Asia was somewhat more familiar in its procedures, but with that flexibility and relative transparency came other problems. While Chinese authorities at Canton opened the port to all comers—so
long as they followed regulations and paid the customary fees—most of
the other ports American vessels visited in the Pacific and Indian Oceans
(Bombay, Madras, Batavia, Port Louis, etc.) were outposts of European colonial empires and thus subject to the same mercantilist codes that bedeviled American traders elsewhere. In an economic arena that required turning over cargoes multiple times in multiple ports to acquire a profitable
mix of commodities and currencies, the restrictions enacted by colonial
administrators increased the risks of each leg of a voyage.[69]

The restrictive trade policies of European empires also put pressure on
the other end of China ventures: where to sell Asian goods. The domestic
American market, though large and expanding, was not large enough to
absorb all that US traders carried, so American merchants complemented
their domestic sales by carrying Asian goods (especially Chinese teas) to
markets in Europe and European colonies. Sometimes these voyages never
touched US shores, but others stopped briefly in the United States to land
goods before reexporting them, following the doctrine of the "broken voyage" that (theoretically) allowed American traders to evade European bans
on foreigners' carrying colonial goods, or goods from areas reserved for
monopoly companies, directly to metropolitan ports. Because European
imperial powers protected their home markets as well as their colonial
ports, reexports were a fragile business, subject not only to policy shifts
in the United States, but also to conditions in Europe—which became a
great deal more unstable after the onset of the French revolutionary wars

in 1792. The structures imposed on the trade by both European and Asian authorities thus fouled one of the hopes of American political leaders: that the China trade would provide an escape from the entanglements of the Old World. Instead, Americans' trade entangled them with more and larger empires, often in subaltern or dependent relationships.

Subject to high taxes and hostile navies, American traders often chose a skulking sort of resistance. At whatever ports they called, even (or perhaps especially) at home, American merchants were no strangers to smuggling and other kinds of dealing outside the customs house. While an American merchant, feeling his patriotism calling, might lament that "in a government like ours smuggling is a heart-rending business," he rarely lost the struggle with his conscience.[70] China traders' biographies often proudly detailed the coast guard cutters and harbor guns they outran in the course of doing business. For subsequent generations these exploits became part of the myth and romance of the old China trade.[71]

It would be a mistake to see these obstacles as insurmountable. Indeed, Americans' early trade with China was (and still is) celebrated largely for the fortunes it made. Estimates of profits across the sector are difficult to ascertain, partly because of the haphazard way the business was organized, but anecdotal evidence suggests that returns could at times be considerable. William Coxe Jr., brother of the Philadelphian publicist Tench Coxe, reported to a business partner that the 1787 voyage of the Philadelphia-based *Canton* had earned its investors a "neat profit of 126 per cent."[72] The Massachusetts congressman Fisher Ames's investments in voyages managed by William Gray saw more modest returns: 11–23 percent per annum in the 1790s, but they also included one jackpot of 130 percent.[73] The sloop *Experiment*, a tiny eighty-five-ton vessel, earned an estimated 8 percent net return for its owners on its only China voyage.[74] But of course other investors and merchants were not as lucky: Samuel Snow, the second American consul in Canton, saw his firm dragged under by bankruptcy; his son, the perhaps too appropriately named Peter Wanton Snow, later followed him in financial ruin.[75]

While China voyages were never easy or completely secure—far from it—they did become prosaic as the trade became more established. The sheer number of American cities serving as home ports for ventures militated against too much exoticism. Though most heavily concentrated in the early republic's major trading centers—New York, Philadelphia, Boston—China-bound vessels called American cities of all ranks home, ranging up and down the East Coast from Charleston, South Carolina, to Salem, Massachusetts.[76] To judge from Vermont farmer Amos Porter's diary, by 1802 pulling up stakes and sailing out to Canton to oversee the sale of a ginseng cargo was almost as banal an affair as planting a new potato field.[77]

Moreover, although individual traders sometimes came to wrack and ruin, the general trend for the sector as a whole was one of impressive, if contingent, growth. From 1784 to 1814, the total number of American ships at Canton, the trade's hub, increased rapidly to a sustained plateau of about thirty ships each year, even after being interrupted by embargoes and war.[78] Other Asian ports saw similar activity: over half the long-distance vessels visiting the French colonies in the Indian Ocean from 1793 to 1810 were American; Manila and Batavia were similarly dominated by the vessels flying the neutral Stars and Stripes.[79] Total American tea imports saw a similar growth. After 1795 American exports to Canton rose sharply, as did imports from China, reaching as much as $5 million a year, but with averages around $2 million and $3 million each, respectively.[80]

The China trade's growth tracks the overall direction of the US economy in the early national period.[81] As they did in the West Indies, American merchants in Asia filled a void left by other trading nations when war interrupted, supplying Europe and America with the Asian products that were ever in demand, especially tea. By the late 1790s they were supplying shipping to the Dutch at their own colonial ports in Asia, and in later years American vessels were even being chartered to service the Dutch trading concession at Nagasaki, Japan.[82] And from 1800 onward, only the British surpassed them in total tonnage and number of ships at Canton.[83]

Perhaps most astonishing was how swiftly Americans came to dominate the export of silver specie to China. From just under 0.5 percent of Western silver exports to China in 1785–91, Americans' share of the silver trade grew to 28 percent in 1792–98, to 64 percent in 1799–1806, and to 98 percent in 1807–13. Even after 1815 the United States supplied the overwhelming majority (74–98 percent) of Spanish silver dollars flowing into China, until countervailing trends reversed the centuries-old flow of silver from the New World to China.[84] The impact of US merchants on the structure and flow of commerce in China, and Asia more broadly, was significant.

The effect at home was more diffuse but still important. A sense of the China trade's share of the American overseas economy can be gained by comparing estimates of the total American trade reported from Canton with summaries of total US trade from the Treasury. In this comparison, American activity in the China trade averaged about 4 percent of the value of total US trade from 1795 to 1820, though it could range as high as 10 percent in particular years.[85] China was consistently an important trading partner for the United States. Americans' commerce there was often of greater value than trade with Spain, Portugal, or Russia, but perspective is important: China's share of US trade always ranked far below Britain's and managed only about half the value of US trade with France or the Netherlands.

The China trade entered the 1790s rich with capital, cultural and monetary, in the politics of the United States. Praising it for its potential as a source of much-needed commercial profits, diplomatic power, and national pride, the first federal Congress protected the trade with special tariffs and drawback provisions, protection that continued as the federal government began more regular administration of trade. Although the newest round of European wars that began in 1793 exposed Americans shipping to more risk—capture, impressment, and destruction—the conflagration worked to merchants' advantage too. In the China trade, as in other branches of commerce, Americans stepped into the gaps war created, feeding hungry European and colonial markets and using their neutral status to build a huge reexport business. Through this trade Americans also reshaped the dynamics of Asian markets. US merchants quickly became the leading carriers of foreign silver specie to China and second only to the British East India Company in the tonnage and number of ships at Canton—with similar market penetration elsewhere in Asia. By the middle of the 1790s, the confidence and special protections American leaders had invested in the China trade were paying handsome dividends, so much so that support for the China trade was not shaken even by renewed partisan conflict. Europe's wars were good for the politics and the economics of the American China trade. But what would happen when they ended?

CHAPTER TWO

The Paradox of a Pacific Policy

As the first era of the American China trade opened, John Jay compared the commerce's growth to Americans' westward migrations. "The Enterprize of our Countrymen is inconceivable," he told Thomas Jefferson in 1787, citing both the burgeoning "East Indies" trade and "the Number of young Swarms daily going down to settle in the Western Country." But while grouping overseas exchange and westward expansion together as examples of American energy, Jay paused to reveal a preference for one of these kinds of growth: he feared that "that Western Country will one Day give us Trouble—to govern them will not be easy," a concern that the flourishing trade with China did not provoke.[1]

Jay's distinction between westward and overseas expansion—and his preference for one—anticipated what would become a recurring divide in US politics. Contrasting notions of what kind of political economy and political culture would best support the new nation's fragile republican institutions underwrote many of the controversies of the 1790s.[2] While Jay's comment to Jefferson anticipated this rift—and prefigured both men's starring roles in helping to create it—the comment, oddly, did not reflect the place of the China trade in the politics of the early republic. Republicans vehemently disagreed with Federalists on many issues, most of all in their approach to the realities of global commerce and international diplomacy; but over the course of the 1790s they nonetheless came to understand the China trade as important to their political project, and they supported it accordingly—with disastrous results.

This chapter investigates how the China trade intersected with the politics of Jeffersonian Republicans and examines the unanticipated consequences this junction had for their policies when in power. Neither Thomas Jefferson nor James Madison was concerned with China's commerce early

in his career. In the broad "country" political tradition they and their allies claimed, commerce was sometimes necessary but always dangerous: it
introduced "luxuries" (like silks or teas) that sapped citizens' virtue, and
if allowed to grow beyond its proper role as a "handmaid" to the productive labor of agriculture, it could create inequalities of wealth that would
threaten domestic harmony. However, the Jay Treaty debate, an early formative moment for the opposition's emerging coalition, led Republicans to
see the China trade differently. The fierce rhetoric of the controversy tied
Republicans' nationalist attacks on British hegemony to the practice of free
trade in Asia while also helping to bring urban merchants into their coalition. Once in office, Republican officials' drive to right Jay's errors and prove
the validity of their theory of commercial coercion informed a wide set of
policies, often to ironic effect—helping to undercut the execution of Jefferson's embargo, scuttle negotiations with Great Britain, and enrage the co-
hort of merchants it was intended to protect. But neither these failures nor
the outbreak of war with Great Britain shifted Republicans' ideas about the
value of US commercial ties with China. Paradoxically, what led Republicans to reconceptualize the role of the China trade in their vision of political economy was peace—and the revolution in world trade that Napoleon's
defeat at Waterloo brought in its train.

Key Federalists had supported the China trade since the end of the War of
Independence. Some, like Jay, even argued that the troubles American traders faced in Asia were a reason to support ratifying the Philadelphia Constitution.[3] By the end of the first year of George Washington's presidency this
support for the China trade had moved from rhetoric to law. Congress created a navigation system that used protective duties to reserve the domestic
market for Asian goods to US traders, while Alexander Hamilton's Treasury
Department provided tea merchants with generous terms for tax payments.
Although federal authorities did not give American China traders every
special consideration they asked for—the need for custom revenues was
keen—they were particularly, and pointedly, solicitous of their interests.

Active support among the politicians and publics that coalesced into the
opposition party developed more slowly, emerging—as the Republican coalition did—in response to fresh controversies in the 1790s. Neither Thomas
Jefferson nor James Madison, the opposition's elite leaders, was a China
trade booster. When China appears in their writings during the 1780s and
early 1790s, they treat it as a philosophical subject, usually a metonym for
autarky or despotism (or both). Despite their support for commercial regulations as a foreign policy tool, Jefferson and Madison thought with the *idea*
of China, not Americans' actual China trade.[4] Neither was the China trade

a major concern of the democratic artisans and farmers who formed the opposition's main base of support and whose parades and public meetings provided its animating force. Instead, the China trade entered into Republicans' calculations because it was a concern of the "merchant-Republicans" whose practical interest in neutral trade made them targets for the belligerent parties in Europe's wars, and thus bargaining chips in US foreign policy.[5]

The controversy over the Jay Treaty jump-started the process.[6] John Jay was dispatched to London by the Washington administration in May 1794 to negotiate an end to the "vexations, spoliations, [and] captures" American mariners had been suffering at the hands of the British navy and to settle the "points of differences" remaining from the 1783 peace treaty, including the continued occupation of Great Lakes forts by British forces.[7] Because American trade and British attacks on neutral shipping were global, Jay's brief included specific instructions to ensure US access to the "East Indies" as well as the Caribbean.[8]

Negotiated from a position of geopolitical weakness, the treaty Jay signed on behalf of the United States on November 19, 1794, found few ardent supporters in the United States. Although it did not settle critical outstanding issues like impressment or the neutral status of US ships, the treaty did offer new ways of regulating boundary disputes and clarified Anglo-American trade relations. Washington's view—he was "not favorable to it" but thought it better to ratify it "than to suffer matters to remain as they are, unsettled"— became the Federalist line on the agreement, carrying it through ratification and then implementation.[9] American merchants, or those claiming to speak for them, concurred. The Jay Treaty settled differences that would otherwise "induce a war, with all its horrors and distresses," so as limited as it was, the agreement would "promote and extend" American commerce rather than injure it.[10]

In the torrent of criticism and public protests that erupted when the treaty's terms became public in the summer of 1795, opponents rejected this premise of certainty. One avenue for this critique centered on Americans' trade in Asia. At issue was Article 13 of the treaty, which governed Americans' access to "British Territories in the East Indies."[11] Treaty supporters argued, alongside Jay, that the article was "a manifestation and proof of good-will," because it made a trade that had existed heretofore "by the mere indulgence" of colonial administrators into a secure legal right.[12]

By contrast, Republicans argued that this "gleam of liberality" was a false dawn.[13] Americans, they pointed out, had for years traded at British ports in Asia, effectively at will, because the commodities they brought—specie, provisions, and naval stores—were in demand.[14] Article 13 did more than simply formalize existing access, however: the new limits it imposed threatened to choke it off. By banning Americans from the coasting trade between ports in Britain's East Indian colonies, limiting the goods they could export from these ports in times of war, and requiring that US vessels only export goods from British Asia to "some Port or Place in America"—instead of allowing them to continue to, say, Canton—the Jay Treaty disrupted the basic patterns of Americans' China trade.[15] As Republican critics noted, Americans' stops at Britain's Asian ports were just one component of more complex trading routes that centered on markets with more profitable goods: Americans carried "salted provisions to Bombay, where they take in cotton and sharks fins on freight to China," to "enable them to lay in a return cargo to great advantage."[16] In this regard, Article 13 was "among the most obnoxious" in the agreement—and similar in effect to Article 12, which so aggressively restricted American trading privileges in the British West Indies that the Senate successfully suppressed it from the final treaty.[17]

Although a notable through-line in the wide-ranging debate over the Jay Treaty, Article 13 was not the provision that overall attracted the most vitriol; Jay was burned in effigy for other sins. But because the Jay Treaty went into force, Article 13's restrictions—and the damage they did to American trade in Asia—remained a sore point for years, especially among those merchants the rising tide of controversy had helped wash into the Republican camp.[18] Further, it helped cement a tie, in Republican leaders' minds, between Americans' success in the China trade and their larger project of aggressively resisting British hegemony. When Republicans began to mount a serious electoral challenge to Federalists in the wake of the Jay Treaty, they held on to the concerns the debate had raised and made consideration of Americans' Asian trade part of their policymaking when they swept to power in the election of 1800.

This interest translated diffusely at first. During Jefferson's first term, other issues—patronage, repealing internal taxes, purchasing the Louisiana Territory from Napoleon, shrinking the central government, and so forth—occupied leading Republicans. But even in this early moment the recommendations that the administration's mercantile allies made reveal the unique place of the China trade in the Jeffersonians' operating theories of political economy and geopolitics. A freshet of memorandums produced by Philadelphia publicist Tench Coxe in late 1801 and early 1802 provide a good example. Anticipating the loss of his position as collector of revenue at Philadelphia (he was to be a casualty of Republicans' drive to eliminate internal taxes) he bombarded the president with fresh policy ideas in hopes of securing a new office.[19] Coxe was a known quantity to Jefferson and his cabinet. As assistant secretary of the treasury, Coxe had helped Jefferson draft his famous "Report on Commerce" in 1793, and in the years since he had continued to offer advice on diverse economic and legal matters to partisans of all kinds.[20] An experienced, if malleable, operative, Coxe understood his audience—and they him.

As Coxe knew, one of the Jefferson administration's goals was to wean the US economy off its reliance on British manufactured goods. Although he was not a devotee of the yeoman republic ideal, his own theories accorded with this goal.[21] More of a realist than his would-be patrons, Coxe knew national self-sufficiency in manufacturing was a long time off, so he thought it would be better to locate alternative sources of manufactures. For years Jefferson and Madison had hoped that the sister republic of France would supply the deficiency, only to be disappointed; but in February 1802 Coxe suggested that there was "one other source of supply which has not yet struck the American mind": China. Trafficking in common orientalist evaluations of China, Coxe noted that the "cheapness of living and of labor, and the imitative talents of that Country & people are well understood and ascertained." Arguing that European capitalists had "discourage[d] the importation of China manufactures, because they interfered with their own," Coxe pointed out that the United States and China faced no such conflict of interests: "We who do not manufacture piece goods, and shall not for some time, are at present situated differently."[22] It was a well-calculated appeal. In the *Notes on the State of Virginia*, Jefferson famously proclaimed his belief in the safety of agriculture over manufacturing for republican institutions: "While we have land to labour then . . . let our work-shops remain in Europe."[23] Stripped of its exoticism, Coxe's plan merely shifted the address of Jefferson's workshops.

In a follow-up letter, Coxe elaborated on the soundness of his "visionary and strange" idea. Playing to Jefferson's Anglophobia, Coxe argued that Americans were too "dependent upon one foreign nation in too great a degree for our supplies, our law notions, the stock of many of our monied institutions, our dresses, furniture & fashions, our didactic books and our credit business." However, if China could be persuaded, through careful commercial diplomacy, to "turn its industry to every species of manufacture [that] would tend to a proper estimation of our consumption," then the United States would have not only broken colonial ties, but also gained a hedge against Britain. Even the colonial products at the core of Americans' reexport trade—coffee, sugar, cocoa, and spices—"would all be procurable from China if they would attend to and improve the cultivation & preparation." By deepening their commercial ties with China and gently directing the Qing Empire toward the production of the goods that dominated the Atlantic, Americans could emancipate Asian commerce from Britain's attempted monopoly and secure their own independence at the same time.[24]

From the perspective of the early twenty-first century, when China's factories do supply American consumers with goods, Coxe's proposed relations between the United States and China seem prophetic. The contemporary practicality of Coxe's proposals was considerably less so; but his plan's resonance with Jeffersonian ideology was pitch-perfect.

Other commercial advisers besides Coxe drew the administration's attention to China, though in less dramatic (or desperate) ways. Recalling his stay in Canton in 1803, William Jones, a merchant and politician from Baltimore, reminded Secretary of State Madison how important a robust consular presence in Asia was in moments when the renewal of European war made the status of American property afloat particularly precarious.[25] The administration also received information through official channels. Reports from consuls in Asia, which trickled in a few times a year, almost always brought news of fresh harassment of American merchants and sailors by European naval or colonial officials. Perhaps reflecting these inputs, the Lewis and Clark expedition to explore the territory of the Louisiana Purchase featured a China trade component. Jefferson instructed the expedition's leaders to find the "most direct and practicable water communication across the continent for the purposes of commerce"—that is, commerce in the Pacific—and to see if the fur trade could be managed overland. He also provided Meriwether Lewis with the names of US consuls in Asian ports whom they could turn to for aid and credit if they needed to return by sea.[26]

By the time Lewis and Clark returned to St. Louis in September 1806, American access to the East Indies trade had become a more important consideration in Republican foreign policy. In late 1804 and early 1805 British authorities once again began capturing American cargoes and impressing sailors from American ships—at times even sealing off New York harbor. Between property seized and spiking insurance rates, the cost to American commerce was considerable.[27] American officials saw these developments as deliberate provocation. James Monroe argued from his ministerial post in London that the British ministry was plotting "to subject our commerce at present and hereafter to every restraint in their power." The British government, he claimed, had made it a "primary object" to "check if not to crush" the United States. In retrospect, Monroe's analysis seems dangerously self-centered—particularly in light of similar French efforts to restrict Americans' neutral trade. But his convictions were shared by his superiors in Washington, up to and including his suspicion that the new impressments and seizures were a tactic intended to force the United States to reinstate the terms of Jay's 1794 commercial treaty.[28]

At Canton, these new aggressions underlined just how little protection American merchants had from either their own government or the Qing

Empire. Although warships were ostensibly banned from Chinese territory, the area downstream from Canton's anchorage at Whampoa—and sometimes the anchorage itself—became a favorite hunting ground of British commanders seeking to press American sailors into service. In response to "this outrageous violence," US officials protested to British authorities, but they also led the American merchant community in an attempt to petition the Chinese government for protection.[29] Lacking any formal diplomatic relationship with the Qing Empire, foreign merchants and consuls in China had to pass the request through the merchant guild—the Cohong—which, in keeping with Qing protocol, almost always declined to push petitions up to Qing authorities. US consular agent Edward Carrington explained to his superiors that he had used his "utmost endeavors" to encourage the Chinese government to stop the British from preying on American ships and sailors but had been met with silence. "It appears," he lamented, "that the Citizens of the United States must rely on their own government to protect them when within the Empire of China against the violence of other nations who visit it."[30]

At home, during the winter of 1805–6 angry and panicked merchants deluged the president and Congress with memorials demanding federal action.[31] Reflecting the global nature of American trade—and of British efforts to arrest it—some of the petitioners from ports with significant trade with Asia took pains to highlight the capture of American vessels as a particularly egregious example of British injustice.[32] Reading these reports and petitions alongside dozens of others, federal officials understood the difficulties faced by China traders as additional instances of an existing problem. Writing to James Monroe in 1807, Madison described the "continued spirit of insolence and hostility" shown by the British squadron nearest to Washington, a quasi blockade of the port of Norfolk, and the harassment of a US revenue cutter carrying Vice President George Clinton and his daughter to New York before mentioning other British "violences against our vessels in foreign ports, as in Lisbon and Canton," which contributed to forming the "mass of injuries and provocations which have justly excited the indignant feelings of the nation and severely tried the patience of the Government."[33]

After lengthy debates over the proper reaction to these provocations, Congress eventually passed a weak non-importation act and recommended dispatching a special diplomatic mission to Britain.[34] After some prodding, Jefferson appointed the Baltimore Federalist William Pinkney to be a special envoy to work with James Monroe, US minister to the Court of St. James's, to make a new treaty with Britain. Secretary of State Madison outlined the mission's aims in a May 1806 letter of instruction. The administration charged Monroe and Pinkney with securing an agreement to end the British impressment of American sailors, as well as a guarantee of neutral rights to trade in colonial goods—one free from Britain's "pretext that a neutral trade, from enemy Colonies, through neutral ports, was a direct trade." But Madison also urged the envoys to broker a legal distinction separating trade with Britain's West Indian colonies from trade with its Eastern holdings. Madison argued that since the East Indian colonies were "generally open in peace as well as war," they should be free of any limitations. And while he admitted that US trade conferred "no particular benefit on the British possessions in the East Indies," he thought American access to British India on a most favored nation basis would be a fair settlement.[35]

Madison's interest in the Asian trade as a component of Anglo-American relations was buttressed by advice from Republican merchants in Congress. In the summer of 1806, Madison had requested from one of these congressmen a report on "American trade to the British West Indies, and generally in relation to our commerce with England and her possessions."[36] His informant, Jacob Crowninshield, was a Salem merchant whose family had leveraged success in Asian trade and Republican politics to come to regional prominence; he was also close to the administration. Crowninshield's response to Madison's request was a lengthy and expansive analysis of US commerce with the British Empire. In his view all subjects were not equal: while he briefly examined trade with the West Indies ("this commerce is held upon the most uncertain tenure"), Crowninshield spent the bulk of the report explaining in great detail the mechanics of Asian trade and the obstacles Britain had consistently placed in the way of US trade there.[37]

Crowninshield's emphasis was not surprising. His family's fortune, as well as his own training as a merchant, had come primarily through the East Indies trade.[38] Nevertheless, he made a thorough case that British efforts to destroy American trade in Asia—in India, China, and all the areas between—were of long standing and, if anything, more underhanded than similar efforts in the West Indies. Crowninshield's report went beyond the items other American merchants had complained of—illegal searches and seizures in Asian waters—to accuse "the English Government" of masterminding bloody attacks on native pepper ports in Sumatra so as to deny Americans the trade there, among other crimes.[39] Some of the wounds to American trade, Crowninshield admitted, were self-inflicted. He focused particularly on the injuries done by the Jay Treaty, which he claimed had "embarrassed" American trade in India by severely (and uniquely) limiting Americans' commercial freedom.[40] The long shadow of Jay's errors continued even in 1806, he averred: owing to the "remarkable" interpretations of international law by the "English Governors and Custom house officers in

India," who "pretend to consider the British treaty as in force at this day though it has expired three years since," Americans could still not trade freely in the subcontinent.[41]

Crowninshield's recommended remedy was Republican orthodoxy: he advised a forthright demand for greater trading rights in Asia, backed by the threat of total commercial exclusion.[42] This calculation was based on what he perceived to be American traders' strength as middlemen. While he noted that British officials were no doubt "desirous of renewing these restraints and prohibitions," he thought there was no danger Americans would be shut out of India because of the special role they played as carriers of silver specie, which the British required for purchases at Canton. "They want our specie," he wrote, "and they would probably exclude us from the Thames as from the Ganges and when they do either we ought to shut up the Chesapeake and Delaware to their flag." If tested, Crowninshield hinted darkly, "we should soon learn who would do best without the commerce of the other."[43] Thus advised, Madison's interest in East Indies affairs increased. Just a month before he would receive the final treaty, Madison revised his instructions to the envoys. In his new orders he lowered expectations for what kind of concessions would be possible but recommended Crowninshield's report as a guide on what to pursue with regard to the East Indies, to avoid the "impolicy" of the Jay Treaty.[44]

These hopes were not met. Instructed to negotiate for the end of impressment and to clear a path for the crucial reexport trade, Monroe and Pinkney instead returned a commercial agreement that effectively reinstated the hated Jay Treaty. There were a few minor concessions on the part of the British: Americans were granted most favored nation status at British ports, and the legality of the "broken voyage" was acknowledged—but only if American trade was hobbled by an import duty.[45] The new agreement recapitulated the Jay Treaty's limits on the carrying and coasting trade—a disaster for American traders, who depended on multiport voyages to generate the cash and cargoes for exchanges in India and shipped Indian goods to other ports, notably Canton.[46] Worse, the treaty lacked any guarantee against impressment and hedged even its protections with a framing note reserving Britain's right to retaliate against the United States should it acquiesce to France's commercial restrictions (e.g., the Berlin Decree).[47]

Monroe and Pickney anticipated that the administration would consider their treaty dead on arrival and sought to explain the concessions they had made—especially with regard to trade in Asia. They admitted, and regretted, that the article "which regulates our trade with the British possessions in India" was worse than the Jay Treaty's. Noting that they were apprised of "the importance attached to this commerce in America," they claimed they had "used the most zealous and persevering efforts . . . to emancipate it from some of those which the treaty of 1794 had distinctly sanctioned"— but that opposition from the East India Company had proved too great. On the matter of American ships being further restricted in their point of departure before arriving at Britain's Asian colonies, Monroe and Pinkney's warnings to their British counterparts about "the passions which it would enlist against the entire treaty" went unheeded; the East India Company preferred this construction of the treaty's language because it would secure their monopoly from American competition. Having explained to Madison how they had been blocked at every turn, the envoys argued that they had at least managed to render the article "less obnoxious, perhaps," by including a clause setting duties for US merchants in India as low as those paid by the "most favored nation."[48]

The envoys were right to have been concerned: the treaty's article covering Americans' East Indian commerce "elicited more criticism than any other" from the administration's commercial experts.[49] Once the administration and its allies had convinced themselves that the article limiting their trade in India would also interfere with other aspects of Asian trade—such as that carried by American ships between China and the West Indies—it became an administration talking point.[50] Maryland senator Samuel Smith, in particular, came out hard against the East Indies restrictions once Madison sent him a full copy of the treaty; Crowninshield came to the same conclusion.[51] Taking these opinions to heart, Madison concluded that the article restricting trade to British colonies "will have a more defalcating operation on our commerce, than was at first noticed," because the logic of the article suggested "that the trade between the Eastern Colonies, and certain Eastern countries and ports as China, Mocha, etc. etc. to which G.B. has not applied her principle [the Rule of 1756] at all . . . will be abolished."[52] When the administration decided to formally approach Britain to request further adjustments to the treaty, concerns about the broad effects on Asian trade—both in India and between China and the Caribbean—were two of the six points the administration requested be amended before ratification could proceed.[53]

The clauses concerning Asian trade were not the deciding factor in the administration's—and particularly Jefferson's—rejection of the treaty. But Britain's harsh line on the East Indies trade was an unexpected, if useful, insult; together with a continued unwillingness to make guarantees on impressment, the administration used it to make a case that the treaty was yet another affront to US sovereignty. The new regulations on the East Indies trade, buttressed by a long-standing feeling that Asian trade was somehow different from the more familiar mercantilist machinations in the Caribbean, gave the administration a plausible reason, beyond impressment, to reject the agreement.

Proof that the Jefferson administration's interest in protecting American trade in Asia was more than a front came quickly, in reaction to a fresh provocation. The HMS *Leopard*'s attack on the USS *Chesapeake* outside Norfolk harbor on June 22, 1807, triggered a crisis in Anglo-American affairs just as the final considerations of the Monroe-Pinkney Treaty were dying out. The main subject of the conflict was once again impressment: the *Leopard*'s commander arrested four sailors from among the *Chesapeake*'s crew who were accused of deserting the Royal Navy. As war threatened in the wake of the attack, the administration moved swiftly to develop and circulate plans for protecting American traders in Asia.

Working with maritime insurance companies to determine what American ships were likely to be in Asia, Jefferson directed his cabinet to devise a plan to warn and protect American traders in the East Indies. The stakes were high: with an estimated $15–20 million worth of American property "now out in that quarter" and potentially at risk of capture in case of war, the administration was keen to develop instructions on what would likely be the safest route back home in case of hostilities. Jefferson relied on Secretary of the Treasury Albert Gallatin, then resident in New York, to take the lead in collecting information from merchants and insurers and to map out the route.[54] The administration concluded that the US consuls at Port Louis in Mauritius, at the western edge of the Indian Ocean, and at Java Head, a cape west of present-day Jakarta on the eastern edge of the Indian Ocean, would have the best chance at contacting American traders as they sailed homeward, without raising a panic. Madison therefore ordered these officials to "exert all your attentions and prudence in apprizing" American captains of the danger.[55]

Without a navy capable of performing convoy duty, the specific advice consisted of sailing instructions, as approved by domestic insurers for maximum safety from British interference.

> The course by which it is supposed the returning Vessels will be least exposed will be to keep as far distant as possible from the Cape of Good Hope, to pass 15 or 20 leagues westward of St. Helena, to cross the line between 23° & 20° West Longitude, [the middle of the South Atlantic] [and] to shape their course afterwards as far as possible Eastward of the West Indies and endeavor to make land between Nantucket & Rhode Island, or to the Southward of the Chesapeake as may best suit the particular destination.[56]

Finding the funds to send out a ship with the directions proved difficult on short notice, but at the last minute Gallatin approved a hurried advance from the customs collector at Baltimore to fill the gap, reasoning that "in case of disaster happening there [in Asia] from want of information, much blame would, and not altogether without foundation, attach to the Administration."[57] Calculations about domestic politics were moved by Asian trade.

War did not break out in 1807. Instead, stymied by a British administration unwilling to recognize the US definition of neutral rights, and further encumbered by a new round of mercantilist strictures emerging from both France and Britain, the Jefferson administration and its Republican allies in Congress attempted to impose their will on the belligerents through other means. On December 22, 1807, they deployed the ultimate in passive-aggressive commercial warfare: a full-scale embargo of American ports. Although Jefferson's intention was to keep American "seamen and property from capture, and to starve the offending nations," the embargo's effects quickly turned a controversial foreign policy measure into an explosive domestic political issue. Like the Louisiana Purchase, the embargo was an example of events' leading to exceptions to the "pure" Jeffersonian ideology of the small, strictly construed federal state. Adding to the irony of opposing interference with some Americans' commerce by interfering with *all* Americans' commerce—fighting fire with self-immolation—enforcing the embargo led Republicans in Congress to arm the executive with unprecedented coercive powers.[58]

The "candid and liberal experiment" was a disaster for American trade.[59] In 1808 exports declined by almost 80 percent, and imports by 60 percent.[60] The China trade suffered similar losses—an 88 percent decline in exports to China and a 76 percent decline in imports—though the full effect was not felt until 1809 owing to the long travel times between North America and Canton.[61] Most of the commercial community regarded the policy as a fatal intrusion into economic affairs—and traders turned to their representatives, partners, and allies (especially in New England state governments) to escape "this Commercial purgatory" by legal and extralegal means.[62]

As soon as the law was signed, merchants inundated Washington with requests for exemptions. Very quickly, one of the primary problems facing the administration became how to answer these requests with fairness and propriety while maintaining the embargo's original purpose. Congress's attempt to resolve this issue through a supplementary act complicated matters. It gave the president authority to grant ship owners and merchants permission "to dispatch a vessel in ballast" to collect property that had been stranded abroad by the embargo.[63] The day after the measure was signed into law, Jefferson recognized the position the legislature had put him in (if he had not realized it sooner), explaining to Gallatin that he had already received enough petitions to "understand there is scarcely a merchant in the United States who has not property somewhere beyond [the] sea."[64]

Gallatin and Jefferson together decided that their aims would best be met if these permits were limited to the "recovery of goods in the West Indies."[65] But they did make exceptions to this rule: of the 594 special permits that Gallatin's Treasury Department reported issuing during the embargo, six were for vessels headed to Asia.[66] (The Treasury was responsible for customs enforcement, and thus for policing the embargo.) Five of these Asian voyages were issued permits on the basis the law described—the retrieval of property from abroad. For example, Willett Coles and Henry and Edmund Fanning petitioned to send the ship *Tonquin* to collect a cargo of sandalwood they had contracted for at the "Friendly islands" and then to sell the wood at Canton, "its only market." Gallatin worried that this last step was a potential violation of the embargo's stricture against any engagement in "traffic, freighting, or other employment" during a voyage, but Jefferson was not concerned. Airily explaining that "the true key for the construction of everything doubtful in a law, is the intention of the law-makers," Jefferson replied that "conversion of the sandal wood into a more portable form,"— into goods salable on the American market, or into hard cash—fulfilled "the object of the law," so he granted permission.[67]

The departure of the ship *Beaver* on August 16, 1808, marked a far more controversial exception.[68] Courtesy of John Jacob Astor, whose vast fur-trading empire had brought him into Asian commerce, the vessel departed New York harbor carrying a special passenger, one Punqua Wingchong, along with $45,000 in what was purportedly Punqua's property.[69] In mid-July 1808, Punqua had traveled to Washington with an interpreter in order to meet Jefferson and "sollict the means of departure . . . to China."[70] Although the meeting never took place—the president had retired to Monticello and so was absent from the capital—Jefferson gave Punqua permission to hire a ship to go to Canton as an act of "national comity," a "means of making our nation known advantageously at the source of power in China." A month later, the man who had been represented to Jefferson as a "Chinese merchant" stood ready to depart from New York in Astor's ship. In contrast to the other permitted exceptions to the embargo, the allowance given to the *Beaver* to furnish transportation homeward for an important Chinese visitor was, in Jefferson's mind, a piece of diplomacy, a "chance of obtaining a permanent national good" that could not be passed up, even within "the great field of the embargo."[71]

Jefferson's evaluation was not widely shared, and just who the Chinese visitor actually was remained an open question. In the letter introducing Punqua to Jefferson, New York senator Samuel L. Mitchill proclaimed him a

"Chinese merchant," and Gallatin followed suit in his orders authorizing the voyage. But Jefferson promoted him, naming him a "mandarin"—a Qing official—a status that public supporters and critics of the *Beaver*'s voyage alike picked up. Those opposed used the title to dramatize Jefferson's error, declaring Punqua to be the mirror image of a potent official, a "petty shopkeeper" who was being used as "an insignificant instrument in the hands of others." An influential account published years after the incident pushed even further, declaring Punqua to be but "a common Chinese dock loafer" that Astor had "picked up . . . in the Park" and dressed up in a mandarin's costume in order to evade the embargo.[72]

It seems most likely that Punqua was a shopkeeper from the suburbs of Canton, not a hong merchant or a mandarin. As one of the many small-time traders working in the cramped shops that lined the side streets of the foreign quarter, he likely lacked official permission from the Qing government to trade with Westerners, much less to voyage abroad.[73] The reason for his voyage to the United States is not clear. Correspondence within the Jefferson administration suggested he had come to America "for the purpose of collecting debts due to his Father's Estate."[74] Though Chinese merchants did pursue collections in the United States, granting power of attorney to trusted American proxies to sue in US courts, Punqua presents the unique case of pursuing his business in person.[75] Perhaps the size of his operation made an attempt at in-person collection the most economical decision; or perhaps he simply wanted to see the world. Likewise, the degree of Astor's management of the situation is difficult to assess. It would be overstating the case to say Punqua was Astor's puppet; but if his goals were compatible with Astor's, it seems logical to conclude that the master of the North American fur trade would know how to take advantage of an opportunity when he saw one. The *Beaver*'s departure thus likely was the result of a coincidental conjunction of interests.

Whatever the rationale for his travel, Punqua's voyage home caused consternation among the forcibly idled American mercantile community. Despite the quiet, indirect approach to the administration, as soon as Jefferson had granted the permit, the *Beaver*'s voyage became common knowledge. Just one day after the administration moved, a notice appeared in the *New-York Evening Post* reporting that one of Astor's ships would carry "the Mandarin Chief and his Secretary" back to China. The news spread quickly, making the rounds not only of the New York commercial and political newspapers, but also of papers up and down the East Coast and into the Appalachian interior.[76] Astor's competitors were quick to criticize the exception as fraudulent and unfair. A group of Philadelphia merchants wrote to inform Gallatin that Punqua was "an imposter" who was neither "Mandarine" nor a "Merchant of distinction," but just a "petty shopkeeper in Canton, utterly incapable of giving a credit." Going beyond the question of Punqua's identity to attack the other embargo exceptions the administration issued, the merchants also declared the idea that any American had property to collect at Canton "equally fallacious," because the cash nature of business in China meant no property was ever left idle between seasons.[77] With a harsher tone but hitting the same points, an editorial in the *New York Commercial Advertiser* declared the permission granted the *Beaver* a fraud because Punqua was not who he claimed to be. The *Advertiser's* editors did see a silver lining to the scandal: perhaps the voyage's success would lead to a looser embargo.[78]

Both Astor and Gallatin disclaimed any fraud or misrepresentation.[79] In a letter to the *New York Commercial Advertiser*, Astor called out his accusers, offering to give "a statement of facts" to whoever had leaked the story, which would, he said "relieve him from the anxiety under which he appears to labor for the honor of the government, and the reputation of all concerned."[80] Gallatin made no excuses, maintaining that the permit was issued under the same rules that affected any other vessel; if the *Beaver's* owners brought back property beyond what was allowed, "their bond will be forfeited." He did state, however, that the merchants interested in the *Beaver* had previously been denied permission to go to China.[81] Gallatin was implying that Jefferson had overruled him in pursuit of what can only be judged a fanciful interest in improving relations with China. Discussion of Punqua's identity continued into the fall, and "Jefferson's mandarin" became a partisan punchline—and an embarrassment to Gallatin, whose efforts to impose some system on the embargo were increasingly in vain.[82]

Because it represented commerce beyond Europe, the China trade was a field of particular importance to the Jefferson administration as it tried to align policy with practical economy. But time and time again, Jefferson and his allies ended up undermining the China trade alongside what the government's Federalist opponents had labeled his "Chinese policy" of economic autarky, the embargo.[83] Although not at the center of Jeffersonian policy, the administration's tight embrace of the *idea* of Asian commerce imposed significant costs on the government's political success. Further, these decisions accomplished all this while simultaneously losing the support of China traders. Concentrated in New England and New York, many repaid the administration's concern for their business with opposition, and smuggling was widespread. Committed Federalist merchants had difficulty understanding why impressments or seizures should have become a political issue in the first place, instead of a business decision. As Essex Junto grandee George Cabot observed, profits could still be had even if just one out of every three vessels escaped capture.[84] But even those that benefited most from Jefferson's choices, like the Perkins brothers of Boston (who shipped cargo on the *Beaver*'s return voyage), made no secret of their distaste for the "mad policy of the Democrats."[85]

This focus on Asian trade as a component of Republican geopolitics did not end with Jefferson's retirement. Though occupied with the fallout from the embargo experiment, Madison at least entertained plans for closer ties with China (as always, positioned as a loose alliance against Europe), and after the onset of hostilities with Great Britain he was subjected to a Punqua-like request to grant a Chinese visitor permission to return home in an American ship.[86] Although in these cases Madison's administration did not embarrass itself as Jefferson's had—and received less publicity for it, too—the political culture that Madison and his cabinet cultivated continued to invite the same kind of propositions.

The War of 1812 was an eventful conflict for Americans' Asian trade, but not a mortal one. The struggle with Britain swept US ships in all lines of commerce off the seas, including those bound to or returning from Asia. At Canton, the advent of war marked an intensification of efforts already under way. Since at least 1806, Americans there had been facing invasive, and sometimes deadly, searches and seizures by the Royal Navy squadron patrolling just outside the mouth of the Pearl River. Great Britain's blockade efforts in North America kept many American ships from even leaving the United States; and as shipping opportunities of all kinds were arrested, many merchants took the opportunity to explore other uses for their capital—notably in manufacturing.[87] The declaration of hostilities did, however, provide some new chances: with the right of armed reprisal against British shipping now open to them, a handful of daring firms sent ships armed with cannon and letters of marque to trade and privateer in Asian waters, with some success.

In 1814, skirmishing between British naval ships and American privateers spilled far enough into Chinese jurisdiction that Qing authorities intervened. Reacting to incidents during the spring and summer of 1814, in the fall the governor-general of Guangdong and Guangxi cut off access to supplies and suspended trade at Canton until the warring parties agreed to keep their "petty quarrels" out of Chinese waters. Admonishing the foreigners to "obey and respect the prohibitions of the Celestial Empire," he reminded them that the empire was "impartial toward all nations, but will not tolerate any nation which dares disobey."[88] For those American traders who managed to reach Canton and then make it back home with a load of scarce teas and silks, the starved domestic market proved a bonanza. The partners from one Boston firm that sent an armed vessel to China crowed about the profit potential to an associate they hoped would invest in the venture: "Teas, sir, Teas are no plus ultra [sic] of Mercantile profit—Young Hysons at $2.45! . . . The several vessels going are small sharp ones & even in case they all go safe . . . cannot bring enough to effect the market here if the war continues."[89] Such successes were, of course, rare in wartime.

The war constricted trade substantially, if temporarily. It did not in itself cause structural changes in the commerce, though by weeding out weaker firms and trading strategies it helped accelerate several ongoing shifts. Notably, the emergencies caused by the embargo and the war helped establish permanent resident agents at Canton as the norm, replacing the older tradition of organizing investors for one-off voyages with supercargoes. War also helped speed consolidation: the total number of firms and ports involved dwindled as New York came to dominate US commerce more generally. And perhaps most consequentially in terms of the human cost, after the war opium, instead of silver, became the major commodity Americans brought to China for trade.[90]

Peace was far more consequential. Federalist opposition to Jeffersonian policies during the embargo and war eras, culminating in the Hartford Convention, was in part a war of the commercial and shipping sectors against other interest groups—and many of the members and supporters of the Hartford Convention traced their own and their families' fortunes to the China trade. One of the country's most successful China merchants, Thomas Handasyd Perkins, even served as one of the three "Lord High Commissioners" (a Republican taunt) who arrived in Washington to deliver New England's shrill demands to President Madison just as news of the peace declared at Ghent and Andrew Jackson's victory at New Orleans arrived in the capital.[91]

But as embarrassing as a China trader's role in the separatist stunt was, it was the structural changes that peace delivered that shifted the political ground. The end of major hostilities in Europe closed off the opportunity Americans had exploited since 1793—serving as the neutral merchant marine for continental Europe and its colonies. Yet even as new competitors and mercantilist restrictions sprouted up again in Europe and European colonies, Americans' China trade, along with the merchant marine as a whole, continued to prosper—which suggested to the new generation of US policymakers in control of Washington that the protections that had been deemed so crucial in earlier years might be ripe for reconsideration. A reevaluation of the value of Americans' trade in China began in the negotiations and legislation that ended the war. And in the new regime of the "American system," Americans came to regard the China trade as a threat to independence rather than a boon.

CHAPTER THREE

Troubled Waters

When the ship *Congress* sailed from Boston bound for the Dutch colonial port of Batavia in 1824, it went using some of the old habits of trade and some new. On the more traditional side of the ledger, Jacaob [*sic*] Caswell and Benjamin Brintnall entrusted "one Hundred Spanish milled Dollars" to an agent who promised to "Carey & Invest" it "from port to port." Caswell and Brintnall were employing a classic cabotage strategy, designed to make the most of limited resources—and characteristic of American trade in Asia since the Revolution.[1]

William Gray, the *Congress*'s owner, adopted a more sophisticated approach. A wealthy merchant whose obituary claimed "there was not a commercial place in the civilized world where his name was not familiar," Gray was a fixture of Boston's mercantile elite and a player in Massachusetts politics. In his prime, he owned and managed one of the nation's largest commercial fleets; in his later years he was instrumental in organizing and leading the Boston branch of the Bank of the United States, New England's most important financial institution.[2] The commercial and financial relationships Gray spent a lifetime cultivating guided his investment in the *Congress*.

His network of correspondents was critical. He instructed the captain of the ship, Nathaniel Kinsman, to consult his contacts in Asia—resident commission merchants—before making purchases, to better profit from local market conditions. Gray also stocked the ship using knowledge those correspondents provided. He packed the hold with $7,786 worth of Western commodities (candles, beef, flour, seltzer water), readily salable at any European colonial port, and invested $19,318 in opium, a smokable narcotic with a large and growing market in Southeast Asia and in China's southern ports.[3] Gray also gave Kinsman access to up to $50,000 in credit with his London bankers, Baring Brothers, so he could take advantage of good prices for return cargoes of Asian products as he encountered them: tea at Canton, sugar at Manila, or cotton at Calcutta. This credit was to be drawn on via bills of exchange, which Kinsman most likely carried as a packet of preprinted forms—making the *Congress*'s lightest cargo simultaneously its most valuable, modern, and secure.[4]

Gray's choices make it clear that he had good intelligence on the new system of global exchange that had taken shape in the aftermath of the Napoleonic Wars. Though not centrally directed, this system depended on capital flowing through London-centered networks in the form of silver dollars, bank drafts, and bills of exchange—a movement of money whose impact increased exponentially with each mile traveled. These workings promoted the expansion of European empires in Asia and the Pacific, as well as the reorganization of the China trade as an opium traffic. The system reached across the Atlantic too, funding the expansion of the cotton frontier in the Southwest United States and helping industrialization take root in the Northeast. Gray's strategy for the voyage of the *Congress* illustrates one of the ways Americans engaged with this modern global capitalist system, and it helps reveal the complex connections capital created between diverse sites, from cotton plantations on the Mississippi River to opium storeships in the Pearl River Delta.[5]

This chapter analyzes the development of the modern system of global capitalism in the early nineteenth century from the perspective of the China trade, and traces its effect on American political economy. It begins by charting the political and economic changes that made Gray's choices about the *Congress*'s cargo possible, and profitable. After the trauma of the French wars, US policymakers tried to minimize reliance on overseas commerce by pushing a suite of policies intended to develop the nation's domestic markets—what its supporters called the "American System." The China trade came under hostile scrutiny in this political environment for its role in creating annual shortages of specie, thought to spark banking panics and inhibit domestic growth. Nicholas Biddle, America's would-be central banker, attempted to use the international reputation of the Bank of the United States to calm these dangerous tides of coin. While he found some success in pushing the Bank's bills as replacements for international specie transfers, his actions empowered his enemies' campaign to destroy the institution and, further, helped crystallize a new global system of capital circulation that linked American cotton, Indian opium, and Chinese tea though the medium of British credit.[6] In part because of the choices of men like William Gray, by the mid-1830s Americans had become close collaborators with a liberalizing British Empire, including in its incursions into China. Attempting to evade the gyres of world trade had, ironically, immersed Americans more deeply in what China merchant John Murray Forbes termed "the troubled waters of speculation"—and subjected them to a fluid system that threatened the solidity of social ties and sovereignty in East and West alike.[7]

When peace broke out in Europe in 1815, old systems of political economy broke with it. After two decades of war in which international shipping exposed the United States and its citizens to depredations by European powers, relying on trade as an engine for prosperity now seemed more dangerous than useful. The reestablishment of European imperial systems also eliminated profitable neutral shipping, driving Americans "to look more to their own internal means and resources."[8] From the perspective of the Republicans ruling Washington, only active government intervention could strengthen the nation's domestic economy sufficiently to withstand the next war.[9] A side effect of this reorientation was that powerful Americans began to regard China traders—for so long exemplars of maritime commerce's national benefits—as at best peripheral to the nation's prosperity, and at worst impediments to it.

One index of China traders' lowered status in an increasingly protectionist environment was their lack of influence over tea tariffs.[10] Under the Hamiltonian system in operation since the 1790s, tea was taxed relatively heavily as one of the "luxury" consumables the state relied on for revenue (spirits, wine, and sugar were others). However, American tea merchants were protected from competition by a high duty on teas carried on foreign ships. But after the War of 1812, legislators began to give consumers' cheap access to tea priority over merchants' profits. Over the course of two decades, and amid significant battles over protectionist policy, politicians from both sides of the aisle increasingly agreed that tea was "one of the necessaries of life" and worked to lower tea tariffs to zero, eliminating protections for American merchants.[11] Though China traders supported these moves, as they did free trade policy generally, they did not drive the change; politicians' desire to appeal to consumers did. (Traders' inability to interest the government in cracking down on tea smuggled from Canada reflected a similar ineffectiveness.)[12]

China traders were also affected by a trend toward tougher enforcement of commercial regulations. After the War of 1812, Congress and the Treasury began to aggressively question merchants' close association with customs house officials and imposed tighter controls. Federal authorities were especially eager to rein in the long-standing practices of letting merchants use customs house bonds to pay import duties, and of relying on merchants to accurately appraise the value of their own goods. Originally expedients intended to provide enough flexibility to enlist merchants' loyalties to the new republic and secure their payment of (at least some) duties, over time these practices had become expected services—and were abused. China traders' notable excesses and frauds in both areas were exposed in the course of federal investigations in the 1820s, contributing to the trade's declining reputation as well as to the more direct unraveling of major import-export firms in New York and Philadelphia.[13]

China traders' peculiar interests did not find a comfortable home in the emerging party coalitions disputing national politics in the 1820s.[14] But that did not mean their commerce was not attended to; far from it. The part of that business that led them to ship millions of dollars' worth of silver to Canton every year attracted a great deal of interest from publicists and policymakers concerned that this "drain" was crippling the nation's currency and destabilizing the republic.

American merchants had always shipped significant amounts of silver specie to Asia. Spanish-minted dollars were the only commodity always welcome in Canton's markets; and because of the United States' considerable involvement in Latin American and Caribbean trade, US-based merchants usually had access to a ready supply. Spanish dollars also held a special place in the American economy. They were legal tender, a common medium for commercial transactions, and functioned as a reserve currency backing banks' paper notes. Silver specie was deeply important to the nation's monetary stability.[15]

Before the boom in state banking institutions that accompanied the War of 1812 (and the interregnum between the First and Second Bank of the United States) China traders' specie shipments attracted some comment but no significant attention. After the war, policymakers' expectations changed. Awash in banks and bank money and nervous about the soundness of the currency, legislators in Washington became alarmed at the rate of silver exports—just as American merchants became the dominant suppliers of specie to Canton.[16] This trend eventually slowed and then reversed in the 1830s as Chinese demand for dollars slackened and opium imports and bills drawn on London replaced silver as key trade commodities and financial instruments, respectively. But in the medium term, this unprecedented flow attracted attention. The steepest parts of the ramping-up of American silver imports coincided not only with the new approach to political economy in the United States, but also with a major economic downturn, the Panic of 1819. Many contemporaries connected the outflow of silver to Asia to the credit contractions, bank runs, and currency instability then plaguing the country—an impression that shaped attitudes toward the China trade for decades.[17]

In the context of a souring economic outlook, some of the same voices that had pushed for tariff reform began arguing that China traders were creating a scarcity of specie. They built on a foundation of existing knowledge in political economy: China merchants' large silver exports were already a mainstay of tracts on banking, Treasury reports, and statistical accounts, and they even appeared as contextual information in articles about the China trade.[18] The arch-protectionist *Niles' Weekly Register* was among the first and most influential to apply this knowledge to the banking crisis. "So great is the present rage for the East India and China trade," *Niles'* reported in November 1818, "that Spanish dollars are at about 9 per cent. premium, over the best bank notes"—in other words, merchants' desire for silver was devaluing the paper of the best American banks. "We are altogether willing to wish," *Niles'* continued, "that many may 'burn their fingers,' [in this trade] for it certainly is disadvantageous to us."[19] A month later the paper reprinted an even more extreme suggestion, from a "northern correspondent of the *National Intelligencer*" who argued that merchants exporting silver coin from the United States should forfeit the coin they sent out of the country and lose their right to vote.[20] Although the protectionist editor of *Niles'* preferred more familiar measures ("levying *rightful* duties"), he nonetheless agreed with the spirit of the suggestion. Traders to China who exported specie were, in his opinion, "destructive merchants . . . whose business ought to be annihilated" for the trouble they caused with the currency.[21]

Cooler heads came to similar conclusions, if not the same solutions. In early 1819 Congress considered banning the export of specie and other precious metals but in the end concurred with Secretary of the Treasury William H. Crawford that such a policy was appropriate only to the "dark ages."[22] (For their part, China traders did not judge any export ban enforceable: "Congress may pass laws for the non-exportation of specie, but we do not think they can prevent it from going out."[23]) Reflecting on the crisis a year later, Crawford decided that paper money was the real underlying problem—but he had not forgotten the role of the China trade in making the panic worse. He told Congress that "the prosecution of the trade to the East Indies and to China" drained "the metallic currency" in amounts that "seriously affected the amount of circulation, by compelling the banks to diminish their discounts."[24] In his own retrospective analysis, Mathew Carey agreed. The Philadelphia entrepreneur, whose writings on political economy provided significant intellectual support for Henry Clay's "American System," described how the "extravagant drain of specie for the China trade" had pressed banks to the breaking point, leaving them "no alternative but to press on their customers, or to stop the payment of specie," creating "great distress and embarrassment" for all.[25]

The ignominy of having helped to cause a major financial crisis proved a stubborn stain. For the rest of the 1820s, supporters of commercial and shipping interests felt it necessary to offer apologias for the China trade's part in currency exports. Some argued that specie exports were a small or unimportant part of the trade compared with its benefits. "We hear the India and China trade denounced, as a commerce conducted on our side, in a great measure, with gold and silver," Daniel Webster lamented in April 1824 in reply to a burst of protectionism from Henry Clay. "These opinions, Sir, are clearly void of all just foundation, and we cannot too soon get rid of them."[26] Answering a congressional inquiry in 1825, well-known Boston China merchant Thomas Handasyd Perkins substantiated his friend Webster's point in his explanation of the trade's operations. The China trade, he said, "cannot be prosecuted with specie alone." Explaining that while his firm "averaged more than a million of dollars annually" in imports from China, they had not "shipped a Spanish dollar for the past *three years to China*," instead exporting "opium from Turkey, British goods from Great Britain, lead and quicksilver from Gibraltar, and the same articles, on a large scale, from Trieste" to Canton. The funds used to make these purchases abroad were from "merchandise shipped from China or this country, and bills of exchange."[27] Replacing coin with credit to solve the problem of specie drain was not just a profitable practice for Perkins's firm—as an answer to the specie drain debate, it became a crucial component of Nicholas Biddle's plan to use the Bank of the United States to domesticate global flows of capital.

Biddle was elected to the presidency of the Second Bank of the United States in 1822. The would-be central banker's ambitious agenda did not at first include the China trade—but a few years of managing operations changed his mind.[28] The trouble was merchants' annual springtime calls on northeastern banks for silver specie to outfit their adventures to India and China. Perkins's claims notwithstanding, by 1825 Biddle had noticed that these annual calls intensified the already significant challenge of maintaining liquidity across the Bank's extensive network of branches. The outflow affected the Bank directly, since China traders were not infrequently major BUS customers—and directors—as well as indirectly, when withdrawals from smaller banks reduced their reserves and forced them to curtail business, producing "a corresponding pressure on all classes of the community" that Biddle felt the BUS must address.[29]

To smooth out these perturbations, in the spring of 1825 Biddle's bank began selling what he called "E India Bills." These were bills of exchange issued by the BUS to American merchants that drew on the Bank's accounts with European banks. They had a number of special features. Denominated in pounds sterling and redeemable at London and sometimes Paris banks, they were designed to find a ready market among private "country" traders in Asia looking for secure remittances back to Europe. Payable at 120 days after sight, much longer than the standard 30 or 60 days, the bills were well suited to the long travel times the China trade required—a premise that the Bank's lending agreement made explicit, requiring that the bills be negotiated only "to the eastward of the Cape of Good Hope." In exchange for using the BUS's credit, purchasers agreed to provide a one-year promissory note as security and to pay a 2.5 percent premium on the sterling-dollar exchange rate. If the bills went unused, merchants could return them to the BUS and get their money back for a 1 percent premium—a small fee, Biddle thought, for guaranteeing "the solvency of a merchant for thirteen months."[30]

In many ways the BUS's East India bills were indistinguishable from other private bills already used in the China trade. But because they were issued by (and drew on) some of the world's most reputable banks, they worked better as currency than private bills; they were readily trusted.[31] This was by design. Biddle and the BUS's directors understood the bills as an extension of methods they had perfected on the domestic scene that used the Bank's institutional power to effect cheap and easy transfers of capital. Since 1817 the Bank had bought domestic bills of exchange and sold drafts on BUS branches, facilitating secure and reliable remittances for long-distance trade within the United States. From 1825, "E India bills" leveraged the Bank's size, expertise, and credit to accomplish the same feat across vaster distances.[32]

But Biddle intended the East India bills to do more than help merchants move money. As the Bank had done in forging connections between American markets, Biddle worked to position the BUS as an intermediary in international commerce, in order to create a buffer capable of absorbing the "sudden and violent fluctuations" of global trade.[33] Specifically, East India bills provided a means to head off the financial panics that could result when the spread in the price of specie in domestic versus foreign markets widened sufficiently to induce the export of silver. As Biddle explained to P. P. F. Degrand, a member of the BUS's stable of friendly publicists, during such moments of crisis, large exports of coin led state-charted banks to "diminish their issues" of notes and restrict their business, "sometimes with great rapidity." While this was a "natural & inevitable remedy" to changing circumstances, it nonetheless was a "harsh corrective" that "may bring in its train the most disastrous consequences": a credit crunch and business failures.[34]

Fall 1825 had threatened just such a crisis. A summer slump in cotton prices and the bursting of an investment bubble in Latin America caused a wave of failures on both sides of the Atlantic and led the Bank of England to contract its credit—difficulties that sharply increased specie calls on American banks, including the BUS.[35] To head off disaster, Biddle worked the BUS as a "balance-wheel," selling coin and issuing notes to provide liquidity and counter prevailing market forces. It was a course, he later alleged, "by which there can be no doubt that much inconvenience & distress was averted." Eager to promote his good work as well as highlight his recent innovations, Biddle further explained to his friend Degrand that the BUS's practice of "furnishing its bills for the trade to countries east of the Cape of Good Hope" had been another important "preservative" for the Bank's specie stocks. In May 1826 Degrand published a glowing account of the Bank's actions in his newspaper, noting that the issuance of "East-Indies" bills was part of an "enlightened plan" and that the phlegmatic courage of the BUS's officers had allowed the United States to "ESCAPE FROM THE MISFORTUNES WHICH HAVE OVERWHELMED THE BRITISH EMPIRE."[36]

Biddle's experiments with bills may have been intended to protect Americans from the misfortunes of the British Empire, but they did little to separate them from the empire itself. In China, Biddle's bills became a part of Americans' entanglement in British imperial schemes. This was partly a result of shifts in business practices as the trade grew, notably the development of a community of American merchants who became full-time residents of Canton; but it was also a consequence of active strategizing, as American merchants scrambled to adapt after the end of the Napoleonic Wars shrank the profits of neutral trade.

In the first decades of the American China trade, the business decisions for each voyage were managed by a supercargo, an agent for the ship's investor-owners who accompanied the vessel and oversaw all transactions in return for a share of the profits. The system was a common and effective one for new trades with uncertain routes. But as they gained experience in Canton and spent longer periods there, some Americans found that having a resident agent was a substantial advantage. Resident merchants knew local conditions better and could cultivate closer relationships with business partners like hong merchants, enabling them to get better rates on commodities and warehouse space, which made it easier to time sales to meet the market; and they could leverage all these services and relationships for further profit by offering them to other merchants on commission.[37]

By the early 1820s the dominant firms in the trade all relied on resident merchants. The families and firms linked in the "Boston Concern"—Perkins, Sturgis, Forbes, and so on—seized on the form early and aggressively, establishing Perkins and Company at Canton in 1804.[38] A formal expansion of brothers James and Thomas Handasyd Perkins's mercantile empire, the outpost was the latest part of a network of firms designed to take advantage of the mutually profitable and interdependent circuits in fur, silver, tea, and cotton goods linking the West Indies, East Asia, Europe, and the Pacific Northwest. But the Canton branch nearly perished as it was born. The man the Perkins brothers had chosen to lead the outpost, Ephraim Bumstead, became ill soon after his arrival, and died while attempting a return journey. All the responsibilities of the enterprise then fell on his clerk, John Perkins Cushing, the teenage son of the Perkins brothers' late sister. After some months of "extreme mortification" waiting for word on which way this disaster would break, Thomas was relieved to find that his nephew was "very competent," shipping well-selected cargoes of teas that made healthy profits for the firm. In 1805 Cushing was elevated to partner, taking full control of Canton operations for the Boston Concern.[39]

"Very competent" proved an understatement. During his nearly thirty years at Canton, Cushing revealed himself as a man dedicated to "doing every thing with system," whose regularity and attention to detail won him the respect and friendship of many, including the leader of the Cohong, Wu Bingjian, better known to Americans under his trade name, Houqua.[40] Their close business and personal relationship made Cushing one of the most influential men in the business—more than even the Select Committee of the East India Company, according to one British trader. Cushing supplemented the advantage his favorable ties to other merchants provided with his own innovations, including finding new ways to exploit loopholes in Chinese customs regulations to reduce his ships' port charges, designing protocols for smuggling opium into the Pearl River, and manipulating the opium market to drive off competitors.[41] Cushing may have been thinking prescriptively rather than descriptively when he described Canton to a business partner as "a place of business where he had had more facilities and less disputes than any other he was acquainted with," but with his acumen and close links to men in Boston, Canton, and London who shared his skills and complemented his interests, he certainly made it work that way.[42]

The opium trafficking system Cushing helped perfect built on earlier experiments, and was in part a response to British colonial policy. Small shipments of the drug had been arriving in China since the early eighteenth century. The first Qing edict against the trade was promulgated in 1729 and reiterated periodically thereafter.[43] In the late eighteenth and early nineteenth centuries, British colonial administrators in India sponsored cultivation of the drug to squeeze more revenue from the peasantry, contracting to produce it directly in Company territory and taxing its transit if grown beyond their monopoly. Pushing opium exports allowed the Company to balance its growing specie deficit in the tea trade. Concerned to maintain peaceful relations with the Chinese, the East India Company did not ship

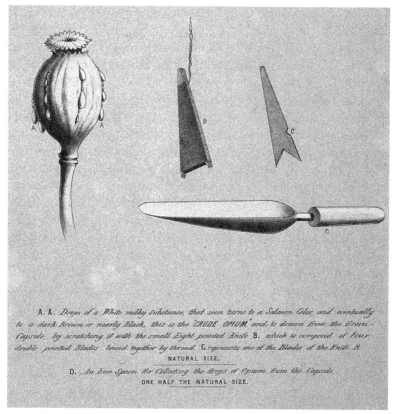

A. A. *Drops of a White milky substance, that soon turns to a Salmon Color, and eventually to a dark Brown or nearly Black, this is the 'CRUDE OPIUM,' and is drawn from the Green Capsule, by scratching it with the small Eight pointed Knife* B. *which is composed of Four double pointed Blades bound together by thread* C. *represents one of the Blades of the Knife* B.
NATURAL SIZE.
D. *An Iron Spoon for Collecting the drops of Opium from the Capsule*
ONE HALF THE NATURAL SIZE.

FIGURE 8. W. S. Sherwill, *A Poppy Capsule Oozing Drops of Crude Opium and Tools for Its Extraction.* Lithograph, c. 1850, https://wellcomecollection.org/works/mb7c3j4g, Wellcome Collection. Attribution 4.0 International (CC BY 4.0).

opium to Canton in its own ships. Rather, it sold the drug, and licenses to traffic in it, to "country" (intra-Asia) merchants. Through these measures, "by 1800, the East India Company had perfected the technique of growing opium in India and disowning it in China."[44]

Americans began experimenting with the trade soon after, but their methods were different. Unable to make purchases in India under the stricter rules imposed by the Jay Treaty, they instead turned to the Ottoman port of Smyrna (modern Izmir) for their supply. Experiments in the commerce likely began in 1804, when merchants from Baltimore and Philadelphia—including the future US consul Benjamin Chew Wilcocks—imported large cargoes of the drug to Batavia and Canton. Other traders soon followed suit, most notably the operatives of the Boston Concern, who used their network of resident merchants to secure a dominant position in opium and support their tea trade out of Canton. The "Turkey" Americans imported from the Anatolian coast was of lower quality than the opium produced in India, but the narcotic still found a ready market—and by contributing to early gluts, it helped expand the population of consumers, too.[45]

American opium shipments came to the East India Company's attention as early as 1807, but Jefferson's embargo and then the Anglo-American war suppressed any concerns Company directors had until peace was restored.[46] However, during the war Americans stranded at Canton began trading in cargoes of Indian opium as well as the Turkish variety, inserting themselves as competitive middlemen able to provide "country" traders in the drug with remittances to Europe, helping drive strong postwar growth in imports—an especially welcome service once the Company's monopoly on Indian trade was withdrawn in 1813 and the number of country traders increased. Here too Cushing was an important figure, using the Boston Concern's capital and his considerable influence in Asia to float the early business of American dealers in Indian opium like Russell and Company.[47] In this way the opium traffic was a species of "collaborative competition" between Britons and Americans of the kind historian Jay Sexton has drawn attention to in Latin America. It was also an enormous business, among the

FIGURE 9. W. S. Sherwill, *A Busy Stacking Room in the Opium Factory at Patna, India*. Lithograph, c. 1850, https://wellcomecollection.org/works/xt2gg8fp, Wellcome Collection. Attribution 4.0 International (CC BY 4.0).

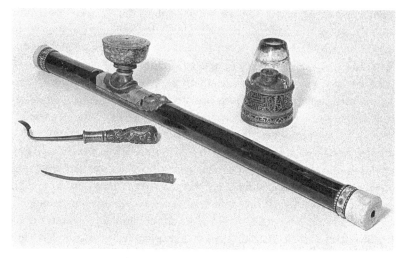

FIGURE 10. Opium pipe. https://wellcomecollection.org/works/djanaf3v, Wellcome Collection. Attribution 4.0 International (CC BY 4.0).

top commodity trades of the period, arguably the largest and most profitable smuggling operation the world had ever seen.[48]

Over the next decade and a half, opium imports doubled, then tripled and nearly quadrupled. The boom cemented the drug as the "keystone" commodity for the China trade, doing for the creation of modern capitalist market dynamics in Asia what tobacco, sugar and tea had done for Europe.[49] The drug trade's growth coincided with an increasing volume of silver flowing out of Qing territory—though whether this was caused by growing opium imports, the minting practices of new Latin American republics, or shifting money preferences within China is unclear. Whatever the root cause, the consequence was that opium imports increasingly replaced silver in exchanges for tea and silk in China.[50]

Or at least opium did so as a trade good. Viscous, bulky, and easily recognized as contraband, the drug did not serve well as currency. Instead, credit instruments took the place of silver coins, mostly in the form of bills of exchange drawn on London. As in their experiments with the opium trade, Americans had intermittently used bills before the War of 1812, but the trade accelerated in the late 1810s and early 1820s as their ability to draw on credit abroad grew. The growth of Southern cotton exports was of particular importance for US China traders because they made larger amounts of British commercial paper available in the United States, where it was issued as payment by the US agents of major London and Liverpool merchant banks who bought bales of raw fiber for British textile firms. Simultaneously, a growing demand in India for new and easier ways to remit funds to England contributed to the wide adoption of London-issued credit instruments among British traders in Asia, including those at Canton. By the late 1820s this complex improvised circuit of global commodity exchanges had crystallized into a new system: "Americans drank Chinese tea paid for by Southern cotton through the medium of London bills and Asian opium."[51]

This system involved multiple rounds of individual negotiations and a large number of intermediaries. A merchant in the United States would first purchase or borrow a bill from an agent of a London merchant bank, or sometimes the Bank of the United States. Then, once in China, he would sell that bill to a "country" trader who had imported English textiles or, more likely, Indian opium and received silver as payment; or the US merchant could use bills to pay for goods from a Chinese merchant directly. Either way, Americans were using London bills to pay for purchases of teas, silks, nankeens, and porcelains, while Chinese merchants used them, along with silver, to buy opium to sell in China. British "country" merchants from India became the end holders of the bills, which they sent to England as remittances, avoiding the expense of shipping specie, saving on insurance premiums and lost interest. If the originating US China merchant had borrowed to acquire a bill, he would answer the claims of the banks in England by sending them London bills that had previously been exchanged for cotton or other slave-produced goods. Much easier to augment or curtail in response to demand than silver had ever been, bills facilitated a growing business in China at the same time that the expanding demand for opium enabled larger and larger purchases.[52]

Even those who were not directly involved in the opium trade relied on its infrastructure to do business. Olyphant and Company, an American commission firm staffed by committed evangelicals who proudly refused to deal in the drug, nonetheless still paid for their teas and silks using bills made liquid by the illicit flow of opium. Opium underwrote their business just as much as the new and fiercely exploitative labor regimes powered the expansion of the textile industry in Europe and the cotton frontier in North America.[53] "Every one trading" at Canton, Robert Bennet Forbes explained to his wife Rose, depended on bills to "get money" for purchases.[54] The flourishing of the American China trade in the postwar era was possible only because of the rapid growth of a global capitalist system whose functioning depended on black markets, dispossession, enslavement, and a continued confidence in the promises encoded in paper credit instruments.

Americans' involvement in the opium trade pushed them to identify more closely with British traders and officials. US merchants forged especially close ties with the British houses of Jardine, Matheson and Company and Dent and Company, who together with the American firm of Russell and Company, took over Canton's trade when the East India Company lost its China monopoly in 1834.[55] These collaborations increased conflict between Anglo-American traders and Qing officials tasked with policing illicit trading. Because of Americans' deep involvement in opium smuggling, two violent incidents involving US vessels—the pirate attack on the ship *Wabash* and the execution of the sailor Francis Terranova of the *Emily* for his role in an accidental death of a Chinese woman—were transformed from simple local policing issues into wide-ranging disputes over the rules of trade and foreigners' sovereignty and security in China, manifestations of the powerful currents that would soon roil Canton's ostensibly calm and profitable waters.[56]

Smuggling incidents that erupted into violence attracted the attention of Canton officials, already primed by theories circulating among Qing elites that suggested opium imports were the cause of the silver outflows destabilizing the empire's money supply.[57] This attention put pressure on American and British traders, who developed new ways to move and market the opium they imported. The result was the "Lintin system," called after the island in the Pearl River Delta where their storeships anchored. An unofficial "second seaport," vessels in the waters around the island operated as a floating warehouse and smuggler haven. Incoming ships carrying opium would stop at the island and transfer their cargo to waiting store ships before finishing their journey upriver to Whampoa, Canton's official port. In lieu of opium, ships would take on rice, using a loophole in the customs laws to lower their port charges.[58] Chinese opium dealers would then purchase chits from foreign merchants at Canton, paying in silver or bills. Redeeming their receipts back at the store ships, they would smuggle the illicit chests to shore in long, narrow vessels known as "scrambling dragons" or "fast crabs" for their speed and their rows of oars.[59] Chinese brokers assumed the most dangerous aspects of the smuggling, such as bribing officials and delivering the product to consumers, while the foreign merchants ran the warehouse, collecting commissions and demurrage fees as they would for warehousing services anywhere.[60] Americans had been posting store ships since at least 1818, but the 1820–21 crackdown the US ship *Emily* sparked spurred these innovations among the smugglers.[61]

Operating store ships gave American merchants a new way to get into the Indian opium trade, and by the 1830s traffic in that variety of the drug had eclipsed trade in Turkish opium.[62] Americans' nationality, and the plausible deniability that came with it, proved valuable during periods when the British trade was closed owing to conflicts with Chinese authorities. As the Lintin system became more firmly established, smuggling expanded.

Store ships "became floating places of deposit *for all kinds of merchandize,* as well as opium," and the mechanisms perfected there spread up the coast to the closed ports of northern China.[63]

These developments were deeply harmful to the Qing state, though the damage was not obvious at first. The growth in opium smuggling also promoted the growth of the legitimate tea trade and thus expanded the revenues sent back to Beijing.[64] This apparent health hid the corruption the Lintin system spread while undercutting the effectiveness of local governance and coastal defense. Eventually Qing officials began to realize the true extent of the problem, but they found it impossible to effect reform. William C. Hunter, a Chinese-speaking Kentuckian employed by Russell and Company, explained how the smuggling system remained stable despite imperial attempts at reform:

> It is needless to say the opium trade was prohibited by Imperial edicts as well as by proclamations of the Canton authorities. The Chinese who dealt in "foreign mud" [opium] were threatened even with capital punishment, but so perfect a system of bribery existed (with which foreigners had nothing whatever to do) that the business was carried on with ease and regularity. Temporary interruptions occurred, as, for instance, on the installation of newly arrived magistrates. Then the question of fees arose, but was soon settled unless the new-comer was exorbitant in his demands. . . .[65]

Smuggling touched all aspects of the American community at Canton, and corroded all relations with the Chinese. Even the missionaries who criticized the drug's deleterious effects were compromised by it, using opium traders' ships to reach their posts, lodging in opium traders' factories, and supporting their ministries from opium traders' donations—and returning the favor by using their language skills to facilitate the opium commerce.[66]

Historian Jacques Downs has argued that resident American merchants' increasing familiarity with China bred contempt. Beyond the polite circle of hong merchants with whom American merchants traded and sometimes socialized, Qing subjects and officials became the object of their racially motivated resentment, fear, and disdain. In Downs's estimation, the "role-myth" of the merchants' relationship with the Chinese made the latter "fair game" for the degrading exploitation of the opium trade, including smuggling.[67] This theory has some explanatory weight, and certainly we need *some* explanation for why pillars of their home communities (many of them well-known philanthropists) could countenance such a harmful trade. But in light of American merchants' literal and figurative investments in white supremacy and their long, storied history of smuggling, it might also be that the perceived "fairness" of selling debilitating narcotics was justified less by the particular circumstances of China than by contempt for non-white people generally, and specifically for any regulations that ate into profits, whether handed down by a Republican Congress or imposed by the Daoguang Emperor.[68] American merchants did not like paying taxes—to anyone—and avoided it whenever they could.

The new business realities that shifted the allegiance of the American mercantile community at Canton influenced the trajectory of US politics during the Bank War. When the Second Bank of the United States came under sustained attack from Jacksonian Democrats, Nicholas Biddle and his allies repeatedly pointed to East India bills as proof of the good the Bank had done. In 1831, the BUS's triennial report noted that the "trade to China and India" had heretofore required "millions of the precious metals" annually, with attendant "abrupt and inconvenient changes in the amount of the currency and of private credit." But then the BUS's experiment in offering bills succeeded, with clear benefits to "the merchants and to the community" alike.[69] Responding to hostile congressional inquiries in 1832, Biddle claimed that once the BUS had led the way, other "capitalists" followed suit, such that "the use of specie in the China trade is almost superseded."[70] *Niles' Weekly Register*, in 1834, called the East India bills "better than dollars, even at *Canton*," and decried those who had slandered the Bank "as an *unsafe* depository of the public money."[71] Even in 1835—after the Bank War was lost, and the BUS was in the last months of its charter—Biddle took time to remind the influential political economist Timothy Pitkin that the Bank's bills lay behind the salubrious decline in American specie exports to Canton.[72]

Much to his surprise, Biddle's claims backfired. They failed to persuade his enemies of his bank's necessity and provided a fresh skirmishing field in the larger Bank War.[73] Like the Bank itself, East India bills had not always been controversial. In his 1831 annual message, no less a figure than Andrew Jackson had celebrated the "increased facilities which the credit and capital of our merchants afford by substituting bills for payments of specie" in the China commerce.[74] But after Biddle and his allies made the Bank's rechartering a campaign issue, East India bills attracted more negative attention. Georgia Democrat A. S. Clayton, one of the leading BUS opponents in the House, seized on the explanation of how East India bills replaced specie exports as evidence that there was "something delusive in the operation." Rather than facilitating legitimate commercial operations, the Bank simply "becomes the shipper of the specie, to pay its bills, in place of the merchant."[75] Specie, Clayton claimed, would still have to flow abroad to settle accounts—but now it would be gold to London instead of silver to Canton.[76] Worse,

There is not a dollar less carried away than before; but there is every probability that there is much more: for this credit plan will enable more persons to engage in this trade than if they had to carry the specie themselves; and they will obtain credit to a larger amount than any amount of specie which they could possibly command. This is dealing without capital, and leads inevitably to overtrading—the curse of any country—and under which it is now experiencing very heavy suffering.[77]

This logic was not unchallenged. Earlier in the same debate, fellow Southern Democrat George McDuffie proclaimed himself "a little surprised" that his colleagues would "question the utility of a measure so beneficial to the planting states." Specie did not need to be sent across the Atlantic to settle accounts: "The cotton, the rice, and the other agricultural productions of the South" would "furnish the means of paying these bills in London." In a minority report on an investigation of the Bank, John Quincy Adams mockingly remarked that Clayton's carping about bills of exchange reminded him of Beatrice's approach to men in *Much Ado about Nothing*—a transparent and willful contradiction.[78]

As in so many other aspects of the Bank War, the dispute over the Bank's experiments in East India bills revolved around conflicting understandings of money in American political economy. The Second Bank of the United States' opponents, like Clayton, saw only dark designs: leery of how credit instruments circulating as currency disintermediated finance from the "real" economy, and skeptical of the long-term consequences of centralizing financial authority in a private corporation with stronger ties to foreign bankers than to citizens at home, they rejected the premise that the bank's management could be trusted to work in the nation's true interests. Friends of the bank, on the other hand, saw in the bills a global extension of the useful work already accomplished by the Bank's notes and domestic bills: they "annihilated time and space" and made commerce more viable and reliable.[79] Curiously, given the Anglophobia of the era, neither pro- nor anti-Bank commentators in this particular debate noted explicitly how the bills bound American traders and financiers more tightly to the financial core of the British Empire and made them a cutting edge of its expansion in Asia—though this was key to both their benefits and their potential drawbacks.

The Second Bank of the United States' East India bills accomplished the opposite of what Biddle intended politically, but their economic effect was more substantive—though perhaps not to the degree he sometimes claimed.[80] Contrary to some of Biddle's declarations, the BUS did not originate the practice of using sterling bills drawn on London to make purchases in China; American trading in China had been shifting away from coin and toward the use of bills and merchandise for longer than the BUS had been in business. Still, American imports of specie into Canton did fall precipitously in the late 1820s, and the Select Committee of the East India Company at Canton blamed "bills upon the Bank of the United States" for the silver shortage that forced them to sell their own bills drawn on Bengal on more "favourable terms" to balance the Company's books.[81] According to documents the BUS produced for a House committee, the Bank issued at least $1.4 million (£303,923) of "East Indies" bills from 1825 to 1831, a significant sum. Given the illicit nature of much of the business, figures for trade at Canton are at best estimates—but from the available evidence, it seems that after their introduction BUS bills made up anywhere from 5 percent to 67 percent of the total value of bills Americans imported into Canton, averaging 23 percent of the total from their introduction to the Bank's demise.[82] Even after the BUS's federal charter ended, major American China trade houses like Russell and Company continued to use its bills, suggesting that they found them a useful—and perhaps necessary—tool for their business.[83]

That business was about to undergo a major trial as tensions about trade in the Pearl River Delta boiled over into direct conflict between Great Britain and China in the late 1830s. During the early stages of the Opium War, American traders found the limits of their cooperation with the British and showed their true colors as agents of capital. Robert Bennet Forbes recounted in his memoir how he had refused to join the English in abandoning Canton in 1839 after Chinese officials seized British stores of opium. He was then the managing partner of Russell and Company, the dominant American firm that had—along with Jardine, Matheson, and Company and Dent and Company—"virtually inherited" the financial and commercial power of the East India Company after the end of its monopoly. Reminiscing, Forbes framed his refusal to flee as a principled dedication to business: "I replied that *I had not come to China for health or pleasure, and that I should remain at my post as long as I could sell a yard of goods or buy a pound of tea.*" But he also put his position in terms of state power: "We Yankees had no Queen to guarantee our losses."[84]

Forbes's retrospective bravado belied a much more complex and conflicted reality. In the moment he was recalling, his fortunes had depended on serving as a middleman, trafficking on commission in British-owned property on behalf of opium merchants exiled from Canton. For decades, Forbes and other Americans had built their Chinese trade on the keystone product of the British Empire in Asia, and they executed their transactions using financial instruments anchored in credit from British banks. In the longer term, they also stood to benefit from the way British guns would force open new Chinese markets. Perhaps drawing on his own experience trading in slaves and sugar during the Haitian Revolution, Forbes's mentor and investor Thomas Handasyd Perkins urged him to embrace the opportunities created by war: "While the trouble lasts you will be enabled to do great things—But one such chance happens in a life time—Il faut en profiter."[85] As they revealed in their actions and their accounts, the ultimate loyalty of the men staffing American countinghouses in Canton was to their profits, not to their flag.

Following the War of 1812, Americans' increasingly close entanglements with British commerce in Asia formed new and influential connections between US political economy and global markets. This development coincided with Americans' rising interest in consuming Chinese objects, texts, and even bodies.[86] Among the rising generation of practical American political economists, enough glimpsed how integral new traffics in silver, bills, and opium were to American fiscal and monetary health to make controlling these flows a significant issue of public concern.[87] In this regard, American politicians and publicists paralleled their counterparts among the official class in China; both worried that their countrymen's profitable enterprises in Canton were destabilizing the money supply—and subverting the state.[88]

The heated debate over specie exports and bank money in the political conflicts of the 1820s and 1830s suggested some of the ways that the new, globally integrated operations of China traders could influence debates over US political economy and the actions of US institutions. When, as Robert Bennet Forbes watched, the simmering conflict between Western smugglers and Chinese officials broke out in war in 1840, American policymakers found themselves with more than new questions about their foreign relations. As they learned why Forbes might want his losses guaranteed (queen or no), deep debates over slavery, sovereignty, and the limits of liberal capitalist marketplaces came out into the open through the medium of discussions of the China trade—influencing US-China relations as well as US domestic politics for the next several decades. The complex system of empire, capital, and sovereignty that had slept in the hold of the ship *Congress* would not stay hidden in the new daylight of Americans' efforts to understand their relationship with China during Britain's war for opium.

* CHAPTER FOUR *

Sovereign Rights, or America's First Opium Problem

It was getting late on March 3, 1843, but Thomas Hart Benton was in the middle of a tirade and it was fruitless to try and stop him. At nearly midnight on the last day of a dying session, "Old Bullion" refused to let a $40,000 appropriation pass quietly. A longtime hard money advocate who helped destroy Nicholas Biddle's bank, Benton was sensitive to the dangers trade with China posed to the US money supply. He was also anxious to maintain his own power over policy. The mission authorized by the bill before Congress was "a studied fraud," he thought, an executive usurpation designed by the Tyler administration to rob the Senate of its authority. Worse, it was all just a complicated and expensive means of patronage, "not created for the country, but invented for a man." The whole enterprise was unnecessary: "China has no political connexion with us," the senior senator from Missouri explained, "She is not within the system, or circle, of American policy."[1] Unlike his youthful combat with Andrew Jackson, this time Benton's bullet points did not find their targets. His colleagues in the Senate endured his harangue and then ignored his objections, quickly approving funding for the United States' first diplomatic mission to the Qing Empire.[2] To Benton's irritation, direct government support for Americans' commerce in China was no longer out of bounds.

This chapter investigates how and why this came to be. The common answer, found in histories of American foreign relations, is that the United States' move to establish a diplomatic relationship with the Qing Empire grew out of a rivalry with Great Britain. The conclusion of the Opium War (1839–42) had netted British traders access to new Chinese markets (four new "treaty ports"), as well as a colonial toehold in Hong Kong; Americans rushing to fulfill their own Pacific destiny did not want to be left out.[3] But while it captures much, this explanation misses the urgency behind Americans' resurgent interest in their commercial relations with China.

This excitement was visible in the way Americans framed, consumed, and debated information about Britain's war. Antebellum editors trumpeted their news stories on the conflict as "calculated to attract the deepest attention" and "fraught with most important consequences." Analysts described it as "of the deepest importance to the civilized world," presenting a "moral spectacle" of which "there is not now, on the whole earth, any grand movement among the world of nations, so interesting or mighty" and as what "may well be the most remarkable event of the nineteenth century"—a superlative of particular note even among antebellum writers' typically enthusiastic declarations.[4]

Americans described the Opium War this way because they saw in it echoes of the ways British power touched their own dearest interests: their national sovereignty and their union. Used to thinking of their nation as an international system unto itself, Americans became keenly interested in Britain's violation of China's imperial borders because it was made by a rival many regarded as a threat, but also because the intervention was made (putatively) in the name of upholding liberal market norms. By justifying their invasion of China this way, the British led Americans to believe that the conflict posed a double threat: to American sovereign independence and to American slavery. These associations between domestic and international politics gave Chinese affairs a new relevance in US politics and led politicians in Washington to initiate direct diplomacy with the Qing Empire.

To understand how Americans shifted their concerns about their China connection from global money movements to British belligerence, this chapter excavates the channels through which information about the Opium War flowed. It begins with a bird's-eye view of the conduct of the war itself and a coincident decline in Anglo-American relations. Next it examines how Americans got their news about the war, finding that they consistently mapped the war's belligerents onto their own political divides, centered on the legitimacy of slavery and the enforcement of the law of nations. Then the chapter turns to how Americans, thus informed, used discussions of China to debate "questions again emerging at home," not merely "abstract theory."[5] Finally, the chapter closes by tracking how all this "intense interest" translated to practical politics—how federal officials created and managed information about Americans' China trade to generate support for the first US diplomatic mission to China, and then to execute it.[6] To defend US sovereignty—and slavery—against what they understood to be a global British threat, American officials sought to widen and deepen their commercial connections with China.

The way the Opium War developed was crucial to the meaning Americans came to assign to the conflict.[7] A dispute between various levels of British and Qing officials that ran alternately hot and cold, the war stretched from 1839 to 1842. While never inevitable, the conflict had roots in a perceived incompatibility between Western and Chinese visions for international order. Since the Ming Dynasty, China's rulers had preferred to keep most Western powers at arm's length, outside their system of close foreign relations (an international order sometimes oversimplified as the "tribute system").[8] Dissatisfied with this distance, many Westerners demanded that Chinese authorities act in accordance with their preferred diplomatic rules: regular contact structured by treaties, mediated through accredited diplomatic representatives, and governed by a vague but purposefully Eurocentric "law of nations" that privileged commercial exchange. These demands went unmet. In practice Chinese relations with Western maritime powers took place only at the local level, negotiated by provincial officials and trading company employees at Canton.

In the early nineteenth century, Great Britain's restructuring of its Asian empire put new pressure on this improvised system. Britons' remittances from Asia relied in large part on private British traders' ability to sell ever-increasing amounts of Indian opium in China. When the East India Company's monopoly on the China trade dissolved after 1833, there was no longer a body of British merchants in China with an interest in restraining the growth of the opium trade, the means to do so, or a way to make amends when smugglers got out of hand. This absence of informal mediation meant that when collisions occurred—as they increasingly did—there were fewer ways to smooth over disputes.

The war's proximate cause lay in the Qing government's efforts to force foreign merchants to stop importing opium. Opium imports had been forbidden in China for decades, but like many of the other regulations governing trade at Canton, the ban was understood to be flexible—ignored for the right price. Following a debate at the imperial court over whether legalization or stricter enforcement would ameliorate the widespread addiction, general lawlessness, and monetary disruptions that officials believed imports of the drug had caused, Beijing adopted more aggressive measures. In March 1839 a special imperial commissioner, Lin Zexu, arrived in Canton to take matters in hand. He confiscated all of the imported opium in the city and arrested Chinese opium dealers. But since the trade was a critical part of the British Empire's political economy, and because most of the merchants dealing in opium were British subjects, Lin's efforts—though successful in the short term—became a disaster in the longer term. While he pressured British (and American) merchants to turn over twenty thousand chests of opium to be destroyed, the transfer of those millions of dollars in commercial property called forth a severe reprisal from London.

The war progressed slowly and fitfully because of the difficulty of communicating between Canton and the political centers of the two empires, London and Beijing. Until fresh orders and reinforcements arrived, the conflict brewed slowly, with minor sea battles, riots, and periods of blockade punctuated by cease-fires and frenzied trading. Because of this dynamic, for years the Opium War was present more as a potential event than as a formal conflict. That began to change when on February 6, 1840, British Foreign Secretary Lord Palmerston ordered a significant naval force to depart from India to blockade—or if necessary invade—the Chinese coast. Palmerston's plan encountered opposition—but after some loud declaiming about national honor, Parliament approved his decision ex post facto. Even so, the denouement was long in coming. Two campaign and trading seasons later, superior gunnery and maneuverable steamships allowed British troops to force their way far enough up the Yangtze River to threaten the "Southern Capital" of Nanking. In August 1842 the Qing emperor's representatives capitulated and signed the Treaty of Nanking, marking the end of hostilities and the beginning of a new era of East-West relations governed by unequal treaties.

The treaty, and a subsequent agreement a year later that expanded its terms, granted the British a bevy of concessions. The most important included a hefty indemnity for opium seized (some $21 million), free trade access to five ports (Canton, Amoy, Foochow, Ningpo, and Shanghai), extraterritoriality within those ports, the cession of Hong Kong, and finally the recognition of Britain's comity as a sovereign nation—that is, acknowledgment that the accredited representatives of Great Britain must be acceded equal status with the representatives of the Qing emperor. The other institutions of the Canton system were also discarded, notably the Cohong, the guild of Chinese "security" merchants that had organized trade, and the Qing-run customs service.[9] With this revolutionized platform for trade and a new base of operations at Hong Kong, Britain emerged as the effective master of the China seas as well as the potential master of all Asian commerce, an ominous situation for American merchants.

The strained state of Anglo-American relations in the 1830s and 1840s motivated Americans' interest in the Opium War and shaped their interpretation of it. Despite a quarter century of peace, in the antebellum era politicians on both sides of the Atlantic expected (and in some cases desired) another war between Great Britain and the United States. While most American politicians before the twentieth century approached US foreign policy with at least some Anglophobia, the degree of bellicosity was a significant point of division between parties (Democrats vs. Whigs) and sections (slave vs. free states) in this period. Most of the active hot spots in Anglo-American diplomacy involved perceived threats to American sovereignty, either on the high seas or at the edges of US territory: revolutionary republican intrusions from US territory into Canada, the right of search claimed by the Royal Navy, the freeing of American cargoes of enslaved people in British ports, and conflicts over the Oregon Territory, the Maine boundary, and Texas annexation. Disputes with Britain, always tense, had grown more intractable after the British Empire abolished slavery in its Atlantic colonies, and Crown officials redoubled their efforts to sweep slave trading off the seas. Both actions aroused a deep (if justified) paranoia among the slaveholders who controlled the federal government, and made keeping up with British actions abroad immediately relevant to politically engaged Americans.

This concern with Great Britain's movements on the world stage helped generate widespread and long-lasting coverage of the Opium War in the US press. As American writers attempted to make sense of Britain's war through the lens of their own ideologies, they linked events in East Asia to political concerns closer to home. In doing so they made the first step toward bringing China itself, and not just Britain's war there, into the circle of American politics. In this sense the Opium War made China real to publics and policymakers alike for the first time.[10]

Most Americans probably learned about the war through the short news bulletins that appeared regularly in almost every newspaper in the country. Usually this content was transmitted to the United States from London through one of the new steamer lines; less frequently the news came directly from Canton or another Asian port, by way of American merchant vessels. It was written up in one of the Northern big-city dailies, then picked up by papers and magazines around the country. Direct reports from British or American missionaries serving in China rarely appeared in anything other than evangelical newspapers—and even in such publications one was more likely to read an article based on mercantile or official British sources.[11] The level of detail and frequency of coverage decreased as one moved away from ports with direct links to China (e.g., Boston, New York, Baltimore), but the depth and extent of American coverage of the war was such that a piece on the life of Commissioner Lin was not out of place even in a Louisville, Kentucky, evangelical newspaper.[12]

Niles' National Register, the closest thing Jacksonian America had to a national newspaper, exemplifies the coverage, sourcing, and transmission patterns of the American press with regard to China. The paper had reported on Chinese affairs before, but beginning with Lin's arrival in Canton in March 1839, *Niles'* began extensive reporting on the Opium War. It offered readers detailed news about the state of commercial, political, and military affairs at Canton and elsewhere, along with extracts from the speeches and

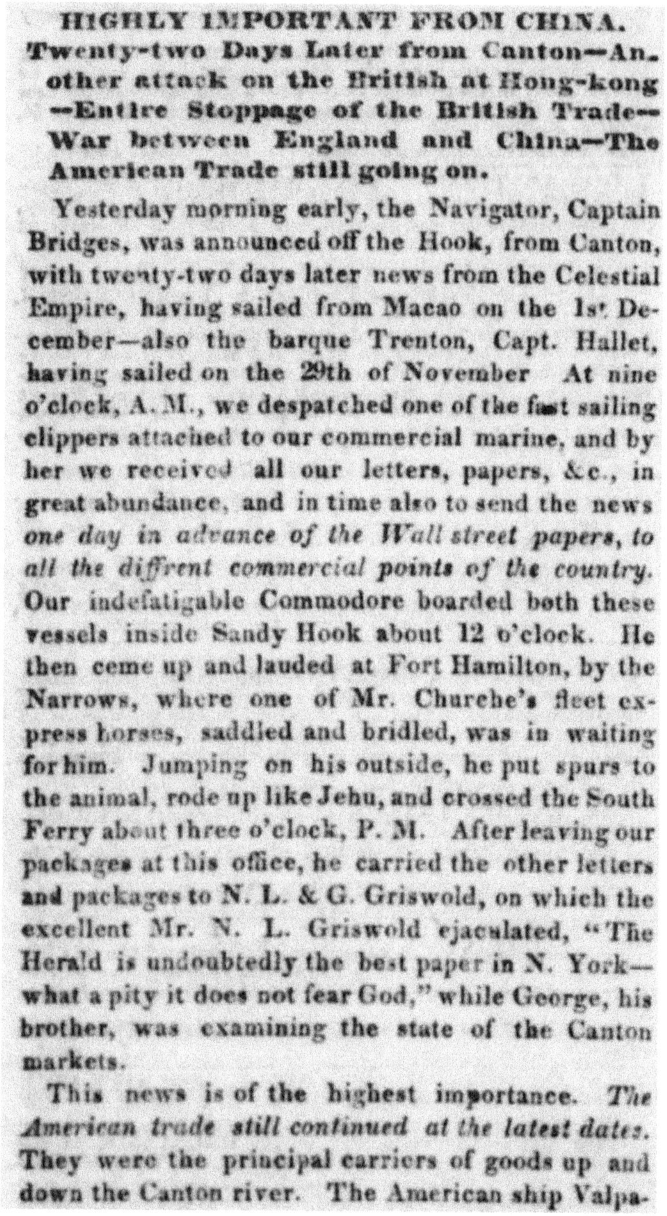

HIGHLY IMPORTANT FROM CHINA.
Twenty-two Days Later from Canton—Another attack on the British at Hong-kong —Entire Stoppage of the British Trade—War between England and China—The American Trade still going on.

Yesterday morning early, the Navigator, Captain Bridges, was announced off the Hook, from Canton, with twenty-two days later news from the Celestial Empire, having sailed from Macao on the 1st December—also the barque Trenton, Capt. Hallet, having sailed on the 29th of November At nine o'clock, A. M., we despatched one of the fast sailing clippers attached to our commercial marine, and by her we received all our letters, papers, &c., in great abundance, and in time also to send the news *one day in advance of the Wall street papers, to all the diffrent commercial points of the country.* Our indefatigable Commodore boarded both these vessels inside Sandy Hook about 12 o'clock. He then ceme up and lauded at Fort Hamilton, by the Narrows, where one of Mr. Churche's fleet express horses, saddled and bridled, was in waiting for him. Jumping on his outside, he put spurs to the animal, rode up like Jehu, and crossed the South Ferry about three o'clock, P. M. After leaving our packages at this office, he carried the other letters and packages to N. L. & G. Griswold, on which the excellent Mr. N. L. Griswold ejaculated, "The Herald is undoubtedly the best paper in N. York— what a pity it does not fear God," while George, his brother, was examining the state of the Canton markets.

This news is of the highest importance. *The American trade still continued at the latest dates.* They were the principal carriers of goods up and down the Canton river. The American ship Valpa-

FIGURE 11. An example of Opium War coverage in an American newspaper. *Morning Herald* (New York, NY), March 23, 1840, 2, https://chroniclingamerica.loc.gov/lccn/sn83030312/1840-03-23/ed-1/seq-2/, Chronicling America: Historic American Newspapers, Library of Congress.

letters of the main participants in the conflict, as well as the major texts in the American discussion of the war. (Sometimes even with a bit of levity: Lin's proclamation demanding foreigners turn over their opium supplies was described in the editorial preface as "a curious document, and quite as much to the point as the greater part of our American gubernatorial messages.")[13]

As an aggregator of other newspapers' material, *Niles'* serves as a useful (if slightly lagging) indicator of both the sources for China news in the United States and the persistence and frequency of that reporting over time. Its sources were generally American commercial papers, especially from New York or Boston, and British newspapers from either India or London. The September 15, 1838, edition of *Niles'*, for example, shared news on China gathered from the *Canton Register*, a British commercial journal based in China, and a "mercantile letter to a house in Calcutta from its London correspondent"—in other words, from a British firm. The news was carried direct from Canton to the United States by the American ship *Rob Roy*, and the article itself was first printed in the *New York Commercial Advertiser*.[14] Or again, on July 25, 1840, *Niles'* reported that the empress of China had died, "Governor" Lin was raising troops, trade to Macao had been reopened, and opium smuggling continued. These were all stories sourced to official British dispatches, first sent "overland" from China by way of the Red Sea and then Egypt, reported in London, then carried to New York by the *British Queen*, a packet steamer. *Niles'* also informed its readers that American merchants were leaving Canton, having "taken the alarm" because of Chinese unrest and an approaching British fleet; this news came to *Niles'* from New York, where the *Charles Forbes*, an American vessel just back from Asia, had recently docked.[15] Although the reports from China were not always accurate, they traveled in well-worn commercial channels, and their transit patterns underscored the Anglo-American nature of trade.

Niles' also followed a common pattern in the increasing frequency of its coverage of Chinese events. In the decade before the opening of hostilities, only one or two articles a year relating to China or the China trade appeared. But beginning in 1839, China articles became a regular feature of the paper: in roughly every other issue an item on China appeared in the "Foreign News" section, sometimes accompanied by a document written by one of the key participants in the conflict, such as an imperial decree or a letter from one of the diplomatic envoys. Though subsequent years saw minor differences in the total number of articles on China, the coverage never dropped back to prewar levels.[16] Because of Great Britain's war, China was now firmly entrenched as part of the foreign news consumed in the United States.

However, *Niles'* coverage does not reflect the full diversity of American news and commentary on the Opium War. All over the United States, and in seemingly every kind of publication, one found coverage and discussion of the war: big-city penny dailies, evangelical newspapers, commercial advertisers, political reviews, agricultural magazines, and literary weeklies. And within this geographic and genre diversity, there was a bewildering array of productions. There were straight news reports or copies of important proclamations and diplomatic documents, as in *Niles'*; but alongside these pieces there were also humorous short stories, poems, romances, catechism-like dialogues for the young, and serious histories of the conflict.

Audience, section, and political ideology all affected how Britain's war in China was treated on the pages of American publications. Charleston's *Southern Patriot*, for example, covered the war closely—but in true Southron form, it emphasized the war's potential effect on the cotton market and sought to expose the sins of majoritarianism perpetrated by American defenders of Britain's war in the public debate.[17] The *New-York Evangelist,* a Presbyterian weekly, relied on British and mercantile sources as well as on missionaries, opposed the opium trade, and hoped that an invasion would open China to Western religion and enlightenment.[18] Horace Greeley's daily the *New-York Tribune* reported on the war in great detail, almost always using multiple sources and depicting neither the Chinese nor the British in a favorable light. After the war Greeley made explicit in an editorial what his coverage had implied all along: that he was critical of British management of the war, though sympathetic to the liberalization of China's trade—the standard Whig perspective.[19] The New York weeklies *Brother Jonathan* and *New World* lived up to their moniker as "periodical sensationals" by covering the war with an eye for controversy and entertainment, giving readers a vicarious experience of the Celestial Empire.[20] In *Youth's Companion*, a children's magazine, the character of a little girl asked her father what the war would mean for her: "The English won't come here, will they father, and kill us if we don't buy their opium and eat it?"[21]

A reader with access to a well-stocked library could have read much more. A detailed selection of primary documents—British and Chinese—was available in any number of widely distributed periodicals such as the *American Eclectic* or the *Museum of Foreign Literature*. In fact, most in-depth American commentaries on the war, including that by John Quincy Adams, were based almost entirely on such sources, either in their original British versions or in the American reprints.[22] Collectively, these textual choices—made by the grubby agents of the New York press and stentorian senators alike—constituted a tacit admission that the information available through American sources was too slight to bear the close reading and scrutiny needed for serious public debate. Discussion of the war, whether it happened in the halls of Congress, on the stage at a lyceum, or in the pages of a newspaper, was defined by a reliance on British sources.

When, based on these sources, Americans ventured to offer a substantive argument for or against Britain's war in China, they hewed closely to the question of the war's justification, using two related frames. First they debated the war's morality, a judgment that usually turned on whether one saw the opium trade as the cause of the conflict. Second, they questioned the war's legality: if indeed the war was about China's trade barriers, as the British government claimed, then the question was whether a war over such an issue was valid according to the law of nations. These questions interested Americans beyond their intrinsic significance: they were part of the debate over slavery that strained the Union.

Speeches by John C. Calhoun and John Quincy Adams exemplified this trend and offered fully articulated and self-consciously political contributions to the debate. When John C. Calhoun rose to speak in the Senate on March 13, 1840, he was not primarily concerned with analyzing Britain's war in East Asia. Rather, Calhoun sought to protect the American slave system. Although not a knee-jerk Anglophobe in the manner of some of his political allies, he linked British threats to Chinese sovereignty with the threats British officials posed to the slave property so dear to the South—an argument that made explicit the subtext of much of the press coverage and debate about the war.[23]

Calhoun spoke in defense of resolutions he had offered a few days before, demanding compensation for losses sustained by the owners of slaves freed from the brig *Enterprize* when bad weather forced the vessel into a Bermuda port.[24] In refusing to compensate the owners of the *Enterprize*, Calhoun believed Britain was trying to abridge international law by applying its own emancipatory regime to territory under American sovereignty—US vessels on the high seas. Britain, he thought, held "either that her municipal laws are paramount to the laws of nations . . . or that slavery—the right of man to hold property in man—is against the law of nations."[25] In either case, Calhoun rejected the claim. Through his resolutions, in effect "abstract declarations against the right of England to emancipate the bondmen of a friendly nation," Calhoun hoped to prod the Van Buren administration into taking a sterner stance against Britain and to build a domestic base for his interpretation of international law.[26]

A key part of the "splendid and powerful argument" Calhoun made on behalf of these resolutions was a detailed indictment of the hypocrisy and corruption of the Pax Britannica.[27] Though in the Atlantic she posed as the champion of "humanity and liberty," Britain's eastern empire, Calhoun contended, was an empire of slaves. "Hundreds of thousands of slaves in the most wretched condition," he claimed, were "held by her subjects in her eastern possessions." Though rejecting the right to hold individual human beings as property, the British government was making a far bolder claim: the right to hold entire nations as property. China, Calhoun argued, was to be the next step in this domination of Asia: "Actuated . . . by a spirit of conquest and domination not surpassed by Rome," Britain was about to wage war against "the oldest of nations" to protect a trade in a drug that was—not incidentally—"the product of her slaves on her Hindoo plantations." Worse, Calhoun claimed, opium caused "a greater destruction of life annually than the aggregate number of negroes in the British West India colonies, whose condition has been the cause of so much morbid sympathy."[28] In Calhoun's view, the British Empire was an empire of slavery, made all the crueler by the pitiful conditions of its slaves, entire nations of them, and all the more morally bankrupt for its hypocrisy. By his logic, there was an equivalence between the American owners of the slaves on board the *Enterprize* and the Chinese: both were threatened by British hypocrisy and greed.

Calhoun's worried observation of Britain's imperial expansion was of long standing. Calhoun was convinced that Britain's master plan—in China as elsewhere—was "to get control of the commerce of the world, by controlling the labour, which produces the articles by which it is principally put in motion." As he put it in a letter to his close associate Duff Green, "humanity is but the flimsy pretext" by which England fixed its grip on the arteries of commerce.[29] His resolutions defending the sovereignty of American law over American ships in all seas and ports were intended to signal to Whitehall that the United States would permit neither Britain's antislavery crusade nor its Asian conquests to restrain the slave system that, in Calhoun's view, powered American development.

The themes that sounded in Calhoun's speech reverberated in other ears, making for some unlikely fellow travelers.[30] Radical abolitionists, looking at Britain's regime in India and the new war with China, saw the same political economy of slavery and potential choke hold on world commerce that Calhoun saw: the *Liberator* called Great Britain "the robber and enslaver of multitudes" in Asia.[31] The coverage of the Opium War in *Hunt's Merchants' Magazine* ran almost entirely along Calhoun's lines, though it stopped short of seeing slavery of any kind as a positive good.[32] Reviewing the costs of Britain's opium trade, a *Hunt's* contributor argued that the "gloomy bondage of millions and tens of millions, chained to the cultivation of a drug, the consequences of which are misery, disease, and death" was a state far crueler and more horrible than any found in the American South.[33] The magazine also consistently argued that the Opium War was motivated by the requirements of the political economy of the British Empire—an argument keyed to the same themes found in Calhoun's speech.

Likewise, the link Calhoun drew between Britain's infringements on American sovereignty at sea and Qing sovereignty on the China coast was not his alone. When Democratic diplomat Lewis Cass defended his (successful) efforts to halt Britain's legitimation of antislavery patrols in international law, he wondered sarcastically why, if Great Britain and the United States "may agree to keep squadrons upon the coast of Africa to suppress the slave-trade," what was stopping them from coordinating patrols "upon the coast of China to suppress the opium-trade"?[34] Cass's opportunistic jab makes it clear that the equation of the slave and opium trades, and Britain's hypocrisy in condemning one while supporting the other, was a useful weapon for anyone interested in undermining British moral authority for the purpose of protecting American slavery, as well as the configuration of domestic and international legal structures it required.

Over a year after Calhoun's speech, when John Quincy Adams ascended the stage at Boston's Masonic Temple on the evening November 22, 1841, his mind was set squarely on China, as it had been for some time. Adams had begun research and writing on the legality and morality of the Opium War almost as soon as he heard of the conflict, while he was also involved in fighting the gag rule in Congress and the *Amistad* case in court—and he juxtaposed his reflections on these matters in his diary. Though he dutifully read widely on the subject, after a year of research his opinions were largely unchanged; from the beginning he had thought that the "very first principles of the Laws of nations are involved in the controversy" and hoped that the war would break down "the impenetrable barriers of the celestial empire of China."[35]

Addressing an audience of well-heeled Brahmins crowded "almost to suffocation," and speaking over a torrential downpour, the septuagenarian former president declared his strong support for Great Britain's war against China. There could be no doubt that the British were on the side of right, Adams argued; the Chinese should be forced—at gunpoint, if necessary—to open their ports to opium.[36] It was a question of freedom: international law demanded that all nations allow free commercial intercourse, just as it demanded freedom for all human beings.

The heart of Adams's argument was the idea that Chinese arrogance and China's policy of isolation—not opium—were together responsible for the war. Or, as he more colorfully put it, "The cause of the war is the Ko-tow! the arrogant and insupportable pretensions of China, that she will hold commercial intercourse with the rest of mankind, not upon terms of equal reciprocity, but upon the insulting and degrading forms of the relation between lord and vassal."[37]

In sharp contrast to Calhoun and many others, Adams described opium as merely incidental to the conflict, "no more the cause of the War, than the throwing overboard of the Tea in Boston Harbour was the cause of the North American Revolution."[38] In Adams's view the shame and dishonor the Chinese inflicted on foreigners in diplomatic rituals, and the Qing rejection of free trade, justified violent reprisal. "It is time," Adams pronounced, "that this enormous outrage upon the rights of human nature, and upon the first principles of the Rights of Nations should cease."[39]

Adams depicted the war in providential terms.[40] It was but the "leading star" in what he called "that *movement of mind* on this globe of Earth."[41] To Adams's mind the higher law that abhorred slavery and guaranteed inalienable rights to life, liberty, and the pursuit of happiness was also in opposition to restrictions on trade; both slavery and trade barriers were intolerable burdens on freedom.[42] As he put it in a later letter to a friend, Britain's war with China was "a branch of that war against <u>Slavery</u> . . . the war of her Democracy," which she was "now waging throughout the globe."[43] This statement reveals that Adams's thinking closely paralleled the perspective of one of the war's main instigators, Chief Superintendent of Trade Charles Elliot, who saw his negotiations with Qing officials through the lens of his prior service as the "Protector of Slaves" in British Guyana.[44] Though he opposed Calhoun's "bastard Law of Nations," Adams was happy to make innovations of his own in international legal theory, as his opponents were quick to point out.[45]

News of the former president's remarks was widely distributed, and it quickly became one of the most hotly debated and commented-on events of the season—and probably of the entire American engagement with the Opium War. Even the American community in China heard about it a few months later, when it was printed in the May issue of the *Chinese Repository*.[46] In the years following the lecture, Adams's argument was discussed in literary and political weeklies, religious reviews, horse-breeding magazines, agricultural journals, and last but not least, the *American Phrenological Journal*.[47]

Running strongly against majority opinion, Adams's arguments were not well received. Reports on the lecture consistently emphasized surprise, and then dismay, at Adams's departure from conventional wisdom.[48] The morality of the Opium War, the *Boston Courier* quipped, was "a question, which was never supposed to have two sides."[49] Others wondered at Adams's motives: even the zealously pro-Adams *North American* found that the speech revealed "a vein of oddity, to say the least, in the old gentleman's composition."[50] Less politely, the *Cleveland Daily Herald* speculated that "the old man must be getting out of his senses."[51]

More thoughtful attacks took pains to shred the logic of his argument about the duty of commercial reciprocity. China's right as a sovereign state to regulate her own trade was upheld as consistent with international practices—including those of the United States—and with natural law. As one New York critic put it, "We maintain, in opposition to Mr. Adams, and upon the authority of all elementary writers on the law of nations, that each nation has the absolute right to determine for herself, whether she will have any, and what, commercial or other intercourse with any other nation."[52] This infamy has secured Adams's speech a permanent place in histories of US-China relations—though, more often than not, scholars have presented it as an idiosyncratic outburst (if perhaps a prescient one), rather than the expression of a coherent politics.[53]

For all the public shock at Adams's opinions, they were not unexpected to those with whom he had discussed his ideas on international law. A year before Adams's speech, C. W. King, an American China trader who had long opposed the opium trade and then strongly opposed Britain's war, recognized the tack Adams was likely to take after discussing the issue over dinner with him in late 1840.[54] Writing to Caleb Cushing a month later, King hoped that "Mr. Adams will not play into the hands of those who are trying hard to cloak these interests [Great Britain's financial interest in the opium trade] under cover of national law & pleas of <u>equality</u>."[55] Unfortunately for King, that is exactly what Adams chose to do.

Adams's speech is important for the way it marks a powerful grouping of ideas around China and Britain's war. His vision of international law was entirely opposed to Calhoun's strong minority-rights view. Adams believed that force could be justified if a sovereign state refused to meet the standards of the larger community—a standard that dovetailed with his vision for limiting slavery in the United States. If, in making this argument, even in reference to China, Adams was not part of the majority, he was emphatically not a voice in the wilderness. As with Calhoun, the stance toward sovereignty that domestic political ideology built around slavery was the not-so-subtle subtext that accounted for his argument's appeal, limited though it was at the time.[56]

Though Adams disagreed with radical abolitionists about the malicious effects of the opium trade, they supported his highly liberal conclusion that the breakdown of China's isolation was in keeping with history's movement toward freedom. As Edmund Quincy put it in the abolitionist standard the *Liberator*:

It is good, at least, that the great doctrine of the natural right of trade should be iterated and reiterated; and monstrous as are Mr. Adams's con-

clusions from this doctrine, it is not in vain that he has repeated it. . . .
China is now enduring the punishment of her selfish policy, which has
condemned her to remain stationary at the point of civilization which she
attained centuries ago. . . . All the restrictions which are put in the way of
the free intercourse of nations, are remnants of barbarism which will dis-
appear before the advancing influences of a true civilization.[57]

A commentator in the New York literary weekly the *New World* found
common cause with Adams in defending British intentions, taking the position that Britain had "assumed a hostile position *grudgingly*" and that China's
intractability was the crux of the issue. To bring this argument home, the
New World's author reminded readers that recent US policy in Asia and the
Pacific was analogous to Britain's actions, citing the repeated shelling of the
Sumatran village of Quallah Battoo by the US Navy in retaliation for piracy,
and a similar reprisal in Polynesia for the murder of a crewman during an
official Pacific exploring expedition. "It would be well," tut-tutted the *New
World*, "as a general rule, before judging too hastily the conduct of others,
to look a little into our own past history."[58] At least some Americans agreed
that at times liberal standards had to be imposed by force.

The salience of international law and notions of sovereignty to American
politics explains the resonance of Calhoun's and Adams's arguments in the
debate over Britain's war in China. For both men, the war raised questions
about issues central to American politics: the limits of state sovereignty,
the proper location of paramount law, and the freedom to define legitimate
commerce. These resonances help to explain why Americans were so deeply
interested in the outcome of the war—as well as some of the vehemence behind critiques of Adams's lecture. Through the wide coverage in the press,
and again through the use of the Opium War as a tool to think through
what are usually considered to be American policy problems, China and
its problems again became an integral part of the American political scene.
But though formation of a China policy in Washington was motivated by
the same themes that attracted so much public discussion, it took some different turns en route to sending an agent to Canton.

Before the Opium War, American officials' attention to events in China
was limited at best. China was most often discussed in relation to the China
trade—how American exports of silver to Canton affected domestic banking and commercial matters. Access to the China trade also received some
mention in discussions of US rights to the Oregon Territory—but, unsur-
prisingly given the nature of the Oregon dispute, these were almost always framed in terms of competition with Great Britain. Small US Navy
squadrons briefly visited China while on longer, globe-circling cruises, but

their instructions there were no different from their general orders. In the 1830s, Chinese affairs appeared only in the peripheral vision of the American state.[59]

However, once reports of Commissioner Lin's actions at Canton began arriving in the United States in the summer of 1839, China began to find its way into serious discussions in Washington. As Congress began to engage with the issue, for the first time the steady trickle of petitions and reports on China and American interests at Canton that had accrued over the 1820s and 1830s became an actively used resource. This archive, compiled and redigested for congressional use through a series of reports, supplemented the copious material published during the press debate and formed the basis for policy discussions. The framework remained the same, however. Tellingly, the first actions the US government made in response, a request through diplomatic channels for clarification over maritime rights and a naval cruise, were both focused on insulating American trade from British, not Chinese, authorities.

American merchants residing at Canton jump-started the process by petitioning Congress. Abbott Lawrence, the prominent manufacturer and Massachusetts Whig who was also a close associate of senior partners in several China trading firms, introduced their memorial to the House on January 9, 1840. The Canton merchants complained that Chinese officials were treating the American trading community unjustly in their campaign against opium smuggling, citing the way they had been briefly imprisoned in their factories to force them to give up their opium stores. The merchants at Canton, led by Russell and Company managing partner Robert Bennet Forbes—and notably, not the US consul—requested naval protection against the Chinese government's "acts of violence and aggression" and recommended that a government agent be sent to negotiate a new treaty to guarantee trade terms, a draft list of which the merchants appended.[60]

Politically canny in some regards, the petition was dreadfully naive in others. The Canton merchants downplayed their involvement in the opium trade, already a bête noire in the American press, by claiming they had "no wish to see a revival" of the odious commerce—but at the same time they suggested (utterly impractically, given the poor state of Anglo-American relations) that the United States "act in concert" with Britain and other European powers to bring the Chinese to heel.[61] In April another memorial, presented by Levi Lincoln, another Massachusetts Whig congressman, arrived from a different set of China merchants. This time the memorial was written by the US partners of those who had written the earlier petition, and they directly contradicted the earlier request from Canton.[62]

More savvy than their Canton partners, the US-based traders were far more circumspect in their recommendations, even framing their memorial as a "statement . . . of intelligence recently received" rather than a request for aid. Counseling a measured response, they recommended that the United States refrain from sending an envoy to negotiate with the Chinese "until the whole subject had been examined and considered in our national councils with all procurable information," as previous attempts by the British to improve conditions at Canton had only harmed the foreign community. However, they did request that a "respectable national force" be sent to protect American lives and property during the coming Anglo-Chinese conflict, especially from the local piracy that they expected to increase during the war. In addition to these petitions, the House received two packets of pamphlets on the China crisis, probably submitted by traders already in touch with individual members of the House.[63]

These petitions and document collections served as a basis for requests for reports from the State and Treasury Departments. As with the petitions, New England Whigs took the lead. On February 7, 1840, the House Committee on Foreign Affairs reported out two resolutions, both written by Newburyport, Massachusetts, representative and later Tyler supporter Caleb Cushing. He asked the president to provide information on how China's anti-opium campaign was affecting "the interests of the people and commerce of the United States" and to clarify whether Great Britain had communicated any plans to blockade China.[64] In December John Quincy Adams, having grown increasingly interested in the China issue, put in a request for "all documents in the Department of State, showing the origin of any political relations between the United States and the empire of China."[65] Then, just a week after Adams's request, Horace Everett, a Vermont Whig, requested yet another report on China, calling for correspondence between the United States and the British government "relative to any proceeding on the part of that Government which may have a tendency to interrupt our commerce with China."[66] The reports arrived unevenly, split into separate documents that arrived in Congress over the next year.[67]

Just as the last of these reports was being delivered in January 1841, the Rev. Dr. Peter Parker, an American missionary famous for using his medical practice in Canton to attract converts, attempted his own lobbying. He devoted part of his stateside vacation from China to "call[ing] the attention of the men in power to the relations of America to China," visiting key officials to share his ideas in person.[68] Though much noted, his impact was diffuse. His policy recommendations were ignored, and his urgent tone failed to motivate action. But, like press coverage and congressional reports, his presence kept China in the eye of policymakers and added to their knowledge.

Collectively these reports, petitions, memorials, and lobbying visits provided Congress with what one historian termed "a documentary history of American relations with China."[69] Without the difficulties with Great Britain, they could have been read the way John Quincy Adams read them, as a chronicle of the dysfunctional, despotic relationship Qing officialdom had with Western traders, a symptom of a larger "civilizational" conflict that justified dispatching gunboats to the China coast. But instead, this new information was digested by a political class whose foreign policy concerns revolved around opposition to Great Britain, and the Opium War was quickly integrated into an existing Anglophobic perspective. On February 13, 1840, for example, Francis Pickens, a South Carolina Whig and the chair of the House Committee on Foreign Affairs, included Britain's "recent movements in the China seas and islands" when describing the worrisome "spectacle of the greatest military and commercial Power in combination ever known" in a report on the *Caroline* affair.[70] And just month later, Pickens's report was followed by John C. Calhoun's speech in the Senate about the *Enterprize*.

Thus, when on March 16, 1840, Caleb Cushing unleashed an anti-British tirade of his own—this one specifically about China—his contribution was neither isolated nor unique. "Somewhat disturbed to learn" that the requests for reports and receipt of petitions on China in Congress were "construed in England as indicating a disposition on the part of the American Government . . . 'to join heart and hand with the British Government, and endeavor to obtain commercial treaties from the authorities in China,'" Cushing rushed to inform the House, and British observers, that this was "a great misconception, if it be not a willful perversion." Cushing, hitting all the concerns about international law (and, through that, domestic state relations) that underlay the disagreement over the Opium War, utterly rejected the "base cupidity and violence, and high handed infraction of all law, human and divine, which have characterized the operations of the British, individually and collectively in the seas of China." "God forbid that I should entertain the idea of co-operating with the British Government," he continued, "I disavow all sympathy with those operations. I denounce them most emphatically."[71] Opining on what US policy in China should be had once again become a means of pursuing domestic and foreign politics simultaneously.

In addition to demonstrating how the standard critique of Britain's war in China reached the floor of Congress, Cushing's speech also illustrates how important a particular fiction was to American anti–Opium War partisans. American merchants' purported abstention, or near abstention, from the opium trade allowed Cushing, Calhoun, and others to attack England with impunity.[72] The lie was promoted by the American merchant community at Canton and appeared in the press from the beginning of the war in widely circulated articles—and proved persistent long after.[73] The lie was necessary because Americans of all kinds were well aware of opium's effects; preparations of opium were a staple of Western medicine, and users, traders, and doctors understood its use—and dangers—as analogous to those of alcohol.[74]

Insofar as American merchants' denials rested on a thin basis in fact, it had to do with their business model in China, not their intent. Americans in China worked on commission, which meant they dealt in much more opium than they technically owned. Most of the opium they handled was not their property but was held for other merchants. Americans directly imported far less opium than their British competitors, but that was because their firms imported less overall than British operations. But these technicalities papered over a deeper complicity: because of the way bills of exchange and opium worked together to replace expensive silver imports as the basic elements of trade at Canton, flagrant smuggling was the basis for all US trade in China, and American merchants knew it.

Perhaps because they were burdened by this knowledge, their disavowals could approach absurd lengths. In the manner of an apostle anxious to get in a few more denials before dawn, US consul Peter W. Snow insisted repeatedly that no Americans were involved in the opium trade. In September 1839 Snow informed Qing officials that it was his "firm conviction that there is not an American in this country that is in any way engaged in the opium trade; and that it is their intention, at all times, to pursue a legal one, such as the Government of China will approve." Less than six months later he repeated the very same lie to his own superior, Secretary of State John Forsyth—even as the American traders remaining at Canton had dug themselves deeper into the business, handling British sales while the English were expelled from the port.[75]

Other Americans danced around the falsehood rather than stating it outright. The Canton merchants petitioning Congress in January 1840 claimed that they had signed a "voluntary pledge" to abstain from trading in the drug, and that "whether we view the subject in a moral and philanthropic light, or merely as a commercial question, we are extremely desirous to see the importation and consumption of opium in China entirely at an end." One of the Canton petitioners, Robert Bennet Forbes, stuck to this line in a later pamphlet on China affairs, claiming he would treat the issue only "as a great political and commercial question"—and thus neatly sidestepped his own moral responsibility.[76] In a policy brief prepared for Secretary of State Daniel Webster, the Rev. Dr. Peter Parker even claimed that "the American nation probably stands higher in the confidence of the

Chinese than any other nation" because "American merchants have had but a limited traffic in the prohibited article."[77] Reports in the press and in government documents of Americans handing over opium to Commissioner Lin—thus proving their involvement in the trade—failed to change the larger impression. Only radical abolitionist newspapers appear to have pierced this veil, taking their cue from William Lloyd Garrison's *Liberator*.[78]

In 1840 the Van Buren administration took two actions in response to congressional pressure. First, in May 1840 the American minister to London, Andrew Stevenson, asked Foreign Secretary Lord Palmerston to clarify whether American neutral rights would be respected in Asian waters if (or when) Britain declared war on China. Stevenson pressed Palmerston on the issue at the request of American merchants concerned that their ships might be seized by the British during military operations. Never one to assuage American fears, Palmerston informed Stevenson that while the admiral on the scene would most likely "confine himself to the detention of Chinese vessels," Britain would be instituting a blockade on the Chinese coast, and any ships trying to break it would be confronted by the Royal Navy. This correspondence plucked at an old string of discord—the power of the Royal Navy over American ships. Not only would the British government neglect to keep the United States informed of its military plans unless questioned directly, but the governments' long-standing disagreement over the interpretation of neutral rights law—a sore point for proslavery ideologues too—would not be suspended for the sake of a united front against the Chinese.[79]

Next, in November 1840 the administration dispatched Commodore Lawrence Kearny to China with a small squadron of two ships.[80] Kearny's instructions, written by Secretary of the Navy James K. Paulding with assistance from China merchant William S. Wetmore, aimed to establish a firm distinction between the United States and Great Britain in East Asia.[81] Kearny was given the standard directive to "give all lawful & necessary assistance, to the person and interests of American Citizens," but he was also instructed to pay "due respect to the laws, authorities & customs of the Chinese People & government." Kearny's orders stressed that he should "take all occasions to impress upon the Chinese, and their authorities, that our great object of your visit [*sic*], is to prevent and punish the smuggling of opium, into China either by Americans or by other nations under cover of the American Flag should it be attempted," because it was "the uniform policy of the Government, which you represent, never to interfere with the Laws or rights of other nations."[82] Paulding sought to use Kearny's cruise to establish the bona fides of the United States as a power fundamentally different from the British in China.

There official matters stood until news of the Treaty of Nanking arrived in late 1842. The announcement of Britain's historic treaty, and the radical restructuring of the China trade that it put into effect, spurred the Tyler administration to more direct action. Its domestic policies stalled, but hoping for a foreign policy success to bolster its anemic supply of political capital, the administration sent a special message to Congress. Written by Secretary of State Daniel Webster but issued under Tyler's name, it requested funds for a diplomatic mission to China and for a consul for the Sandwich Islands—two expansions of US power in the Pacific in one.[83] The British treaty, the administration argued, had radically altered the terms of trade in China, but the agreement provided "neither for the admission nor the exclusion of the ships of other nations."[84] America had to make its own new treaty with China to secure its own trade.

Congress passed the matter into committee. John Quincy Adams, now chair of the House Committee on Foreign Affairs, drafted the official committee report and its attendant legislation in consultation with Webster.[85] Adams's report recommended a $40,000 appropriation for the China mission. Noting that "access to the heart of the Chinese empire has . . . been obtained by conquest" of "questionable morality," the report distanced the United States from British aggression but stopped short of condemning the war. Congruent with the interpretation Adams had advanced in his lecture, the report welcomed China's "opening" as "auspicious to the hopes of the philanthropist, and to the anticipations of the philosophical well-wisher to the progressive improvement of the condition of mankind upon earth." Britain's stated *object* in the war, at least, the report declared "lawful."[86] After some minor debate, primarily about the fitness of the reviled Tyler administration to handle such a large sum, the House passed the measure recommended by Adams's report on February 21, 1843.[87] A few weeks later, at the very end of the session, the Senate did so as well—with a surprising lack of opposition (Benton aside), given the difficulties the upper chamber had given the Tyler administration that same day.[88] China was now once again officially within the purview of the US government as an object of policy.

A familiar character put this legislation into action. Unable to make his way into the cabinet (yet), Caleb Cushing was instead appointed commissioner, envoy extraordinary, and minister plenipotentiary to China during a congressional recess. He departed from the naval station at Norfolk, Virginia, on August 5, 1843. A restless intellect with a tireless pen, Cushing used his journey as an opportunity to gather and compile information. He sent home voluminous and detailed reports, dividing his attention between those on political and commercial matters, which the State Department and the president received, and those on scientific issues, which he sent to the National Institute, a forerunner of the Smithsonian Institution.[89] As his voyage progressed and he saw more of the European empires expanding through Asia and Africa, he elaborated new theories of racial hierarchy in an attempt to reconcile white American attitudes toward slavery with European (and especially British) colonialism—a vision similar in its belief in the necessity of white supremacy to the one that had been uniting Americans at Canton with their British colleagues for over a decade.[90]

Though American merchants at Canton worried that the vain, scholarly congressman who arrived at Macao on February 24, 1844, would only bring unwelcome scrutiny to their business, the treaty Cushing eventually signed at the Pearl River temple village of Wangxia exceeded Americans' hopes.[91] Aided and advised by Peter Parker and Elijah Bridgman, American resident missionaries with Chinese-language skills, through tedious negotiation Cushing gained for the United States all the advantages the British had won through force of arms, and then some. Beyond the opening of new ports to trade, his most important achievements were a most favored nation status for customs rates, a set of formal rules governing port procedures, duty collections, guarantees of formal diplomatic access to Chinese authorities all the way to Beijing (without any intervening bodies like the Cohong) and assurances that the Chinese authorities would protect the foreign communities now springing up at ports beyond Canton. The United States also agreed to control their own citizens and discipline them for crimes committed in China via consular authority—a procedural implementation of extraterritoriality already in practice in the Near East—and also promised to prevent opium smuggling. In practice these terms were honored only in the breach: in making these promises, the United States was "putting on for the first time some of the garments of imperialism, only to find that the nation itself had not at all grown up to such ample vestments."[92]

But if the empire's new clothes did not fit yet, the new suit nonetheless advertised real changes. The Treaty of Wangxia reestablished China, and Americans' China trade, as a concern in American politics—though in a far different way than for the founding generation or in the Bank War dispute. Notably, it committed the United States to a significant official presence in China. Henceforth it would be uncommon for China to be without a high-ranking American diplomat for any length of time, and the same was true for American naval vessels.[93] The consular system also grew quickly, extending to the new treaty ports. These officials created a new, government-controlled flow of information. Distant dispatches were now not only read by policymakers, but avidly followed within a framework that linked domestic and foreign politics in a larger ideological and economic conflict.

American China traders did not always benefit from this new channel of information. But it did have the effect of making China a more consistent part of American discussions of political economy—with diverse and wide-ranging results, informing topics from US relations with the Caribbean to interest in constructing a transcontinental railroad, and even the fate of the Union itself.

* CHAPTER FIVE *

The Empire's New Roads

The proof was in the plotting. When Asa Whitney addressed the Pennsylvania legislature on his proposal to build a transcontinental railroad, the former China merchant appealed to hearts and wallets alike, making his case with flourishes of rhetoric as well as detailed "facts and figures."[1] The key to his March 1, 1848, lecture was a visual aid, a "skeleton map" created for the purpose. Whitney began his remarks with this chart, he explained, so that his audience might clearly "see our actual position on the globe."[2] An accurate awareness of the place of the United States in the world was crucial; only once this act of imagination was accomplished would his listeners understand why his unprecedented road must be built—and why he was the man to build it.

Whitney designed his map to correct an epistemological error. Standard world maps, he averred, placed at their centers the meeting place of "Europe, Asia and Africa," shifting North America "to one side of all, as if of no importance." Whitney's cartography unskewed this bias, showing America as it "really" was: "in the centre of all." More than a salve to national geographic pride, Whitney's map showed that the "belt of the globe," the east-west band running across Europe and Asia that contained "the population and the commerce of all the world," was incomplete. He observed that if one followed this "belt" it "makes a straight line across our continent"—and here lay the opportunity. The United States could completely redraw the "present route for the commerce of Europe with Asia" by connecting the world's wealthy population centers, but only if it had the necessary infrastructure.[3]

Whitney's proposal for a railroad running from the shores of Lake Michigan to the Oregon coast would provide the missing continental buckle for the space between oceans. The case for what he touted as "the grand thoroughfare for all the nations of the earth" turned on basic commercial

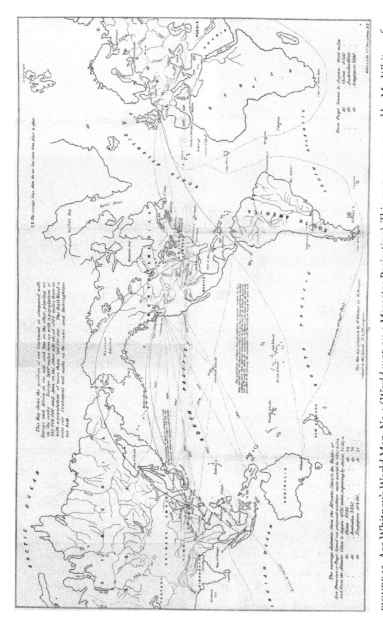

FIGURE 12. Asa Whitney's World Map. *No. 1 (World map on a Mercator Projection).* This map was prepared by Mr. Whitney for Mr. Breese's report to the Senate, US 29 Cong. Miller's Lith. 102 Broadway, NY (on the lower margin) 1235. (To Accompany) a Project for a Railroad to the Pacific. By Asa Whitney, of New York, https://purl.stanford.edu/vm954qw5346. Courtesy of David Rumsey Map Collection, David Rumsey Map Center, Stanford Libraries.

principles: a railroad across North America would reduce the cost of freight so significantly that it would out-compete all other modes of transport, rejiggering global commercial networks to deliver all the traffic of "the commerce of all Asia" into American hands. This "Pacific road" (his term, subsequently widely adopted) would enable the quick settlement and "civilization" of the American West, and supply the means for US domination of the Pacific Ocean. Whitney's road would make the United States the owner, and toll taker, of the world's highway, as well as "the grand exchange for all the world."[4] Providing cheap, convenient transit would benefit all mankind, of course, but as Whitney later explained, the road's "first great object" was a nationalist one: "to change the route for the commerce and intercourse of Europe with Asia, and force it, from interest, to pay tribute to us."[5] In other words, Whitney's railroad was a scheme for making the American republic a global hegemon by securing for it a monopoly on the most important artery of world trade.

Though not the first to imagine such a transcontinental railroad, Whitney was instrumental in making it seem not only desirable, but inevitable.[6] He inaugurated a new conversation, one in which Americans no longer talked about finding a passage to the East but began seriously planning to build one. A colorful character who aroused intense feelings among his fellow Americans, Whitney has persisted as a leitmotif in histories of United States railroads—but not much more.[7] This is partly because we know, or think we know, the universe of forces, events, and individuals that led to the extension of the American "empire of liberty" to the Pacific littoral and beyond. Certainly neither Whitney nor his plan was sui generis. His scheme, and discussions of it, drew on discourses that had long been at the center of historical studies of antebellum expansion, including ideologies of white supremacy, the growth of an increasingly ravenous capitalist economy, and the dynamics of sectional, national, and imperial politics.[8] Still, Whitney's plan fits imperfectly within these categories. His proposal sought to redefine the United States' place in the world, whole and round, not just on the North American continent—and perhaps this is why he has remained outside our explanations of antebellum American political culture.

Whitney's road was not the only project supported by dreams of inaugurating a new era of American-dominated Asian commerce. Plans for a trans-isthmus canal, mail contracts for Pacific steamer lines, and Commodore Matthew Perry's mission to "open" Japan all floated on the prospect of increased trade. The rhetoric and supporting data for Whitney's proposal are broadly representative of the efforts made on behalf of these other projects. Where it was different—and analytically useful—is in the way it helped shift the political conversation toward transcontinental infrastructure. Canals, steamers, and gunboats all attracted political attention, and to varying degrees actual capital; but transcontinental railroads differed in their consequences. They were not only legislated, but built; and the corporate form, physical infrastructure, and political corruption they introduced fundamentally reshaped the political economy of the United States.[9]

This chapter examines the origins, discussion, and results of Whitney's plan for a "Pacific road" in order to better understand how and why Americans imagined they would build a transcontinental empire using trade with China. A closer look at the movement Whitney's plan instigated reveals a unique and formative moment in antebellum American politics, one in which Americans first endorsed the plausibility of a transcontinental railroad out of a widespread conviction that commerce, and particularly Chinese commerce, was crucial to their national project of imperial expansion. The self-consciously global perspective found in Whitney's proposal, and in others like it, sought to leverage commerce not only to enable expansion, but to solve the persistent problems of union. This study of Whitney's road reveals that the China trade and the global perspective it encouraged were critical components of the political economy of manifest destiny, as well as crucial to the creation of one of the principal means and ends of the nineteenth-century American empire: the transcontinental railroad.

To make this case, this chapter will first examine Whitney's full plan and suggest what experiences may have led him to conceive of his scheme. It will then move outward from Whitney to examine how his plan was received by the politically engaged public and what factors led editors, politicians, and others to find his vision persuasive, useful, or necessary. The warm hearing Whitney's plan received partly depended on contingent domestic and geopolitical alignments, but it also grew out of long-standing tensions in republican political theory. Tracing these deeper roots, the essay turns to the antecedents of Whitney's plan—and specifically to the national road imagined by Thomas Hart Benton during the Missouri Crisis—to show that links between the China trade, transcontinental infrastructure, and national aggrandizement have been a persistent feature of American political economy since the beginning of the republic. The penultimate section of the chapter will explain how arguments for transcontinental railroads changed in response to rising sectional tensions and offer some reasons why all transcontinental railroad proposals, including Whitney's, failed to pass Congress before the Civil War. It concludes with a consideration of what "transcontinental" meant for antebellum Americans and what consequences the commercial and global contexts they infused into the term have had for our present understanding of manifest destiny's historical moment.

Whitney's journey toward his plan for a transcontinental railroad began when he set sail from New York City's Pike Slip wharf on June 18, 1842.[10] Twice widowed, his finances had collapsed in the lingering downturn following the Panic of 1837; he shipped out to recover his fortunes as well as his spirits.[11] His destination was the rich port of Canton, where the chaos of the recent Anglo-Chinese conflict, the First Opium War, was creating new commercial opportunities for enterprising foreign merchants. A pious man but not an unassuming one—his physical resemblance to Napoleon was noted—Whitney hoped the voyage would improve his circumstances and perhaps lead to something grander.[12] "It certainly is a great tryal at my time of life to recommence the work, too in a strange foreign Land," he confided to his diary, but he hoped "above all things that I may yet be enabled to do some good to mankind & in some small degree make amends for the abuse of all God's providences to me."[13]

He arrived in Canton on November 24, 1842, a few months after the Treaty of Nanking had confirmed the consequences of Britain's successful invasion and opened new Chinese markets to Western traders. Amid the continuing commercial and political upheaval that followed the war, Whitney spent sixteen months engaged in business. During that time he conceived the plan whose scope and "vast importance" he hoped would rival the deeds of his doppelgänger and hero, Bonaparte.[14] Returning to New York on September 9, 1844, with his finances restored, Whitney set about writing up his ideas and preparing to memorialize Congress about his railroad project.[15]

The core details of Whitney's plan remained largely the same from his first congressional proposal in 1845 to the end of his major public efforts in 1852.[16] His plan's outline was simple: Whitney proposed that the federal government set aside a sixty-mile-wide swath of public land, thirty miles on either side of his proposed road, running from the shores of Lake Michigan to the mouth of the Columbia River in the Oregon Territory. After building ten miles of track as a proof of concept, he would then sell five-mile-long blocks of this land grant to finance the rest of the road's construction—all under government oversight. He estimated that the road would cost a little over $68 million, and to raise those funds he would need to sell seventy-eight million acres of what he termed "waste."[17] Crucially, he denied any pecuniary interest: the land would be sold only for construction costs, and the road's tolls would go only to maintenance. If the road failed, all the property would revert to government ownership. "I have but one motive," he explained, "and that is, to see this great work successfully accomplished."[18]

The prospect of reserving that much land for one individual raised eyebrows and even helped cause a minor riot at a meeting in New York.[19] Paradoxically, it was also one of the plan's key selling points. Construction of the road by one person, as opposed to a corporation or government agency, circumvented constitutional objections that the politics of strict construc- tionism might have otherwise raised—the same scruples that repeatedly killed attempts to create any national institution, like a national bank, with significant economic power. As an 1850 Senate report noted, "the constitu- tional difficulties" for a railroad were otherwise daunting: "large and formi- dable sections and parties of the country" objected to "to the building of this work by the government directly, or to putting it indirectly on the national treasury; or to loaning the public credit to a company incorporated for this object; or to the setting apart of a specific part of the national revenue, the latter leaving the work still in the hands of the government." These "insur- mountable difficulties," the report explained, could only be "superseded by substituting *the principle of private enterprise and private responsibility*"— what Whitney alone proposed to do.[20]

The benefits Whitney envisioned from his land-locked Northwest Pas- sage were millenarian in scope. The road would unite all sections and inter- ests of American society, strengthening the union; settle the American West and make its "wastes" productive; unleash "a flood of light, life, and liberty, which would spread over, enlighten, and enliven the heathenism of all Asia"; and end all war by removing the grounds for armed conflict through "a free exchange of commodities." Its construction would employ the world's poor, many of whom were already migrating to the United States, and eradicate endemic poverty by opening vast new areas for settlement. (Whitney spared a thought for the "removed Indians" living on his proposed route, but only to consider how his road might be protected from them.) The road's geopo- litical results would be no less epochal. Drawing on the Anglophobia that powered much of antebellum politics, Whitney argued that his railroad would sap the strength of the British Empire by denying its merchant ma- rine and naval forces their employment in Asian maritime trade. The effect would be to reduce Great Britain's commercial tonnage by a third, choking off the empire's source of wealth while inflating American coffers: "What a blow, what a reduction to England's power!"[21]

The economic argument behind these prophecies was more pragmatic. It all came down to distance and position. Whitney took pains to prove that transit directly across the North American continent would be cheaper and more efficient than purely maritime travel, either by the standard routes around Cape Horn and the Cape of Good Hope or through proposed ca- nals in Central America or Egypt. In this effort he amassed detailed tables of travel times and compiled statistics on the cost per pound of shipping tea, cotton, or wheat, in addition to creating new maps to better visualize this data. All put North America at their center.[22]

Creating a more efficient channel for shipping and exchanging goods would not just benefit the United States as a toll taker, Whitney argued. Better access to old and new markets would unleash the nation's productive capacities, enabling Americans to "take our vast products, both from the soil and manufactures" to "the Atlantic coast and Europe with 250,000,000 of souls on the one side, and, on the other side, the Pacific coast and all Asia, with 700,000,000 of population."[23] New markets and easy transit would attract productive and permanent citizens instead of the "poor workers of mines" then being drawn to California gold; and a securely supplied outlet onto the Pacific would give the American fishery advantages that no other nations' fleets could best. Finally, all this new trade and settlement would spur a boom in secondary financial activity, concentrating the world's banking and insurance business in the cities of the United States.[24]

With the potential for such power and wealth, it was no wonder Whitney's rhetoric escalated to the eschatological. "Here, then," he proclaimed, "would be the consummation of all things; and here it would be as fixed, as fast as time and earth itself. Here we should stand forever, reaching out one hand to all Asia and the other to all Europe, willing that all may join the great blessing which we possess, claiming free intercourse and exchange of commodities with all, and seeking not to subjugate any; but all, the entire, the whole, tributary, and, at our will, subject to us."[25] Whitney asked for a public investment and promised the world's trade, and global hegemony, in return.

Whitney first presented his plan in a brief memorial to Congress on January 28, 1845.[26] After his memorial was published, Whitney led a western surveying expedition to confirm his route's practicality, then barnstormed the nation as a lecturer, explaining his plan to audiences from Alabama to Maine at special meetings, railroad conventions, and legislative assemblies—all while barraging Congress and prominent newspapers with new letters, reports, and petitions.[27] The ink he spilled and the miles he traveled paid dividends. Whitney's ideas were soon hotly debated at the highest levels of government and intensely discussed across the entire country. He became a minor celebrity; in addition to his being indelibly associated with his railroad project, the workings of his mind were analyzed in a leading phrenology journal.[28] More important, by 1849 a majority of states had passed resolutions supporting his project.[29] By 1856 Whitney's advocacy had made the construction of a road linking "the Atlantic and Pacific coasts" to open "the rich commerce of Asia" a major policy plank in the platforms of both the Republican and the Democratic parties, a rare point of agreement in antebellum politics.[30]

His timing mattered. Whitney began promoting his plan just as the Polk administration began moving to expand the nation's territory by force. Indeed, post hoc celebrations of Polk's negotiations with Mexico trafficked in predictions quite similar to Whitney's. Democratic spokesman Lucien Chase declared in his apologia for the administration that "in the Bay of San Francisco will converge the commerce of Asia and the model Republic," while a Democratic pamphlet in 1848 argued that "from our cities on the Pacific, a speedy communication will be opened with China, and a profitable trade enjoyed, which must soon pour the wealth of that nation into our laps."[31] Likewise, Whitney adapted his plan in response to the Mexican-American War: after the capture of California, he added a second western terminus on San Francisco Bay to his original route.

As Whitney inaugurated a new conversation about transcontinental infrastructure and tried to capitalize on events like these, they also helped to make his case. For some the settlement of the Oregon dispute in 1846, the Mexican cession of 1848, and the subsequent California Gold Rush did much to settle debate on the necessity of a Pacific railroad, even apart from Asian commerce. The editors of the St. Louis *Western Journal*, for example, were moved by these events to finally embrace Whitney's arguments. They explained their new perspective as an accommodation to changing conditions: "The project of a railway to the Pacific," that "a short time ago appeared so like the offspring of a disordered imagination," was now "a work of national necessity."[32]

While there were detractors who rejected the plan as impractical or dangerous, Whitney consistently met with significant enthusiasm and support. Critics varied in the strength and tone of their opposition. The *New York Herald* waged a vituperative and lengthy campaign against him; the *American Railway Times* was genteel by comparison in alleging that granting Whitney land would be a "great national misfortune."[33] But the reluctant acceptance expressed by the *Western Journal* forms a repeated theme in many statements. Supporters were won over in spite of themselves, worn down by his masses of evidence and dogged assertions of the "practicability" of his project. The legislators of Kentucky reported that they had been struck "with astonishment" at the "idea of undertaking and accomplishing such an enterprise." But after a "very lucid explanation" by Whitney, the statesmen of the Bluegrass State became convinced that despite its audacity, the plan "deserves the strong arm of the government" (or at the very least they knew of "no plan less obnoxious" for using public lands).[34] The New York Chamber of Commerce praised Whitney's "practical views, detailed information, and untiring zeal"—but issued a statement of support only after exhaustively investigating other plans and finding their capital requirements too high.[35] Even supporters who publicized his public meetings were uncomfortable with the scale of his ambitions: "Having been acquainted with Mr. Whitney for many years, and heard his arguments and explanations, based upon statistical facts," one Philadelphian wrote, "I may confess that there is more ground to sustain his scheme than any one would imagine who had not heard him."[36]

A chorus of competitors augmented the volume and reach of Whitney's pitch to the public. After his memorial to Congress in 1845, "proposing Pacific railroads became an industry."[37] Transcontinental plans proliferated, hawked by opportunistic politicians, ambitious boosters, and sharp-dealing land speculators across the country. They diverged on many matters, from the funding structure to the estimated pace of construction, and, most critically, on routes and endpoints. But what remained constant during this infighting is revealing. All the plans on offer agreed on the road's motivation: to capture Asia's trade for the United States. George Wilkes, a self-proclaimed Oregon expert and rival railroad promoter, only stated the now-conventional wisdom when he noted that "the commerce of the East, in every age, has been the source of the opulence and power of every nation which has engrossed it."[38] This perspective was so commonplace after the publication of Whitney's plan that it hurt his claim to distinctiveness. Professional proslavery advocate and editor J. D. B. De Bow argued that "the world having dreamed so long of reaching the Indies by reduced travel," it would be pointless to try to determine the true originator of the idea of a transcontinental railroad scheme. "Such is the progressive nature of American mind," he opined, that "we may argue that this idea of a passage across the continent must have occurred to many simultaneously with the first successful railroad results among us."[39]

De Bow's belittlement raises an interesting question: Why, in the late 1840s, did the idea of access to "the Indies" gain such a hold on the American imagination, even when separated from the clever constitutional politics of Whitney's plan? The opportunities Whitney profited from while he was a merchant in China are part of the answer. His voyage to Canton was itself a product of an increased American awareness of China's commercial potential—an awareness generated by Britain's successful prosecution of the First Opium War, waged to secure wider access to China's markets at the cost of Qing imperial sovereignty. The violence not only "opened" the Qing Empire to Westerners by creating new protected free trade zones (known as "treaty ports") and granting foreigners extraterritorial rights, it also encouraged American attention to China, which later brought an official foreign policy response. Occurring during a fraught period in Anglo-American relations, Britain's invasion of the China coast in 1839–42 was closely covered by the American press. Editors, and their readers, saw in the war not only a major world news event ("the most remarkable event of the nineteenth century" in Horace Greeley's overheated phrase), but an analogue to their concerns about Britain's power in Oregon, Mexico, and the Atlantic Ocean.[40]

Public attention to Britain's war in China prompted a burst of congressional attention to American interests in Asia and, subsequently, a formal treaty mission to China. The 1844 Treaty of Wangxia that the Tyler administration negotiated with the representatives of the Daoguang Emperor granted Americans trading rights in China equal to those won by British arms, including access to new commercial enclaves and extraterritorial rights. It also made the United States a stakeholder in the colonial treaty port system, under which every economic advantage and exception to Chinese law accrued by one foreign power was automatically guaranteed to all others through the mechanism of most favored nation treaty clauses.[41]

This investment in "jackal diplomacy" quickly took on a life of its own, leading to the regular posting of diplomats and naval squadrons to China and other parts of Asia to protect and enlarge on new commercial and missionary opportunities. The presence of new groups of American merchants, missionaries, and federal officials regularly injected information about Asia's economic and political value into the American body politic. At first interested in China because Britain's aggression there seemed related to the empire's moves striking closer to home, American policymakers and publics soon became invested in China, and Asia more broadly, as a core part their own global strategy.[42]

The consequences of this new perspective can be found in discussions of transcontinental railroad projects. A widely disseminated 1846 Senate report, for example, supported Whitney's proposal with detailed descriptions of commercial opportunities in "Manchoo Tartary," China, Japan, Polynesia, Australia, India, and Singapore as well as a dozen tables of trade statistics about all these areas and more—all of which Congress would have been hard-pressed to compile before the Opium War.[43] The reach of this new information spread well beyond railroads, too: projectors advocating canals, scientific expeditions, and more esoteric schemes all used as their keystone the promise of a new era of American dominance in global commerce, premised on Asia.[44]

Still, the distribution of this new information does not fully explain why early transcontinental railroad plans were so closely tied to the China trade. Indeed, one early twentieth-century historian concluded that the "fundamental idea" that "Asiatic trade" would support a transcontinental railroad "can only be described by the word absurd."[45] In hindsight, promoters' more excited claims about antebellum transcontinental railroad projects can certainly appear fatally flawed. Establishing a new route across North America did not, in point of fact, reroute global trade from the high seas, nor did it immediately usher in an age of American global hegemony.

But analyzing railroad proposals like Whitney's as if they were narrow business proposals is not a contextually appropriate approach, nor is it the most profitable one. Just as the rules of household accounting function poorly when applied to a nation, antebellum transcontinental railroad plans should not be assessed like less grand private investments. Their scale and ambition worked with a different logic. Further, such plans were not fantasies of a moment: Whitney and others were drawing on an established tradition of trying to solve the political problems of republican union by expanding Americans' engagement with the global economy through China.

In 1848, as he was threatening to derail a bill granting Whitney the land needed for his railroad plan, Senator Thomas Hart Benton reminded his colleagues that he had "studied the history of California long before Mr. Whitney thought of it."[46] Though given to dramatic posturing, Benton was stating facts. His long political career was rooted in a vision of American empire extending to the Pacific coast and powered by Asian commerce—a vision he had first sketched out almost thirty years earlier in a series of editorial essays in the *St. Louis Enquirer* in the fall of 1819.[47] Benton's ideas shed light on the tradition that railroad promoters like Whitney drew on when they plotted a part for Asian commerce in the political economy of an American continental empire.[48]

Written as the future of Missouri's statehood and the expansion of slavery hung in the balance, Benton's 1819 essays advanced a complex development program. At its core was what Benton called an "American road to India": an overland route consisting of a series of roads and improved rivers that would link the Missouri River valley to Oregon's coast. (Following older conventions, Benton used the term "India" as a metonym for Asia, and especially East Asia; his usage is reminiscent of the sources he was fond of citing, ranging from the Bible to the Jesuits to Abbé Raynal.) Benton's road was intended to clinch the case for Missouri's admission as a state based on how it would help the United States capture Asian trade, and thus secure the nation's independence.[49] In this he was following the ideas of his elders. The revolutionary generation had thought of Americans' success in the China trade as a lever with which to extricate themselves from the mercantilist and monarchist Atlantic world—not unlike the way some among them viewed settlement in the North American interior. The first federal Congresses had granted American traders unique tariff protections to promote commerce with Asia, and particularly China. Similarly, the Washington, Adams, Jefferson, and Madison administrations all worked to protect the neutral status of Americans' lucrative China trade. However, their successors in post-

1812 Congresses turned against the trade, and against overseas commerce more generally, interpreting the experience of the recent war as proof that an overreliance on merchant shipping exposed the nation to too much European interference without enough economic benefit.

Early in his public career Benton synthesized these conflicting perspectives. Like Whitney later, Benton took the sectional economic integration imagined by Henry Clay's "American System" and expanded it outward to include the entire world in order to resolve tensions between rival visions for the republican experiment. With Asian commerce secured through an overland route, the nation could be simultaneously agrarian and commercial, extensively and intensively developed, globally dominant but peaceful—overrunning and enclosing a variety of partisan and ideological categories within one imagined political economy.[50] Benton saw his commercial system as the next stage of the American experiment, the commercial revolution needed to complete the political turn of 1776—even attributing its key points to Thomas Jefferson.[51]

In theory, Benton's new "overland" path had many potential benefits to recommend it. Not only would it be shorter than the maritime routes favored by American China traders, it would also be safer, cheaper, and better for the balance of trade, replacing payment in "gold and silver" with "an exchange of commodities."[52] It was also durable: so long as people across the globe continued "to love spices and aromatics, silks and teas," Benton explained, the trade in those Chinese goods would ever be "*sought after by all nations.*" Given these advantages, he thought it clear that "instead of going to the *east*, Americans should therefore go to the *west* to arrive in Asia."[53] (The inscription on the westward-facing bronze statue of Benton his daughter had placed in Lafayette Park, St. Louis, repeats this sentiment for posterity: "There is the East. There is India.")[54]

Despite this bold statement, for twenty years Benton's ideas commanded little support; he wavered on the details himself. Although he never questioned whether Americans should settle the Pacific coast, Benton was undecided about whether it would be possible for the United States to reach the new ocean in one piece. In an 1825 Senate speech that was much quoted by eager expansionists in the 1840s, Benton made a thorough case for the right to fully occupy Oregon; but then he reasoned that eventually settlers would want their own independent government—and he agreed they should have it. "This Republic should have limits," he declared, and the "convenient, natural, and everlasting" boundary was the continental divide, where "the Western limit of this republic should be drawn, and the statue of the fabled god, Terminus, should be raised upon its highest peak, never to be thrown down."[55] The prospect of founding a rival nation on the other side of the continent did not seem to trouble Benton, who, like many Americans, regarded republics as natural allies against the perfidious monarchies of the world. As he explained to the Senate, all the benefits of a "road to India" would continue even if half of it ran through a separate republic.[56]

In the 1840s, amid the Tyler and Polk administrations' aggressive pursuit of new territory, Americans' political thinking shifted. Where opinion on white American settlement on the Pacific coast had once divided on whether the new polities there would join the Union or become separate republics, in the discussions of transcontinental railroad plans that followed Whitney, these roads were explicitly sold as a means to a unified expansion. Indeed, a key part of Whitney's brief was that the railroad would be the thread that would bind the continental republic "together as one vast city" and bring its people into harmony of interests "as one family."[57] One of the key benefits of the Pacific railroad was the national consolidation—physical, economic, and spiritual—that it promised.[58]

But even if the road provided the means for harmonious communication between the east and west coasts of North America, trade with China would still be needed to grease that path with traffic; settlement in the West was just too slow to justify the expense of a road on its own. But the concept of commercial expansion premised on access to Asia was widely picked up only after the first Anglo-Chinese war reactivated American political interest in the China trade in the early 1840s. In this context Benton's early editorials were republished as part of the Democratic campaign effort for the upcoming presidential election.[59] After the first US diplomatic mission to China departed, the language about the lure and luxury of Asian commerce that Benton wielded with such imagination began to surface in Congress once more, reappearing in speeches and reports about Oregon, Texas, Cuba, and slavery in the territories, among other topics that concerned expansionists.[60]

Whitney was thus able to plead his case to a national political class recently reacquainted with Benton's arguments about the need to transform the global trading system to suit the needs of a burgeoning continental democracy. Indeed, Benton's arguments helped form the context for Whitney's entire public career. But the changes Whitney made were critical. Replacing impractical transmontane trails and canoe portages with steel rails, government management with private (individual) enterprise, and any lingering doubts about the Pacific coast's eventual independence with a firm emphasis on the power of steam engines and magnetic telegraphs to secure union through the annihilation of distance through speed, Whitney took the opportunity Benton sketched and fundamentally altered the common wisdom of American politics.

But important as these adaptations were, they were not enough to make the dream of transcontinental rails real—at least not in the moment. Though they sought to resolve major tensions in the practice of republican political economy, Benton, Whitney, and other "Pacific road" promoters failed to reckon with the partisan and sectional politics that bedeviled national infrastructure projects. Almost immediately upon the introduction of bills into debate, plans for a national railroad incurred the full rancor of late antebellum politics. Railroad plans' agreed-on importance became their greatest weakness, as discussion triggered the involvement of too many strongly felt, but divergent interests. Choosing a route required decisions about which section would be favored by the road and who would control nearby land; therefore the question of slavery in western territories would be raised, which in turn would offer new opportunities for quibbling about the legitimacy of the federal government's power. Together, national party rivalries based on explicit disagreement over constitutional construction, sectional divides over slavery, and differences among the multitude of state and local boosters advocating for their own petty claims effectively spoiled the chance that any railroad plan would get through any antebellum Congress. No legislation creating a transcontinental railroad was able to pass until after Fort Sumter had fallen.[61]

Whitney realized his plan was doomed well before the shelling started. Long insistent that his plan needed to pass quickly, before the land needed to fund the venture was sold off, in March 1851 he came to the conclusion that his project could no longer succeed even if passed into law.[62] Unwilling to abandon what had by now become a quixotic personal quest, he traveled to Great Britain hoping to get backing for a Canadian version of his scheme.[63] Meeting with no more success in Westminster than he had in Washington, he returned to the United States, remarried, and retired to obscurity in suburban Maryland. (Whitney's retreat from public view after 1852 was so complete, yet his association with the transcontinental project still so strong, that during a House debate on the 1862 Pacific Rail Road Act one frustrated representative groused that "the shade of Whitney—for I believe he is dead" should have been enough to convince his colleagues that such a road would be useful for more than the transport of "silks and opium." This last burst of influence was indeed a miracle of astral projection, as Whitney was still alive at his farm in Maryland, a short distance from the Capitol, where he remained until he died from typhoid fever on September 17, 1872.)[64]

His withdrawal from the field did not prevent others from continuing the cause, however. If anything, interest in transcontinental railroad projects increased alongside rising sectional tensions, providing fertile ground for new proxy battles over patronage and slavery.[65] But the chaotic struggle that erupted in the Thirty-Second Congress (1851–53), when the national legislature openly debated a Pacific railroad in a sustained way for the first time, illustrated how just how gridlocked the political system had become on the issue. After much acrimony, Congress postponed taking any action, instead ordering Secretary of War Jefferson Davis to use the resources of his department to make official surveys of potential routes.[66] It was a vain effort to settle a divisive issue by collecting data; no topographical survey, however well executed, could overcome the array of local, sectional, and partisan preferences arrayed against any particular plan. The disaster of Senator Stephen Douglas's later efforts to tie the repeal of the Missouri Compromise to legislation favoring his preferred transcontinental route in the Kansas-Nebraska Act only drove a final stake through proposals already dead on arrival.[67] The very road that supporters had claimed would become "a commercial and political bond of union" and "an imperishable link to make the Union of the States perpetual" instead provided new ammunition in the conflict that would lead to civil war.[68]

As these obstacles increased, the animating role of the China trade in arguments for the railroad diminished—though it never wholly disappeared.[69] By the mid-1850s supporters began to emphasize the military necessity of the road above other factors. Like Whitney's one-man/one-railroad proposal, this was largely a tactic aimed at overcoming constitutional objections. Advocates like President James Buchanan argued that the Constitution's war-making power granted Congress the unquestionable right to fund railroad construction.[70] As Buchanan repeatedly explained, with increasing frustration, in each new annual message, "It is our imperative duty to construct such a road" because without it "we can not 'protect' California and our Pacific possessions 'against invasion.'" While the commercial possibilities of the road remained important—Buchanan considered access to Asia "the great question of the day"—it was based on national defense that he repeatedly asked Congress to pass a Pacific railroad bill. But in keeping with the course of his entire administration, Buchanan was unwilling to commit himself "to any particular route," thus helping to ensure that the controversy only continued to fester.[71] The shift from trade to national defense was a lasting one, continuing beyond secession as a rhetorical device among Republicans.[72]

The "projectors" of the early and antebellum republic were wrong in their operating assumptions, at least in part. The integration of western territory was indeed a threat to the republic—but it was the boundary marked by Mason and Dixon, not the Rockies, that would serve as the tear line. Instead of binding East to West, the transcontinental railroad contributed to

North-South sectional animosity. Partly as a result, the road advocated by Benton, Whitney, and others was not built until after the Civil War—and even then the flow of global commerce never poured across the continent as they predicted. But though it was unsuccessful in the short term, their advocacy was by no means inconsequential: the road they dreamed of did finally come into being, and largely along the route they had planned.

The word "transcontinental" did not come into common use until after the Civil War, when there were multiple continent-crossing railroads and railroad corporations to talk about.[73] The word serves as signpost for the appearance of a new approach to an old problem—finding a shortcut across the Western Hemisphere from Europe to Asia, a goal of Western explorers from Columbus onward. The new word nonetheless marks a significant change, a native antebellum American creation "born of the railroad and bred in a new phase of federal expansion and national identity."[74] However, our genealogies for the term are incomplete.[75] Beyond Columbus, Benton, or Whitney, they ignore an important contribution to the concept behind the word: the China trade.

The common misdating of the term's first appearance helps to explain why Asian commerce has been overlooked. According to the reports of lexicographers and geographers, "transcontinental" made its first appearance in a brief news bulletin in the March 1853 issue of *Harper's New Monthly Magazine*, which mentioned a plan by a company of New York's "wealthiest" capitalists to petition Congress for the right to build a railroad from New York to San Francisco—but said nothing about Asian trade.[76] In fact, the term had come into printed use a few years earlier, just months after Asa Whitney, former China trader, had introduced his own plan for a railroad linking the Pacific and Atlantic coasts.

The first apparent users of the word, the editors of the *Ohio Statesman*, deployed it on November 5, 1845, to warn their readers that the latest news from South America suggested the United States would soon face fierce competition with European powers over the "Route to the East Indies." Reports that the navigable portion of the Amazon River might extend to within "*eight miles*" of the Pacific port of Callao, Peru, led the *Statesman* to believe that there would soon be a dramatic confrontation. Of course, the United States' "proximity to the line of transcontinental navigation" on the Amazon would be a "decided advantage" in any trade war, but that proximity would not be enough on its own: "Should this passage to the Indies prove as easy and available, as seems to be anticipated, it will render prompt and decided action on the part of our government in relation to Oregon, and the communication to the Pacific through that portion of the Territories of the United States, still more necessary than ever. *We must* have the control of the commerce of the East, and that commerce *must* pass through the American Union."[77]

Though the editors left it unspecified, it is possible that they had Whitney's project in mind when they urged a "communication to the Pacific" running through US territory.

In the *Ohio Statesman* and far beyond, Whitney's plan, and his promotion of it, ensured that for the next decade discussions about integrating far western territories into the United States, or connecting the Atlantic and Pacific, were also inevitably discussions about securing Americans privileged access to Asian commerce. This connection was so strong that it not only infused the term "transcontinental" with meaning, it helped to define the ideology of American empire itself. In the same article where *Democratic Review* editor John L. O'Sullivan hailed the annexation of Texas as part of the nation's "manifest destiny" (perhaps coining the phrase), he also declared that an American railroad linking "the Empires of the Atlantic and Pacific" was a "necessity" that "cannot remain unbuilt." This "iron clasp" would be needed to bind the "fast-settling Pacific region with that of the Mississippi valley" and hold the Union together. And what would support such a project? Why, the same "commerce of the world with the whole eastern coast of Asia" that Whitney's plan proposed to capture.[78] O'Sullivan was not alone in internalizing Whitney's logic. Indeed, in the minds of antebellum Americans, the transcontinental railroad, Asian trade, and the future of the United States' western empire were deeply interdependent concepts.

"Transcontinental" thus concentrates into five syllables the story of how trade with China was yoked to the belief in the transformative power of locomotive technology and a confidence in Providence's design for the United States' westward-moving imperialism, melding all three ideas as one concept in the American political imagination. The central place of Asian commerce in plans like Whitney's illustrates the global scope of American ideas about commerce and empire. It is a discrete example, if an extraordinarily influential one, of the continuous interaction between global concerns and North American territorial questions that historian William Earl Weeks has argued characterized antebellum American expansionism generally.[79]

A fuller understanding of Whitney's proposal, and the context of its reception, changes how we see the political culture of the United States in the mid-nineteenth century. Of course, highlighting the global and commercial components of American political culture does not make the project of manifest destiny any simpler or more innocent. If anything, Whitney articulated Americans' dangerous ambitions more nakedly than his peers did. However, it does suggest some of the ways that demands beyond those imposed by white supremacy, growing markets, or sectional conflict influenced the development of transcontinental thinking in American politics.

For Whitney and his supporters, a road to the Pacific supported by commerce with Asia was a means to empire, but it was also a solution for the political problems posed by a continent-spanning federated nation-state. Promising speedy communication and a means to consolidate the interests of white settled Easterners and Western settlers, transcontinental roads like the one Whitney planned answered fears that republican institutions would split and fray as the United States stretched across the continent's wastes. The argument Whitney and other promoters made—successfully—was that the bonds of union should be rails of iron, bought, laid down, and worn smooth by China's endless commerce. However manifestly designed or not, the practical reality of the nation's expansion to the Pacific was first made plausible by this abiding faith in the importance of trade with China to the United States' political economy.

* CHAPTER SIX *

This Slave Trade of the Nineteenth Century

Newly arrived at Macao in early March 1853, Humphrey Marshall found himself with too many fresh problems. While the new US commissioner to China was still busy finding an official residence and trying to persuade the US Navy to lend him the gunships he wanted to intimidate Qing imperial authorities, Marshall discovered a new existential threat to the American republic: the ongoing emigration of indentured Chinese workers to the Western Hemisphere, popularly known as the "coolie trade." Observing the traffic from one of its primary centers, Portuguese-controlled Macao, Marshall wasted no time in informing the State Department that "there is not another movement among nations, at the present moment" to compare with it in importance—or danger.[1]

A note on terminology: Following the norms of current scholarship, I have not used quotation marks around every instance of the terms "coolie" or "coolie trade." As other scholars have noted, using this kind of punctuation to mark off some racial categories makes others seem more permanent and concrete, to the detriment of our understanding of the unstable nature of these designations. During the nineteenth century "coolie" was as much a term for a particular imagined legal and class status as it was for an imagined racial one pertaining to Asians alone, and in this it was similar to "slave" (and similarly pejorative). Indeed, the precise relation of "coolie" to "slave" and "free" was the subject of much debate. Insofar as this chapter attempts to track that debate around these categories, and its implications, rigorous use of such punctuation has seemed a hindrance rather than an aid.

In the analysis that follows, I do not refer to historical human beings as "coolies," but rather use Chinese "migrant laborers" or "indentured workers." My choice here follows the same logic as the scholarly convention preferring "enslaved" (an adjective) rather than "slave" (a noun). The conditions of life under which Chinese laborers worked and traveled were mutable, unstable, and temporary—and not, as many white Americans claimed at the time, an inherent characteristic.

See Moon-Ho Jung, *Coolies and Cane: Race, Labor, and Sugar in the Age of Emancipation* (Baltimore: Johns Hopkins University Press, 2006), 10; Matthew Frye Jacobson, *Whiteness of a Different Color: European Immigrants and the Alchemy of Race* (Cambridge, MA: Harvard University Press, 1998), ix–x; P. Gabrielle Foreman, et al. "Writing about 'Slavery'? This Might Help," community-sourced document, accessed September 30, 2020, https://docs.google.com/document/u/1/d/1A4TEdDgYslX-hlKezLodMIM71My3KTNozxRvoIQTOQs/.

Encountering the coolie trade directly for the first time, Marshall found the threat it posed worthy of "deep interest" by "an Enlightened American Administration" invested in protecting slavery. Marshall was concerned that coolie labor seemed to be both better quality and more cheaply acquired than slave labor. The masses of male Asian workers he saw leaving China to work on plantations in South America and the Caribbean were skilled, "tractable" agriculturalists, "accustomed to hard labor," who would, he was sure, "compel from the Earth the maximum production of which it is capable." Their numbers "may said to be exhaustless," and they worked for low wages, making for competition, he feared, that would depress "the entire planting interest of the United States."[2]

Moreover, the coolie trade was geopolitically dangerous. By creating an alien population in plantation zones that was disenfranchised yet in some sense free, the traffic would destabilize other American republics and limit the United States' ability to expand slavery's empire, tilting control of the global economy even further in Great Britain's favor. A patriotic Whig as well as a loyal Southerner, Marshall did not entirely despair: strong federal action, like a ban on American ships' engaging in the coolie trade, "might, possibly" halt "the scheme, so at war with any established principle of American policy."[3] Though his official brief in China was to ensure Americans free access to Chinese markets, Marshall's commitment to maintaining slavery as a central part of the US political economy convinced him that arresting Americans' commerce in Chinese people was necessary to protect the national interest.

Marshall's urgent report was quietly interred in the State Department's archives upon receipt. But his concerns about the traffic in indentured Asian labor were not buried with it; to the contrary, Marshall's analysis was a common one among the proslavery voices that shaped antebellum US politics, and of a piece with enslavers' other efforts to shape foreign policy to their benefit.[4] Though the coolie trade had attracted some limited notice in the United States before slaveholders and slavery-friendly politicians began to investigate it, it was their use of the information generated by new government and commercial networks in China that transformed the public consensus on the meaning of the traffic in the United States. Despite having little direct contact with China, the masters of slavery's growing empire successfully convinced first themselves and then the American political class that the commerce in Chinese labor was a dire "free labor" threat to slavery that was also *worse* than chattel bondage—and therefore needed to be addressed by policy. The discussion they started defined the meaning of Chinese labor in American politics for generations, shaping not only US relations with the Qing Empire, Great Britain, and Latin American republics, but also the discursive and legal formulations at the core of the post-Civil War American state.

The coolie trade was a transimperial response to labor shortages triggered by emancipation and stricter enforcement of transatlantic slave trade bans. Like the word "coolie" itself, the traffic originated in South Asian labor practices but had gone global through an officially sanctioned pilot program in 1838 that linked "overpopulated" British territories in India to "understaffed" plantation societies in the colonial Caribbean.[5] Though unpromising at first, the practice of bringing indentured Asian laborers to postemancipation plantation zones soon proved popular among imperial administrators and planters. After the First Opium War weakened Qing sovereignty, the practice of transferring contracted Asian laborers to the Americas spread well beyond the British Empire. American merchants and shipowners, unable to tap the pool of laborers in South Asia, instead chose to become major players in the traffic in Chinese migrants to other areas, specializing in using their vessels to transport workers to Peru and Cuba.[6]

As this Anglo-American division of the traffic suggests, there was no "one" coolie trade; there were many. Further, the trade itself was merely a small part of much larger patterns of nonindentured migration out of China's main coastal population centers, including migration to California, Manchuria, and other parts of Southeast Asia. Historian Adam McKeown estimated that 750,000 Chinese migrants "signed indenture contracts with European employers, including 250,000 to Latin America and the Caribbean before 1874," a figure dwarfed by the "11 million Chinese" who went to the "Straits Settlements" (Malaysia/Singapore) and the "between 28 and 33 million Chinese [who] migrated into Manchuria and Siberia" during the nineteenth century. Indentured labor on plantations in the Americas was by far the exception, not the rule, for out-migrating or sojourning Chinese people.[7]

What united different coolie trades were the legal terms. Whether originating in South Asia or China, the standard eight-year indenture was officially contracted with free persons (mostly men), making them employees, not slaves. In practice, "recruitment" involved debt peonage, drug addiction, and kidnapping; cruel, crowded conditions on shipboard and unchecked exploitation by employers also linked migrant laborers through shared traumatic, dehumanizing experience. Partly because of these systemic abuses, white observers took to lumping all laboring Asians into the same subhuman category of "coolie" as Asian emigration increased, no matter their contractual status or mode of migration.

Almost as soon as it was under way in the Caribbean, white Southern politicians and editors incorporated attacks on the coolie trade into their existing critiques of Britain's imperial, abolitionist project. Their rhetoric built on long-standing criticisms of Britain's Eastern empire as a unique zone of hypocrisy and despotism—criticisms the Opium War had recently reenergized.[8] For fire-eaters like John C. Calhoun, James Hammond, or J. D. B. De Bow, Britain's imperial aggrandizement, support of abolition, and importation of Asian labor were components of the same plan for a "monopoly of the world" that aimed to control commerce by controlling the labor that produced its most necessary commodities. For these ideologues, any pretensions toward "philanthropy" through the use of "free" labor were simply lies covering greater crimes.[9]

Shortly after their first appearance in the mid-1840s, these arguments began reaching a national audience on the floor of Congress during debates over territorial questions. On this essential battleground of the slavery controversy, influences were reciprocal: California's admission to the Union in 1850 gave Senator R. M. T. Hunter of Virginia the opportunity to not only tar his opponents as abolitionist Anglophiles, but also to create one of the most enduring characterizations of the coolie traffic, when he termed it "a new species of the slave-trade, equal, perhaps, in the horrors of the middle passage."[10] But while the coolie trade had been effectively incorporated into slavery's apologia by 1850, it had not yet become a primary subject for Southern policymakers and political agents; they had more pressing concerns.

That nonchalance ended when Cuban planters began importing Chinese laborers en masse in the 1850s.[11] Long a target of American imperialists, the Spanish colony was assumed by many to be manifestly destined to become the newest frontier of the slave South. The prospect of coolie labor replacing slave labor in Cuba alarmed proslavery advocates far more than such replacements in the British West Indies did; the suggestion of a functioning nonslave system of labor on the island struck at the core of their arguments for annexation. If Cuba would not be more productive under American administration, what rationale could expansionists offer for taking it?

The first to pick up on this threat, at least publicly, were moderate antislavery politicians and commentators. In a mirror image of slaveholders' alarm, they viewed Chinese emigration to Cuba as proof that free (or at least freer) labor could outcompete slavery and thwart filibusterers' imperial designs. As annexation fever was heating up in the spring of 1852, the *New York Times* took up the subject from the perspective of antislavery political economy, articulating what had become the conventional wisdom on the topic. Noting that in Cuba the "experiment" in Chinese labor "has proved successful," the *Times* wondered if Cuba's labor system would not be "coveted by the Planter in the neighboring American States?" A few weeks later the editors went further, suggesting that "the real malady of the South is defective labor, and the remedy the same as that now employed in Cuba—the introduction of the Chinese Coolies." Should contracted Chinese labor be successful, the *Times* editors thought, "the peculiar institution will at once give way to imitation; and so will end the great economical pestilence of the South." The *Times* spoke for the Northern bourgeois elite: for this class, indentured Chinese labor had briefly become a potential panacea for the economic and political ills of slavery.[12]

Ohio congressman Joshua R. Giddings deployed the same argument in the House, arguing that the economic advantage of Chinese labor in Cuba was an important part of the eradication of slavery. Pointedly avoiding the term "coolie," Giddings argued with intentional irony that the greater productivity of "free" Chinese labor would "slowly but surely" lead to "the redemption of Cuba." This trap laid, one imagines Giddings—who made his career spit-roasting hot-blooded fire-eaters on the points of their own arguments—grinning like the Cheshire cat as he concluded that the Cuban annexation slaveholders so earnestly desired would only "hasten the overthrow of slavery, both there and in our slave states."[13] Proslavery advocates' response was to extend their earlier attacks on Britain's coolie trade to encompass Cuba. Reflecting the island's close association with the American slave system, they added to their denunciations by stressing the direct threat coolie labor posed to American political economy. Humphrey Marshall's 1853 dispatch was the first to make this connection in official channels, but soon enough other fire bells were sounding in the night.

No alarm rang louder than the 1854 Ostend manifesto. A clear and forceful rallying cry in favor of Cuban annexation, drafted by proslavery American diplomats assembled in Europe—though without Washington's prior approval—the widely publicized report depicted coolie labor in Cuba as a national security threat. It grouped rumors of new imports of North African "apprentices" together with coolie shipments as signs of an effort to "Africanize" Cuba—that is, to install a nominally free labor system that was in practice coerced, in the manner of new European colonies in Africa. The manifesto warned that this "system of immigration and labor, lately organized," threatened "insurrection at every moment."[14] The likely author of this particular part of the message was also the driving force behind the manifesto itself, Pierre Soulé, a Louisiana politician and rabid expansionist. Soulé's fears about insurrection in Cuba were consistent with reports received from the acting US consul at Havana in 1855, William H. Robertson. Revealed in response to a request from another Louisiana politician, Senator Judah Benjamin, Robertson's reports from Cuba argued that coolie immigration was "daily becoming more worthy of serious consideration" there. Stirring up centuries-old fears of foreign-led slave insurrections, Robertson related rumors that "an affiliation" between Chinese coolies and African slaves had taken place on certain plantations, giving rise to "great uneasiness," though Robertson fretted that "the people of the island do not appear to see the danger."[15]

The logic behind the fears expressed in the manifesto was identical to that which drove much of the slavery controversy: concern for the future. "Is it not easy to see," declared a widely reprinted column in the *New York Journal of Commerce* in 1855, "in the very fact of the substitution of free Asiatic for African slave labor, in Cuba, an evidence and an acknowledgement that Slavery is about to die out in Cuba; when it dies, will it not die everywhere?"[16] This death, warned the *Journal*, could come either "by a legal or a natural process," but it would come if the coolie trade was left unchecked.

The traffic terrified slaveholders not only because it would prevent slavery's growth or undermine the current labor system's effectiveness; it struck fear into their hearts because it would also effectively rob them of their electoral edge, loosening the Slave Power's grip on the national government. As a Boston columnist explained, "the ownership of slaves confers a power in the apportionment of representatives which is not conferred by the ownership of anything else. . . . The idea, therefore, of substituting Coolies, for slaves, is simply preposterous . . . for the South, without their negroes, would be, to a considerable extent, politically crippled; and of this they are sufficiently aware." The presence of indentured Chinese laborers in Cuba was as threatening as the presence of Free Soilers in Kansas.[17]

This vision of the coolie trade as an existential threat explains the tenacity of Southern opposition to the commerce. This fear did not paralyze, however; the South's proslavery politicians and editors were able to transmute opposition to the coolie trade into a powerful force for their interests. Through good timing, agile rhetoric, and the release of government documents, Southerners were able to reinforce and amplify their critique in national debates. They were able not only to overturn antislavery Northern support for the coolie trade, but also to make it impossible for partisans of any kind to respond to the traffic without accepting that the trade was essentially immoral, as well as contrary to American interests, however defined.

In the wake of the panic over Chinese laborers in Cuba, proslavery partisans began to portray their opposition to the traffic as a matter of principled humanitarianism. In slaveholders' carefully calibrated telling, the coolie was a deceived victim of short-sighted and greedy abolitionists, foreign and domestic, who were so eager to end slavery that they called an even crueler modern bondage into being. This new pose allowed slaveholders to secure national traction for their opposition to the coolie trade, even among their enemies.

The anticoolie position drew on multiple strands of the proslavery apologia. Perhaps most curiously, proslavery commentators sometimes described the Chinese as "white." This was not an acknowledgment of racial equality, but shorthand for East Asians' position ahead of Africans in white supremacists' imagined racial hierarchy, a place likely due to the widespread belief that the Chinese were skilled agriculturalists.[18] In sharp contrast to other descriptions of China, which emphasized the Qing Empire's "backwardness," proslavery politicians described the Chinese as motivated to work without needing violent compulsion and therefore deserving of freedom. Louisiana Democrat Miles Taylor explained in the House that

> the African slave is not only accustomed to bondage, but, from his very nature, he is unfitted for any other life than one of dependence and servitude. . . . But it is not so with the subjects of this other traffic. They [the Chinese] have enjoyed what men call freedom through all time. They have those feelings which make them industrious without compulsion, and provident without necessity, so as to be qualified to contribute to the progress of the world in agriculture and the arts, by their individual and independent action.[19]

Such categorization heightened the immorality of the commerce. On the floor of the House, T. L. Clingman of North Carolina moaned that "in sight of our own coast"—meaning Cuba—"white men are regularly sold into slavery," simultaneously adding rhetorical shock value to his argument and perverting abolitionists' repeated complaints about the slave markets operating "in sight of" the halls of Congress in Washington, DC.[20]

Second, the coolie was depicted as the tropical version of the wage slave, a familiar character in proslavery propaganda. Powerful Louisiana Democrat John Slidell included a fully articulated version of this character in his official report in support of his bill to fund the acquisition of Cuba, lamenting that "philanthropists" (i.e., abolitionists), ever ready to shed tears "for those of ebon hue," had not expanded their sympathies to suppress "the infamous Coolie traffic." Slidell noted American and British involvement in the trade, then drew a direct line between the "temporary slavery" of an indenture contract and the Dickensian horrors of modern factory work. The coolie's death, he argued, "is to the master a matter of as much indifference as is the fate of the operative employed in his mill to the Manchester spinner."[21]

But the coup de grâce of the proslavery argument against the coolie trade, the rhetoric that found the most purchase beyond the fire-eaters of New Orleans and Charleston, went much further. It was composed of two propositions: first, that the coolie trade was akin to the African slave trade, a claim founded on government and informal reports that described the voyages from China that coolies endured as re-creations of the horrors of the middle passage; and second, that the actual commerce in coolies was conducted by none other than the opponents of slavery. As *De Bow's Review* put it in 1857, "Abolitionism has, by setting the negroes free . . . made filibusters and buccaneers of more than half of Christendom"—and it had done so primarily through the coolie trade, that terrible "filibustering philanthropy."[22]

This advance in proslavery rhetoric would not have been possible without a steady stream of eyewitness reports on the coolie trade and its effects. These were all generated and distributed by networks of Americans active in Asia, in circuits of information exchange that had only recently gained thick connections to metropolitan centers in the United States, mostly as a result of the first commercial treaty between the United States and China, signed in 1844. Before that treaty, the United States had had only a sporadic official presence in Asia, and the merchants active there mostly had kept their business to themselves. However, in the wake of China's "opening," American diplomatic and naval officials began visiting China regularly and sending regular reports back to Washington. They were joined by a flood of journalists, small-time entrepreneurs, missionaries, and tourists, who began filling American newspapers and magazines with stories about all the people, things, and events they witnessed in East Asia. Because the circle of American foreign policy had expanded, knowledge that had once been the province of a privileged few now became accessible to a wider public—with consequences for how Americans imagined their own political economy and their place in the world.

Among the earliest and most influential of these reports were George W. Peck's 1853 news stories on what Chinese laborers endured at the Chincha Islands. A group of three small guano-rich islands off the coast of Peru, the Chinchas were worked by Chinese laborers imported by English merchants with a concession to export the valuable fertilizer. Visiting the islands while on his way to Australia, Peck described the workers' situation as worse "than that of the negroes on our Southern plantations." Citing the regular suicides among the workers, Peck argued that the Chinchas revealed the truth of British hypocrisy: "the poor Chinamen are sold into absolute slavery—*sold by Englishmen into slavery*—the worst and most cruel perhaps in the world."[23] Peck's reports were published in the *New York Times*, and the Chinchas instantly became a byword for the cruelty of the coolie trade. But though he noted both American and English ships serving the islands,

Peck attributed the evils of the coolie traffic there wholly to the British—and left Americans out of it.

That associative gap disappeared in dramatic fashion over the course of the presidential election year of 1856. During that spring, waves of damaging revelations about the coolie trade broke upon the American public, revealing Americans' involvement in the trade, the extent of violence and death that inhered in the commerce, as well as an "official" condemnation of the traffic by the head American diplomat in China. These revelations arrived in the form of three distinct news stories, all spread quickly by the new American networks in Asia that had sprung up in the years after the Treaty of Wangxia. First came news that the master of an American ship, the *Waverly*, had suffocated hundreds of indentured migrants below decks while suppressing a mutiny.[24] Second were reports that the US commissioner to China, the famous Yale-trained medical missionary Peter Parker, had issued a proclamation comparing the coolie trade to the transatlantic slave trade—specifically claiming that some of its "horrors" exceeded those of the middle passage—and condemning American participation in it.[25] Finally there came news that American firms—in particular the respectable Boston firm of Sampson and Tappan, one of whose partners was a nephew and namesake of Lewis Tappan, the famous abolitionist—were transporting coolies to Peru and Cuba to sell their contracts on the open market.[26] The combination of these waves of new information proved too much for public figures to countenance any further embrace of the trade's antislavery potential. That was in part because these stories, and others like them, were widely discussed and publicized by the same Southern politicians who had long been concerned about the coolie traffic. This publicity, in turn, launched further investigations and even more coverage, solidifying the image of the trade as a new slave traffic, and migrating Chinese workers as a new kind of slave.

The tragedy of the *Waverly*, American news readers soon discovered, was no rarity. Long voyages and crowded conditions aboard ships led to disease, frequent mutinies, and suicides. Americans learned that United States officials in Asia had from Humphrey Marshall's tenure forward attempted to curtail the trade, but with no success; the Rev. Dr. Parker's proclamation against the trade, as ineffectual in China as it was widely reported at home, was merely the latest effort.[27] Finally it was revealed that the partnership of Sampson and Tappan, while saddled with the additional irony of a family connection to the famous abolitionist brothers, was but one of many American firms directly or indirectly involved in coolie transport.

Most important, the American reading public learned that comparisons between the coolie trade and the Atlantic slave trade were accurate.

Migrants were coerced—though deception was the norm, rather than outright physical force, at least until resistance was encountered. Local Chinese agents lured migrants with promises of work or the repayment of debts accrued from gambling or opium addiction, but there was also outright kidnapping. Brokers gathered laborers into private prisons on the China coast known as "barracoons" and held them under guard until vessels were ready to depart. At some point before sailing, all migrants would sign labor contracts attesting to their voluntary departure and laying out the terms of their service while abroad—a nicety intended to satisfy Western law, not Chinese, since officially the Qing banned emigration entirely. These contracts were almost always a farce, composed with no regard to the truth of the laborers' pay, the length of their terms, or their final destinations. Upon arrival at Callao or Havana, these contracts were sold to the highest bidder, and the migrants were delivered to their new employers. Indeed, the distribution of laborers at the final port reminded many observers of a slave auction; migrants' bodies were examined and their origins and temperaments probed as plantation overseers searched for hardy but malleable workers. One fierce Northern critic of the trade reported that coolie traders even adopted the same iconography as slave traders and slave catchers, placing the classic image of a runaway slave—a *"facsimile of a black slave, in the act of running away, with a bundle on his shoulder, and his head turned backward"*—in an advertisement in a Peruvian newspaper announcing the arrival of a new shipment of coolies from China.[28]

The similarity to the slave trade was even more striking at sea. Like the slave trade before it, the coolie trade was dangerous or deadly for all involved. The constant threat of mutinies was managed using techniques perfected in the Atlantic slave trade. Migrants, though not commonly bound or chained, were housed belowdecks, separated from the crew and other passengers. Many coolie ships had a tall barrier running perpendicular to the keel across the deck, a construction borrowed from slave ship design.[29] This half-wall, topped with swivel guns, gave crewmen protection and better sight lines from which to sweep the deck with grapeshot in case of resistance.[30] Long voyages, unhealthy conditions aboard the ships, and the bloody consequences of frequent mutinies led to high mortality rates; even on successful voyages, they ranged from 10 percent to 20 percent—similar to those in the Atlantic slave trade.[31] "Middle passage" described the experience of the midcentury coolie trade very well.

Journalists and editors augmented the impact of these reports by circulating them widely and analyzing them as evidence for the proslavery, anticoolie position. One of the most important examples was an essay that appeared on April 5, 1856, in the *New York Journal of Commerce* under the title "The White Slave Trade." The article's key rhetorical move was to collapse the distinction between the Northern merchants engaged in the trade and more radical antislavery Northerners, both abolitionists and Free Soilers, such that all antislavery Northerners were portrayed as hypocrites—just like the British. It was "very likely," the article's author claimed, that "some of the same men are engaged in this nefarious business, who are loud in denouncing the Southern man for not turning a large part of his family out of doors, or sending them to the snows of Canada." This approach had the benefit of defending Southern interests while allowing the *Journal of Commerce* to continue occupying the political middle ground, on the side of humanity and common sense, by condemning the "modern slave trade."[32]

The *Journal of Commerce* article was intended to provoke antislavery partisans, who responded with immediate and forceful pushback. Horace Greeley's Republican standard-bearer, the *New-York Tribune*, characterized the concern of the *Journal of Commerce* over coolies' welfare as "Satan Rebuking Sin"; another editor called such complaints "crocodile tears . . . streaming down its columns in great profusion."[33] The *Tribune* argued that instead of antislavery men behind the trade, "it is ten to one that every New-York and Boston African slave trader and Cooly trader is an habitual reader and an enthusiastic admirer of the *Journal of Commerce*" who had "first duly served an apprenticeship and graduated with distinction under our domestic kidnapping act"—the Fugitive Slave Act—of which the *Journal of Commerce* was a strong supporter.[34] Garrison's *Liberator* made the same connection: "The fact is, beyond all question, that the Northern men engaged in this Coolie trade, as well as those engaged in the African slave trade, are Northern doughfaces," men known for "continually clamoring against sectional parties and finding excuses for the projects of the slavery-extensionists."[35]

By reacting in this way, antislavery partisans turned the coolie problem into a wedge issue among Northerners, particularly Whigs. Like the *Tribune*, the *Liberator* attributed any traffic in human beings to the outlook propounded in papers like the *Journal of Commerce*: "So long as the North is cursed with doughface politicians and newspapers . . . of course there will be men enough found to engage in the slave trade, or any other nefarious traffic that promises to be profitable."[36] The *Concord Independent Democrat* turned the accusation of hypocrisy back on the proslavery journals, arguing in colorful language that "making themselves hoarse in croaking about the 'slave trade' in Chinese coolies" was merely the latest effort of "canting demagogues" to "play the common and persevering lick-spittle" of the Slave Power.[37] Even as they were effective in shifting the terms of debate, sudden onsets of conscience like the *Journal's* were not universally convincing.

Hypocritically reported or not, published revelations about the coolie trade attracted congressional attention. Proslavery advocates, having neatly collapsed the distinctions between different streams of Asian migration as well as different types of Northerners, called for further investigation while decrying antislavery hypocrisy. Antislavery politicians, outflanked by this maneuver and embarrassed by their fellow sectionalists, responded by taking on the issue as one of their own. By the end of April 1856, both the House and the Senate had initiated inquiries into the facts of the American coolie trade as well as parallel investigations into whether and how it should be banned.[38] This bicameral symmetry was replicated in the sectional allegiances of the politicians involved, though not in their partisan allegiances; both Northerners and Southerners called for attention to the issue—but no Democrats seemed interested, perhaps because their allegiances across sections were more secure.[39]

These efforts produced two executive reports, each titled "Slave and Coolie Trade." They used correspondence from US officials in China and Cuba to explain the workings of the trade, the status of migrants on plantations, and accounts of particular instances where American diplomats had attempted to intervene to prevent coolie trafficking (almost always unsuccessfully).[40] This new government consensus on the trade, its myriad cruelties, and Americans' deep involvement in it, all supported the critique of the coolie trade originally developed by proslavery commentators. By late 1856, the coolie trade was officially indefensible.

Despite their navigational skills, the American China traders engaged in the traffic failed to discern which way the political wind was blowing. Responding to anti–coolie traffic arguments, some China merchants reiterated long-discarded arguments touting the benefits of the free movement of labor, as one merchant who signed himself as "Oolong" did in a letter to the editors of the *New York Journal of Commerce*. Though careful to note that he was not now involved in the trade, Oolong rejected the idea that the trade was prima facie an evil one: "I should like to know why, in a country overburthened with population as China is, engagements may not be made with them to emigrate. . . . And if I obtain such emigrants, or send my ships to carry them, why should I be accused of being engaged in the slave trade, or worse?" Oolong's sentiment was close to that expressed by Boston merchant Robert Bennet Forbes in an 1854 letter to the secretary of state: "The effect of it [the coolie trade], *on those who get safely to their destination* is generally beneficial to them and to the countries to which they go."[41] Others clung to the idea that coolie labor could end slavery.[42]

But as the spring progressed, the number of the traffic's friends dwindled. The Boston *Atlas*, the standard of Massachusetts Cotton Whigs, began the year by defending the trade once the editors learned that respectable merchants—their supporters and subscribers—were involved in it. But a few months later, when congressional reports started to arrive, the *Atlas* quietly retreated from its pro–coolie-trade position. Offering no further editorials defending the traffic or the American merchants involved in it, the editors of the *Atlas* instead did what many other American publications had already done: they filed stories on the trade under headlines that associated it with the African slave trade, tacitly accepting the analogy between the two that they had earlier worked so hard to reject.[43]

Seeing that even their best friends in the press were finding the coolie trade too toxic to support, the more astute American China trade firms began to revise their public position on it—though their private practices shifted more slowly, if at all. An 1856 circular from Russell and Company, the leading American commission house in China, for example, affected ignorance, explaining that "we have been under the impression all along, that except some individual cases of hardship at the Chincha Islands, the Chinese were well treated" and that "encouraging this sort of emigration would tend to check the slave trade itself." However, recent notices had encouraged them to look further into the "irregularities" of the trade, "such as kidnapping—holding out false pretences, &c, &c., &c.," and to ask the shipowners they represented if they should stop chartering freights for it. (The circular was dated June 1, 1856, six months after Parker's anti-coolie trade proclamation, and roughly the same time as early news of the fracas in the United States over the trade would have become known in China). By 1860, agents connected to Russell and Company were rejecting "coolie charters" outright—proclaiming themselves "astonished" at a correspondent's "mortifying" assertion that they were still involved in transporting coolies to Cuba, "a business which we disapprove."[44] These public relations moves closely mirrored what the same traders had attempted when the opium traffic became controversial in the late 1830s.

The sea change in public interpretation of the coolie trade in the United States and China did not translate into political action against it—at least not at first. In the aftermath of the wave of reports in 1856, Congress took no substantive action. Neither, in subsequent years, did the executive branch; indeed, both the Pierce and Buchanan administrations actively resisted the efforts of US officials in China to use anti–slave trade statutes to arrest American traffickers in migrant Chinese laborers.[45] The political calculation here was simple, if depressing: while coolie trading in Asia complicated affairs for American officials and other merchants there, efforts to clamp down on it would have risked the greater ire of slaveholders at home, because it would have necessarily involved the federal government's claiming the power to control a commerce in bound labor.

Committed to servicing the needs of enslavers in all regards, the

Buchanan administration was particularly egregious about preventing official action against the trade while mouthing official condemnations to score political points. Belatedly responding to China commissioner William B. Reed's request for a ruling on the applicability of anti–slave trade statutes, the attorney general declared that, despite his agreement that "the Coolie trade is sometimes accompanied by cruel circumstances calling for restraint or prohibition," he could find no basis for applying existing laws to prevent it. Later, during the summer of 1860, the administration went out of its way to deride a plan offered by the British foreign secretary, Lord John Russell, to promote Chinese emigration via the coolie trade as a method of decreasing slave trading. In response to Russell's proposal, William H. Trescot, acting secretary of state, publicly aired the talking points of the proslavery critique of Britain's emancipatory imperialism in a form seemingly designed to appeal to both sections of the Democratic coalition. Loyally toeing the Southern line, Trescot described the coolie trade as "scarcely less horrible" than the "middle-passage" and coolie labor a force that would only "exert a most deleterious influence upon every portion" of the United States, demoralizing the happy, Christian slaves of the South and cheapening the labor of the Northern workers "who constitute so large a portion of our best citizens." Despite this bluster, however, the Buchanan administration committed no resources to arresting the trade, leaving American officials in China to their own devices.[46]

Not that American officials in China needed much instruction on the matter from Washington. Working as an interpreter during the Tientsin treaty negotiations in 1858–59, missionary Samuel Wells Williams thought he saw "the habit of living among slaves" behind US Minister to China John E. Ward's refusal to push Qing officials on the coolie issue when he had the chance. The Georgia native, Williams confided to his journal, "does not look upon his fellowmen as possessing some of the rights of humanity," and so ignored opportunities to secure "the lives and safety of thousands of Chinese coolies."[47]

The beginning of the next presidential election cycle breathed new life into the coolie controversy—but the revival came through the efforts of one man, not a movement. Thomas Dawes Eliot was a vociferous antislavery Republican from the whaling port of New Bedford, Massachusetts; before 1860 he had focused his energies in Congress on preventing slavery's westward extension.[48] During the 1860 session he opened a new front, attempting to push through a ban on the trade he found "unchristian and inhuman, disgraceful to the merchant and the master, oppressive to the ignorant and betrayed laborers, a reproach upon our national honor, and a crime before God."[49] Frustrated in these efforts by procedural objections of several soon-to-be Confederates, in April 1860 Eliot did manage to produce and distribute a fresh congressional report that summarized the history of the commerce and the pernicious aspects of Americans' involvement in "the fearful character of this slave trade of the nineteenth century."[50]

There the matter rested until the Civil War was in full roar. An amended version of Eliot's ban (H.R. 109) finally passed the House on January 15, 1862, a few weeks after the Lincoln administration answered Eliot's plea for yet more documents on the "Asiatic coolie trade" to support his case.[51] Eliot's bill prohibited American participation in the "Chinese coolie trade," vaguely defined as the sale or transport of "the inhabitants or subjects of China known as 'coolies'" without their consent. It explicitly allowed "any free and voluntary emigration of any Chinese subject" but put the burden of proof for free and voluntary status on the migrant and the carrier—a "'permit' or certificate" had to be obtained from a US consul in China attesting to the migrant's status before departure.[52]

The bill did not pass exactly as Eliot intended. In the Senate, the Commerce Committee made one major change. John C. Ten Eyck of New Jersey proposed an amendment removing the qualifying phrase "against their will and without their consent," thus altering the meaning of the text from a ban on the *involuntary* transportation of the "subjects of China known as coolies" to a much more expansive ban on the transportation of "coolies" full stop—with no consideration of the migrants' wishes and no further definition of that status. The New Jersey senator explained that his committee was "of the opinion that persons of this description"—coolies—"should not be transported from their homes and sold, under any circumstances"; this was because "as is well known," they were of "an inferior race," and so could not give proper consent to migrate—"words will afford very little protection to this unfortunate class of people."[53] Making the latent logic of Eliot's act now explicit, the Senate's amendment constructed "coolie" as a racial category all its own and made it law. "An Act to Prohibit the 'Coolie Trade' by American Citizens in American Vessels" was signed by President Lincoln on February 19, 1862.[54]

Though initially targeting only Chinese migrants, the anti–coolie trade bill set up a system of federal control over migration, a novelty for the United States. It built on the shaky foundations of the American consular service in China, and never worked smoothly or efficiently.[55] But the problem lay as much with the statute's racial logic as with institutional capacity. As late as 1869, American consuls in China were still writing to the State Department for clarification about "What is a 'coolie' as here defined, and what is a free emigrant?"—questions that would recur in treaty negotiations and congressional debates for decades. Nor did the emerging US bureaucracy feel it could depend on other imperial powers for guidance on the matter; one minister to China strongly recommended that the American port authorities desist from relying on British certificates issued in Hong Kong to verify a migrant's status, since the inspectors there did not inquire fully enough about the terms of indenture contracts, but just asked about migrants' stated volition.[56]

The debate over the 1870 Naturalization Act showcased the continuing power of the antebellum logic defining Chinese migrants as coolies and coolies as slaves in the postwar era. The same Congress that contributed some of Reconstruction's most important accomplishments—the final ratification of the Fifteenth Amendment and the passage of the Force Act to ensure that the franchise would not be denied "on account of race, color, or previous condition of servitude"—almost failed to enact a national naturalization law over the issue of Chinese migrant laborers. Proposed by New York senator Roscoe Conkling to eliminate voting fraud and regularize the extension of civil and political rights (and, not incidentally, boost Republican turnout in large cities), the Naturalization Act was nearly derailed by an antiracist amendment proposed by Massachusetts senator Charles Sumner that threatened to open the door to Chinese citizenship.

Sumner had been working for years to eliminate discrimination on the basis of "race or color" in the naturalization process. Conkling's bill presented him with an opportunity to achieve this end, and he proposed that the word "white" be struck from "all acts of Congress relating to naturalization." Caught up in the effort to consolidate the gains he had already won, Sumner underestimated how thoroughly proslavery rhetoric had become mixed into his colleagues' politics, providing them with the direction and precedent needed to successfully exercise their anti-Chinese animus.[57]

After Sumner offered his amendment, intraparty chaos erupted among Republicans, who dominated the session. Senators from western states threatened to sink the entire bill over the issue. Leading this group, Senator William M. Stewart of Nevada claimed to speak as a "friend of the Chinese," but he argued that the conditions of Chinese laborers' migration—through the "coolie trade"—made them categorically unfit for citizenship, "They were brought here under the same system under which they were taken to the West India islands," he explained, "the same system that has made slaves of them in the Spanish dominions." The "contracts made in Asia" that governed the terms of their slavery would give their votes to their employers, he argued, and that made naturalization impossible as well as unwise.[58]

Stewart protested that it was common sense, not "prejudice against the Chinese" that brought him to this position. Indeed, he noted that he had in that same session proposed a bill that would "relieve [the Chinese] from odious exactions and persecutions" by defining any contract whose terms ran beyond six months' work as mandating servile labor, and thus illegal (it did not pass).[59] Echoing arguments antebellum slaveholders had made, Stewart and other opponents claimed they were moved by a respect for migrants' humanity and the value of their lives. Sumner's amendment, Stewart alleged, would make the naturalization bill into an incitement for mob violence in the mining camps of the West. He claimed there was no inconsistency in this approach: "The Republican party has never done anything to commit itself to the policy which is here proposed" but had only extended the rights and duties of citizenship to nonwhites as they were able to bear it, and as it was safe for the republic to do so.[60] After two days of strenuous debate, Sumner's proposal failed, voted down on July 4, 1870. In its place, and on the anniversary of the Declaration of Independence, the Naturalization Act of 1870 passed with a semirestrictive section extending naturalization laws "to aliens of African nativity and to persons of African descent," but notably not to anyone of Asian nativity or Asian descent.[61]

In following his color-blind convictions, Sumner chose to ignore the way that since 1862 statutes and treaties focused on the coolie trade had built anti-Chinese discrimination into American law. This was as true of "friendly" legislation as of explicitly exclusionary measures. The Burlingame Treaty of 1868, signed at a high point in Sino-American relations and arguably the most "equal" treaty China had made with a Western power to that point in the nineteenth century, included an article that mandated that each party institute penalties for involuntary migration—and another section, inserted by the Senate, explicitly abjured any interpretation of this guarantee of freedom to voluntarily migrate as a step toward naturalizing "the subjects of China in the United States."[62] The *Revised Statutes* of 1875, the first official federal code, made the identification of nascent American immigration law and the coolie trade ban quite directly: Title 29, the section of the code covering "Immigration," consisted *entirely* of procedures designed to prohibit the maritime transport of "the subjects of China, Japan, or of any other oriental country, known as 'coolies.'"[63]

Subsequent efforts to exclude ever more Chinese migrants from American shores built on these precedents, and they were supported by the pervasive assumption that all Chinese arriving in the United States had come through some kind of slave-like traffic. The Page Act of 1875, for example, effectively barred the immigration of Chinese women by empowering US port officials to deny entry if they were suspected of being trafficked as prostitutes (surprising no one, officials decided that many were).[64] Likewise, debates over other restrictive measures, like the Passenger Act of 1879, all turned on the question of how free Chinese migrants could truly ever be imagined to be. With decades of public agitation and positive law all carved out from the discursive field defined by proslavery attacks on the coolie trade, in 1882 policymakers in Washington decided that their imaginations were, in the end, quite limited—the passage of the Chinese Exclusion Act proved the old association between Chinese migrants, the coolie trade, and slavery was just too strong, or too useful, to abandon.

In April 1860 railroad magnate and China merchant John Murray Forbes wrote to Massachusetts congressman Thomas Dawes Eliot to support the trade in indentured Chinese laborers. Having heard that Eliot had "got in charge a Cooley Trade Bill" that threatened to ban the commerce outright, Forbes wished to relay his conviction that it instead "ought to be regulated and not prohibited." While he readily admitted that the system supplying Asian laborers to plantations in the Americas had serious problems—it was toxic enough that he claimed he had never personally engaged in it—Forbes nonetheless wished to see it corrected, not abandoned.

Forbes's comments to Eliot repeated what were by then outmoded arguments in favor of the coolie trade. His contention that the "admirable labor of over populate [sic] China" could be profitably and safely put to work improving American soil as a free and productive replacement for slavery had years before been rejected by the politically engaged classes in Washington, New York, and Boston. However, Forbes did hit on an interesting analysis in his letter. Knowing firsthand the "jealousy which the planters have of any scheme of labor outside of their 'peculiar institution,'" Forbes had no doubt that any effort to prohibit American participation in the coolie trade would only benefit the Slave Power—something he thought Eliot, as a committed and vocal radical Republican, would surely wish to avoid. "There might be and would be danger to the value of slave property from Chinese labor," Forbes told the congressman—but that, he thought "is no reason why we Republicans should lend ourselves to their prohibitory schemes." At stake, according to Forbes, was not only "the interest of our commerce, but of Civilization and Freedom."[65]

Forbes knew about planters' "jealousy" from personal experience: first, from his acquaintance with Humphrey Marshall (who owed him money), and second from his failed efforts to set up a Florida plantation staffed by indentured Chinese laborers in the mid-1850s, exactly at the moment the public turned against the coolie trade.[66] His tone-deafness to the shift on the issue was common among China merchants—and, as with other traders, it is doubtful that Forbes's intentions toward China or the Chinese were truly beneficent. (For years he had helped manage Russell and Company, the dominant American firm in China, overseeing a large trade in opium.)

Still, from the perspective of later anti-Chinese developments in American immigration law, Forbes's analysis turned out to be a surprisingly accurate. Banning the coolie trade in 1862 solidified a particular approach to Chinese laborers within the constellation of American racial ideology, one that leveraged the logic of slaveholders' self-serving attacks on the coolie trade to attach the disabilities of the slave's status to Asian migrants, even as African American men and women were (briefly) able to carve out more space for themselves in the polity. Over time that logic had proved very powerful, promoting the growth of the US administrative state in Asia and at home, and provided subsequent generations of white politicians with tools to narrowly define the composition of the body politic, restricting the admittance of Chinese migrants before expanding the list of racially defined "undesirables." In the end, Rep. Eliot's attempt to bar the nineteenth century's newest "middle passage" did little to end the evils of the coolie trade; instead, it raised a bridge between the political economy of slavery and the modern age of racially restricted immigration.

Chinese exclusion is often narrated as a story of the local or state politics of the American West pushing upward to the national level, and of racial ideologies developing slowly and then hardening across sectional lines. It is also a narrative of how the major parties courted white voters in particular (western) states by enacting new strategies to restrict, oppress, and demean Asian migrants living within their borders during the 1850s, 1860s, and 1870s, in a repetition of the pattern of herrenvolk democracy all too familiar in other eras and other sections of the country. These narratives are valid: popular activism from below, organized by overarching and intersecting hierarchies of race, class, and gender, was crucial to creating a national restrictive immigration system out of the more open and decentralized borders of the pre–Civil War period. But these accounts also miss a crucial step, failing to account for the way the incremental accretion of restrictions on Chinese migration was argued at the federal level within the constraints of a particular set of arguments—constraints that left a small opening in the ensuing decades for Chinese migrants who could convince US authorities they were not, and never would be, laborers.

In explaining this gap, however small, the patterns set by the antebellum coolie trade debate are crucial. Following the lines of that conflict, regulations excluding Chinese migrants from the United States expanded gradually, first by giving American officials license to broaden the definitions of who counted as a "coolie," then by using the logic of the coolie-trade ban—which turned on the problem of labor trafficked unfreely—to encompass almost all Chinese migrants. Thus by 1882 the coolie trade, perpetrated by American merchants and given political power by threatened American slaveholders, ultimately proved to be the evil that justified the denial of civil rights and voluntary migration in the United States to all but a few people from China, an unhappy but stable legal equilibrium that continued until 1943—and one whose re-creation is a goal of powerful players in twenty-first-century American politics.

CHAPTER SEVEN

A Propped-Open Door

Seeking to explain the world-historical importance of his appearance in the Hall of the House of Representatives as the envoy of China's emperor, Anson Burlingame mixed his metaphors. Speaking on Tuesday, June 9, 1868, as the head of the first formal diplomatic mission ever sent by the Qing Empire to the capital of a Western power, Burlingame announced that the "warm and unusual reception" he received was more than a "personal compliment." The "greeting of one great people by another," he declared, was an "electric contact whose touch makes the whole world kin." Then, perhaps reflecting on the recent past of civil war in both China and the United States, or maybe just the usual effects of electric contact, he added that he hoped it would "go on without those convulsions which are too apt to mark great changes in human affairs." Still searching for a phrase to encompass the occasion, he lifted his gaze from the body, electrified, to look heavenward, describing the congressional audience as a meeting of "two civilizations which have hitherto revolved in separate spheres": a "mighty revolution."[1]

Elocutionary exuberance was a hallmark of Burlingame's career as a politician and diplomat.[2] During his tour of the United States and Europe from March 1868 to February 1870 as China's official envoy, the Yankee Republican's oratorical flourishes earned both fame and infamy for him and the mission alike. However, Burlingame's mission presents more than a tangle of verbiage. Because of its unique features and timing, the mission—and the treaty between the United States and China that resulted from it—poses a real interpretive problem for historians.

On one hand, almost everything about the mission is so extraordinary that its significance seems unassailable. Burlingame's own rise from antislavery Boston politician to US minister to China and then to the head of the first multinational, multiethnic embassy from the Chinese empire—

from "the representative of little more than a third part of Boston" to "the representative of more than a third part of the human race," as Senator Charles Sumner noted—was remarkable enough.[3] The months of official pomp and media attention that followed the embassy as it crisscrossed the globe were unprecedented. That Burlingame and his Chinese fellow envoys, Zhigang and Sun Jiagu, would go beyond their instructions to successfully negotiate the first equal treaty between the Qing Empire and a Western power would seem to justify even the most enthusiastic declamations about the mission.

On the other hand, this uniqueness underscores how briefly the mission's impact was felt. The moderate "cooperative policy" that Burlingame had helped forge between his Chinese and European diplomatic colleagues in Beijing—and that his mission was intended to promote—came undone shortly after the embassy ended, unraveled by aggressive lobbying by American China traders, fresh outbreaks of xenophobic violence in China, and a resurgence of Western powers' gunboat diplomacy. While the mission received a great deal of public attention, signs of changing attitudes toward the Chinese among Americans (or vice versa) were scarce. Likewise, bilateral relations between the United States and China proceeded on much the same course after the mission as they had had for decades before: American officials made gestures toward the importance of Chinese sovereignty but did little to prevent other powers from forcing new trading concessions, performing an opportunistic Open Door routine in Asia while simultaneously closing the gates to Chinese migration to the United States. Contributing to its transient power, Burlingame did not live beyond his own tour, dying of pneumonia on February 23, 1870, while visiting the czar's imperial court at St. Petersburg.[4]

Exceptional but ineffectual, historians of the United States have found it difficult to contextualize Burlingame's mission.[5] Among scholars of foreign relations, it is most often covered as a curious, temporary exception to longer arcs that bent toward injustice, a hitch in the longer march toward hegemonic commercial empire, democratically enforced white supremacy, or, most benignly, the continuance of official American neutrality (but practical imperialism) in China. Insofar as there is a debate about the mission, it centers on who was the main author of the impermanent and ultimately unenforceable set of policies enacted by the 1868 treaty: Burlingame or his former superior at the State Department, William H. Seward.[6] There is also another strain of scholarship, in which legal scholars place Burlingame's treaty as a brief, partial reversal of the anti-Chinese immigration restriction schemes that grew out of state regulations on the West Coast.[7] But these are small disagreements. The "electric contact" between "the oldest nation of history" and "the newest republic of the world" that Americans of 1868 celebrated is understood, generally, to be just a bit of static.[8]

Burlingame's characterization of the mission as a "mighty revolution" suggests a more profitable approach. Like many of his contemporaries, he regarded the embassy he led as a sign of a new epoch of world history—an era of "progress" that would be marked by China's increasing acceptance of Western, liberal norms for international comportment and economic integration. But this diplomatic revolution was not the only one on tap. The United States that welcomed China's embassy in 1868 was struggling with massive shifts in political, social, economic, and cultural structures as a result of slaveholders' ignominious secession and subsequent defeat at the hands of a greatly empowered and consolidated federal union, one governed by a Republican Party wedded to an ideology of free labor and enthusiastic about state-directed capitalist development. The Qing Empire, too, was emerging from its own apocalypse, the Taiping Civil War (1850–64). Far bloodier than the American struggle, this conflict was further complicated by a simultaneous foreign invasion during the Second Opium War (1856–60) that saw Beijing occupied, the emperor forced to flee, and his birthplace, the nearby Summer Palace, looted and burned.[9] In the Chinese case, the coincidence of the winding down of a massive civil war, the end of a foreign invasion, and the accession of a new emperor still in his minority led the metropolitan and provincial leaders of the Tongzhi Restoration (1862–74) to experiment with using the "practical knowledge" of the West for "self-strengthening" to improve the empire's fortunes in foreign relations as the Neo-Confucian order retrenched. For both the United States and China, then, the late 1860s were protean moments—"unfinished revolutions," to adopt Eric Foner's phrase—that were still in process after the near-annihilation of the state.[10]

Flipped on itself, Burlingame's own framing can help us understand how the revolution in "foreign relations" he was attempting was embedded in fundamental "domestic" reform projects. Considering the Burlingame mission as a link between the "mighty revolutions" reforming the American and Chinese polities, as well as within the context of a global postslavery economy, can offer a new perspective on the geopolitical goals of the US government during a fraught moment in the life of Reconstruction and the Republican Party.[11]

The Reconstruction-era Republican vision for the political economy of American empire was a liberal one, premised on mutually reinforcing policies intended to ensure "peace, prosperity, and fullest development."[12] Proceeding from this perspective, the architects of the Burlingame Treaty understood that progress toward full equality among nations as well as among men was necessary for maintaining peace, as well as for the operation of a prosperous global regime of capitalist development. Burlingame's mission was thus a Reconstruction project: one aimed at remaking both sides of the US-China relationship through a new foundation of equality—and through that relationship, at remaking the world.

These ideas were not airless theory, but were developed out of the traumatic experience of the struggle between the democracy of self-governed men and the despotism of slaveholders. Burlingame had gained national fame by challenging Rep. Preston Brooks to a duel in retaliation for his attack on Charles Sumner in the Senate; so when he branded opponents as agents of "that tyrannical school" and counted slaveholders and opium traders among them, he was naming for his audiences the international brigades of an enemy whose insupportable pretensions to superiority had led to vast bloodshed and suffering—and positioning himself, and Republican policy, as a "check to these aggressive pretensions."[13]

Emerging out of the material and ideological struggle with slavery, the geopolitical component of Reconstruction Republican political economy was defined by its opposition to autocratic impulses. Instead of insisting that complete control of human property in the bodies of "lesser" races was necessary to produce the "tropical" commodities the modern global economy depended on, Reconstructed Republican political economy required that the movement of laborers be certified as the free choice of self-owning individuals. It likewise insisted that decisions about the technological and regulatory infrastructures guiding flows of commerce must be made freely by sovereign nations. Without that freedom, the progress in culture and commerce that would flow from these arrangements could be neither democratic nor sustainable.

In practice, this vision did not survive the evolving political realities of the postbellum period in either the United States or China. As in domestic politics, Republican geopolitics in the Reconstruction era was premised on unstable ideas about racial equality and the capability for self-government. In the same way that white Republicans like Grant and Sumner understood the formerly enslaved as in need of instruction, the vision Burlingame and his allies championed sought space and time for "uncivilized" or "half-civilized" peoples like the Chinese to make the "progress" necessary to be accorded full equality. By embracing the language of tutelage that harder-edged white supremacists used, Reconstruction Republicans ceded critical ground. When the fragile, contingent recognition of shared humanity was refused to the Chinese—by merchants eager for fatter profits, laborers desperate for work, or government bureaucrats keen to consolidate police powers—the Republican coalition against hegemonic white supremacy cracked into its component parts at home, and the foreign policy informed by these visions of equality collapsed abroad.

Burlingame's death in February 1870 is often held responsible for this retreat, for good reason. The loss of his loud voice coincided with a diplomatic crisis over mob violence against foreign missionaries in China, as well as the dissolution of the coterie of foreign ministers who had helped support his "cooperative policy" for a decade. But while it was a blow, Burlingame's death did not dissolve the US government's commitment to his China policy.

That retreat came only after the Republican Party had retreated from Reconstruction in a strategic attempt to maintain a grip on power. This withdrawal began during the second Grant administration but fully took effect only after 1876, when the incoming Hayes administration, acting to further sectional reconciliation, acceded to more aggressive actions by Western congressmen to restrict Chinese immigration and narrow the scope of US-China relations. The components that Burlingame's tenure helped weld together—the free movement of commodities, capital, and people—became disaggregated despite the best efforts of experienced American diplomats in China like Samuel Wells Williams and George F. Seward.

The disbanding of the pro-Reconstruction Republican coalition in Washington created the opportunity for the emergence of a more familiar constellation of domestic and foreign policies. Racialized restrictions on migration, backed by consolidated federal police powers, were combined with more aggressive pursuit of "open door" access to Asian markets for American manufactured goods. Burlingame's "mighty revolution" was effectively finished when the American experiment in multiracial democracy was defeated. Thereafter the American government's embrace of white supremacy led to a fundamental shift in US-China relations. No longer eager to use commerce in China as an opening onto the world, US policymakers instead sought to channel people, goods, and capital into discrete flows—each managed for maximum national benefit, now defined as maintaining white supremacy and accumulating industrial capital.

Anson Burlingame never set out to go to China. A Harvard lawyer by training, he had spent his youth on the Ohio and Michigan frontiers before making a name for himself in Boston. His first and best skill was oratory, which he put to use in campaigning for political and reform causes, including Martin Van Buren's presidential campaign on the Free Soil ticket, protests against the Fugitive Slave Act, and fund-raisers for Louis Kossuth's Hungarian revolution. He served in Congress for three successive terms, beginning in 1855 as a member of the nativist (and antislavery) American Party but quickly following his radical Massachusetts colleagues into the Republican Party, where he was zealous enough to gain national fame through his aggressive defiance of the Slave Power.[14]

He ran for Congress again in 1860 but lost, in part because his stumping for Abraham Lincoln took him away from his district. To reward his loyalty—and under pressure from the Massachusetts Republican Party—Lincoln appointed Burlingame minister to Austria. This proved a temporary placement; in retaliation for his earlier support of Kossuth's revolt, Vienna declared him persona non grata while he was still traveling to his post.[15] After some scrambling, he was offered the position of minister to China instead. Though he had not shown any particular interest in Chinese affairs to this point, he accepted the position as soon as it was offered, and spent the time between his appointment and the arrival of his commission interviewing retired American China merchants and bankers in Paris and London.

If he felt any anxiety about his fitness for the post, it does not appear in his official correspondence. Leaving Marseille on a steamer bound for Hong Kong, he closed his first report to Secretary of State William H. Seward breezily: "I proceed to my new post with diffidence but still with pleasure for there is a fine field and I am yet a young man."[16] Unearned at first, Burlingame's confidence in himself and his mission was borne out over a long and productive tenure. He arrived in China in October 1861 and served as US minister plenipotentiary and envoy extraordinary there through November 1867, with a break to visit Europe and America from May 1865 to September 1866.[17]

Seward did not intend for his new minister to revolutionize the Sino-American relationship. In 1861 and 1862, Lincoln's secretary of state was busy with many other matters, and his instructions to Burlingame reflected the administration's general policy of using diplomacy to keep external crises—and foreign aid to Confederates—to a minimum. But amid the exigencies of ongoing civil wars in China and America, the old policy of cooperating with European allies to gain greater access to China's markets while also maintaining a neutral pose presented a fierce dilemma, exacerbated because Burlingame could not expect any monetary or military support from home—limiting his capabilities.

The recapture of Ningpo from Taiping forces in spring 1862 revealed the conflicting pressures the American minister faced. Replying to news of the imperial government's victory—and the renewed threat the rebel forces posed to foreigners in the enclave of Shanghai—Seward observed that "revolutions are apt to effect sudden and even great changes in very short periods," so Burlingame "ought not to be trammelled with arbitrary instructions." But even in granting his envoy this freedom, he reminded Burlingame to support the forces of order and national sovereignty and "lend no aid, encouragement, or countenance to sedition or rebellion against the imperial authority."[18] This was something of a change from earlier in China's civil war, when American (and other Western) observers had looked to the Sinicized Christian millenarian theology of Hong Xiuquan's "Heavenly Kingdom" as evidence that the faction was a "Christian, pro-Western alternative to the universally reviled Manchu rulers in Beijing."[19] By 1862, Western publics and the expatriate community in China had soured on the Taiping, and Western governments began to more regularly support the imperial government over the alternative. This shift was useful for Seward, who was working in a moment when the threat of European recognition of the Confederacy still hung in the balance—and with it the fate of the American war—making Union support for any rebellion, anywhere, impossible without weakening his own government's position. So he told Burlingame to trust that other Western powers would protect American interests—but gave him cover in case they did not. Burlingame was to "consult and cooperate . . . unless, in special cases, there shall be very satisfactory reasons for separating from them."[20] Demonstrating his political skill, Burlingame took these muddy comments and turned them into clear authorization for his independence, thanking Seward for his approval of "the policy thus far pursued by me."[21]

Burlingame's major contribution while in China was the development of what he termed the "cooperative policy." This was something much more than the standard instructions the State Department had been issuing to China ministers since the 1840s about the need to coordinate with other Westerners in China. Though the US policy had long been grounded in a conviction that Western nations had a union of interests on China's coast, Burlingame's innovation, made at the intersection of two civil wars that were both shaped by the threat of international intervention, was to recognize that that this shared interest required stabilizing centralized Qing authority. Without a stronger imperial government, Western traders, missionaries, and diplomats could not reasonably expect secure access to China or avoid a scramble among themselves for access and territory.[22]

Formally, the "cooperative policy" described an agreement among Western powers to coordinate in their dealings with Qing officials. In practice it was something more: it meant cooperating with their negotiating partners at the Zongli Yamen, the new foreign ministry Qing imperial authorities set up after the 1860 European invasion.[23] Working together, the "Yamen" (as it was known in Western diplomats' internal correspondence) and the foreign diplomatic corps could construct a united front, facing outward toward their respective domestic audiences, who were more ready to abandon peaceful methods of international integration (the "antiforeign party" in China, the "force party" in European capitals). As Burlingame concisely defined the "cooperative policy," it required Western officials to

> consult and co-operate in China upon all material questions; to defend the treaty ports so far as shall be necessary to maintain our treaty rights; to support the foreign customs service in a pure administration, and upon a cosmopolitan basis; to encourage the Chinese government in its efforts to maintain order; to neither ask for nor take concessions of territory in the treaty ports, nor in any manner interfere with the jurisdiction of the Chinese government over its own people, nor even menace the territorial integrity of the Chinese empire.[24]

This "substitution of fair diplomatic action for force" was designed to limit unproductive Western avarice and aggression in order to encourage Chinese openness, to the benefit of all. In the small diplomatic community in China, where excuses for conflict where readily found, its success depended on the constant support of forceful personalities.[25] Conscious of the fragility of such arrangements, Seward approved of Burlingame's cooperative policy from the start but warned that it was precarious: it would "fall into disuse" if any one of the "intelligent and able statesmen" who represented foreign powers and the Chinese at Beijing were replaced.[26]

Like most examples of great diplomacy, the results of the "cooperative policy" lay mainly in what it prevented. With the support of Prince Gong and imperial officer Wenxiang on the Chinese side and the other European ministers resident in Beijing—Frederick Bruce (Great Britain), L. D. Baluzek (Russia), and Jules Berthemy (France), who made up the rest of the "four Bs"—Burlingame helped smooth over a number of potentially explosive incidents.[27] These ranged from the serious but low-burning controversy over whether Western diplomats would ever gain an in-person "audience" with the underage Qing emperor, or more incendiary affairs like the suspicious sale of a British naval fleet, a Prussian invasion of Chinese waters, the arrest of Western mercenaries in the employ of the Taiping, or the murders of European missionaries.[28]

In doing his part to keep China free of new invasions—and open for business—Burlingame was carrying out the work of any far-sighted American diplomat, if unusually well. He also actively sought to bridge Chinese and American politics by making the struggles of one relevant to those of the other. In part this was just a smart career move—successful service abroad could burnish his credentials at home—but it also prepared the way for later implementing a Republican Reconstruction geopolitics. Following orders from Washington, shortly after he arrived in China he had administered loyalty oaths to US diplomatic and naval personnel in China to weed out Confederate sympathizers.[29] Throughout his tenure he used consular courts to discipline Americans in China, most prominently the "fillibusters" that California had "vomited upon China" after the Civil War began—though he was willing to support American military adventurers in China as long as they found favor with Qing authorities.[30] And by working with his colleagues in Beijing, Burlingame was able to provide intelligence that helped the State Department coordinate a multicontinent campaign against the construction and sale of steam-powered warships that would have otherwise fallen into Confederate hands.[31] After the Confederate raider *Alabama* was spotted in the China seas, Burlingame successfully petitioned the Qing government to ban "rebel cruisers" from its waters to protect US commerce.[32]

(These efforts were reciprocated. Early in his tenure, Chinese authorities sought assurances that American shipyards would not supply the Taiping with steamships, which Burlingame duly conveyed.[33] Over time, Burlingame and his interlocutors in the Zongli Yamen, including Prince Gong and Wenxiang, became more adept at drawing out the parallels between their two nations. They congratulated each other on victories over rebellions and together mourned the loss of important leaders.)[34]

Like many foreigners, Burlingame understood China primarily through the lens of his own country's experience, which happened in that moment to be as unsettled and precarious as China's. Explaining why the "cooperative policy" was needed to strengthen Beijing's hand in maintaining its empire, for example, Burlingame told his chief that "as in our own country," "a portion" of China's population had rebelled "because they have felt too little the influence of the central government."[35] Not everyone applied American politics to China this way, of course. Writing a few years later, Samuel Wells Williams, the most experienced and learned American official serving in the nineteenth century, offered a more condescending comparison. He saw in China's ambivalent participation in the international system the same kind of political "education" that the formerly enslaved were then receiving: "she finds, like the slaves in the old Southern states, that as an inferior she gets one kind of treatment and as an equal another."[36]

Burlingame shared other Westerners' desire to reform China. By his own lights, he had made significant strides toward that goal by refusing the old "force policy." Under the cooperative regime, he explained to Seward in April 1867, "great development has occurred, missions have extended, trade has increased three-fold, scientific men have been employed, 'Wheaton's

International Law' translated and adopted, military instruction accepted, nearly one hundred men received in the civil service, steamboats multiplied, the way slowly opened for future telegraphs and railroads, and now we have this great movement for education."[37]

Later Burlingame would look back on his time as US minister and describe this progress as the "origin" of the Sino-American treaty, when momentum shifted to make way for a new era. At the time he simply expected to continue going "cautiously and steadily forward" with "those in authority," using careful diplomacy to stave off a backlash from Chinese traditionalists and impatient outsiders.[38]

Though many foreigners, including Burlingame, had recommended that the Chinese send an embassy to the West, he did not anticipate leading one. This unexpectedness is what makes the Sino-American treaty of 1868 so revealing. Until the December 1867 farewell dinner when Chinese officials surprised Burlingame with a request that he lead a diplomatic mission abroad, American officials did not expect any new treaty, at least for a few more years.[39] Even after he had entered on the mission, a formal agreement was not predicted. Burlingame's official brief as he left China was not to enter into negotiations, but rather to demonstrate China's willingness to engage in Western diplomatic formalities. He was supposed to show the flag and shake hands, not remake international law.[40]

The personnel for the embassy were selected to bolster the mission's legitimacy in China and the world beyond. Burlingame was chosen to head the mission as minister plenipotentiary and envoy extraordinary, with a formal position as "minister of the first rank" in the Qing imperial bureaucracy.[41] Accompanying him were two high-ranking Qing officials seconded to the service of the Zongli Yamen: Zhigang, a Manchu official who normally served in the Imperial Maritime Customs Service, and Sun Jiagu, a Chinese secretary to the Board of Rites, a major ministry that oversaw the ceremonies that legitimated imperial authority. They were each denoted "ministers of the second rank"—or "commissioners" for the purposes of Western conventions. J. McLeary Brown, formerly Chinese secretary of the British legation, and one Mr. Deschamps, a Frenchman who had accompanied a Chinese official on an informal tour of Europe the year before, were named as secretaries of the mission, and the group was rounded out by six Chinese interpreters plus a suite of copyists, military orderlies, and servants (including, for a short time, a "bard").[42]

A fully staffed and empowered embassy gave Burlingame and his former superior Secretary Seward a freer hand then they might otherwise have had. The choices they made—and the way they were received politically—reveal important aspects of the Reconstruction Republicans' approach to political

FIGURE 13. The personnel of the "Chinese Embassy," photographed in 1868. J. Gurney and Son, Chinese Embassy, China, 1868, Photograph, https://www.loc.gov/item/2008680540/, Prints and Photographs Division, Library of Congress.

economy and geopolitics. The first and most important thing they did was to redirect the conversation about China's relationship with the world away from "access" and toward "equality." They did so by refusing to focus on the further "liberalization" of China's trade or expanding Westerners' rights in China at the expense of Qing sovereignty—the bread-and-butter issues of "opening" China that had been the primary aim of Western treaty powers for decades. Instead, they drafted a treaty that emphasized formal equality between nations and created mechanisms meant to ensure the reciprocal recognition of civil rights for individuals as they moved within and between those territories. These aspects of the treaty mirrored and extended Republican domestic policies in development since the early 1860s. Further, according to the statements of the principal negotiators, they were also intended to foster hospitable conditions for the easy movement of cheap foreign labor and American capital into profitable development projects, especially infrastructure. The establishment of equality in Sino-American affairs aimed as much at ensuring the viability and prosperity of American capitalism in a global context as at ensuring China's continued stability.[43]

Burlingame left Beijing on November 25, 1867. After an overland journey moderately plagued by bandits, he assembled with the rest of his embassy at Shanghai and departed by steamer for San Francisco, via Japan, on February 25, 1868.[44] To Burlingame's surprise, California's golden metropolis welcomed the embassy warmly, if guardedly.[45] San Francisco was the main port of entry for Chinese in North America and had long been a hotbed of anti-Chinese xenophobia. But in the mission's first public events in the United States the politics of Chinese immigration remained mostly submerged. At a banquet in honor of the embassy, the state's Democratic governor, a thoroughly anti-Chinese politician, lauded the "near future" of a "vast commerce springing up between the Chinese empire and the nations of the West," but he made it clear that he had in mind "an interchange of products," not people. Burlingame, for his part, emphasized that the mission was about international affairs and human brotherhood—but he refrained from discussing specific plans and avoided mentioning Chinese immigration. The mission, he cryptically remarked, "means progress"—but he did not specify which kind or how it would be achieved. Zhigang, his Chinese fellow envoy, responded to a toast in his honor by reminding the Chinese in America to "be careful" and "obey the laws and regulations" of their new country of residence, a message likely intended to reassure a wary room of the mission's benign intentions.[46]

In Washington a few months later, the message was substantively different. The embassy took the water route to go east, crossing the Central American isthmus, and reached New York in late May.[47] Their journey was delayed just enough to allow Congress's impeachment proceedings to wrap up with an acquittal, and a cowed President Johnson received the embassy in the Blue Room of the executive mansion on June 5, 1868. Flourishing impressive credentials—including a parchment "imperial Letter" some twenty-five feet long—the "Americo-Chinese minister" repeated the message he had offered in San Francisco: that the mission was charged with proving that China had "accepted the laws of nations as they are allowed and practiced by the western powers."[48]

The president's reply contained much more than protocol required. Johnson welcomed Burlingame with an unusually long and detailed speech—containing only a "touch of patronage" toward the Chinese, according to the mission's first historian, Frederick W. Williams—and lauded the recent successes of Secretary of State Seward's foreign policy. (Seward, not coincidentally, had written the speech.)[49] Beyond niceties about China's "progress," the core of Johnson's message was that the United States had won the respect of other nations, defended its hemispheric hegemony, and was expanding its commerce and its territory peacefully in responsible accordance with its newly demonstrated power. Eager to use the opportunity of Burlingame's visit to enhance this project, the president closed his remarks by enjoining the envoy to "commend" the construction of a trans-isthmus canal to the governments of Colombia, China, and the "several European States" he would visit.[50]

This odd conclusion suggests one of the ways China, and Asian trade more generally, was crucial to the geopolitical imagination that animated much of American politics in the late 1860s. Like many Americans in the mid-nineteenth century, Seward imagined that when China was "opened," its trade would naturally flow to US holdings on the Pacific (Asa Whitney's vision, updated). These new territories and states, if provided with appropriate infrastructure—like the transcontinental railroad then under construction, the line of transpacific steamers whose government mail subsidy was then pending in Congress, or the contemplated trans-isthmus canal—would link Asian commerce to West Coast gateway ports and East Coast capital and unlock the North American continent's vast resources, granting the US hegemony over global trade.[51] This vision of an American commercial empire quickened by China's commerce was not new, but secession had granted the Republican Party power enough to begin making the infrastructure for it a reality—a project, that by 1868, was well under way.

Seward was concerned with more than just promoting commerce, narrowly construed. His ambitions for United States hegemony required infusions of cheap labor to build a vast new continental infrastructure, as well as new markets for American products and capital. Though he did not always see eye-to-eye with other Republican leaders, during his long tenure at the State Department Seward was able to advance these goals. Early in the first Lincoln administration he promulgated an international call for skilled immigrants, ordering American consuls and diplomats to advertise the liberal "recompense" that "industrious foreigners" might earn through work in the nation's "agricultural, manufacturing, or mining interests."[52] During the war he also worked with Congress to create and administer a new State Department office tasked with facilitating the entry of immigrant workers and preventing the abuse of those entering the country under a new class of one-year indenture contracts.[53] Although Chinese migrants do not appear to have fallen under this bureau's auspices (in part because it was based in New York, and in part because of the existing prohibition on the coolie trade), Seward and Burlingame's draft treaty attempted to accomplish similar ends.[54]

The treaty negotiated at Seward's estate in central New York and signed at Washington on July 28, 1868, was not a wholly new agreement but a set of eight "Additional Articles" expanding the 1858 Treaty of Tientsin.[55] Unlike the earlier agreement, which forced China to open new ports and accord new privileges and protections to foreigners of the wake of the Second Opium War, the new treaty was notable not only for recognizing both China's and the United States' equality as states, but also for how it practiced that principle with reciprocal rights. Repudiating long-standing European efforts to develop enclaves in China, the United States agreed to respect China's territorial integrity and pledged not to interfere in its internal affairs. The treaty guaranteed nationals of both parties freedom to create and attend schools, as well as freedom of religion.[56]

These provisions, while important, do not reveal as much as the three articles that touched directly on the issues facing Chinese migrants, and through them, broader Reconstruction-era debates about race, citizenship, and labor. (These were also the articles that most perplexed Burlingame's bitterest opponents, the foreign merchants resident at Shanghai.)[57] Article 5 recognized "the inherent and inalienable right of man to change his home and allegiance" and the "mutual advantage" of "free migration" and obligated both parties to make it a criminal offense to promote involuntary emigration. In a brief compass, the article combined two concerns that had been troubling Republican policymakers for years: the threat of new kinds of involuntary servitude and the right of voluntary expatriation. The former condition was already codified in existing anti-coolie trade laws and the Thirteenth Amendment, but it likely was included in part to emphasize that not all migrant Chinese were "coolies" excluded by existing law.[58] As Burlingame's friend Mark Twain explained in an apologia for the treaty (written with Burlingame's aid), far from sending "coolies," China was sending "the best class of people" to the United States.[59]

The affirmation of the right to expatriation fit with other US efforts to make the "naturalization principle" international law.[60] Reacting to high-profile arrests of naturalized Americans in Europe, in July 1868 Congress passed the Expatriation Act to protect the rights of naturalized American citizens abroad. The statute declared the right of expatriation a fundamental "natural and inherent" human right and authorized the president to "use such means"—short of war—as might be necessary to protect naturalized American citizens from arrest on grounds of their former national identification.[61] The act complemented another of Seward's diplomatic triumphs that year, the "Bancroft treaty" with Prussia, which defined a protocol for establishing the naturalization of American citizens in Germany and Germans in America.[62] Both were efforts to graft the American understanding of mutable allegiance onto international law; but the Burlingame Treaty went further than anything Congress had agreed to by implying that free migration should be a right of nonwhites as well.[63]

Article 6 touched even more directly on the great domestic political arguments over the rights of nonwhites within the United States. It secured Americans in China "privileges, immunities or exemptions" equal to those provided to visitors from the most favored nation—then offered Chinese subjects visiting the United States the same guarantees. This article leveraged the federal treaty power to check state laws abusing Chinese migrants. It was exactly the kind of federal oversight of loyal states that anti-Chinese politicians in Congress, Democrats as well as conservative Republicans, had been attempting to forestall for months as they watched the Fourteenth Amendment come closer to ratification.[64]

Reflecting the growing worries among congressional Republicans about their ability to maintain control of the federal government in the face of threats from Democrats in the West and elsewhere, this provision was altered before ratification. The Senate amended Article 6 to include the significant caveat that "nothing herein contained shall be held to confer naturalization" on Chinese subjects.[65] Federal naturalization was already restricted to "white persons," but the Pacific Coast senators who asked for the restriction wanted additional security that Chinese nationals could not gain citizenship, just in case the courts or the executive interpreted the treaty expansively.[66] (They had reason to worry; even weakened, the treaty's provisions delayed the passage of federal restrictions on Chinese immigration for the next dozen years.) This new language was made a condition for the treaty's approval, and it laid down a clear marker in the ongoing national controversy over the racial limits on citizenship, one that would be revisited during the 1870 debate over the Naturalization Act. Thus, while conservative West Coast Republicans were increasingly unwilling to deny African Americans the rights of citizenship, including suffrage, because it was proving crucial to the continued health (and legitimacy) of their party, admitting Chinese immigrants into that circle was untenable to any beyond the Radical Republican faction.[67]

Even the diminished protections the treaty offered would have been dead without Article 3, which created a potentially powerful enforcement mechanism by granting China the right to appoint consuls in the United States. Although consuls were the lowest grade of diplomatic officers, they were nonetheless a tested means of protecting nationals' rights abroad, at least among Western powers. As recognized foreign agents, they had the power to make local issues into international incidents; in the United States that would mean bringing federal protection of civil rights into states and localities where courts and juries were unlikely to offer it. As Mark Twain explained in a *New-York Tribune* article defending the treaty, with consuls appointed to offer a "strict account" of wrongs perpetuated, "the days of persecuting Chinamen are over, in California."[68]

The treaty was intended to bolster the US-China relationship by ensuring more hospitable conditions for the laborers desired in the American West. As negotiations were under way, chargé d'affaires Samuel Wells Williams warned from Beijing that the murder, robbery, and discriminatory taxation Chinese migrants endured in California was exerting "an unhappy influence upon those Chinese who are going and coming between the two continents."[69] Seward thought he had taken these complaints seriously. As he explained in 1868 to J. Ross Browne, Burlingame's replacement as minister to China, the treaty negotiators had "endeavored to provide a remedy for the existing evils" afflicting the "Chinese immigrants and laborers" in the "States and Territories on the Pacific Coast."[70] After all, as one of the State Department's informants explained, "it is not dear, but cheap labor that develops and enriches a nation"—and especially after the passage of the Thirteenth Amendment, there were few better sources of cheap labor than China.[71]

After his retirement from the State Department, Seward defended the Burlingame Treaty as part of his legacy as a statesman who championed humanity, justice, and democracy. He informed an Oregon audience in 1870 that "no state or nation has ever flourished that was unsocial, inhospitable, or intolerant." While he admitted that there were objections to "the policy of freedom and immigration which I advocate," he firmly rejected them. Such complaints were as "old as the Republic" and for decades they had "threatened to strangle" what Seward considered to be the great experiment of the United States: "whether men of all nations are capable of self-government." Time and again these objections had been overridden to the benefit of the country. After all, he pointed out, "What would have been our condition now, and our prospects, if the country had listened to objections of the same nature against the abolition of African slavery—a measure to which we are indebted for the entire and complete national independence?" After Black, Irish, and German laborers had proved themselves, Seward thought "we have no excuse for admitting such objections or prejudices now" with regard to the Chinese.[72]

Burlingame leaned even more heavily on the morality of the issue. Promoting the treaty to a friendly audience in Boston, he described its protections as the just reward of the "sober and industrious people by whose quiet labor we have been enabled to push the Pacific Railroad over the summit of the Sierra Nevada." He also defended it as an act of political nerve: "I am glad the United States had the courage to apply their great principles of equality. I am glad that while they apply their doctrines to the swarming millions of Europe, they are not afraid to apply them to the tawny race of Tamerlane and of Genghis Khan."[73] He was not above drawing attention to how other powers had profited from Chinese labor—particularly Great Britain, in its Asian colonies—but he kept his allusions to imperial competition subtle, instead framing the policy as a matter of equity. All China asked in return for this gift of labor was fair treatment, he said: "that you will be as kind to her *Nationals* as she is to your *Nationals*."[74] The treaty's authors saw these provisions not only as crucial to equal relations with China, but as important to the crafting of a new American empire that fulfilled the best ideals of free labor ideology.

These were not priorities shared by Americans in China, or by their European associates. In the context of Civil War politics, most American merchants and missionaries in China were conservative Unionists: generally drawn from the ranks of Cotton Whigs or the most moderate of Republicans, they supported the interests of capital, not revolution.[75] In China they were maximalists: maximally frustrated with the Chinese government and maximally dismissive of Chinese people, eager to see the empire "reformed" in ways that would maximize their ability to profit—from expanded trade, the construction of new infrastructure, and other "modern" projects.

Still, at first Burlingame's embassy to the West was welcomed by the foreign expatriate community—though not warmly. *The North-China Herald*, the newspaper of record for the Anglo-American business community at Shanghai (motto: "Impartial, Not Neutral"), expressed cautious optimism, accepting "the step gained" by the mission as "one more notch in the wheel of progress."[76] The choice of Burlingame to lead was uncontroversial: as the leader of the famous "cooperative policy," he seemed to the editors the obvious favorite of the Zongli Yamen—and his reputation would make it "impossible for any political faction to treat him with contempt."[77] Burlingame's gregariousness had won him friends in the treaty ports; a year and a half later, looking back on the embassy's beginning, the American residents of Shanghai recalled that they had "supported, and rejoiced in the mission," at least when they still "had reason to believe that it was in the interest of progress."[78]

The honeymoon did not last long. News of a speech Burlingame gave at a June 1868 dinner at Delmonico's in New York City reached China by early fall and marked the moment when the foreign community in China turned against the mission. At the dinner, Burlingame had attacked opponents of the cooperative policy as men of "that tyrannical school" and promised that China was now "open."[79] The *North-China Herald*'s hot reaction to this "post-prandial" speech suggests Burlingame was correct about the sentiment among the commercial classes, as the editors assailed the mission mercilessly for the rest of its journey, concluding that its "effect will be retrogressive instead of progressive."[80]

The expatriate commercial community became convinced that Burlingame's purpose was the same as that of other Qing officials: to delay and frustrate their schemes for "opening" China. The vision of progress they desired could be said to have arrived only when China was "thoroughly converted to Christianity, when her territory is chequered with rail-roads, her foolish notions about Fung-shui eradicated, and the masses of her people brought from the darkness of sin and heathen superstition into the light of the gospel."[81] By late 1868, white Shanghai residents were labeling Burlingame's mission a "failure," and soon after—feeling particularly grieved that Burlingame had labeled opposition to his policies as akin to "upholding the principle of slavery"—began claiming the ambassador was a "dupe" of his Chinese masters.[82] True to its British orientation, the *North-China Herald* framed the American treaty as shirking the white man's burden: by deferring further treaty revisions and relieving China of the need to respond to foreigners' "pressing wish" to build "railways and other scientific improvements," Seward and Burlingame had shifted the "onus of advocating progress" onto "other powers."[83]

Perhaps the clearest expression of the Anglo-American merchant community's united antipathy to Burlingame's mission came in their encomiums for his successor, J. Ross Browne. Browne was a late Andrew Johnson appointee, whose embrace of the foreign merchant community's aggressive anti-Chinese perspective did not sit well with Grant administration, which cashiered him in 1869.[84] Though Browne had nodded agreement to Burlingame and his policies when they crossed paths en route to their respective missions in 1868, once in China he quickly came to favor the views of the resident American community, mercantile and missionary, with whom he socialized.[85] That warm feeling was returned when Browne appeared in Shanghai to bid his farewells in July 1869. First the American residents and then the British community tendered long addresses applauding Browne for his service. The Americans regretted that Browne's "valuable services to American interest in China" were being lost because of his "dissent from the declarations of Mr. Burlingame," who had spread abroad such dangerous "misapprehensions" about China.[86] The Anglo-American community's farewell memorials articulated an anti-Burlingame policy, one in which China was so "low in civilization" as well as in "wealth and power" that it could not be trusted to reform without the judicious application of "pressure." Browne responded at length, "fully concurring" with the celebration of the aggressive approach to "progress" that "Anglo-Saxon blood" demanded.[87]

As sweet as they may have sounded in Shanghai, these plaudits caused an awful noise when they reached the United States. The *New York Herald* headlined its reports on Browne's final acts as US minister bluntly: "Our Chinese Diplomacy—Mr. Browne Botches It"; "J. Ross Browne's Departure from China. HIS GREAT MISTAKE."[88] In part his remarks received this reception because they arrived first as rumors—that Browne, in responding to the merchant community, had "denounced" Burlingame's embassy; that "the Pekin Government" had rejected the US treaty—which were subsequently contradicted and corrected in hastily telegraphed statements.[89] But the arrival of fuller accounts did not smooth things over. The *New York Times* castigated Browne's policy as "Gunboat Diplomacy" and excoriated him for the insults he had offered China as minister as well as for his unrepublican toadying to British imperialists. Mirroring Browne's accusations of Burlingame's naivety, the *Times* argued that Browne "fell headlong into the traps set for him by the foreign traders," becoming "a mere echo" of Britain's policy of "'cringe to the strong and bully the weak.'" The British merchants' "entire and unanimous approbation" of Browne was an "excellent reason for his recall."[90]

While Browne's questionable loyalties and inept diplomacy were roundly condemned, responses in the United States to Burlingame's treaty and his mission were more complex. Public opinion divided largely on partisan lines, with Democrats suspicious and Republicans more warmly disposed.[91] The way friends of the mission and the treaty described their detractors as opposed to both the rights of nations and the rights of individuals supports this picture, albeit with negative space. Burlingame preemptively defined the treaty's opponents as men motivated by the same spirit that animated "the old indigo planters in India," "the old opium smuggler in China," and "such as opposed Emancipation in the West Indies."[92] In his private correspondence, Burlingame dropped the evasion of describing his opponents—the Yankee merchants of the American community in China—as nabobs and declared them as akin to the "slaveholders of South Carolina," a framing that friendly Republican sheets picked up in their coverage.[93] In a widely reprinted article that roused the Shanghai community to unprecedented howls of outrage, the *Boston Journal* described the battle over Burlingame's treaty as "the old fight again between freedom and slavery," with the "Englishmen in China" reacting as "exactly as the slaveholders did when the Emancipation Proclamation was issued by Mr. Lincoln."[94]

Opponents of equal treatment of China and Chinese migrants were not shy about linking them to Reconstruction. One opponent cried that the radical Republican efforts were "a consolidation of government, and will result in a consolidation of empire" that would make "citizens not only of the pet negro but also of the filthy Chinese."[95] For opponents and proponents, Burlingame's treaty was part of the same struggle that defined Reconstruction domestically: whether the American empire would continue as a fundamentally white supremacist state.

During Reconstruction, Republicans put the full force of the federal government behind Burlingame's treaty. It was ratified unanimously by the Senate on July 24, 1868.[96] Writing from his State Department desk, Seward advised Burlingame to make use of the US legations in Europe to sound out his target governments before talks, and to maneuver Paris and Berlin to put pressure on London.[97] His sentiments were no secret. When the Chinese embassy boarded a Cunard steamer in September, the *New York*

Herald was fully justified in declaring that Burlingame went "backed by the moral power of the United States":

> No minister was ever received in this country as he has been and no mission was ever more popular. The Embassy was honored by a reception on the floors of Congress, the treaty was ratified by a unanimous vote of the Senate, the press of all parties endorses the action of the government, the President heartily approves of the objects of the mission, and the people everywhere, irrespective of political parties, are in favor of the policy established toward the Chinese.[98]

The *Herald* exaggerated the bipartisan comity, but it did not inflate Washington's support, which was consistent even across a rancorous election year and presidential transition. Although the administrations were driven by very different politics—Johnson fighting until the end for a reconciled white man's government, Grant (at first) embracing a firmer commitment to multiracial democracy—they both found the Chinese embassy useful as an example of the persuasive power of American diplomacy.

Secretary of State Hamilton Fish explained the continued official support in a long letter to historian George Bancroft, then serving in Berlin as US minister to North Germany. The "great principle" of the 1868 treaty, Fish said, was "the recognition of the sovereign authority of the imperial government at Pekin over the people of the Chinese empire and over their social, commercial, and political relations with the western powers." Burlingame's treaty, Fish averred, "was a long step in another direction" from both the "European-Chinese policy" of "isolation" and "disintegration" and the high-toned isolationism that Chinese statesmen had pursued out of fear of the political and economic consequences of greater trade with the West.[99] Like Williams, Burlingame, and Seward, Fish saw Chinese immigration to the United States as critical to the development of the Pacific Coast and the nation's "new position in the commerce of the world" that the Pacific Railroad was making a reality. Fish also predicted that the growth of US commercial power—underwritten by migrant labor—would call forth a corresponding increase in the number of Americans settling in China's treaty ports, because it would augment overall trade. To promote this virtuous cycle and encourage the continuance of the "cooperative policy" more generally, Fish directed Bancroft, and other US diplomats, to support the Burlingame mission's efforts in Europe.[100]

An eminently respectable conservative in Grant's cabinet, Fish managed the State Department with the same controlled diligence and attentive care he took with his large New York estates. Once he adopted them, the principles of the 1868 treaty guided Fish's personnel decisions as well as his policy statements—leading to J. Ross Browne's firing and informing the instructions to his replacement, Frederick F. Low. Fish even cautioned the navy to be wary of trusting any officers who took foreign merchants' peculiar "views of the Chinese character and government" too seriously, lest US influence in Asia be weakened through rash anti-Chinese actions, as Britain's had been.[101]

President Grant's first annual message, issued in December 1869, made this support for Burlingame's mission public. After reviewing how the United States was faring after "emerging from a rebellion of gigantic magnitude" and recommending plans to pay down the debt, restore commerce, and protect and foster "free labor," the president lauded "the sagacity and efforts of one of our own distinguished citizens" in bringing about "a more enlightened policy than that heretofore pursued toward China," one that would enable "increased relations with that populous and hitherto exclusive nation." Since Americans had initiated this new policy, Grant—and the nation—was invested in its success.[102] Preparing to depart for what would become his mission's final destination, Saint Petersburg, Burlingame wrote to a friend that he was cheered by the "noble backing" in Grant's message.[103]

The US government's interest in Anson Burlingame's mission lasted beyond his life but was also bound up in it. When Burlingame died unexpectedly on February 23, 1870—after a short, vicious infection—the US minister to Russia immediately reported his fears that the mission would "fall into foreign hands" as European governments sought to "control the policy of the Chinese government." (He was worried that John McLeavy Brown, the mission's first secretary, would aid efforts to "get it under English control, now that Burlingame is dead.")[104] While this fear proved unfounded—the mission fizzled out instead, leaving Russia in April 1870 and accomplishing only some sightseeing in Southern Europe before leaving from Marseille to return to China in late August—it suggests the geopolitical stakes that Burlingame's contemporaries saw in his diplomatic mission of reconstruction.[105]

Burlingame was widely and expressively mourned. From Berlin, George Bancroft reported that "on every side from scholars and from statesmen," he heard "the strongest expressions of regret at the premature close of his career"; the historian Leopold von Ranke told George Bancroft that "he looked upon his death as a loss to the human race."[106] The same civic organizations in New York and Boston that had arranged banquets for the mission now assembled honor guards and somber eulogies to accompany his remains as they were transferred from ship to train to hearse to lie in state at Faneuil Hall before a funeral at Arlington Street Church and then interment, under American and Chinese colors, at Mount Auburn ceme-tery.[107] Posthumously, the emperor's court at Beijing accorded Burlingame the honorary title of a first rank mandarin, "the highest rank possible to be given anyone" outside of the royal family, and added the scroll conferring it to the imperial archives.[108]

Although it effectively ended after Burlingame's death, the embassy's supporters did not see it as a failure. Rather, they understood it as an ex-pression of the work a revitalized and reformed American power could ac-complish. Burlingame's death was not "premature," William H. Seward told Wenxiang, a Qing imperial official who had supported the mission, because he had succeeded in bringing China and the West "into relations of mutual friendship and accord." Though work remained—China needed to fulfill its obligation to send diplomats of its own abroad—the US diplomat had "raised an honorable fame on a firm foundation," laying the groundwork for reciprocity in international relations and equality of protection of "the rights and interest of Chinese immigrants" flowing to the United States.[109]

Just as the Thirteenth, Fourteenth, and Fifteenth Amendments were not intended by their authors to be the end of the Union's progress toward per-fection, neither did the authors of the Burlingame Treaty intend it to be the final word on China's relationship with the United States. Rather, it was supposed to be a foundation for a new beginning. By codifying the coopera-tive policy in "unbending text," the treaty, Burlingame argued, recognized China "as an equal among the nations"—providing the "footing," the po-litical framework, for future peace and prosperity by recognizing China's sovereignty and the shared humanity of its people.[110] Or it could have, had Burlingame's vision survived his own death and the collapse of the Ameri-can government's support for full equality for individual nations as well as individual human beings.

Looking back on Burlingame's embassy from the perspective of the early twentieth century, the sons of men close to the mission depicted it as sepa-rated from the rancorous politics of its day. Frederick W. Seward, William H. Seward's son, explained this as strategic. Because Johnson's impeach-ment had engendered such "intense political excitement and bitterness," only by suspending the "ordinary methods of diplomacy" and working in secret could the treaty have been drafted.[111] Frederick Wells Williams, the son of Burlingame's close associate in China and a sinologist of interna-tional reputation himself, regarded the mission as doomed by later com-plications. When Burlingame visited California, he said, "the spectre of a yellow peril had not yet harassed the American imagination nor had fears of undesirable emigrants disturbed its dreams of the future."[112] By these lights, only 1868's unexplained (and imaginary) vacation from the pervasive white supremacy of the nineteenth century could have made the treaty possible.

But in separating Burlingame's mission from the politics of Reconstruction, the two Fredericks excised vital context. William H. Seward's dreams for a free labor empire and Anson Burlingame's advocacy for international equity, both encoded in the final treaty, were of a piece with Republican attempts to remake the United States after the Civil War. The opposition their agreement attracted was not just analogous to a broader opposition to Reconstruction, it was an organic component of that opposition. The Burlingame Treaty was not merely part of the "springboard" to later imperial formations, nor was it a forgettable deviation from the normal patterns of Sino-American relations.[113] The brevity of the mission's moment—in China and the United States alike—was tied to the "unfinished revolution" of which it was a part. Considered within the geopolitics of Reconstruction, the treaty was not an aberration, too unique to be usefully understood within the context of American or Chinese history; rather, it was another expression of the difficulty of translating even the mightiest of revolutions into lasting institutional form. The failure of both those revolutions underwrote the end of the American China trade as a free-flowing commerce in goods, people, and capital—and the beginning of the United States' new approach to the political economy of globalization.

CHAPTER EIGHT

Death of a Trade, Birth of a Market

Worried in early 1871 that an "irrepressible conflict" was brewing between Chinese and Westerners, US minister to China Frederick F. Low outlined some observations and "speculations" in a long report to the State Department. A California Republican who rose to his post in part because of his stout support for Reconstruction and his opposition to harassment of Chinese immigrants, Low saw two possible futures. If China's "masses" could be "educated" by Christian missionaries into Western modes of social organization and its rulers tutored by foreign diplomats about the benefits of integrating further into the global economy, then together they could achieve a peaceful "regeneration" of the Qing Empire. The alternative was war, an invasion of China by one or more Western powers, aimed at overthrowing the ruling dynasty to bring this "progress."

Low termed this path the "'popular course'" because it was favored by foreign missionaries, merchants, and governments. Like his predecessor, Burlingame, Low believed support for it was rooted in bigotry. Westerners in China, he thought, had been curdled by the same racist ideology that had perverted justice in the Dred Scott case: they believed that "'a Chinaman has no rights that a white man is bound to respect.'" Low found this an impossible position, and advised that foreign powers like the United States should "be prepared to exercise patience and forbearance" in their dealings with the Qing government and the Chinese people as they introduced reforms piecemeal, through negotiation.[1]

Still, if war came, Low thought it would be motivated most immediately by material concerns, not racist ideology. The "suffering" of workers in European factories whose livelihoods depended "upon maintaining and increasing the market for manufactures in India and China" would provide the tinder and the spark for a conflagration. "Happily," Low noted, "no such considerations are likely to enter into the policy which the United States may choose to pursue toward this or any other nation."[2] The United States did not want for territory, and the nation was content, he and other Republicans thought, to develop its own resources. As one of his contemporaries explained in Congress, the United States' true interests in Asia lay in encouraging the "closer relations" that a "liberal commerce" and "an increasing tide of emigration" would create—not in trying to capture distant markets with gunships and marines.[3]

Writing thirty years later, from the other side of Reconstruction and the Gilded Age, Charles Denby saw things differently. Denby had served as US minister to China from the first Cleveland administration through to the first year of McKinley's term, an unprecedented thirteen-year run in the post. In his memoir, *China and Her People*, the lifelong Democrat argued that American interests now required what Low had once characterized as a European orientation to China.[4] "For us," Denby claimed, "China must remain simply a market," "an outlet for our superabundance of manufactured goods." While ambivalent about whether "protection or free trade" would secure "the greater market for our manufactures," Denby was sure that "our condition at home is forcing us to commercial expansion."[5]

By "condition at home," Denby meant the pressure cooker of industrial capitalism in a globalized age. Since the Civil War, massive influxes of capital and people had helped the United States produce a large and growing output of commodities of all kinds on a massive scale—a success that created its own seemingly endless supply of new victims of low wages, low prices, and mass unemployment. This "condition" led Denby, like many of his contemporaries, to offer vociferous support for restrictions on Chinese immigrants. The Chinese, he told his readers, were a dangerous and "stubborn" population that resisted "everything which pertains to good government, public hygiene, police rules and regulations."[6] White American workers could never compete with their low-cost labor, and American political institutions could not survive their presence. The "yellow peril" was therefore a "permanent menace" that Americans had every right to resist by excluding "whom we please."[7]

In their respective eras, Low and Denby expressed the consensus orientation toward China among US political elites. Where Low linked expanding equality and commercial progress in US-China diplomacy to a domestic Reconstruction Republican program of expanding equality and commercial progress in the United States, Denby thought the Sino-American relationship was more mixed, and in need of strong direction. Instead of understanding China's markets and Chinese migrants as aspects of the same commercial relationship—much less as equally beneficial, the way Low did—Denby attempted to treat them as separate issues, cordoning them off into discrete chapters of his memoir, in much the same way as his government tried to divide flows of goods and people.

In the period between Low's report and Denby's reflections, Americans' conception of China's role in their nation's political economy broke up, dividing a coherent relationship into its constituent parts. Globalization was the solvent that dissolved these bonds. New global financial and transportation networks linked markets across the world, allowing goods, people, and capital to move more quickly and in greater quantities than ever before. Neither these networks nor the goods they moved were accidents of nature; they were the products of actively expanding imperial states embedded in capitalist economies, and they reordered lives and markets across the world, with massive and lasting effects on the scale and distribution of wealth. In China, globalization helped usher in a new era of colonial competition and local capitalist growth, killing the business model American merchants had relied on for decades. In the United States, globalization helped produce a political appetite for using federal power to restrict the movements of (some kinds of) people and (some kinds of) goods through racialized immigration restrictions and protectionist tariffs.[8]

Shifts in Americans' commercial situation in China helped spark shifts in the United States' political and policy response to globalization more generally. Instead of conceptualizing US relations with China around access to a system of global commerce—as the *China trade*—at the end of the nineteenth century Americans began framing their economic relations in China primarily as a discrete source of new consumers, kinds of labor, or specific commodities—the *China market*. Developed as the ills of cheap money, cheap labor, and cheap goods became more concerning to US elites, the China market model began to have a concrete influence on US policy in the 1870s—two decades before historians like Thomas McCormick have dated its emergence in national politics.[9] Embedded in a post-Reconstruction white supremacist politics that co-opted antislavery rhetoric to justify new restrictions on migration and new policing powers at the border—as well as new forms of competitive imperialism—this conceptual shift reverberated in US efforts to reshape monetary policy, immigration law, and diplomacy.

This chapter will examine the death of the China trade, as a business model, and the rise of the China market, as a focus of American policy. The China trade began to die in the 1870s when the storied commission agency houses that had defined US-China commercial relations for two generations started to collapse, victims of competition unleashed by globalization. As the commission merchant business evaporated, leaving only nostalgic traces, the shift from "China trade" thinking to "China market" thinking found expression in US policy: first in the creation of the trade dollar, then in restrictions on Chinese migration, and finally in the growing consensus among US business and official elites that China's 400 million consumers were the antidote to the "overproduction" crisis. The result, by the end of the nineteenth century, was a revolution in American China policy and a fundamental restructuring of the US-China relationship. By tracking the development of US interest in accessing the "China trade" into manipulating the "China market," this chapter seeks to shed light on the motives and mechanics of globalization in the late nineteenth century and on Americans' engagement with it—and to recast our understanding of how developments in international business, racial politics, economic thinking, and foreign relations laid the groundwork for the modern era of outwardly imperialist but domestically restrictive US political economy.

The soaring rhetoric surrounding the Burlingame Treaty set high expectations for a new era of US commercial partnership with China, but reality proved disappointing. Direct trade between the United States and China began to stagnate in the late 1860s, a fact well documented in official trade statistics. In 1861, US trade with China accounted for $18 million ($3 million in exports and $15 million in imports), a healthy 3.5 percent of total US trade—and in keeping with antebellum levels. By 1870, total US commerce was $907 million—an increase of 56 percent over pre–Civil War levels, despite the decimation of the merchant marine and slowdowns in cotton production—but trade with China still rested at just $18 million. This pattern held through the rest of the century. While there were moments when US trade with China increased—as in the early 1870s, when cheaper tea, easier credit, and the anticipation of lower tariffs inflated a small bubble in imports, only to be undone by the Panic of 1873—slow growth and stagnation was the overall trend.[10] As US gross national product tripled and US international trade quadrupled between 1865 and 1900, trade with China grew in tiny increments or not at all, hovering between 1 percent and 2 percent of US trade volume overall.[11]

Of course the China trade had never been simply a matter of bilateral exchange, and its value was not fully captured in national accounting. American China traders had historically functioned as middlemen in complex commercial circuits between and among ports in Asia, Latin America, and Europe as well as the United States. But statistics from Chinese sources attest to the decline of their business in China. In 1873, US firms accounted for 15 percent of foreign firms in treaty ports (52 out of 345 firms), but that fell to just 5 percent (18 out of 354) a decade later, a position maintained for the rest of the century. The decline in commercial organizations was not the product of consolidation—mergers or acquisitions—but rather resulted from failures and withdrawals from business. During the same period, the American share of the foreign population in Chinese ports fell from 15 percent to 8 percent; even the expansion of US missionary efforts could not compensate for the disappearance of traders. (Overall numbers of foreigners did not decline. Instead, continued expansion by British firms, and new imperially backed ventures by German, French, and Japanese traders ate into Americans' presence in treaty ports.)[12] Americans' share of China's total foreign trade stagnated in the last quarter of the century too, inching upward only in the wake of the 1898 war.[13] This retreat stood out in what was otherwise a period of significant commercial growth in both the United States and China.[14]

Changing business conditions drove this decline. Until the 1870s, the largest and most successful American firms in China were commission agency houses. Firms like Russell and Company, Heard and Company, and Olyphant and Company were organized as simple partnerships, not corporations. Far from being anonymous market participants, they traded on their partners' long-standing and reliable relationships in ports across the globe to organize the efficient purchase and marketing of Chinese goods abroad and of foreign commodities within China—often using as their agents firms run by trusted relatives. Though such businesses were often quite lucrative, they did not have deep pockets; working with a few hundred thousand dollars in operating capital instead of the millions that increasingly characterized "big" American businesses in the period, they depended on clients' capital to buy cargoes and charter ships. Their profits were earned on fees, usually assessed as a percentage of transactions processed and capital managed, and from ancillary services like banking and insurance. Volume was key to their success.[15]

Although stable in their organizational form since the early nineteenth century, these businesses had adapted—or tried to—as conditions changed. In the 1850s and 1860s, as the twin disasters of the Taiping revolution and Western invasions forced the Qing court to expand the treaty port system, US merchant houses grew to exploit these new markets, shifting their headquarters to the booming metropolis of Shanghai and creating networks of branch offices that reached deep into the river ports of the interior. This heyday, and its lavish physical manifestations in company hongs, was the basis for China firms' celebrated (and exaggerated) reputation as representatives of American "commercial genius" abroad, and as wielders of great influence in Asia.[16]

However, as disorder in China retreated, and as the Qing Empire's ties to the world's increasingly dense network of steamship, railroad, and telegraph lines increased, American merchant firms began to struggle. Easy credit and global linkages fostered "undue inflation, and consequently collapse" among merchants on the China coast generally, but American firms fared especially poorly.[17] In contrast to US firms like Russell and Company, which "maintained enormously expensive establishments in the Chinese cities, employed hosts of servants, and entertained lavishly," new competitors were smaller and nimbler. Lower overhead allowed these firms to compete on costs, while their abandonment of the strict commission business—in favor of shipping cargoes on joint account—allowed them to offer customers more value for lower risk.[18]

Some of these competitors were new foreign entrants in the market, part of the commercial expansion of industrializing nations (German and Japanese companies, in particular). They benefited from state support in the form of diplomatic and military aid as well as government contracts for shipping companies. In earlier decades, the United States had made similar efforts—subsidizing the Pacific Mail Steamship Company, for example—but as rivals muscled in during the 1870s, official funding for steamer lines and related ventures sputtered and died.[19] Other competitors were Chinese firms run by men who had previously served as local agents for Western establishments—"compradors" in treaty port parlance. Thomas Knox, an American journalist, borrowed the racist language of xenophobic restrictionists to describe "John Comprador" as the merchant equivalent of the laborer "John Chinaman"—a homo economicus supposedly capable of living on "wonderfully small profits" that no white American merchant could endure.[20] (A tolerance for lower margins mattered, but fluency in local languages—which most American merchants lacked—and easier access to more extensive local social networks probably played a larger role in these firms' competitive advantage.) By the 1880s, foreign and native firms not only were outcompeting American firms in China, they were extending their reach to American markets.[21]

The partners of major American firms like Heard and Company, Olyphant and Company, and Russell and Company tried to adapt to these challenges. They founded short-haul steamship lines in China to capture intra-treaty port and intra-Asian trade, manufacturing enterprises to make maritime and export products in China and British-ruled Hong Kong, and new banks and insurance firms to finance and secure all these enterprises. Some of these ventures met with success—some even outlasted the parent firms—but the old firms were ultimately unsuccessful in reformulating their business to fit the times.[22]

The trouble was capital—or rather, rates of return on capital. Ventures in China could not compete with investment opportunities in the United States. Instead, the "members and materials" of merchant houses were "absorbed and overwhelmed" by what one retired trader called the "a sea of corporate rail-road and other bonds."[23] John Murray Forbes, a Russell and Company partner who left trade to become a master of railroad investing, framed his retreat as an acknowledgment of reality. By the 1870s, he recalled, "the whole of our foreign trade had changed," so he directed his privately held investment firm to wind up "old concerns" in commerce, dissolve the partnerships that managed it, and direct funds fully to domestic affairs.[24] "When the ledger books said go," established American China traders acted like rational investors—they went.[25] Abandoned by their founders, the major US firms failed, one by one, after being caught short of capital in a crisis: Heard and Company in 1875, Olyphant and Company in 1878, and Russell and Company, largest and last, in 1891.

Lacking personnel, profits, and prospects, American commission firms disappeared and were not replaced. This was in keeping with larger trends in US business in the Gilded Age, which was increasingly defined by sprawling railroad corporations, industrial giants, and massive financial trusts. Merchant firms, long the face of American business abroad, decreased in influence and importance. After the 1870s, the new and growing US firms in China were not full-service commission agency houses managing global circuits of trade, but specialized import/export businesses that extended the overseas marketing efforts of industrial enterprises like Standard Oil, Singer Sewing Machines, Sherwin-Williams Paint, and British American Tobacco.[26] Focused on single businesses—and sometimes single products—these businesses did not reestablish broad currents of trade or recreate Americans' former prominence as pilots helping to steer China's engagement with the world. Overmatched by competition and out of sync with US commercial expansion, the US-China commercial connection dried up; China would not become an active area of economic growth for US commerce again until the First World War.[27] Instead, as American China traders retreated, China became an object of official American anxiety centered on concerns about glut.

The shift in the business environment for US firms in China dovetailed with changes in the way American officials understood the relation between the nation and the global capitalist system. "Blessed among nations" by waves of capital investment and immigration from Europe and Asia, the United States in the late nineteenth century experienced rapid economic growth, particularly in the development of railroads, commercial farms, western mines, and manufacturing enterprises.[28] By the mid-1870s, the nation's exports were outpacing imports for the first time—setting a pattern for the next century. But the same close ties to global markets that boosted the nation's productive capacity also made the United States fragile, subject to financial panics and declining commodity prices, and to the widespread suffering, social unrest, and political revolution those shocks caused.

In the aftermath of the Civil War, American politicians—and their voters—conceived of economic policy primarily in terms of the "Money Question." In many ways this was a continuation of antebellum debates in which periods of economic hardship were understood to be primarily the result of ill-advised monetary or financial policies, with the chief battle line drawn between advocates of "hard" and "soft" money (coins vs. specie-backed paper money). The financial exigencies of the Civil War and the triumph of Republican policy had reshaped the field, somewhat; after Appomattox the debate over the "Money Question" was not about whether there should be federally regulated paper currency—millions of fiat greenbacks and national banknotes were in circulation—but about whether and how quickly fiat notes should be withdrawn and replaced with specie and specie-backed bank money, and about how soon the government could resume paying its debts in gold. The conflict was about whether US monetary policy should benefit debtors or creditors—and which ones.

Because debates over the "Money Question" turned in part on what role internationally traded precious metals should play in American money, they involved foreign policy—and were marked by white supremacists' ideas about racial hierarchy. Supporters of the gold standard drew the boundary between "civilization" and "barbarism" along the color line, justifying a currency convertible into gold as the "natural" order, as they claimed white supremacy was.[29] When Republican congressman and future president James A. Garfield made his case for a gold-based currency in the pages of the *Atlantic Monthly* in 1876, he described it as "the real, the certain, the universal standard" of value, pointing, tautologically, to its centrality in Western international transactions for proof of its universality.[30] Goldbugs like Garfield condemned silver and fiat currencies together as "barbaric" kinds of money because they were "local" rather than universal—used only by undeveloped or "degenerate" societies. (That this divide was largely an artifact of British monetary and imperial policy—not a "natural" formation—did not seem to enter into Garfield's fustian explanation.) Bimetallism supporters sometimes shared these ideas about racial hierarchy, but they saw a potentially advantageous role for silver in the US system because the "lesser" of the precious metals would give the United States a trading advantage in "barbaric" regions where silver dominated, like China and India, while gold would maintain integration with the "commercial nations" of Europe—a vital consideration for a nation looking for new "natural outlets" for both agricultural staples and manufactured goods.[31]

It is in this context that Americans first attempted to use the "China market" to address a glut created by overproduction. In the late 1860s, owners of new western silver mines, Treasury and Mint officials, and senior Republican politicians began to grow concerned that cheap silver was about to flood the American market, threatening the stability of the US monetary system—then bimetallic—and plans for the resumption of government debt payments in specie, as well as mine owners' solvency. This group—which included powerful senator John Sherman, secretary of the treasury George Boutwell, Treasury employees John Jay Knox and Henry R. Linderman, former China minister J. Ross Browne, and California banker and mine owner William C. Ralston, among others—first became concerned when considering the consequences of new silver discoveries in the American West, like the vast Comstock Lode, and advances in the techniques used to mine and refine the ore found there. As they began working through the implications of a massive increase in US silver production, the new imperial German government promised to adopt the gold standard following the 1871 Franco-Prussian War. This oncoming tide of demonetized German silver became the group's more proximate cause for alarm and political action.[32]

By late 1872 this group of monetary experts and mine owners had gelled and began coordinating a campaign to push for the abandonment of the bimetallic standard and the creation of a silver trade dollar. As Henry R. Linderman, the Treasury official who served as the group's primary advocate, explained in *Bankers' Magazine:* "The true policy of this country under these circumstances is to seek a market in CHINA for its silver bullion; and to do this it must be put in form to meet a favorable reception in that empire." If the Mint could create a trade dollar—an official coin of known weight and fineness, made expressly for export—that dollar could supplant the Spanish and Mexican coins that had been the preferred money on the China coast since the seventeenth century. Then, Linderman argued, the China market would be secured as a "safe outlet" for US silver and the "perplexing proposition as to the decline in price of this metal, and its increasing production, be at once solved in a most satisfactory manner."[33]

After several false starts, this group successfully pushed the Coinage Act through Congress in early 1873. In addition to all the supporting committee reports that Treasury agents like Linderman provided and the backroom maneuvering of Senator Sherman, the bill's congressional manager, another member of the group, Secretary of the Treasury George Boutwell, provided a nudge from China in the form of a consular report. In October 1872 David H. Bailey, an ambitious but thoroughly corrupt US consul at Hong Kong, sent an unsolicited memorandum to the State Department, arguing that American traders were "paying enormous tribute" to British banks for credit in Asia. Instead of paying a 4 percent "tax" (i.e. interest rate) for the use of English funds abroad, Bailey suggested the United States should set up a transpacific exchange bank using the output of American gold and silver mines as capital. As a "corollary," the consul recommended the United States coin a trade dollar "to serve for currency in China." Once the United States had recognized the "vast market for her coins in the East," Americans would "get, thereby, an enormous hold on this great trade." Passing Bailey's timely report on to Congress, Boutwell highlighted how well the consul's suggestion for a new coin fit with the coinage reform bill then pending and lauded Bailey's views as being of "great importance."[34]

Once public, Bailey's report attracted immediate, derisive criticism from experienced China merchants. Edward Cunningham, a Russell and Company partner, scorned it as "founded on misconceptions so palpable that he cannot live six months in Hongkong without discovering for himself the futility of his suggestions." The higher rate of return for capital in the United States made any notion of a transpacific bank laughable, and as for the trade dollar Bailey proposed, Cunningham thought it would require selling it at a loss in China for a decade and cost the country "a million or two of dollars" in silver before it would become currency in China's treaty ports.[35]

Cunningham's critique came too late to stop the Coinage Act. Passed late in the session, its supporters, led by Senator Sherman, pushed it to President Grant's desk, where he signed it into law on February 12, 1873. A complex measure not fully understood by most legislators who voted for it (indeed, Grant himself seemed confused about its effects), the bill reorganized operations at the US Mint, eliminated the production of standard silver dollars—effectively putting the United States on the gold standard—and created a silver trade dollar to Linderman's specifications.[36]

In addition to detailing the trade dollar's weight and fineness, the act also contained a number of provisions to induce its export. Its nominal value was lower than the then-current price of silver in Asia, making it profitable to ship abroad. It was also designated a "subsidiary" coin, legal tender only for sums "not exceeding five dollars in any one payment"—rendering it useless for any substantial domestic use (theoretically, at least; in practice it became a regular component of Americans' small change). Finally, charges for coining were left up to the discretion of the director of the mint—one Henry R. Linderman, conveniently appointed just after the act's passage—who set charges at cost, saving the Western mine owners who had lobbied for the legislation large fees they would otherwise have had to pay to remove the trace amounts of gold typically found in their mines' silver ore in order to meet the Chinese market's purity standards.[37] In design and implementation, the trade dollar was a union of marketing and government policy: a private surplus of silver production packaged by the US government into a

FIGURE 14. A US trade dollar, intended for export to China. One trade dollar, United States, 1876, http://n2t.net/ark:/65665/ng49ca746a9-2d24-704b-e053-15f76faob4fa, Division of Work and Industry, National Museum of American History, Smithsonian Institution.

standardized, sovereign-approved form that, its creators hoped, would appeal to customers on the China coast.

The coin was a moderate success as an export but a disastrous political venture. From 1873 to 1885, when production was discontinued, some 35,965,939 coins were struck, 81 percent of which were exported, primarily to China through the port of San Francisco.[38] Endearing himself further to his allies in Washington, Consul Bailey reported excitedly in 1877 that the "success of the United States trade-dollar in the east is well established"— but as before, more objective observers were less impressed.[39] After a decade's trial, the trade dollar never displaced the Mexican dollar or "found a market to any great extent" outside a narrow use in a few southern China ports.[40] It absorbed a significant volume of US-produced silver, for a time—

some 23 percent of the Comstock lode's silver was turned into coins from 1873 to 1878—but not enough to prop up silver prices.[41] William C. Ralston, the president of the Bank of California and an owner of a silver mine who had funded Linderman's lobbying, was not saved by it. Just over two years after the bill passed, his bank collapsed; shortly thereafter, Ralston was found drowned in San Francisco harbor, a presumed suicide.[42] The trade dollar had not buoyed him enough.

Further trouble for the coin came in domestic politics. "America's Only Unwanted, Unhonored Coin" was attacked soon after its production began, first for causing confusion in US markets because of its status as legal tender for small debts, and, later, for encouraging the export of silver that "loose" money proponents argued should have been kept for domestic circulation. In 1878, concerned that too many trade dollars were coming home to be exchanged for other nonsilver currencies of equal face value but greater market value, Congress revoked the coin's status as legal tender. In 1887, responding to reports of its continued domestic circulation, Congress recalled the coin outright: holders were given six months to exchange their trade dollars for standard silver dollars, after which the coin would cease to have any recognized legal value beyond its metal content. This was widely seen as a giveaway to holders of trade dollars, because at the time of the bill's passage the silver content of the coin was worth only seventy-five cents.[43]

Despite its creators' intentions, the trade dollar did not consume America's surplus of silver, keep domestic money on the gold standard, or lead to a rebirth of American commercial influence in China. But the episode does reveal what would become a regular feature of the thinking of late nineteenth-century American policymakers. When faced with a crisis they understood as driven by glut, US elites turned to the "China market" to engineer a solution.

Unlike the trade dollar, Chinese migration to the United States had aroused controversy since the 1850s. Chinese migrants faced such lasting and intense hostility from whites, historian Gordon Chang notes, that the question is not why the United States passed anti-Chinese restrictions, but only why these laws took "*so long*."[44] But if the eventual passage of xenophobic migration restrictions is historiographically interesting only in how late it came, what is perhaps more surprising is that partisans on both sides of the "Chinese Question" consistently framed their arguments in terms of glut—specifically, the need to attract or remove "surplus" Chinese labor because of the benefits and dangers it posed.[45]

During Reconstruction, Republican elites regarded the free movement of voluntary Chinese migrants as a net positive for all parties involved—a critical part of commercial exchange and foreign relations. William H.

Seward, touring the world in his retirement, encapsulated this perspective when he declared in Hong Kong in 1871 that he

> look[ed] for the practical advancement of civilization in China chiefly to commerce. . . . Say what they may the whole world cannot prevent this commerce from regenerating China and Japan. . . . The free emigration of the Chinese to the American and other foreign continents is the essential element of that trade and commerce. Chinese emigration to the American continent will tend to increase the wealth and strength of all Western nations; while, at the same time, the removal of the surplus population of China will tend much to take away the obstructions which now impede the introduction into China of art, science, morality, religion.[46]

Seward had more reason than most to praise free and open commerce between China and the United States, because of his role as architect of the Burlingame Treaty while serving as secretary of state. The first "equal" treaty between the Qing Empire and a Western power, the 1868 agreement established equal protections for Chinese migrants in America, propping open the door to Chinese immigration that Pacific states' regulations had sought to close. In grouping free commerce and free migration together, Seward was working within a "China trade" approach to US-China relations that saw free movement of goods, people, and capital as strategically, and necessarily, linked—as did most supporters of Chinese immigration to the United States.[47] But his early emphasis on the "surplus" Chinese population hinted at what soon became the key feature of the debate over Chinese immigration.

When enemies of Chinese migration attacked positions like Seward's, they did so by emphasizing that Chinese migrants were "cheap" and "degraded" and "servile" labor—an unwelcome "importation."[48] The rhetorical association between Chinese migrants and enslaved laborers was forged in the 1850s by enslavers fearful of the consequences for their investment in human chattel if "coolies"—indentured Asian workers—came to the South in large numbers.[49] Opposition to the "coolie trade" attracted the support of antislavery partisans, especially the moderates in the Republican Party, leading to the first ban on American participation in the coolie trade in 1862.

After the Civil War, concern over the coolie trade became part of the official justification for sustained diplomatic attention to human trafficking generally and Chinese migration specifically. Beginning under Seward but increasing during Hamilton Fish's term as secretary of state (1869–77), American ministers and consuls produced a steady stream of reports on the movements of laborers rumored to be involuntary, and the markets in which they were sold. Like similar British efforts in the aftermath of the emancipation of the 1830s, these investigations served as a means of pressuring other powers while accumulating moral capital, internationally. They were also global in scope: dispatches on slave markets in Russian provinces, suspected slave ships in Malta, and the "slavery question in Egypt" all were deemed important enough to merit the State Department's attention and were featured in official publications.[50] But the movements of Chinese migrants deemed "coolies"—out of Chinese ports, on US-bound or American-chartered ships, or onto South American plantations and mines—were the object of special concern, because they had direct implications for the Republican Party's electoral success on the West Coast.

Fish and his staff in Washington became a clearinghouse for information on the coolie trade, collecting and organizing reports on the state of the traffic and the treatment of laborers in Peru, Cuba, and Hawaii and forwarding them to the US legation in Beijing. Ensuring the application of US law prompted some of this attention, but they were called on to do so by others, too. Chinese migrants in Lima and Quito routed pleas for the Qing government's aid through US consuls, while British officials' actions to curtail trafficking in Hong Kong and elsewhere—itself a product of pressure from antislavery groups—provided a rationale for American attention to the China coast.[51] At times the propaganda generated by the overlapping oversight claims by British, American, and Chinese officials was used to justify new ventures in the coolie trade, as when the *Overland China Mail* assured its readers that the American firm of Olyphant and Company's new steamer line and coolie supply contract with the republic of Peru would be free of fraud because the "lynx eyes," "cautious observations," and "special and minute supervision" of diplomatic officials and merchants would "form a sort of Protectorate which it will be all but impossible to mislead or avoid."[52] (Olyphant and Company's scheme failed, as did the firm—brought to ruin by Hong Kong and Chinese officials who barred the company from loading migrants onto their chartered steamers. Unusually for the failure of a China trade firm, the story was covered extensively in US papers, perhaps because of Olyphant's well-known reputation as the "moral" China trade house.)[53]

American ministers in China used these reports as opportunities to advise Prince Gong and other members of the Zongli Yamen (the Chinese foreign ministry) on policy, positioning themselves as critical intermediaries. In practical terms, American diplomats urged the Chinese to actively embrace the tools of international law to ensure migrants' well-being—to send out fact-finding missions to investigate mistreatment and establish consular posts abroad to protect their rights. Occasionally, US diplomats also acted as agents for Spain or Peru, helping these powers write fresh treaties with China to secure new laborers (incidentally making shipping business for struggling American China firms like Olyphant and Company), but also building mechanisms for oversight into the new agreements.

American diplomats pursued this intermediation to burnish their reputation among Chinese officials as a "friendly" power, and to position themselves as brokers between the Qing court and the rest of the world. Although they hoped the Chinese would start to treat international law as sacrosanct and thus enforce the maximum interpretations of treaty rights in China that they and most other foreigners favored, American officials' faith in international law to protect migrants was mostly a front. In a moment of candor, Samuel Wells Williams, a mainstay of the US legation, admitted to his superiors that the idea that "consular agents" could eradicate or even reduce the "evils of the coolie system" was "very fallacious." As he well knew, consular protests meant little without political leverage or military force.[54]

Still, under certain conditions consular reports could be influential. From almost the moment he started as the US consul to Hong Kong in late 1870, David H. Bailey was an avid writer, using his official correspondence (and position) to go deep into the "true crime" genre, in multiple senses. He wrote regular reports on the state of trade, but he supplemented this mandated output with memorandums on banking and currency in China, opium smuggling in San Francisco, and bribery in Macao. But Bailey's favorite subject, one he returned to again and again, was what he alternately termed the "coolie trade" and the "Chinese slave trade."[55] In his most popular report, cited profusely by xenophobic congressmen and nativist editors for years afterward, Bailey averred that emigration from China was fundamentally unlike that from "other parts of the world." It was an "organized business or trade, in which men of large capital, and hongs of great wealth, engage as a regular traffic," buying and selling men "for so much per head, precisely as a piece of merchandise is handled." This "new mode of enslaving men" was bad enough for those caught by the "now world-famed atrocities at Macao," but Bailey also spared a thought in his report for the "great free-labor interests of our own country" facing an oncoming wave of "servile" and "heathen" labor. There may be some "free and voluntary emigration" to the United States, but "it is so surrounded, mixed up, and tainted with the virus of the coolie trade, as to require the utmost vigilance and scrutiny to separate the legitimate from the illegitimate." He promised his superiors he would neither lend aid to this "nefarious traffic, nor bow to the behests of the great houses" invested in "forcing this great wrong"; he promised to do his duty "and let the consequences care for themselves."[56]

If one only read his dispatches, Bailey would seem to have been a man of his word. Collectively, his reports were zealous to the point of obsession; he worked (seemingly) tirelessly to expose the horrors of the trade and cajole British, Chinese, and Portuguese authorities in the Pearl River Delta to work together to suppress it. But Bailey's accounts were not the full story. Although the consul spoke no Chinese dialects—his alarming dispatches were often summaries of others' reports or hearsay—he did have firsthand experience in the "organized business or trade" of Chinese migration. As John S. Mosby, his successor at the Hong Kong consulate revealed in 1879, Bailey leveraged his post for enormous personal gain, cooking his books for almost a decade to hide the huge haul in illegally assessed fees he collected for certifying that Chinese migrants bound for the United States were voluntary migrants. According to Mosby, Bailey skimmed some $38,375 during his tenure. He maintained his distance by sending cronies, including an illiterate innkeeper and a suspected pirate, to do the ticket stamping and fee collecting in his stead; but these cutouts did not lend his later denials much credibility. In his private accounts and public career, Bailey got ahead by knowing just enough about the business of Chinese migration to exploit it.[57]

Bailey's reports were as suspect as his ledgers, but they gained currency among US politicians looking to justify xenophobic policies.[58] The shift to an anti-Chinese politics gathered strength in the long depression that followed the 1873 financial panic. After losing the House to Democrats in the midterm elections of 1874, the Republican Party began to retreat from its Reconstruction-era commitments to radical equality and multiracial democracy. Along with weakening support for using federal power to uphold African Americans' civil rights in the South, party leaders and voters began to shift toward the nativist position on Chinese migration, embracing xenophobia as a solution to the "Labor Question" that would not threaten the interests of capital or other policies—the protectionist tariff, the return to the gold standard—that the party's leaders prioritized.

In this political environment, the insistence of experienced China diplomats like Samuel Wells Williams, Frederick F. Low, and George F. Seward—to say nothing of the Chinese sojourners themselves—that Chinese labor was "free labor" counted for little.[59] Instead, informed by reports like Bailey's, the federal government imposed new restrictions. At first these measures continued in the mold of 1862's anti–coolie trade measure and were framed as laws preventing forced "importations" of unwilling workers. In 1874 President Grant used his annual message to inform Congress that a "great proportion of the Chinese immigrants who come to our shores do not come voluntarily" but arrived under contracts "with headmen who own them almost absolutely." Chinese women, Grant continued, were likewise trafficked sex workers, "brought for shameful purposes." In response, Congress passed the Page Act in 1875, requiring US consuls to certify that "any subject of China, Japan, or any Oriental country" was migrating voluntarily, not under any contract, and not for "immoral purposes," and made it a felony for US citizens to import, or arrange to supply, migrants in a manner considered an "illegal importation," either "cooly" laborers or prostitutes.[60]

The Page Act whetted restrictionists' appetites. West Coast politicians increased pressure on their eastern colleagues in Congress and the State Department, while western state legislatures tested the courts with new anti-Chinese statutes. In the 1876 presidential election the "Chinese Question" made it to national party platforms, though as before the Democratic Party led the debate with more extreme anti-Chinese (and anti-Black) policies. Republicans promised to "investigate the effects of the immigration and importation of Mongolians," while Democrats pledged to "demand" treaty modifications to "prevent further importation or immigration of the Mongolian race."[61] Only at the end of the decade, amid the death of US China trade firms, did Republicans begin to support full national restriction as a means to win white votes in western states and thereby shore up their increasingly tenuous hold on power. In making this shift they built on language laid out in State Department reports, framing their opposition to Chinese "importations" as an extension of antislavery policy. It was "China market" thinking with the direction reversed: instead of a market that could absorb excess silver, the Qing Empire was a source of surplus unfree laborers, unfit for a modern, industrial republic.

The final turning point came in the run-up to the 1880 presidential election. Political weathervane James G. Blaine signaled what the consensus Republican position would soon be in a speech on the Fifteen Passenger Bill, delivered in the Senate on Valentine's Day, 1879:

> You cannot work a man who must have beef and bread, and would prefer beer, alongside a man who can live on rice. It cannot be done. . . . Slave labor degraded free labor; it took out its respectability; it put an odious caste upon it. It throttled the prosperity of a fine and fair portion of the United States; and a worse than slave labor will throttle and impair the prosperity of a still finer and fairer section of the United States. We can choose here to-day whether our legislation shall be in the interest of the American free laborer or for the servile laborer from China.[62]

Blaine used this speech—and a subsequent article in the *New-York Tribune*—to send a love letter to the nativists he thought would carry him to the presidency in 1880. The bill under discussion proposed to break the

Burlingame Treaty by limiting the number of Chinese passengers allowed to sail in ships bound for US ports. Blaine framed his intervention on the question in the language of free labor ideology, fusing the core of the Republican Party's heroic founding myth—Unionists united to eradicate the Slave Power!—to the race science equation of immigrants and slaves that was common to both Hong Kong consuls and San Francisco sandlot orators. Decrying the threat that the "incalculable hordes of China" posed to good order and American workers, Blaine articulated a sort of Gresham's law for immigration policy. Instead of "bad money" driving out the good, "bad labor" Chinese migrants threatened to drive out the "good labor" of white American citizens. Blaine's formulation yoked the hard money monetary politics of his party to white voters' xenophobic nightmares.[63]

Blaine's support for the Fifteen Passenger Act failed to secure him his party's nomination, and it didn't succeed in making the bill into law. Shortly after it passed, Rutherford B. Hayes vetoed the Fifteen Passenger Act as an abrogation of the Burlingame Treaty. But the ground had shifted. In his veto message, Hayes observed that the "very grave discontents of the people of the Pacific States" with the Chinese deserved "the most serious attention."[64] In early 1880 he authorized the State Department to send a special three-man diplomatic commission to China to negotiate a new agreement that would allow the United States to restrain immigration. Led by historian and University of Michigan president James B. Angell, the negotiation was brief and successful, largely because the Zongli Yamen, facing new aggression from Russia and Japan and ambivalent about emigration, was willing to move quickly to eliminate a source of friction.[65]

The result was two new treaties, both signed in Beijing in November 1880. One addressed immigration and allowed the United States to "regulate, limit or suspend" the "coming or residence" of Chinese laborers but—crucially—not to "absolutely prohibit it."[66] (The next few decades of American immigration legislation largely consisted in increasingly aggressive attempts to enact a complete prohibition on Asian migrants.) The other dealt with "Commercial Relations and Judicial Procedure"—it reaffirmed each country's most favored nation status with regard to tariffs and fees, banned Americans from shipping opium into China and Chinese from shipping the drug into the United States, and confirmed Americans' rights to extraterritorial courts in China.[67] What's notable about these agreements is how they formally separated in law what Americans had already separated in political discourse. Unlike all previous US agreements with China, the 1880 treaties divorced the movement of people from the movement of goods—declaring one to be "immigration" and the other "commerce." Ironically, this separation occurred because the US political class refused to consider any Chinese laborers as legitimate travelers, and saw them only as involuntarily trafficked goods.

Angell's treaty negotiations wrapped up just after the 1880 election, a contest in which both major parties adopted platforms promising to end "unrestricted immigration of the Chinese" (Republicans) or simply "no more Chinese immigration" (Democrats).[68] Courting working-class votes with policies that would eliminate the "importations" of Chinese—albeit in a way opposite to how they had previously tried to address the problem of silver oversupply—Republicans won the election. After a few attempts at restrictionist legislation that President Chester Arthur found overzealous, Congress passed the Chinese Restriction Act—better known later as the "Chinese Exclusion Act"—in May 1882.[69] Together with the Immigration Act, the first session of the Forty-Seventh Congress laid the legal and bureaucratic foundations for a modern restrictive immigration system that distinguished—and deported—migrants on the basis of their nationality, race, and class. It expanded the policing power of the federal state, building up new capacity to restrain the movement of people across borders, as the tariff already did for goods.[70] As they were intended to do, the Angell Treaty and the Chinese Exclusion Act altered relations between the United States and China. Chinese migration fell, though not as quickly or as dramatically as restrictionists wanted—so they pushed for complete exclusion. Coupled with the spectacular violence targeting Chinese living in United States and US authorities' unwillingness to uphold their own treaty obligations, Americans actions' were sufficient to cool relations with the Qing government and to spark boycotts against US goods in China in the early twentieth century.[71]

But restrictionist policies did nothing to moderate crises of the globalized industrial economy, and the search for effective solutions continued. Between the two great financial panics of the late nineteenth century, 1873 and 1893, leading American political economists, corporate executives, and union leaders came to embrace "overproduction" or "glut" theory explicitly to explain why the nation's economy regularly suffered distress, and as a guide for what could be done about it. As articulated by theorists from David A. Wells to Jeremiah Jenks, the core of this explanation was that that surplus capital created overinvestment in production that turned out goods at a rate and on a scale far beyond what could be consumed. Unchecked, firms and individuals trapped in this disequilibrium competed ruinously, lowering prices, wages, and rates of return on capital. While this understanding of economic dynamics did not dictate a specific policy response—as the gulf between the public statements of Populist leaders and corporate executives demonstrated—it did tend to deemphasize monetary policy, and to some extent immigration policy, as critical issues. What emerged as something of a consensus, however, was that the problem of a glut of capital or production could be addressed with commercial expansion—venting surplus goods to overseas markets.[72]

The shift to "China market" thinking was intertwined with the growing consensus on the "glut" thesis. In 1883 Chester Arthur's annual message noted that, under his guidance, the State Department had declined to enforce some of its treaty rights in China. Prevented by Shanghai officials from opening a cotton yarn factory, William S. Wetmore, an American merchant, had appealed to the US legation in China for aid, arguing that the right to form a manufacturing company in China was established by the most favored nation clause of US treaties. The State Department agreed with this interpretation but declined to pursue it. As Arthur explained in his message, "The transference to China of American capital for the employment there of Chinese labor would in effect inaugurate a competition for the control of markets now supplied by our home industries."[73]

Although not interested in helping Americans export capital to China, the US government did try to provide American exporters with information on foreign markets. Before the late nineteenth century, US consuls in China spent most of their energies reporting on shipping and commercial statistics and agitating for diplomatic action on local issues like transit duties or lighthouse placement. But in the 1870s they began to pay more attention to what American goods were popular in a given port and what new opportunities there might be for exports. This shift in reporting was in part a play for establishing the importance of consular expertise—one of the consistent themes of such reports was that manufacturers were "strangely forgetful of their interests" in not attending to information consuls provided—but the net effect was to help broaden and regularize government attention to export markets.[74] In 1897 the new Bureau of Foreign Commerce began issuing annual surveys of the state of American international trade under the title *Review of the World's Commerce*. Despite the plenary label, these pamphlets were concerned not with the work of merchants or the shipping industry, but rather with how global commercial trends affected US industrial and agricultural exporters.

During the export boom of the late 1890s, the report was often a statement of confidence in American competitive capacities, always understood in the context of rival industrial powers. In a typical moment of bombast, Frederic Emory, head of the Bureau of Foreign Commerce, reported that "the industries of the United States have, in fact, been developed to the point where it seems to be not only practicable but comparatively easy to supply a considerable portion of the world as well as the home market." As Emory quoted him, the president of the newly formed National Association of Manufacturers agreed: US manufacturers "have acquired a position in the world's markets from which they can not be dislodged. With the start that has been made, our foreign trade is bound to grow, and no opposition from our strongest competitor can bar our progress."[75] What had been "overproduction" was now a source of strength.

China figured prominently in these reports as a major market with limitless prospects. Notably, while the United States' consuls were eager to find opportunities for Chinese consumers to learn to "appreciate our goods," they assumed that potential entrants into the "trade" were agents of manufacturing concerns—not merchants—and in need of advice on "cater[ing] to the trade here." China was presented as a market for US goods, and the issue was one of marketing—and of competition with other imperial rivals for consumers and consumer loyalties. As the consul-general at Shanghai explained in 1898, "If this trade is to be taken and kept by America, its needs, customs, and superstitions must be studied on the ground by experts in each department."[76]

As the search for overseas markets for American products became the guiding principle of US commercial policy in the last decade of the nineteenth century, notices of the decline of the "old China trade" became regular features in commentary on US affairs in East Asia. Russell and Company's failure in 1891 was a theme in many of these elegies. John Russell Young, Grant's protégé and a former US minister to China, marked the "fading-away of American influence in China" by the "failure of Russell and Co."—which he argued could have occurred only through the malign influence of "British interests" playing great-power politics.[77] Less invested in sparking an international rivalry, a *Harper's Weekly* correspondent in 1894 described seeing the "towering warehouse of Russell & Co." on the "splendid Bund" of Shanghi and thought that its "its abandonment by that firm speaks volumes on the decay of our influence!"[78]

China traders themselves made more accurate assessments. Charles Tomes, a Russell and Company junior partner who had been left holding the bag when the firm failed, blamed the failure on his colleagues' unwise investments in silver speculation—along with simply "not making any money" in other lines.[79] Surveying a slightly grander prospect, the former head of a different China house blamed the decline of US trading firms in China on the changes in the business environment: "the establishment of Banks, the substitution of steam for sails, and the use of the telegraph," as well as the "the passing of local trade into the hands of the Chinese." Rejecting the "stock argument of the American politician"—specifically, that of John Russell Young—Augustine Heard Jr. parsed the death of the China trade and the "decline of American influence" as a business matter: it was "no longer profitable."[80]

At the end of the nineteenth century the United States emerged from a period of disorder and civil war as a self-conscious—and unusually confident—first-rank power. Globalization and industrialization had reshaped the nation's political economy, destabilizing the producerist ethos underlying its governing ideologies; the uneven pace of growth had led to a reconfiguration of the nation's borders and of its policies. As the new restrictionist state took shape, the ambitions of its leading businessmen and politicians were not hard to discern. Hailing the nation's ability to produce the key commodities of modern "commercial power"—iron and steel—more cheaply than any other nation, Joseph C. Hendrix, president of the American Bankers' Association, predicted that the United States would soon "dominate the commerce of the world." He further predicted that Americans would not stop there: "We have long been the granary of the World; we now aspire to be its workshop. Then we want to be its clearinghouse."[81]

Agricultural, industrial, and finally financial power: Hendrix's sequence for world domination did not include the core of American activity in China in earlier eras: commerce. The banker likely avoided it because the dire state of the nation's merchant marine, destroyed during the Civil War, did not lend itself to a rousing, confident speech; but times and thinking had also changed.[82] In an industrial political economy where productive capacity had exploded to the point of being a threat to social and political stability, trade's benefit lay primarily in the ability to quickly and efficiently ship the glut of goods to new consumers. Organizing the logistics of mediating markets—commission merchants' work—was no longer valued as an area of expertise, but taken for granted as infrastructure. The era of looking to China's great port cities as opportunities to build power through arbitrage and mediation—a "China trade" that could support American development without threatening US institutions—was over.

In this new context of industrialization, globalization, and imperial expansion, Americans understood China primarily as a market, not as a trade. The events that defined the Sino-American relationship at the turn of the twentieth century—the colonization of the Philippines, intervention in the Boxer Rebellion, circulation of the Open Door Notes—were in this regard quite different from previous eras. Despite the superficial continuities in guaranteeing "access" to China, US leaders undertook these imperial acts to compete with other industrial powers. These policies all aimed at a new kind of commercial expansion because the basis for American business abroad was new. Finding consumers for an overabundance of mass-produced goods, rather than a place to do commerce, was the new reason for American interest in China.

Globalization killed the China trade and the political imaginary that grew out of it. On its grave, Americans built a new outward-facing state, one that attempted to control the nation's connections to the rest of the world by controlling how freely (some kinds of) people and (some kinds of) goods flowed across borders. As they had in earlier eras, the policymakers behind this shift hoped to use commerce with China in multiple ways: as a tool for geopolitics as well as a solution to domestic problems. But if the ways Americans imagined the role of China in their political economy had changed, their stubborn insistence that it *did matter* had not. As it had been since the nation's birth, their commerce with China was at the heart of Americans' definition of themselves.

Acknowledgments

Like organizing a venture to China, writing a book involves many people and incurs many debts. While this particular voyage has gone on so long that I am sure my tally is incomplete, I have tried my best to warmly acknowledge, even if I cannot fully repay, all those who have done so much to make this work—and my life with it—possible. Particularly since the coronavirus pandemic has cut away so much of it, I feel keenly the dearness of the social dimension of scholarship. I hope readers will forgive my extravagance with gratitude.

Many institutions have supported this project. Princeton University offered research and writing fellowships. The foundational research was supported by the Massachusetts Historical Society and collaborating institutions of the New England Fellowship Consortium. The Program in Early American Economy and Society at the Library Company of Philadelphia hosted me twice for short-term fellowships, providing intellectual support and access to critical collections. A fellowship from the McNeil Center for Early American Studies saw me through the final lap of my dissertation and brought me fully into the wide and vibrant world of the Greater Philadelphia Early Americanist community. The Bernard and Irene Schwartz Postdoctoral Fellowship, hosted by the New-York Historical Society and the New School, gave me a secure home base from which to launch my post-dissertation research, and the Cassius Marcellus Clay Postdoctoral Fellowship at Yale University gave me the breathing room—and scholarly community—to sketch out the second half of the book. I am grateful to Binghamton University for providing me with course releases during my Dean's Research Semester. Thank you to the University of Delaware for granting me a course release during my first semester in Newark and funds to support the final years of writing and book production.

I sincerely thank the staffs of all the libraries and archives whose collections I have relied on. These include the archives at Andalusia Historic House, Gardens and Arboretum; the American Philosophical Society; Baker Library at Harvard Business School; the Boston Athenaeum; the Glenn G. Bartle Library at Binghamton University; the Boston Public Library; Butler Library at Columbia University; the Franklin D. Roosevelt Presidential Library and Museum; Houghton Library at Harvard University; the Historical Society of Pennsylvania; the Lackawanna Historical Society; the Library Company of Philadelphia; the Library of Congress; the Massachusetts Historical Society; the Middlesex County Historical Society (Middletown, Connecticut); the US National Archives in Washington, DC, College Park, Maryland, and Philadelphia; the UK National Archives at Kew; the New-York Historical Society; the New York Public Library; Bobst Library at New York University; the Phillips Library at the Peabody Essex Museum; the Princeton Theological Seminary Library; Firestone Library at Princeton University; the Smithsonian Institution Archives; Morris Library at the University of Delaware; Special Collections Research Center at the University of Michigan Library; the University of Pittsburg Library Digital Collections; and Sterling Memorial Library and the Beinecke Rare Book and Manuscript Library at Yale University. I am also thankful, particularly in this moment, for the digital collections created and managed by HathiTrust, the Internet Archive, the Digital Public Library of America, and their coordinating institutions.

I deeply appreciate the wonderful scholars who have mentored me as I tried to rechart the world of China merchants and others interested in their business. I walked into Sean Wilentz's reading seminar convinced I would rather be a historian of any time and place other than nineteenth-century America, and left it committed to studying the United States' messiest century (so far). As my adviser, Sean gave me as much rope as I wanted for this project—then helped reel me back when I got lost. The other members of my dissertation committee—Dirk Hartog, Dan Rodgers, and Peter Onuf—pushed me to expand my ambitions for the project and to follow the story to its end. Cathy Matson saw something useful in this research long before I did, and helped me see it too; and through the PEAES seminars she hosted, I learned to think rigorously and expansively about political economy. She also led me to Delaware, which has been such a warm and welcoming place. Joanne Freeman invited me to join the thriving community of Yale Early American Historians, and over lunches she taught me to think differently, and more humanely, about writing, teaching, and researching. I am especially grateful to Joanne for organizing the colloquium that helped solidify the course the book should take. Her critiques, and those of the colloquium's other participants, Jay Sexton and Ed Baptist, proved immensely productive. It turns out that following the money—as they suggested—pays off.

Thank you to everyone at the University of Chicago Press who made this book real. Robert Devens, who saw the promise in this project in the first paper I gave on it; the series editors, Stephen Mihm, Edward Gray, Mark Peterson, and Emma Hart, who were sounding boards throughout; the anonymous readers at the press; and executive editor Tim Mennel, editorial associate Susannah Engstrom, and all the members of their fabulous production team. Their expert eyes and seemingly inexhaustible patience are what enabled me to finally bring this ship of text into port, even as new and more thrillingly distracting calamities unfolded in the wider world around it.

I shared portions of this book as works in progress at panels and seminars, and benefited from the generous and thoughtful criticism of audiences at those events. Thank you to all the hosts and seminar participants who shared their ideas and suggestions, including those at the Massachusetts Historical Society Brown Bag series; the PEAES Fellows Colloquium; the Colonial Americas Workshop (Princeton University); the McNeil Center for Early American Studies Friday Seminar; the History Workshop (New School); the Nineteenth-Century United States History Workshop and the Early American Money Symposium (Brown University); the Washington Area Early American Seminar Series; the Yale Early American Historians Seminar; the Upstate Early American History Workshop (Binghamton University); the Columbia University Seminar on Early American History and Culture; the Migration and Rights Working Group (Binghamton University); the Center for Legal Studies (Northwestern University); the Missouri Regional Seminar on Early American History (University of Missouri); the Hagley Center Brown Bag series; and last, but by no means least, my colleagues at the History Workshop (University of Delaware). I am grateful too for the suggestions made by commentators and audiences at the annual meetings of SHEAR, SHAFR, BHC, OAH, and AHA, as well as at other conferences.

I owe more thanks than I can properly express to the brilliant folks I was lucky to be surrounded by on C Floor while I wrote the first draft pages of this project as a student at Princeton: thank you to Sarah Milov, Jamie Kreiner, Dan Bouk, Chris Moses, Anne Twitty, Christienna Fryar, Lo Faber, Jessica Lowe, Ben Schmidt, Anne O'Donnell, Alex Bick, and Nealin Parker. The community at the McNeil Center is too enormous and important to name, but I want to thank Jess Roney, especially, for her many years of friendship, expert advice, and advanced mixology. At N-YHS I joined Drew Lipman, Kevin Butterfield, and Robin Vandome in exploring the archives and had the great joy of seeing up close the immense possibilities for public history by watching Valerie Paley and Marci Reaven work. At the New School, Elaine Abelson, Julia Ott, and Jeremy Varon provided kind introductions to the rhythms of faculty life, and Cyp Stephenson, in addition to his able department administration, was a great lunch partner. In both places I shared comically small work spaces with the extraordinary Catherine McNeur. She was a tolerant officemate then and has been a great and good friend ever since, as well as a keen and insightful reader. I remain impressed by her good humor in the face of the Pacific Northwest's baffling reluctant capitalism.

My time as part of the excellently acronymed Yale Early American Historians (YEAH) was enlivened by the warm intellectual community of Michael Hattem, Michael Blaakman, and David Gary. Ariel Ron, Caitlin Rosenthal, and Matt Karp kindly included me in their book writers' group and kept me moving on slow days. Susan Gaunt Stearns, Craig Hollander, and Andrew Fagal are all adventurers whose willingness to get up and go has gotten me to more fun spots than I had any business being. I have long shared with Hannah Farber an irritated fascination with antique accounting and outdated economic history, a mutual concern that has profited me in so many ways that traditional interest rates are useless to explain it. Ann Daly, Seth Rockman, Jessica Lepler, and Sharon Murphy have helped me comprehend the business of money, a service more valuable than negotiating a bill at par. When I started this project, I was (I thought) one of just a handful of scholars plowing these waves, but now there is a regular fleet—a delightful development. It is a privilege to sail the same waters as Rachel Tamar Van, Dane Morrison, Fred Grant, John Rogers Haddad, Dan Du, Gwenn Miller, Laurie Dickmeyer, and many others.

The History Department at Binghamton University gave me the great gift of ongoing employment as a professor. My thanks go to John Chaffee for stepping in to rescue me from an awkward question about opium smoking during my interview and for conversations about Chinese maritime history afterward. The collegiality of Diane Miller Sommerville, Rob Parkinson, Wendy Wall, Jon Karp, John Cheng, Steve Ortiz, Liz Casteen, Heather Welland, and Nancy Appelbaum made seminars, exams, defenses, and department meetings so much better than they had any right to be. I appreciate Kathy Fedorchak, Keith Limbach, and Colleen Marshall, whose administrative labor made them possible. Conversations with Binghamton's brilliant graduate students improved my work immeasurably; special thanks to Jason Tercha, Jonathan Jones, and Chelsea Gibson for their productive questions. Finally, Bat-Ami Bar On, director of the Institute for

Advanced Studies in the Humanities, was a champion for rigorous transnational research across the university, including mine. May her memory be a blessing.

My time in the Southern Tier was busy and enlivening for other reasons too. Though it often took me away from book writing, the solidarity of my friends in Fair Deal Binghamton, and the important work we did, was a bright light in dark times. Thank you and solidarity to Amanda Licht, Doug Jones, Jessie Reeder, Kevin Boettcher, Beau Brammer, Ayşe Baltacıoğlu-Brammer, Meg Leja, Alex Chase-Levenson, Julia Walker, Kevin Hatch, Frank Chang, Sean Dunwoody, John Kuhn, Bridget Whearty, and Tina Chronopoulos.

My colleagues at the University of Delaware have helped me see this project to its completion. No one could ask for a more welcoming, supportive work environment. I am grateful to Arwen Mohun, Jim Brophy, and Alison Parker for their steady leadership during uncertain times, and to Deb Hartnett, Amy Dolbow, Diane Clark, Meg Hutchins, and Doug Tobias for making everything run so smoothly (and answering all my questions). Zara Anishanslin invited me into the community and has been my guide in all things; it's a true joy to collaborate with her on all sorts of projects, now and into the future. Owen White and Patricia Sloane-White sealed the deal with bagels and, with Peter Kolchin and Anne Boylan, are my models of how to thrive as brilliant scholars and effective teachers at Delaware, as well as good neighbors. Weekly writing sessions with Rebecca Davis have helped keep me on track and sane—no small thing at any time, but especially during a pandemic.

My family is both more practically minded than I am and more creative, and their good sense and smart perspective have inspired me for many years. My father, Dan Norwood, passed before I began this project, but I like to imagine that he would see his fascination with the sea in this book. My mother, Phyllis Humphrey Norwood, taught me that asking questions was the way to live, and through her own example she showed me how to take action when needed. My siblings Catherine, Patrick, and Sean are all brilliant, funny, and eminently capable people who have brought more wonderful folks into my life through their partners and children—a great joy. (A special shout-out to my sister-in-law Lauren for sharing her Boston Public Library card at a crucial juncture.)

Michelle Paul has been the light of my life for seventeen million years (approximately) and I hope for many, many millions more. She did not do any of the intellectual labor of this book—she has her own important work to do and does it extraordinarily well (including writing her own book, finished many years before this one). But she has lived every stage of it with me and offered critique, corrections, and encouragement throughout. I could not imagine the world, much less this work, without her.

Though this book took shape amid too many disasters to name, I entertain some aspirations that it is not one itself. But if there are any tragic mistakes, irritating oversights, or enraging errors, I, reluctantly, must take full responsibility—for, unlike a trading venture, there is no insurance for authors; we trade on our own risk.

Appendix: Accounting for the China Trade

Americans' trade with China is notoriously difficult to quantify.[1] That is not because data are difficult to find; statistics on the commerce can be found in many sources, from government reports to merchants' files to credit rating agencies' books. The problem is that, collectively, data on the trade are incomplete, discontinuous, and often incommensurable.[2]

For government data the availability of reliable information varies depending on the capabilities of central bureaucracies and their local agents. In the eighteenth and nineteenth centuries, state capacity was often minimal. The early United States lacked the apparatus—and the will—to report rigorous, comparable statistics on any branch of commerce. The early Treasury reports to Congress were based on irregularly recorded customs house records and were frequently prefaced by letters explaining the absence of data from major ports. Official Treasury reports were also inconsistent in how they reported data: some years include figures for both exports and imports for China and "the East Indies," while others include just one, or neither; at times European possessions in Asia are separated out as distinct entities, and at other times not; and the figures for particular commodities are sometimes denoted by monetary values, but more often are given as units of measurement or piece numbers (X pounds of tea, X bales of cloth), with no values or current prices.

Similarly shifting inconsistencies in definitions and jurisdictions afflict reports produced by the customs services and statistical bureaus run by Great Britain and China, the other powers most interested in Americans' China trade. What each state saw depended on who was collecting data and for what purpose. Goods moved on Chinese ships on the China coast, or trafficked at Hong Kong, for example, are not accounted for in any one series, and frequently occur in none, because they were not of specific inter-

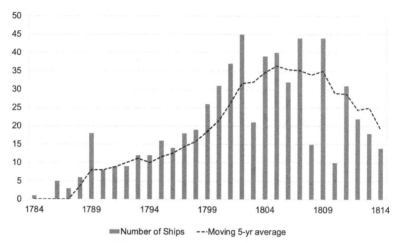

FIGURE A1. American ships at Canton, 1784–1814. Rhys Richards, Mary Malloy, and Briton C. Busch, "United States Trade with China 1784–1814," *American Neptune*, 54, no. 1 (Winter 1994): 5–74. The drop in American ships in 1803 is likely a consequence of the temporary peace in Europe (the Peace of Amiens); that in 1808 is likely a result of Jefferson's embargo.

est to revenue officials or were beyond their legal authority. Financial data on currencies or banking facilities were collected even more haphazardly.

Accounting for the China trade runs into deeper issues than the scope or reliability of official reports. By its nature, much of Americans' activity related to their China commerce took place beyond the sight of official clerks: sea otter furs collected on the coast of Oregon, or credit extended by hong merchants, for example, were not counted in US, British, or Chinese figures, yet they played a critical role in Americans' purchase of teas. Also, traders had an interest in keeping their affairs hidden. A great deal of the trade Americans conducted in China was smuggling; and even if the commodities were not contraband, secrecy could bestow a significant market advantage. Thus Americans' business in China is almost certainly undercounted in any given extant report.

These problems are not unique to the analysis of Americans' China trade; rather, they define the study of transnational and international trade generally. As Paul Yates (and many others) has observed, trade data, whether historical or contemporary, is not suited to "exact measurements" but "rather as general indications of broad orders of magnitude."[3] In my analysis (and the charts that follow below) I have endeavored to focus on trends and flows rather than specific details, while also being as clear and specific as possible about my sources, so that the limits of the data can be readily observed and understood.

 Tea, in lbs − −Tea, in lbs, 5-yr moving average

FIGURE A2. Tea exports from Canton to the United States, 1784–1814. Foster Rhea Dulles, *The Old China Trade* (1930; repr. New York: AMS Press, 1970), 210. Dulles draws on several sources for his figures. For the years up to 1810, his source is a table compiled by an East India Company servant using Canton Factory reports: William Milburn, *Oriental Commerce: Containing a Geographical Description of the Principal Places in the East Indies, China, and Japan, with Their Produce, Manufactures, and Trade* (London: Black, Parry, 1813), 2:486. For the post-1810 figures he references a Senate report that does not contain national tea trade estimates; however, the series seems more likely to have been drawn from a published account: "The China Trade," *Hunt's Merchants' Magazine and Commercial Review*, January 1845, 50. On the whole, Dulles's estimates run slightly higher than those reported by US government sources, as excerpted by Pitkin and later by Downs, but the trend line is roughly the same. I use his series here because it is more complete than others. See Timothy Pitkin, *A Statistical View of the Commerce of the United States of America* (New Haven, CT: Durrie and Peck, 1835), 246–47; Jacques M. Downs, *The Golden Ghetto: The American Commercial Community at Canton and the Shaping of American China Policy, 1784–1844* (Bethlehem, PA: Lehigh University Press, 1997), 353–54.

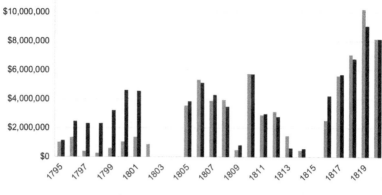

American Exports to Canton (from anywhere)
American Imports from Canton (to anywhere)

FIGURE A3. American exports and imports, to/from Canton, by value, 1795–1820. Pitkin, *A Statistical View of the Commerce of the United States of America*, 257–62, 302; Downs, *Golden Ghetto*, 351–52. NB: Pitkin describes the pre-1805 data as "China and the East Indies" because he is drawing from Treasury reports that use that language. After 1805 he is drawing from a Canton report. Downs reproduces Pitkin's figures but does not distinguish between the numbers Pitkin draws from a Treasury report (which records the data on "imports" and "exports" from a US perspective) and the later Canton report (which reverses these labels, such that "imports" signify things Americans brought into China, not took from it). I have corrected for that: the "imports" here are "exports" from the Treasury table, and vice versa. The upshot is that my numbers for these tables do not line up with Downs's; before 1804, what I use as "imports to China" are equal to Downs's "exports from Canton."

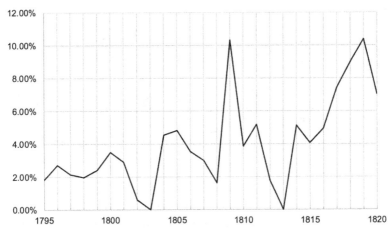

FIGURE A4. American trade at Canton as a percentage of US foreign trade, 1795–1820. Figures on total US imports and exports in Susan B. Carter et al., eds., *Historical Statistics of the United States: Millennial Edition Online* (New York: Cambridge University Press, 2006), Ee424, Ee365. The figures on China trade imports and exports, on the other hand, are drawn from reports made from Canton, as published by Timothy Pitkin and reprinted by Downs. While comparing statistics compiled in two locations with different scopes is not ideal, Pitkin's figures provide the only series that approaches completeness for this period. Pitkin, *Statistical View of the Commerce of the United States of America*, 257–62; Downs, *Golden Ghetto*, 351–52.

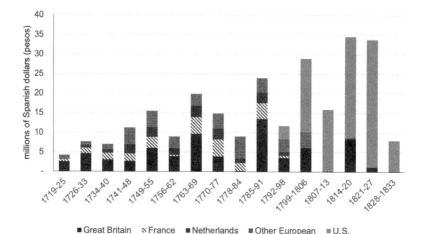

■Great Britain ⬠France ■Netherlands ■Other European ■U.S.

FIGURE A5. Imports of silver to China, by country, 1719–1833. Louis Dermigny, *La Chine et L'Occident: Le commerce à Canton au XVIIIe siècle, 1719–1833* (Paris: SEVPEN, 1964), 2:735. This chart follows the form of "Figure 1: Country Share of China's Silver Imports, 1719–1833 (in pesos)," in Alejandra Irigoin, "The End of a Silver Era: The Consequences of the Breakdown of the Spanish Peso Standard in China and the United States, 1780s–1850s," *Journal of World History* 20, no. 2 (June 1, 2009): 211.

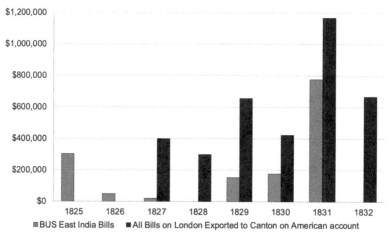

■BUS East India Bills   ■All Bills on London Exported to Canton on American account

FIGURE A6. Bills of exchange in the US-China trade, 1825–32. "No. 26: STATEMENT of all the bills of exchange on London and Paris, furnished by the Bank to go circuitously; stating the places they were conditioned by the purchasers to be sent to, and the amount to each place; the amount each year; and the amount now unsettled for," in "Bank of the United States," H.R. Rep. 460, 22nd Cong., 1st Sess. (April 30, 1832), 206, and Pitkin, *A Statistical View of the Commerce of the United States of America*, 303. Between 1826 and 1832, £1 was on average = $4.875 (https://www.measuringworth.com/exchange/).

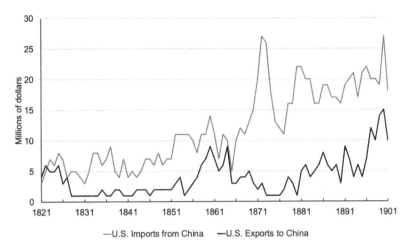

FIGURE A7. US-China trade, by value, 1821–1901. Carter et al., *HSUS*, Ee546, Ee564.

FIGURE A8. Total US-China trade (imports plus exports) as a percentage of total US foreign trade (imports plus exports), 1821–1901. Carter et al., *HSUS*, Ee533, Ee546, Ee551, Ee564.

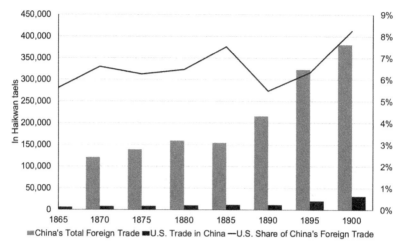

FIGURE A9. US trade in China as a share of China's total foreign trade, 1865–1900. Liang-lin Hsiao, *China's Foreign Trade Statistics, 1864–1949* (Cambridge, MA: East Asian Research Center, Harvard University, 1974), 22–23, 162–63. Hsiao's figures summarize various reports issued by the Chinese Imperial Maritime Customs Service, a government agency staffed and organized by foreigners at senior levels, but under the control of the Qing imperial court.

Notes

Introduction

1. Thomas Handasyd Perkins Papers, Massachusetts Historical Society, ser. 3, Bound Volumes, reel 4, vol. 26, Diary, July 18, 1846 (Saratoga Springs), 56–57.

2. For a full exploration of the Canton system's history and development, see Paul Arthur Van Dyke, *The Canton Trade: Life and Enterprise on the China Coast, 1700–1845* (Hong Kong: Hong Kong University Press, 2005).

3. Charles Toogood Downing, *The Fan-Qui in China* (London: Colburn, 1838), 3:225.

4. R. G. W. Jewell, "Canton," in *Commercial Relations of the United States with Foreign Countries [CRUS]* (Washington, DC: Government Printing Office, n.d.), 1872, 127.

5. Thomas Handasyd Perkins to Robert Bennet Forbes, Boston, February 14, 1840, in Thomas Handasyd Perkins Papers, Massachusetts Historical Society, ser. 1, Loose Papers, 1789–1853, reel 2 (box 2), folder 10, part 1.

6. Carl Seaburg and Stanley Paterson, *Merchant Prince of Boston: Colonel T. H. Perkins, 1764–1854*, Harvard Studies in Business History 26 (Cambridge, MA: Harvard University Press, 1971), 37–44. Magee had made himself in demand as a shipmaster through daring privateering and blockade-running escapades during the war and by captaining—and nearly dying on—the ship that carried the first US consul to China. Henry Lee, "The Magee Family and the Origins of the China Trade," *Proceedings of the Massachusetts Historical Society*, ser. 3, 81 (January 1, 1969): 104–6.

7. Thomas Handasyd Perkins Papers, Massachusetts Historical Society, ser. 3, Bound Volumes, reel 4, vol. 26, Diary, July 18, 1846 (Saratoga Springs), 28.

8. George Granville Putnam, "Salem Vessels and Their Voyages: The Ship *Astrea* of Salem," *Essex Institute Historical Collections* 60, no. 3 (July 1924): 193–94. On the *Astrea*'s size, see "To be Sold, by Elias Hasket Derby, the fast-sailing Ship *Astrea*, about 360 tons," *Columbian Centinel* (Boston), July 7, 1790.

9. For a recent analysis of the political valences of independently acquired tea, see Jane T. Merritt, *The Trouble with Tea: The Politics of Consumption in the Eighteenth-Century Global Economy* (Baltimore: Johns Hopkins University Press, 2016).

10. "Donation of Curiosities," *Columbian Centinel* (Boston), August 28, 1790, 3.

11. "Manifest of the Cargo on Board Ship *Astrea* . . ." in Putnam, "Salem Vessels and Their Voyages: The Ship *Astrea* of Salem," 194–96. The rest of the ship's cargo comprised a diverse array of consumables salable at any port (beer, wine, butter, chocolate, tar, fish, steel, beef, flour, tobacco) and some more specialized manufactured goods, including handkerchiefs,

196 * NOTES TO PAGES 8–15

women's shoes, and "one phaeton and harness complete, with saddles, bridles, etc." On the *Astrea*'s departure, see "Ship News," *Salem* (MA) *Mercury*, February 17, 1789. For a brilliant analysis of how social and family networks structured this venture—and the American China trade generally—see Rachel Tamar Van, "Free Trade and Family Values: Kinship Networks and the Culture of Early American Capitalism" (PhD diss., Columbia University, New York, 2011), 52–61.

12. Elias Hasket Derby to Capt. James Magee Jr. and Mr. Thomas H. Perkins, Salem, February 1789, in Putnam, "Salem Vessels and Their Voyages: The Ship *Astrea* of Salem," 196–200.

13. For an example of Perkins comparing his travel to published accounts see June 16, 1789, in Journal of Thomas Handasyd Perkins, 1789, Thomas Handasyd Perkins travel diaries, Massachusetts Historical Society, available through *China, America and the Pacific* (Adam Matthew Digital). Perkins's preferred reference was William Herbert, William Nichelson, and Samuel Dunn, *A New Directory for the East-Indies*, 5th ed. (London: H. Gregory, 1780). Guides like Dunn's were "methodized, corrected, and further enlarged" by the collection of standardized data of the kind Perkins compiled using his preprinted log book produced by "James Hawkins, No. 8, Well Court, Queen Street, Cheapside."

14. For a sustained consideration of these port cities in their early modern configurations through to the late eighteenth century, see Leonard Blussé, *Visible Cities: Canton, Nagasaki, and Batavia and the Coming of the Americans* (Cambridge, MA: Harvard University Press, 2008).

15. On the *Astrea*'s return, see "Maritime Intelligence," *Salem Gazette*, June 1, 1790.

16. Petitions of Elias Hasket Derby, Salem, Mass., June 10, 1789, June 23, 1790, in Linda De Pauw et al., eds., *Documentary History of the First Federal Congress of the United States of America, March 4, 1789-March 3, 1791* (Baltimore: Johns Hopkins University Press, 1972), 8:407–8.

17. 1 Stat. 145, "An Act: To provide more effectually for the collection of the duties imposed by law on goods, wares, and merchandise imported into the United States, and on the tonnage of ships or vessels" (August 4, 1790); 1 Stat. 219, "An Act: Making farther provision for the collection of the duties by law imposed on teas, and to prolong the term for the payment of the duties on wines" (March 3, 1791); De Pauw et al., *Documentary History of the First Federal Congress*, 8:403–11; Walter Lowrie and Matthew St. Clair Clarke, eds., *American State Papers: Finance* (Washington, DC: Gales and Seaton, 1832), 1:107; Seaburg and Paterson, *Merchant Prince of Boston*, 56.

18. Report of the Secretary of the Treasury, March 2, 1791, in De Pauw et al., *Documentary History of the First Federal Congress*, 8:411.

19. Gautham Rao, *National Duties: Custom Houses and the Making of the American State*, American Beginnings, 1500–1900 (Chicago: University of Chicago Press, 2016).

20. Thomas Handasyd Perkins Papers, Massachusetts Historical Society, ser. 3, Bound Volumes, reel 4, vol. 26, Diary, July 18, 1846 (Saratoga Springs), 49. Joseph Ingraham, fresh from his experience in the Pacific Northwest as chief mate of the Boston ship *Columbia Rediviva*, was his key informant.

Chapter One

1. John Adams to Secretary Livingston, Paris, July 16, 1783, in "M247: Papers of the Continental Congress, 1774–1789," Records of the Continental and Confederation Congresses and Constitutional Convention, RG 360, National Archives, 1957, reel 113, item 84, 5:1–7; reprinted

in John Adams, *The Works of John Adams, Second President of the United States: With a Life of the Author, Notes and Illustrations*, ed. Charles Francis Adams (Boston: Little, Brown, 1850), 8:99–103.

2. The business and sailing of the *Empress of China*'s voyage is most fully described in Philip Chadwick Foster Smith, *The Empress of China* (Philadelphia: Philadelphia Maritime Museum, 1984). Many other historians have touched on the venture: Kenneth Scott Latourette, *The History of Early Relations between the United States and China, 1784–1844*, Transactions of the Connecticut Academy of Arts and Sciences 22 (New Haven, CT: Yale University Press, 1917); Tyler Dennett, *Americans in Eastern Asia: A Critical Study of the Policy of the United States with Reference to China, Japan, and Korea in the 19th Century* (New York: Macmillan, 1922); "Appendix I: Early Records of Robert Morris's Involvement in American Trade with China," in Robert Morris, *The Papers of Robert Morris, 1781–1784*, ed. E. James Ferguson (Pittsburgh: University of Pittsburgh Press, 1973), 8:857–82; Jacques M. Downs, *The Golden Ghetto: The American Commercial Community at Canton and the Shaping of American China Policy, 1784–1844* (Bethlehem, PA: Lehigh University Press, 1997); James R. Fichter, *So Great a Proffit: How the East Indies Trade Transformed Anglo-American Capitalism* (Cambridge, MA: Harvard University Press, 2010); Kariann Akemi Yokota, *Unbecoming British: How Revolutionary America Became a Postcolonial Nation* (New York: Oxford University Press, 2011); John Rogers Haddad, *America's First Adventure in China: Trade, Treaties, Opium, and Salvation* (Philadelphia: Temple University Press, 2013).

3. Mariners from British North America had traded in Asian waters before. The voyages by "Red Sea men" (so called because they practiced piracy near the Horn of Africa) were a source of Asian goods for the Atlantic world into the eighteenth century. Caroline Frank, *Objectifying China, Imagining America: Chinese Commodities in Early America* (Chicago: University of Chicago Press, 2012), 27–57.

4. On the formal end of the War of Independence see Francis Wharton, ed., *The Revolutionary Diplomatic Correspondence of the United States* (Washington, DC: Government Printing Office, 1889), 6:754–57. The *Empress* got under way on Sunday, February 22, 1784. Samuel Shaw, *The Journals of Major Samuel Shaw: The First American Consul at Canton; with a Life of the Author*, ed. Josiah Quincy (Boston: Crosby and Nichols, 1847), 133–34; Smith, *Empress of China*, 3. Smith notes that the ship departed on George Washington's birthday, as calculated by the revised Gregorian calendar—a coincidence, as the *Empress* had been trying to leave port for days. On the ship's design and characteristics, see Smith, *Empress of China*, 25–26, 67, 129, 306n15; Shaw, *Journals of Major Samuel Shaw*, 337.

5. Dael A. Norwood, "The Constitutional Consequences of Commercial Crisis: The Role of Trade Reconsidered in the 'Critical Period,'" *Early American Studies* 18, no. 4 (Fall 2020): 490–524.

6. On the role of China goods for North American consumers in the colonial and revolutionary eras, see Frank, *Objectifying China, Imagining America*, and Yokota, *Unbecoming British*. On the place of China among American philosophes, see Alfred Owen Aldridge, *The Dragon and the Eagle: The Presence of China in the American Enlightenment* (Detroit: Wayne State University Press, 1993).

7. Fichter, *So Great a Proffit*, 45–55. Fichter argues that this moment of "public economy" was short-lived, as merchants quickly abandoned the idea of accomplishing public goals as well as private profit in the wake of the difficulties faced by the *Empress* and other early ventures. However, Fichter's periodization does not fully account for policymakers' continued zealous interest in the trade, or for its incorporation into several successive schemes for reshaping American political economy. This separation is likely a product of the chronology of his work,

which focuses on the period from 1784 to 1815—and thus closes before the commerce's political stock rose again in the 1830s.

8. Robert Morris to John Jay, Philadelphia, November 27, 1783, in John Jay, *The Correspondence and Public Papers of John Jay*, ed. Henry Phelps Johnston (New York: Putnam's, 1890), 3:96–97.

9. "Philadelphia, February 28," *Maryland Journal and Baltimore Advertiser*, March 5, 1784.

10. According to Smith, accounts of the *Empress*'s return cargo differ in their particulars, in some cases by a great deal; but the common thread is that teas made up most of the cargo, by bulk and value, followed by silks and nankeens (cotton cloths), and finally by porcelain—the classic items, in the classic proportions, of the American China trade. Smith, *Empress of China*, 172–73. For a sample of newspaper commentary on the ship's return, see *New York News Dispatch*, May 12, 1785, as quoted in Smith, *Empress of China*, 224–25. The *Dispatch* article was reprinted: "New-York," *Independent Journal* (New York, NY), May 14, 1785; "New York, May 12," *New-Jersey Gazette* (Burlington, NJ), May 16, 1785; and "New York, May 12," *Connecticut Courant* (Hartford, CT), May 16, 1785.

11. Drew R. McCoy, *The Elusive Republic: Political Economy in Jeffersonian America* (Chapel Hill: University of North Carolina Press, 1980), 88.

12. Richard Henry Lee to Samuel Adams, New York, May 20, 1785, in Paul Hubert Smith, ed., *Letters of Delegates to Congress, 1774–1789* (Washington, DC: Library of Congress, 1976), 22:397. Lee also discussed the *Empress*'s voyage in letters to Thomas Jefferson, John Adams, and James Madison, among others. See Smith, *Letters of Delegates to Congress*, 22:392–93, 409–10, 417–18. Lee's interest in Asian trade was of long standing; while serving on the Committee for Foreign Affairs in 1777, he recommended that new French-built ships be used to harass British shipping in China; see Committee for Foreign Affairs to Commissioners at Paris, York Town, Pennsylvania, December 2, 1777, in Smith, *Letters of Delegates to Congress*, 8:367.

13. "On the First American Ship, (*Empress of China*, Capt. Greene) That Explored the Rout to China, and the East Indies, After the Revolution, 1784," in Philip Freneau, *Poems Written and Published during the American Revolutionary War*, 3rd ed. (Philadelphia: Lydia R. Bailey, 1809), 2:181–82. The poem's opening gives a sense of Freneau's intent: "With clearance from Bellona won / She spreads her wings to meet the Sun, / Those golden regions to explore / Where George forbade to sail before."

14. South Carolina Delegates [Charles Pinckney, David Ramsay, John Kean] to William Moultrie, New York, January 28, 1786, in Smith, *Letters of Delegates to Congress*, 23:115–16.

15. William Grayson to James Madison, New York, May 28, 1785, in Smith, *Letters of Delegates to Congress*, 22:406–7.

16. June 9, 1785, Worthington Chauncey Ford et al., eds., *Journals of the Continental Congress, 1774–1789* [JCC] (Washington, DC: Government Printing Office, 1904), 28:442–43; Charles Thomson to John Jay, New York, June 16, 1785, and John Jay to Samuel Shaw, New York, June 23, 1785, in United States, *The Diplomatic Correspondence of the United States of America: From the Signing of the Definitive Treaty of Peace, September 10, 1783, to the Adoption of the Constitution, March 4, 1789*, ed. William Weaver (Washington, DC: Blair and Rives, 1837), 7:436–37; MSS. of these letters can be found in *M247: Papers of the Cont. Congress*, reel 28, i19, 5:323 and reel 68, i55, p. 275.

17. Appendix, fig. A1, "American Ships at Canton, 1784–1814."

18. Paul Arthur Van Dyke, "Bookkeeping as a Window into Efficiencies of Early Modern Trade: Europeans, Americans and Others in China Compared, 1700–1842," in *Narratives of Free Trade: The Commercial Cultures of Early US-China Relations*, ed. Kendall Johnson (Hong Kong: Hong Kong University Press, 2012), 17–31; Downs, *Golden Ghetto*; Rhys Richards, Mary

Malloy, and Briton C. Busch, "United States Trade with China 1784–1814," *American Neptune*, 54, no. 1 (Winter 1994): 5–74.

19. Wingrove does not appear to have ever suggested a full-fledged monopoly corporation, though others appear to have tried (unsuccessfully) to create a corporation with a name that suggested that purpose. See Rufus King to John Adams, New York, February 3, 1786, in Smith, *Letters of Delegates to Congress*, 23:132. Richard Henry Lee to John Adams, Chantilly, December 12, 1785, in Richard Henry Lee, *The Letters of Richard Henry Lee*, ed. James Curtis Ballagh (New York: Macmillan, 1911), 2:408; East India Company of North America, *Constitutional Articles of the Association of the East India Company of North-America* (Philadelphia: John Ward Fenno, 1799). Cf. Fichter, *So Great a Proffit*, 39, 146.

20. Samuel Shaw to John Jay, New York, May 19, 1785, in Shaw, *Journals of Major Samuel Shaw*, 337–41. Mathew Carey later published Shaw's reports: Samuel Shaw, "Letter from Mr. Shaw, Agent for the Owners of the Ship *Empress of China*, in Her Voyage to Canton, Addressed to John Jay, Esq. New York, May 19, 1785," *American Museum, or Universal Magazine* 1, no. 3 (March 1787): 194–97.

21. Samuel Shaw to John Jay, New York, May 19, 1785, in Shaw, *Journals of Major Samuel Shaw*, 338. This treatment led Jay to recommend to Congress that the US minister to France, Thomas Jefferson, tender formal thanks for "these pleasing Acts of Kindness," which he did. John Jay to the President of Congress, September 1, 1785, in Ford et al., *JCC*, 29:673–74; Thomas Jefferson to Comte de Vergennes, Paris, October 21, 1785, in Thomas Jefferson, *The Papers of Thomas Jefferson*, ed. Julian P. Boyd, Main Series (Princeton: Princeton University Press, 1953), 8:656.

22. Some even went so far as to report that the British were the first to salute the American flag upon its appearance at Whampoa Reach, Canton's anchorage. "New York, May 12," *Connecticut Courant* (Hartford, CT), May 16, 1785.

23. Emphasis in original. Samuel Shaw to John Jay, New York, May 19, 1785, in Shaw, *Journals of Major Samuel Shaw*, 338. For an analysis of this anxiety about identity expressed in China and through Chinese goods, see Yokota, *Unbecoming British*, 115–52.

24. John Adams to Richard Henry Lee, September 6, 1785, and John Adams to John Jay, November 11, 1785, in *The Adams Papers*, ed. Gregg L. Lint, C. James Taylor, Sara Georgini, Hobson Woodward, Sara B. Sikes, Amanda A. Mathews, and Sara Martin, *Papers of John Adams* (Cambridge, MA: Harvard University Press, 2014), 17:412–13, 584–85.

25. Samuel Shaw to John Jay, Canton, December 21, 1787 in Shaw, *Journals of Major Samuel Shaw*, 353–54.

26. John Jay, "No. 4," in Alexander Hamilton, James Madison, and John Jay, *The Federalist*, ed. George W. Carey and James McClellan, Gideon ed. (Indianapolis: Liberty Fund, 2001), 14. Jay had expressed similar fears in correspondence with Jefferson. John Jay to Thomas Jefferson, New York, July 14, 1786, in Jefferson, *Jefferson Papers: Main Series*, 10:135.

27. On nationalists' efforts to push back against their opponents on the issue of economic freedom, see Cathy D. Matson and Peter S. Onuf, *A Union of Interests: Political and Economic Thought in Revolutionary America*, American Political Thought (Lawrence: University Press of Kansas, 1990), 76–81.

28. John Adams to Thomas Jefferson, Braintree, March 1, 1789, in Jefferson, *Jefferson Papers: Main Series*, 14:599; "Annapolis Convention: Address of the Annapolis Convention," in Alexander Hamilton, *The Papers of Alexander Hamilton*, ed. Harold Coffin Syrett and Jacob Ernest Cooke (New York: Columbia University Press, 1962), 3:686–690; February 21, 1787, in Ford et al., *JCC*, 32:71–74.

29. These were the second, third, and fifth laws passed by Congress, respectively; the first

act passed was to regulate oaths: 1 Stat. 23, "An Act: To regulate the time and manner of administering certain oaths" (June 1, 1789); Tariff: 1 Stat. 24, "An Act: For laying a duty on goods, wares, and merchandises imported into the United States" (July 4, 1789); Tonnage, 1 Stat. 27, "An Act: Imposing duties on tonnage" (July 20, 1789); Collection, 1 Stat. 29, "An Act: To regulate the collection of the duties imposed by law on the tonnage of ships or vessels, and on goods, wares, and merchandise" (July 31, 1789).

30. Before the advent of the federal income tax, scholarship on the history of American commercial policy was a thriving subfield of economic and political history; since 1913 the subject has been less thoroughly examined. Helpful analyses of the first Congress's actions include Frank William Taussig, *The Tariff History of the United States: A Series of Essays* (New York: Putnam's, 1888); William Hill, "The First Stages of the Tariff Policy of the United States," *Publications of the American Economic Association* 8, no. 6 (November 1, 1893): 9–162; Edward Stanwood, *American Tariff Controversies in the Nineteenth Century*, 2 vols. (Boston: Houghton, Mifflin, 1903); Leonard Dupee White, *The Federalists: A Study in Administrative History* (New York: Macmillan, 1948); Douglass C. North, *The Economic Growth of the United States, 1790–1860* (New York: Norton, 1966); Merrill D. Peterson, "Thomas Jefferson and Commercial Policy, 1783–1793," *William and Mary Quarterly*, ser. 3, 22, no. 4 (October 1, 1965): 584–610; Vernon G. Setser, *The Commercial Reciprocity Policy of the United States, 1774–1829* (1937; repr., New York: Da Capo Press, 1969); Jacob Ernest Cooke, *Tench Coxe and the Early Republic* (Chapel Hill: University of North Carolina Press, 1978), 134–39; John R. Nelson, *Liberty and Property: Political Economy and Policymaking in the New Nation, 1789–1812* (Baltimore: Johns Hopkins University Press, 1987); Drew R. McCoy, "Republicanism and American Foreign Policy: James Madison and the Political Economy of Commercial Discrimination, 1789 to 1794," *William and Mary Quarterly*, ser. 3, 31, no. 4 (October 1, 1974): 633–46; McCoy, *Elusive Republic*; Matson and Onuf, *Union of Interests*; Stanley Elkins and Eric McKitrick, *The Age of Federalism: The Early American Republic, 1788–1800* (New York: Oxford University Press, 1993); Robin L. Einhorn, *American Taxation, American Slavery* (Chicago: University of Chicago Press, 2006), 111–56; Douglas A. Irwin, *Clashing over Commerce: A History of U.S. Trade Policy* (Chicago: University of Chicago Press, 2017). There has been some dissent from this general framework among diplomatic historians, but it has been muted. See James A. Field, "1789–1820: All Œconomists, All Diplomats," in *Economics and World Power: An Assessment of American Diplomacy since 1789*, ed. William H. Becker and Samuel F. Wells, Political Economy of International Change (New York: Columbia University Press, 1984), 12.

31. Elkins and McKitrick correctly note that the debates over the tariff of 1789 were conducted with "a minimum of hard feelings," but they imply that this cordiality was due to an absence of political import. This gets things backward: that the tariff schedule passed with relatively little struggle demonstrates that commercial regulation was regarded as crucial to factions across the political spectrum. Minutes of debate can reveal critical agreements as well as fractures. Elkins and McKitrick, *Age of Federalism*, 65–66.

32. June 11, 1789, in William Maclay, *Journal of William Maclay, United States Senator from Pennsylvania, 1789–1791*, ed. Edgar S. Maclay (New York: Appleton, 1890), 73.

33. The tariff discrimination was a revised version of an idea floated in the April 1784 congressional report on commerce. See April 22, 1784, in Ford et al., *JCC*, 26:269–71.

34. Einhorn, *American Taxation, American Slavery*, 117–56, esp. 117, 120, 150–51, and 293n4.

35. Einhorn, *American Taxation, American Slavery*, 111–56. On Madison's clever debate management, see 153.

36. 1 Annals of Congress 185 (April 21, 1789).

37. 1 Stat. 25; cf. Stanwood, *American Tariff Controversies in the Nineteenth Century*, 1:59.

38. In differentiating between varieties and modes of transport, these rates built on precedent already established by several states, including New York, Pennsylvania, and South Carolina. Albert Anthony Giesecke, *American Commercial Legislation Before 1789* (Philadelphia: University of Pennsylvania, 1910), 130; Latourette, *History of Early Relations between the United States and China, 1784–1844*, 78n138; Stanwood, *American Tariff Controversies in the Nineteenth Century*, 1:62–71.

39. 1 Stat. 25, "An Act: For laying a duty on goods, wares, and merchandises imported into the United States" (July 4, 1789); 1 Stat. 180, "An Act: Making further provision for the payment of the debt of the United States" (August 10, 1790).

40. 1 Stat. 26.

41. Thomas Fitzsimons to Tench Coxe, New York, April 25, 1789, in Linda De Pauw et al., eds., *Documentary History of the First Federal Congress of the United States of America, March 4, 1789–March 3, 1791* (Baltimore: Johns Hopkins University Press, 1972), 15:354–55. Madison, too, was aware of the importance of a drawback for US commerce; one of his influential correspondents, Tench Coxe, advised him that "it appears necessary." See Tench Coxe, "Notes on American Revenue," March 24, 1789, in De Pauw et al., *Documentary History of the First Federal Congress*, 15:104.

42. Oddly—or perhaps not, given the smallness of the early republic—Fitzsimons and Robert Morris each represented equal 50 percent shares of the final dispensation of the *Empress of China*'s cargo: Morris on his own account as an original investor, and Fitzsimons as the assignee of Daniel Parker and Company, whose proprietor had fled the United States as a bankrupt before the *Empress*'s return. See Shaw, *Journals of Major Samuel Shaw*, 217–18. For the questions Parker's case raises about mercantile practice and honor, see Tom Cutterham, "'A Very Promising Appearance': Credit, Honor, and Deception in the Emerging Market for American Debt, 1784–92," *William and Mary Quarterly*, 3rd ser. 75, no. 4 (November 1, 2018): 623–50.

43. On Fitzsimons's political associations, see E. Wayne Carp, "Fitzsimons, Thomas," in *American National Biography Online*, February 2000.

44. 1 Annals of Congress 141 (April 14, 1789).

45. Edward Dewey Graham, *American Ideas of a Special Relationship with China, 1784–1900*, Harvard Dissertations in American History and Political Science (New York: Garland, 1988), 17.

46. 1 Annals of Congress 169 (April 18, 1789).

47. 1 Annals of Congress 170 (April 18, 1789).

48. During a discussion of the drawback provision of the tariff—which Madison opposed in general—he conceded that he "thought that there were very few cases in which drawbacks ought to be allowed, perhaps none but what related to the East India trade." See 1 Annals of Congress 174 (April 20, 1789).

49. Thomas Fitzsimons to Tench Coxe, New York, April 25, 1789, in De Pauw et al., *Documentary History of the First Federal Congress*, 15:354–55.

50. "It is something like a perversion of history to represent that there was substantial unanimity in Congress upon the act, or that it embodied a 'compromise.'" Stanwood, *American Tariff Controversies in the Nineteenth Century*, 1:71.

51. June 5, 1789, and June 8, 1789, in Maclay, *Journal of William Maclay*, 67–68, 71. See also 1 Annals of Congress 45 (June 8, 1789).

52. The reason for their behavior may have been tactical; the diarist William Maclay thought they were trying to delay a bill for their own reasons. June 5, 1789, in Maclay, *Journal of William Maclay*, 68.

53. June 5, 1789, and June 8, 1789, in Maclay, *Journal of William Maclay*, 67–68, 71.

54. On Butler's suspicion of the utility of the "India" trade in service of the general interest, see June 9, 1789, in Maclay, *Journal of William Maclay*, 71–72; "Notes of Pierce Butler . . . ," June 9, 1789, in De Pauw et al., *Documentary History of the First Federal Congress* (Baltimore: Johns Hopkins University Press, 1988), 9:452.

55. For example, although Morris declared he was "in sentiment" with Dalton's monopoly proposal, he opposed it because it had not been demonstrated to be necessary. June 9, 1789, in Maclay, *Journal of William Maclay*, 71–72; "Notes of Pierce Butler . . . ," June 9, 1789, in De Pauw et al., *Documentary History of the First Federal Congress*, 9:452.

56. Emphasis mine. June 1, 1789, in Maclay, *Journal of William Maclay*, 60–61. For more on Maclay and his point of view, see De Pauw et al., *Documentary History of the First Federal Congress*, 9:ix–xviii.

57. Of students of Americans' China commerce, only Graham offers an in-depth analysis of the tariff. See Edward Dewey Graham, "Special Interests and the Early China Trade," *Michigan Academician* 6, no. 2 (Fall 1973): 233–42; Graham, *American Ideas of a Special Relationship with China*, 13–21.

58. Mathew Carey, *The New Olive Branch* (Philadelphia: Carey, 1820), 214–16.

59. Arthur Lee to Francis Lightfoot Lee, May 9, 1789, in De Pauw et al., *Documentary History of the First Federal Congress*, 15:491–93.

60. John Wendell to Elbridge Gerry, Portsmouth, NH, July 23, 1789 in De Pauw et al., *Documentary History of the First Federal Congress*, 16:1120.

61. May 10, June 3, June 5, 1789, in Maclay, *Journal of William Maclay*, 29, 63, 67. Maclay also suspected Richard Henry Lee of using the same delaying maneuvers as Morris and Fitzsimons.

62. On Hamilton's statements on Asian trade as it mattered to the nation's finances, see Alexander Hamilton, *The Works of Alexander Hamilton*, ed. Henry Cabot Lodge, Federal ed. (New York: Putnam's, 1904), 2: 272–73, 277, 279, 291–327, 349–51; "Report of the Secretary of the Treasury, March 2, 1791," in De Pauw et al., *Documentary History of the First Federal Congress*, 8:411. For a summary of legislation and federal government acts related to Americans' Asian commerce, see Latourette, *History of Early Relations between the United States and China, 1784–1844*, 78n138.

63. For example, extensions on duty payments were allowed in 1790 and recommended by Hamilton in his second report on public credit. See 1 Stat. 145, "An Act to provide more effectually for the collection of the duties imposed by law on goods, wares, and merchandise imported into the United States, and on the tonnage of ships or vessels" (August 4, 1790), and "Report on Public Credit" in Hamilton, *Works of Alexander Hamilton*, 2:349–51.

The government's lenience was the result of lobbying by Elias Hasket Derby, a prominent Salem merchant who found himself underwater on his duty payments because he overestimated the American market for teas. "Collection Act [HR-11]: Duties on Teas," in De Pauw et al., *Documentary History of the First Federal Congress*, 8:403–11. Derby's complaints about competition are echoed in a separate petition in which traders complain that their European competitors were making it impossible to procure insurance for China ventures. "Petition on East India Trade, January 22, 1791," in Thomas C. Cochran, ed., *The New American State Papers: Commerce and Navigation* (Wilmington, DE: Scholarly Resources, 1973), 1:27–28. After the 1790 session, Congress and the Treasury were together much less responsive to additional requests from merchants. "Report on Tea Imports, February 27, 1792," in Cochran, *New American State Papers: Commerce and Navigation*, 1:64. For additional documentation, see 3 Annals of Congress 121, 431, 482, 483, 549–50, 559, 896, 899; *House Journal*, 2nd Cong., 1st Sess., 469, 517, 519, 521, 523, 529–30, 545, 547, 571, 581; *House Journal*, 2nd Cong., 2nd Sess., 720, 734; *Sen-*

ate Journal, 2nd Cong., 1st Sess., 423, 429. This inaction was not all on one side: counterpetitions in favor of lower trade discriminations were also allowed to lie fallow. *House Journal,* 2nd Cong., 1st Sess., March 24, 1792, 541; "Philadelphia, Congress, House of Representatives, Wednesday March 7," *National Gazette,* March 12, 1792 (Philadelphia), 154; 3 Annals of Congress 477 (March 21, 1792). On the politics of federal accommodation of merchants' needs, see Gautham Rao, *National Duties: Custom Houses and the Making of the American State,* American Beginnings, 1500–1900 (Chicago: University of Chicago Press, 2016).

64. June 18, 1789, in Maclay, *Journal of William Maclay,* 82–83; De Pauw et al., *Documentary History of the First Federal Congress,* 9:83. Punctuation and paragraph structure appear to have been added by Maclay's 1890 editor, Edgar S. Maclay.

65. Emphasis in original. George Washington, "Farewell Address," September 17, 1796, in James D. Richardson, ed., *A Compilation of the Messages and Papers of the Presidents, 1789–1908* (New York: Bureau of National Literature and Art, 1908), 1:222.

66. Beginning with Latourette, the trades in these goods have often been described by historians as a series of successive boom-and-bust cycles—a wave of demand for ginseng, then furs, then sandalwood, etc.—with each new commodity taking over for previous items. However, Block's examination of China trade commodities on the California coast suggests that while the peak interest in these commodities might have been successive, ventures trading in the previously fashionable commodity by no means disappeared; rather, their operations were coincident over long periods. Latourette, *History of Early Relations between the United States and China, 1784–1844,* 53–60; Michael D. Block, "New England Merchants, the China Trade, and the Origins of California" (PhD diss., University of Southern California, 2011), 19–20, 202–410. On silver's supposed restraining effect on speculation, see Fichter, *So Great a Profit,* 120–21. On the extension of credit to American traders by Chinese and European partners, see Dan Du, "Green Gold and Paper Gold: Seeking Independence through the Chinese-American Tea Trade, 1784–1815," *Early American Studies: An Interdisciplinary Journal* 16, no. 1 (2018): 151–91.

67. A. Barton Hepburn, *History of Coinage and Currency in the United States and the Perennial Contest for Sound Money* (New York: Macmillan, 1903), 20–33. For estimates on the combined American specie import into Canton, see Appendix, fig. A5, "Imports of Silver to China, by Country, 1719–1833," and "Appendix 3: A Note on the Silver Trade," in Downs, *Golden Ghetto,* 358–60. Downs bases his figures on Hosea Ballou Morse, *The Chronicles of the East India Company: Trading to China, 1635–1834* (Oxford: Clarendon Press, 1926), 4:385; Timothy Pitkin, *A Statistical View of the Commerce of the United States of America* (New Haven, CT: Durrie and Peck, 1835), 303.

68. The hong merchants were the best known to Americans at home and arguably the most important resources for Americans in Canton. Ann Bolbach White, "The Hong Merchants of Canton" (PhD diss., Philadelphia, University of Pennsylvania, 1967); Anthony Ch'en (Ch'en Kuo-tung), *The Insolvency of the Chinese Hong Merchants, 1760–1843,* Institute of Economics Monograph Series 45 (Nanking, Taipei: Institute of Economics, Academica Sinica, 1990); W. E. Cheong, *The Hong Merchants of Canton: Chinese Merchants in Sino-Western Trade,* Nordic Institute of Asian Studies Monograph Series, no. 70 (Richmond, Surrey, UK: Curzon, 1997); John D. Wong, *Global Trade in the Nineteenth Century: The House of Houqua and the Canton System* (Cambridge: Cambridge University Press, 2016). For details on the exhaustive rituals, procedures, and exchanges that made up the Canton system, see Paul Arthur Van Dyke, *The Canton Trade: Life and Enterprise on the China Coast, 1700–1845* (Hong Kong: Hong Kong University Press, 2005), 19–115.

69. For specifics on colonial Asian ports, see Seward W. Livermore, "Early Commercial

and Consular Relations with the East Indies," *Pacific Historical Review* 15, no. 1 (March 1, 1946): 31–58.

70. The merchant in question—a member of the Perkins network—had added "a just and reasonable charge" of 2.5 percent to a customer's bill in light of the potentially "dangerous consequences." In this case the charge was for smuggling slaves from Saint Domingue, but the morality expressed was fungible; the same merchants would go on to found the largest American opium smuggling concern. See Perkins and Burling to William Gray, Cap-Français, December 16, 1787, in James Elliot Cabot, ed., "Extracts from Letterbooks of J. & T. H. Perkins et al.," Boston Athenaeum, available through *China, America and the Pacific* (Adam Matthew Digital) and Thomas Handasyd Perkins Papers, Massachusetts Historical Society, ser. 3, Bound Volumes, 1783–1892, reel 6.

71. For example, see Amasa Delano, *A Narrative of Voyages and Travels, in the Northern and Southern Hemispheres Comprising Three Voyages round the World, Together with a Voyage of Survey and Discovery, in the Pacific Ocean and Oriental Islands* (Boston: E. G. House, for the author, 1817), esp. 562–72. For an analysis of the process of creating mythic figures out of China traders, see Emily Axford Murphy, "'To Keep Our Trading for Our Livelihood': The Derby Family of Salem, Massachusetts, and Their Rise to Power in the British Atlantic World" (PhD diss., Boston University, 2008), 236–50.

72. Coxe's letter was intended to influence policy, and thus it likely exaggerates; forwarded and excerpted, it was intended as much for his business associates as for the information of Thomas Jefferson and John Adams (both then serving out diplomatic terms in Europe). William Coxe Jr. to John Brown Cutting, Summer 1787, in Jefferson, *Jefferson Papers: Main Series*, 13:3–4.

73. Samuel Eliot Morison, "The India Ventures of Fisher Ames, 1794–1804," *Proceedings of the American Antiquarian Society* 37 (April 1927): 14–23.

74. Paul E. Fontenoy, "An 'Experimental' Voyage to China 1785–1787," *American Neptune* 55, no. 4 (September 1995): 295.

75. Jacques M. Downs, "A Study in Failure—Hon. Samuel Snow," *Rhode Island History* 25, no. 1 (1966): 1–8; Jacques M. Downs, "Bad Luck in the China Trade: Peter Wanton Snow," *Rhode Island History* 25, no. 3 (1966): 73–80.

76. The most comprehensive study of American ships at Canton in the years before the War of 1812 lists more than a dozen American ports among the "home" ports of active trading vessels, including (in no particular order) New York, Philadelphia, Boston, Salem, Providence, Newport, Bristol (RI), Baltimore, Nantucket, New Bedford (MA), New Haven, Stonington (CT), and Charleston (SC). In addition to these seaports, American captains often used foreign ports as their base of operations during multiyear voyages, so that Lisbon, London, Canton, Manila, Bombay, and Calcutta, along with the Northwest Coast of North America, Hawaii, and the fur-seal islands off the southern South America are not uncommon as observed points of origin for US vessels arriving at Canton. Rhys Richards et al., "United States Trade with China, 1784–1814," *American Neptune* 54, no. 1 (Winter 1994): 5–74.

77. Amos Porter, *The China Journal of Amos Porter, 1802–1803*, ed. Sally Fisher and Eleanor Broad (Greensboro, VT: Greensboro Historical Society, 1984).

78. Appendix, fig. A1, "American Ships at Canton, 1784–1814."

79. Fichter, *So Great a Proffit*, 149–57. For more on Americans in these ports, see Blussé, *Visible Cities.*

80. Appendix, fig. A2, "Tea exports from Canton to the United States, 1784–1814"; fig. A3, "American exports and imports, to/from Canton, by value, 1795–1820"; fig. A4, "American trade at Canton as a percentage of U.S. foreign trade, 1795–1820."

81. North, *Economic Growth of the United States, 1790–1860*; Curtis P. Nettels, *The Emergence of a National Economy, 1775–1815*, Economic History of the United States 2 (New York: Holt, Rinehart and Winston, 1962).

82. Fichter, *So Great a Proffit*, 151, fig. 6.1 "Percent Share of Known Vessels Arriving in Batavia by Flag, 1793–1807"; Blussé, *Visible Cities*.

83. In 1800 the American traffic surpassed that of the Dutch; however, British trade remained substantially larger than American: thirty thousand tons (combined direct voyage and country trade) to Americans' six thousand tons. That gap closed somewhat in subsequent decades, but even in their best years US traders rarely carried more than one-third of the combined total of Britons conducting "country" (intra-Asian) and direct (West-East) trade. See "Trafic à Wampou," in Louis Dermigny, *La Chine et L'Occident: Le commerce à Canton au XVIIIe siècle, 1719–1833* (Paris: SEVPEN, 1964), 2:523–25.

84. Appendix, fig. A5, "Imports of silver to China, by country, 1719–1833"; Dermigny, *La Chine et L'Occident: Le commerce à Canton au XVIIIe siècle, 1719–1833*, 2:735; Alejandra Irigoin, "The End of a Silver Era: The Consequences of the Breakdown of the Spanish Peso Standard in China and the United States, 1780s-1850s," *Journal of World History* 20, no. 2 (June 1, 2009): 207–43.

85. Appendix, fig. A4, "American trade at Canton as a percentage of US foreign trade, 1795–1820." For data on American trade at Canton, see Pitkin, *Statistical View of the Commerce of the United States of America* (1835), 252, 257–62, 302. Figures on total US imports and exports are from Susan B. Carter et al., eds., *Historical Statistics of the United States: Millennial Edition Online* (New York: Cambridge University Press, 2006), Ee424, Ee365. Field, working only from Pitkin's early (1817) figures for a slightly different period, finds the trade to be a somewhat smaller proportion of exports. Field, "1789–1820: All Œconomists, All Diplomats," 21–22.

Chapter Two

1. John Jay to Thomas Jefferson, New York, April 24, 1787, in Thomas Jefferson, *The Papers of Thomas Jefferson*, ed. Julian P. Boyd (Princeton, NJ: Princeton University Press, 1955), Main Series, 11:313–14.

2. Key works on how ideas about political economy informed partisan division include Major L. Wilson, *Space, Time, and Freedom: The Quest for Nationality and the Irrepressible Conflict, 1815–1861* (Westport, CT: Greenwood Press, 1974); Drew R. McCoy, *The Elusive Republic: Political Economy in Jeffersonian America* (Chapel Hill: University of North Carolina Press, 1980); Andrew Shankman, *Original Intents: Hamilton, Jefferson, Madison, and the American Founding* (New York: Oxford University Press, 2017).

3. John Jay to Thomas Jefferson, New York, July 14, 1786, in Jefferson, *Jefferson Papers: Main Series*, 10:135; John Jay, "No. 4," in Alexander Hamilton, James Madison, and John Jay, *The Federalist*, ed. George W. Carey and James McClellan, Gideon Edition (Indianapolis: Liberty Fund, 2001), 14.

4. Thomas Jefferson to G. K. van Hogendorp, Paris, October 13, 1785, in Jefferson, *Jefferson Papers: Main Series*, 8:631–34; "Notes on the Influence of Extent of Territory on Government," ca. December 1791, in James Madison, *The Papers of James Madison*, ed. William T. Hutchinson (Charlottesville: University of Virginia Press, 1983), Congressional Series, 14:132–33. China and East Indies trade appear briefly, but not substantively, in "Report on Commerce," in Jefferson, *Jefferson Papers: Main Series*, 27:532–81; "Commercial Discrimination," January 14–31, 1794, in Madison, *Madison Papers: Congressional Series*, 15:191, 212, 229–30, 239–40.

5. On the term "merchant-Republican," see Roland M. Baumann, "John Swanwick: Spokes-

man for 'Merchant-Republicanism' in Philadelphia, 1790–1798," *Pennsylvania Magazine of History and Biography* 97, no. 2 (April 1, 1973): 131–82.

6. Key works: Samuel Flagg Bemis, *Jay's Treaty: A Study in Commerce and Diplomacy*, rev. ed. (New Haven, CT: Yale University Press, 1962); Jerald A. Combs, *The Jay Treaty: Political Battleground of the Founding Fathers* (Berkeley: University of California Press, 1970); Todd Estes, *The Jay Treaty Debate, Public Opinion, and the Evolution of Early American Political Culture* (Amherst: University of Massachusetts Press, 2006); Lawrence B. A. Hatter, "The Jay Charter: Rethinking the American National State in the West, 1796–1819," *Diplomatic History* 37, no. 4 (September 1, 2013): 693–726; Amanda C. Demmer, "Trick or Constitutional Treaty? The Jay Treaty and the Quarrel over the Diplomatic Separation of Powers," *Journal of the Early Republic* 35, no. 4 (2015): 579–98.

7. Edmund Randolph, "Instructions to Mr. Jay," Philadelphia, May 6, 1794, in *American State Papers: Foreign Relations*, ed. Walter Lowrie and Matthew St. Clair Clarke, 6 vols. (Washington, DC: Gales and Seaton, 1833), 1:472–73.

8. In the list of "general objects" to be achieved by a treaty, the administration listed "1st. Reciprocity in navigation, particularly to the West Indies and even to the east Indies." Randolph, "Instructions to Mr. Jay (Philadelphia, May 6, 1794)," 473.

9. George Washington to Edmund Randolph, July 22, 1795, in George Washington, *The Papers of George Washington*, ed. Carol S. Ebel (Charlottesville: University of Virginia Press, 2015), Presidential Series, 18:404. Jay himself judged that nothing better was "attainable" in these circumstances. John Jay to Edmund Randolph, London, November 19, 1794, in John Jay, *The Correspondence and Public Papers of John Jay*, ed. Henry Phelps Johnston (New York: Putnam's, 1890), 4:138.

10. "Proceedings of the Boston Chamber of Commerce. . . . held at Their Hall, on Tuesday, August 11, 1795," in Mathew Carey, ed., *The American Remembrancer, or An Impartial Collection of Essays, Resolves, Speeches, &c. Relative, or Having Affinity, to the Treaty with Great Britain* (Philadelphia: H. Tuckniss for M. Carey, 1795), 1:129. Merchants in other cities offered similar sentiments: "The Address of the Subscribers, Merchants, and Traders of the City of Philadelphia," in Carey, *American Remembrancer*, 1:122–25.

11. "The Jay Treaty," in David Hunter Miller, ed., *Treaties and Other International Acts of the United States of America*, Publications of the Department of State (Washington, DC: Government Printing Office, 1931), 2:255.

12. John Jay to Edmund Randolph, London, November 19, 1794, in *Correspondence and Public Papers of John Jay*, 4:142; "Camillus—Nov XXVI," in Carey, *American Remembrancer*, 3:155. There is no consensus on which side introduced Article 13, but historians have tended to agree with Jay that the provision was a concession made by the British—a trade-off made in order to secure the Empire's Atlantic interests. Bemis, *Jay's Treaty*, 293, 355, 417, 469–71; Vernon G. Setser, *The Commercial Reciprocity Policy of the United States, 1774–1829* (1937; repr., New York: Da Capo Press, 1969), 127–30; Holden Furber, "The Beginnings of American Trade with India, 1784–1812," *New England Quarterly* 11, no. 2 (June 1, 1938): 243–45; Susan S. Bean, *Yankee India: American Commercial and Cultural Encounters with India in the Age of Sail, 1784–1860* (Salem, MA: Peabody Essex Museum, 2001), 67–85; James R. Fichter, *So Great a Proffit: How the East Indies Trade Transformed Anglo-American Capitalism* (Cambridge, MA: Harvard University Press, 2010), 177; Jonathan Eacott, *Selling Empire: India in the Making of Britain and America, 1600–1830* (Chapel Hill: University of North Carolina Press, 2016), 336–38.

13. "Remarks on the Treaty . . . by a Citizen of the United States," in Carey, *American Remembrancer*, 3:296.

14. Eacott, *Selling Empire*, 333–81; Furber, "Beginnings of American Trade with India, 1784–1812"; Bean, *Yankee India*.

15. "The Jay Treaty," in Miller, *Treaties and Other International Acts of the United States of America*, 2:256.

16. "Decius—No. IV," in Carey, *American Remembrancer*, 2:136.

17. "Decius—No. V," in Carey, *American Remembrancer*, 2:140. On article 12, see Miller, *Treaties and Other International Acts of the United States of America*, 2:266–73.

18. Samuel Smith of Baltimore, Stephen Girard and John Swanwick of Philadelphia, James Nicholson of New York, and the Crowninshields of Salem, Massachusetts, are all well-documented examples of merchants with Republican sympathies and China trade interests. John S. Pancake, *Samuel Smith and the Politics of Business: 1752–1839* (Tuscaloosa: University of Alabama Press, 1972), 44–46; Jonathan Goldstein, *Stephen Girard's Trade with China, 1787–1824: The Norms versus the Profits of Trade* (Portland, ME: MerwinAsia, 2011); Brenna O'Rourke Holland, "Free Market Family: Gender, Capitalism, and the Life of Stephen Girard" (PhD diss., Temple University, 2014); Baumann, "John Swanwick"; William T. Whitney, "The Crowninshields of Salem, 1800–1808: A Study in the Politics of Commercial Growth," *Essex Institute Historical Collections* 94, nos. 1–2 (1958): 1–36, 79–118. For more on the determinants of merchants' political sympathies, see John R. Nelson, *Liberty and Property: Political Economy and Policymaking in the New Nation, 1789–1812* (Baltimore: Johns Hopkins University Press, 1987), 90–93; James A. Field, "1789–1820: All Œconomists, All Diplomats," in *Economics and World Power: An Assessment of American Diplomacy since 1789*, ed. William H. Becker and Samuel F. Wells, Political Economy of International Change (New York: Columbia University Press, 1984), 1–54.

19. Tench Coxe to Thomas Jefferson, Philadelphia, February 17, 1802, in Jefferson, *Jefferson Papers: Main Series*, 36:600. Other examples of his memorandums are in Jefferson, *Jefferson Papers: Main Series*, 35:264, 36:41–42, 562–63, 600–601, 623–25. My thanks to James P. McClure, general editor at the *Papers of Thomas Jefferson*, for first pointing me to Coxe's memos.

20. The best description and analysis of Coxe's contribution to Jefferson's signal policy document as secretary of state can be found in the Jefferson papers: "Report on Commerce," in Jefferson, *Jefferson Papers: Main Series*, 27:532–81.

21. Jacob Ernest Cooke, *Tench Coxe and the Early Republic* (Chapel Hill: University of North Carolina Press, 1978), 100–108 et passim; Lawrence A. Peskin, *Manufacturing Revolution: The Intellectual Origins of Early American Industry*, Studies in Early American Economy and Society from the Library Company of Philadelphia (Baltimore: Johns Hopkins University Press, 2003), 93–118 et passim.

22. Tench Coxe to Thomas Jefferson, Philadelphia, February 22, 1802, in Jefferson, *Jefferson Papers: Main Series*, 36:623–25.

23. Thomas Jefferson, *Notes on the State of Virginia*, ed. William Peden (Chapel Hill: University of North Carolina Press, 1955), 165.

24. Tench Coxe to Thomas Jefferson, Philadelphia, March 1, 1802, in Jefferson, *Jefferson Papers: Main Series*, 36:664–66.

25. William Jones to James Madison, Philadelphia, February 23, 1805, in James Madison, *The Papers of James Madison*, ed. Mary A. Hackett (Charlottesville: University of Virginia Press, 1986), Secretary of State Series, 9:62–64.

26. Thomas Jefferson to Meriwether Lewis, June 20, 1803, reprinted in Thomas Jefferson, *The Writings of Thomas Jefferson*, ed. Andrew Adgate Lipscomb, Albert Ellery Bergh, and Richard Holland Johnston (Washington, DC: Thomas Jefferson Memorial Association of the United States, 1903), 18:148–49, 154–55. Lewis understood his chief's interests, and his report upon returning to the Mississippi Valley focused on the practicality of using a continental portage to access the markets of the East Indies (he judged a portage across the Rocky Moun-

tains impractical). Meriwether Lewis to Thomas Jefferson, September 23, 1806, in *Original Journals of the Lewis and Clark Expedition, 1804–1806*, ed. Reuben Gold Thwaites (New York: Antiquarian Press, 1959), 7:335. See also Joseph Schafer, "The Western Ocean and Oregon History," in *The Pacific Ocean in History: Papers and Addresses Presented at the Panama-Pacific Historical Congress Held at San Francisco, Berkeley and Palo Alto, California, July 19–23, 1915*, ed. Henry Morse Stephens and Herbert Eugene Bolton (New York: Macmillan, 1917), 289–91; Henry Nash Smith, *Virgin Land: The American West as Symbol and Myth* (Cambridge, MA: Harvard University Press, 1950), 20–21.

27. Setser, *Commercial Reciprocity Policy of the United States, 1774–1829*, 161–62; Donald R. Hickey, "The Monroe-Pinkney Treaty of 1806: A Reappraisal," *William and Mary Quarterly*, ser. 3, 44, no. 1 (January 1, 1987): 70–73; Gordon S. Wood, *Empire of Liberty: A History of the Early Republic, 1789–1815*, Oxford History of the United States (New York: Oxford University Press, 2009), 624–25, 640.

28. James Monroe to Secretary of State [Madison], London, October 18, 1805, in James Monroe, *The Writings of James Monroe, Including a Collection of His Public and Private Papers and Correspondence Now for the First Time Printed*, ed. Stanislaus Murray Hamilton (New York: Putnam's, 1898), 4:361–62.

29. Edward Carrington et al. to His Excellency John Tuck, Governor of the Province of Canton, Canton, October 23, 1805, Enclosure, Edward Carrington to James Madison, Secretary of State, Canton, November 25, 1805, in "M101: Despatches from U.S. Consuls in Canton, China, 1790–1906," General Records of the Department of State, RG 59, National Archives, 1964, reel 1. This and similar material are also excerpted in "Political Relations between the United States and China," H.R. Exec. Doc. 71, 26th Cong., 2nd Sess. (January 25, 1841).

30. Edward Carrington to Samuel Snow, Canton, November 26, 1806, in "M101: Despatches from Canton," reel 1.

31. Walter Lowrie and Matthew St. Clair Clarke, eds., *American State Papers: Foreign Relations* (Washington, DC: Gales and Seaton, 1833), 2:737–73; Merchants of Baltimore, *Message from the President of the United States Transmitting a Memorial of the Merchants of Baltimore on the Violation of Our Neutral Rights; January 29th, 1806, Read, and Committed to a Committee of the Whole House, on the State of the Union* (Washington, DC: Way, 1806); *Memorial of the Merchants of the Town of Boston in the State of Massachusetts, February 3, 1806* (Washington, DC: Way, 1806).

32. For example, the account of the seizure and condemnation of the *Indus*, returning to Boston from Batavia by way of Mauritius (a common route) in *Memorial of the Merchants of the Town of Boston*, 6.

33. James Madison to James Monroe, Department of State, July 17, 1807, in James Madison, *The Writings of James Madison, Comprising His Public Papers and His Private Correspondence, Including Numerous Letters and Documents Now for the First Time Printed*, ed. Galliard Hunt (New York: Putnam's, 1900), 7:463.

34. Bradford Perkins, *Prologue to War: England and the United States, 1805–1812* (Berkeley: University of California Press, 1961), 106–17.

35. James Madison to James Monroe and William Pinkney, Department of State, May 17, 1806, in Madison, *Writings of James Madison*, 7:375–95. Other items of concern in Madison's instructions—a list described by one historian as "ridiculous" and by another as "largely an exercise in wishful thinking"—included a narrower definition of a blockade, a wider understanding of the extent of American territorial waters, and the settlement of existing spoliation claims. Bradford Perkins, *Creation of a Republican Empire, 1776–1865*, Cambridge History of American Foreign Relations 1 (New York: Cambridge University Press, 1993), 123; Hickey, "Monroe-Pinkney Treaty of 1806," 74.

36. As quoted in Jacob Crowninshield, "Some Remarks on the American Trade: Jacob Crowninshield to James Madison 1806," ed. John H. Reinoehl, *William and Mary Quarterly*, 3rd ser., 16, no. 1 (January 1, 1959): 90.

37. Crowninshield, "Some Remarks on the American Trade," 92.

38. John H. Reinoehl, "Post-Embargo Trade and Merchant Prosperity: Experiences of the Crowninshield Family, 1809–1812," *Mississippi Valley Historical Review* 42, no. 2 (1955): 229–49; Whitney, "Crowninshields of Salem."

39. Crowninshield, "Some Remarks on the American Trade," 105.

40. Crowninshield, "Some Remarks on the American Trade," 111.

41. Crowninshield, "Some Remarks on the American Trade," 110, 114–15.

42. On other occasions, such as in congressional debate, he was more bellicose. See 15 Annals of Congress 555 (March 5, 1805).

43. Crowninshield, "Some Remarks on the American Trade," 110.

44. James Madison to James Monroe and William Pinkney, Washington, February 3, 1807, Madison, *Writings of James Madison*, 7:403.

45. Hickey, "Monroe-Pinkney Treaty of 1806," 66.

46. "Treaty of Amity, Commerce and Navigation, between His Britannic Majesty and the United States of America" (Monroe-Pinkney Treaty), in Lowrie and Clarke, *American State Papers: Foreign Relations*, 3:147–51.

47. Hickey, "Monroe-Pinkney Treaty of 1806," 65–66.

48. "Mr. Monroe and Mr. Pinkney to Mr. Madison," London, January 3, 1807, in Lowrie and Clarke, *American State Papers: Foreign Relations*, 3:142–43.

49. Hickey, "Monroe-Pinkney Treaty of 1806," 80.

50. Smith's first impression was that the East India articles were "much more like a Boon now, then when Jay made his Treaty," but he later changed his mind. Samuel Smith to James Madison, March 14, 1807, in *The James Madison Papers, 1723–1836* (American Memory from the Library of Congress), accessed May 28, 2012, http://hdl.loc.gov/loc.mss/mjm.25_1504_1511. Original in reel 25, ser. 2, Additional Correspondence, James Madison Papers, Manuscript Division, Library of Congress.

Tench Coxe seems to have changed his opinion depending on the day, waffling between seeing the reshipment restrictions as a deadly hindrance to American merchants and as a lucky break for domestic producers of sugar and cotton. Tench Coxe to James Madison, April 1, 1807, April 2, 1807, in *The James Madison Papers, 1723–1836* (American Memory from the Library of Congress), accessed May 28, 2012, http://hdl.loc.gov/loc.mss/mjm.09_0620_0621 and http://hdl.loc.gov/loc.mss/mjm.09_0624_0632. Original in reel 9, ser. 1, General Correspondence, James Madison Papers, Manuscript Division, Library of Congress.

51. Pancake, *Samuel Smith and the Politics of Business*, 77; Frank A. Cassell, *Merchant Congressman in the Young Republic: Samuel Smith of Maryland, 1752–1839* (Madison: University of Wisconsin Press, 1971), 136. See also Albert Gallatin to Thomas Jefferson, Washington, April 13, 1807, in Albert Gallatin, *The Writings of Albert Gallatin*, ed. Henry Adams (Philadelphia: Lippincott, 1879), 1:332–33; Jacob Crowninshield to James Madison, August 18, 1807, in *The James Madison Papers, 1723–1836* (American Memory from the Library of Congress), accessed May 28, 2012, http://hdl.loc.gov/loc.mss/mjm.09_0947_0949. Original in reel 9, ser. 1, General Correspondence, James Madison Papers, Manuscript Division, Library of Congress.

52. James Madison to Thomas Jefferson, Washington, April 13, 1807, Thomas Jefferson and James Madison, in *The Republic of Letters: The Correspondence between Thomas Jefferson and James Madison, 1776–1826*, ed. James Morton Smith (New York: Norton, 1995), 3:1466.

53. "Mr. Madison to Messrs. Monroe and Pinkney," Department of State, May 20, 1807, in Lowrie and Clarke, *American State Papers: Foreign Relations*, 3:166–67.

54. Albert Gallatin to Thomas Jefferson, New York, August 26, 1807, in Gallatin, *Writings of Albert Gallatin*, 1:354; Thomas Jefferson to Robert Smith (secretary of the navy), Monticello, September 4, 1804, in Jefferson, *Writings of Thomas Jefferson*, 11:358–59.

55. James Madison to John McClallan (consul at Java) and James Madison to William Buchanan (consul at Isle of France), Department of State, September 4, 1807, in "M78: Consular Instructions of the Department of State, 1801–1834," General Records of the Department of State, RG 59, National Archives, 1945, reel 1, 1:297–98, 298–300. The administration also considered sending warnings to consuls in British India and Canton but feared they would not arrive in time or would create "an alarm which would increase the danger." Albert Gallatin to Thomas Jefferson, New York, August 26, 1807, in Gallatin, *Writings of Albert Gallatin*, 1:354; Thomas Jefferson to Robert Smith, Monticello, September 4, 1804, in Jefferson, *Writings of Thomas Jefferson*, 11:358–59.

56. James Madison to John McClallan (consul at Java), Department of State, September 4, 1807, in "M78: Consular Instructions," reel 1, 1:298–300. See also Seward W. Livermore, "Early Commercial and Consular Relations with the East Indies," *Pacific Historical Review* 15, no. 1 (March 1, 1946): 39–40; Tyler Dennett, *Americans in Eastern Asia: A Critical Study of the Policy of the United States with Reference to China, Japan, and Korea in the 19th Century* (New York: Macmillan, 1922), 33.

57. Albert Gallatin to Thomas Jefferson, New York, September 2, 1807, in Gallatin, *Writings of Albert Gallatin*, 1:357.

58. Thomas Jefferson to Albert Gallatin, April 8, 1808, in Jefferson, *Writings of Thomas Jefferson*, 12:27. The embargo was a simple law, but implementation difficulties led Congress to enact three supplementary acts in the spring of 1808 and, finally, an enforcement act during the embargo's last months, before it was replaced by a more targeted nonintercourse act banning trade with France and Britain. For the relevant legislation, see The Embargo Act: 2 Stat. 451, "An Act Laying an Embargo on All Ships and Vessels in the Ports and Harbors of the United States" (December 22, 1808); First supplementary act: 2 Stat. 453, "An Act Supplementary to the Act, Intituled an 'Act Laying an Embargo on All Ships and Vessels in the Ports and Harbors of the United States'" (January 9, 1808); Second supplementary act: 2 Stat. 473, "An Act in Addition to the Act, Intituled, 'An Act Supplementary to the Act, Intituled an Act Laying an Embargo on All Ships and Vessels in the Ports and Harbors of the United States'" (March 12, 1808); Third supplementary act: 2 Stat. 499, "An Act in Addition to the Act, Intituled, 'An Act Laying an Embargo on All Ships and Vessels in the Ports and Harbors of the United States,' and the Several Acts Supplementary Thereto, and for Other Purposes" (April 25, 1808); Enforcement act: 2 Stat. 506, "An Act to Enforce and Make More Effectual an Act Intituled 'An Act Laying an Embargo on All Ships and Vessels in the Ports and Harbors of the United States,' and the Several Acts Supplementary Thereto"(January 9, 1809); Embargo repeal and non-intercourse act: 2 Stat. 528, "An Act to interdict the commercial intercourse between the United States and Great Britain and France, and their dependencies; and for other purposes"(March 1, 1809).

For evaluations of the law's effectiveness—and particularly the growth in federal administrative apparatus it engendered—see Leonard Dupee White, *The Jeffersonians: A Study in Administrative History, 1801–1829* (New York: Macmillan, 1951), 423–74; Burton Spivak, *Jefferson's English Crisis: Commerce, Embargo, and the Republican Revolution* (Charlottesville: University of Virginia Press, 1979), 102–225; Jerry L. Mashaw, "Reluctant Nationalists: Federal Administration and Administrative Law in the Republican Era, 1801–1829," *Yale Law Journal* 116, no. 8 (June 1, 2007): 1636–1740.

59. Thomas Jefferson, "Eighth Annual Message," November 8, 1808, in James D. Richard-

son, *A Compilation of the Messages and Papers of the Presidents, 1789-1908* (New York: Bureau of National Literature and Art, 1908), 1:452.

60. Douglass C. North, "The United States Balance of Payments, 1790-1860," in *Trends in the American Economy in the Nineteenth Century*, National Bureau of Economic Research, Studies in Income and Wealth 24 (Princeton, NJ: Princeton University Press, 1960), 590-92. While most historians agree the embargo was an enormous disaster, one economist has argued that the policy could have succeeded had there been more political will behind it: Jeffrey A. Frankel, "The 1807-1809 Embargo Against Great Britain," *Journal of Economic History* 42, no. 2 (June 1, 1982): 291-308.

61. Americans' exports to Canton fell from $3,940,090 in 1808 to just $479,850 in 1809; Americans' imports from Canton tumbled from $3,476,000 to $808,000. See fig. A3, "American exports and imports, to/from Canton, by value, 1795-1820."

62. Emphasis in original. J. and T. H. Perkins and Company to Le Roy, Bayard and McEvers, December 30, 1807, in James Elliot Cabot, ed., "Extracts from Letterbooks of J. & T. H. Perkins et al.," Boston Athenaeum, available through *China, America and the Pacific* (Adam Matthew Digital) and Thomas Handasyd Perkins Papers, Massachusetts Historical Society, ser. 3, Bound Volumes, 1783-1892, reel 6.

63. 2 Stat. 475 § 7.

64. Thomas Jefferson to Albert Gallatin, March 13, 1808, in Gallatin, *Writings of Albert Gallatin*, 1:377.

65. Mashaw, "Reluctant Nationalists," 1661.

66. Others included 577 permits for ships destined for the Caribbean or the Gulf of Mexico; the remaining 11 were for voyages to Europe or Africa. United States Department of the Treasury et al., *Message of the President of the United States, Transmitting List of Vessels Permitted to Depart from the United States, since 22d December, 1807*, Shaw and Shoemaker 16486 (Washington, DC: Roger Chew Weightman, 1808).

67. Albert Gallatin to Thomas Jefferson, Washington, May 16, 1808, in Gallatin, *Writings of Albert Gallatin*, 1:387-88; Thomas Jefferson to Albert Gallatin, Monticello, May 20, 1808, in Jefferson, *Writings of Thomas Jefferson*, 12:59-60. In one of his memoirs, Edmund Fanning gives an account of the voyage of the *Tonquin* but misremembers who was president during the embargo—he refers to "President Madison" as having given permission for the venture. Edmund Fanning, *Voyages to the South Seas, Indian and Pacific Oceans, China Sea, North-West Coast, Feejee Islands, South Shetlands, &c.: With an Account of the New Discoveries Made in the Southern Hemisphere, between the Years 1830-1837: Also, The Origin, Authorization, and Progress of the First American National South Sea Exploring Expedition . . .* (New York: Vermilye, 1838), 114-36.

68. The story of Jefferson's permission for Punqua Wingchong's voyage on Astor's ship the *Beaver* has been retold many times, including in Joseph Alfred Scoville, *The Old Merchants of New York City by Walter Barrett, Clerk* (New York: Knox, 1885), 3:5-10; Dennett, *Americans in Eastern Asia*, 77-78; Kenneth Wiggins Porter, *John Jacob Astor, Business Man*, Harvard Studies in Business History 1 (Cambridge, MA: Harvard University Press, 1931), 1:143-50, 420-28; Robert Greenhalgh Albion, *The Rise of New York Port, 1815-1860* (New York: Scribner's, 1939), 197; Carl Seaburg and Stanley Paterson, *Merchant Prince of Boston: Colonel T. H. Perkins, 1764-1854*, Harvard Studies in Business History 26 (Cambridge, MA: Harvard University Press, 1971), 192-98; Michael H. Hunt, *The Making of a Special Relationship: The United States and China to 1914* (New York: Columbia University Press, 1983), 13, 322n14; John Kuo Wei Tchen, *New York before Chinatown: Orientalism and the Shaping of American Culture, 1776-1882* (Baltimore: Johns Hopkins University Press, 1999), 41-43, 312-13; Mashaw, "Reluctant Nationalists," 1661.

69. As is common with Chinese names transliterated into English, particularly during this period, the spelling of Punqua's name varies from writer to writer. I have here followed the convention of most writers on the matter in using "Punqua Wingchong," partly for easy comparison but also because there is a chance that this is how Punqua himself may have written his name in English. The evidence for the latter point comes from a series of advertisements that ran in New York and Boston commercial papers in the fall of 1811, inviting American China traders to visit Punqua's new silk shop on China Street in the foreign quarter at Canton. In the absence of clearer evidence of writing at Punqua's direction, or by his own hand, using the spelling found in these advertisements seems the best alternative. "New Silk Store," *Columbian Centinel* (Boston), September 7, 1811; reprinted in *New-York Gazette*, October 31, 1811.

70. Samuel Latham Mitchill to Thomas Jefferson, July 12, 1808, in Porter, *John Jacob Astor, Business Man*, 1:420–21. The interpreter was Aaron Palmer of New York.

71. Thomas Jefferson to Albert Gallatin, Monticello, July 25, 1808, in Porter, *John Jacob Astor, Business Man*, 1:421–22.

72. Thomas Jefferson to Albert Gallatin, July 25, 1808, in Jefferson, *Writings of Thomas Jefferson*, 12:106–7; Porter, *John Jacob Astor, Business Man*, 1:420–22, 425; Scoville, *Old Merchants of New York City*, 3:8. See also "Mr. Jefferson's Mandarin," *New-York Evening Post* (September 5, 1808).

73. For details on the geography of the foreign quarter, and Americans' experience of street life there, see Downs, *Golden Ghetto*, 25–36.

74. Albert Gallatin to David Gelston, Treasury Department, August 3, 1808, in Porter, *John Jacob Astor, Business Man*, 1:423; "Columbus" to James Madison, August 11, 1808, Papers of Albert Gallatin, New-York Historical Society, box 6, as quoted in Tchen, *New York before Chinatown*, 43, 313n4. After his return to China, Punqua sent the Madisons a gift through Philadelphia merchant Jesse Waln (he had perhaps encountered the couple while visiting Washington in search of Jefferson in 1808). Jesse Waln to James Madison, Philadelphia, April 23, 1810, in James Madison, *The Papers of James Madison*, ed. Robert Allen Rutland (Charlottesville: University of Virginia Press, 1984), Presidential Series, 2:322–23.

75. On hong merchants' bringing suit, see Frederic Delano Grant, "Hong Merchant Litigation in the American Courts," *Proceedings of the Massachusetts Historical Society* 99 (1988): 44–62; Frederic Delano Grant, *The Chinese Cornerstone of Modern Banking: The Canton Guaranty System and the Origins of Bank Deposit Insurance, 1780–1933* (Leiden: Brill Nijhoff, 2014), 146–65. For a long-distance petition over a debt, see "Conseequa vs. Willing & Francis," Willings and Francis Records (Collection 1874), Historical Society of Pennsylvania, folders 1–8; Conseequa (or Ponseequa), Petition to the President (Madison), February 10, 1814, enclosure, in B. C. Wilcocks to James Monroe, Canton, January 6, 1816, in "M101: Despatches from Canton," reel 1; Lo-shu Fu, trans., *A Documentary Chronicle of Sino-Western Relations, 1644–1820* (Tucson: University of Arizona Press, 1966), 1:391–93.

76. The notice appeared in the *New-York Evening Post*'s editorial column and was quite brief—perhaps helping it spread quickly through reprints in other newspapers. *New-York Evening Post*, August 4, 1808. Other notices of the *Beaver*'s departure include "The Ship *Beaver*," *Repertory* (Boston, MA), August 9, 1808, reprinted in the *Connecticut Journal* (New Haven, August 11, 1808, and *Political Censor* (Staunton, VA), August 24, 1808.

77. William Jones et al. to Albert Gallatin, Philadelphia, August 10, 1808, in Porter, *John Jacob Astor, Business Man*, 1:424–25.

78. "The Ship *Beaver* and the Mandarin," *New York Commercial Advertiser*, August 13, 1808.

79. Interestingly, the other merchants involved in the *Beaver*'s voyage, the firm of J. and T. H. Perkins and Company, were not mentioned in the press, nor did they offer any public

comment—though they sold their share of the *Beaver*'s return cargo for $113,000 in July 1809. Seaburg and Paterson, *Merchant Prince of Boston*, 198. The Perkins brothers were otherwise active opponents of the Jefferson administration and played a significant supporting role in the Federalist politics of New England.

80. "To the Editor of the *Commercial Advertiser*," *New York Commercial Advertiser*, August 15, 1808. For a detailed account of the ship's return voyage, including a description of its encounters with British cruisers, see "Ship News," *Democratic Press* (Philadelphia), June 13, 1809. For Astor's advertisements, see "For sale by J. J. Astor . . . ," *New York Commercial Advertiser*, July 6, 1809, and "For sale by J. J. Astor . . . ," *New-York Gazette*, June 29, 1809. In a passage many later writers reference, Albion reports that the *Beaver*'s profits were in the neighborhood of $200,000, though he does not specify a source for the figure or tell how the money was shared between the merchants invested in the property on the ship. This amount would be high for profit—but not unusual for the overall revenue from sales of full cargo. Albion, *Rise of New York Port, 1815–1860*, 197.

81. Albert Gallatin to Capt. William Jones, Treasury Department, August 17, 1808, in Porter, *John Jacob Astor, Business Man*, 1:426–28.

82. "Mr. Jefferson's Mandarin," *New-York Evening* Post, September 5, 1808; "The Candid Reader . . ." *Monitor* (Washington, DC), August 20, 1808; reprinted in *L'Oracle and Daily Advertiser* (New York), August 24, 1808. Reports summarizing the *Monitor*'s argument also appeared in a few places: "The name of the Mandarin . . ." *Mercantile Advertiser* (New York), August 24, 1808; reprinted in *Alexandria (VA) Gazette*, August 27, 1808.

It seems likely that Punqua visited the United States multiple times: in 1808, then again in 1811 (when advertisements for his Canton shop appeared), and once more in 1818, when his presence was noted in published passenger lists and mail calls. See "New Silk Store," *Columbian Centinel* (Boston), September 7, 1811 (reprinted in *New-York Gazette*, October 31, 1811); "Shipping Intelligence. Port of Boston . . . Monday, Jan 19," *Boston Daily Advertiser*, January 20, 1818 (reprinted in *New-York Gazette*, January 23, 1818); "Lang, Turner & Co's Marine List," *New-York Gazette*, March 9, 1818; *New-York Evening Post*, March 25, 1818; "List of Letters, Remaining in the Post Office on the 1st of May, 1816," *National Advocate* (New York), May 8, 1818. Thomas Hill Hubbard, a New York congressman, recorded meeting him in the House's gallery. Thomas Hubbard to Phebe Hubbard, Washington City, March 25, 1818, Thomas H. Hubbard Papers, Library of Congress, box 1. My thanks to Professor Cassandra Good, Marymount University, for pointing me to Hubbard's letters.

For Gallatin and Jefferson's correspondence on the affair, see Thomas Jefferson to Albert Gallatin, Monticello, August 15, and August 26, 1808, in Jefferson, *Writings of Thomas Jefferson*, 12:134, 150–51. Albert Gallatin to Thomas Jefferson, New York, August 9, 1808, and August 17, 1808, in Gallatin, *Writings of Albert Gallatin*, 1:402–7.

83. For Jefferson's opinion of this accusation see Jefferson, *Writings of Thomas Jefferson*, 12:235–38, esp. 237–38.

84. Samuel Eliot Morison, *The Maritime History of Massachusetts, 1783–1860* (Boston: Houghton Mifflin, 1922), 191.

85. J. and T. H. Perkins to R. H. Wilcocks, February 29, 1809, in James Elliot Cabot, ed., "Extracts from Letterbooks of J. and T. H. Perkins et al."

86. For the China relations plan, see Augustus B. Woodward to James Madison, New York, May 27, 1809, and June 12, 1809, in Madison, *Madison Papers: Presidential Series*, 1:208, 244–47. For the Chinese visitor ("Mr. Washing") requesting permission to sail home, see Jonathan Russell to James Madison, Mendon [MA], September 27, 1813, and "Washing" to James Madison, Washington, October 9, 1813, in Madison, *Madison Papers: Presidential Series*, 6:661, 685–86.

87. Fichter, *So Great a Proffit*, 252–54. The Perkins brothers of Boston provide a useful if not typical example of splitting the difference between new and old pursuits. During the embargo, they had invested in an iron forge in Vermont, and at the outset of the war they secured a government contract for cannonballs; but they also funded privateering expeditions, including one ship, the *Jacob Jones*, that was caught up in the Anglo-American skirmishes near Canton. Seaburg and Paterson, *Merchant Prince of Boston*, 199–247, 263–65.

88. Fu, *A Documentary Chronicle of Sino-Western Relations, 1644–1820*, 1:393–94; Kenneth Scott Latourette, *The History of Early Relations between the United States and China, 1784–1844*, Transactions of the Connecticut Academy of Arts and Sciences 22 (New Haven, CT: Yale University Press, 1917), 50–52; Hosea Ballou Morse, *The Chronicles of the East India Company, Trading to China, 1635–1834* (1926–29; repr., Taipei: Cheng-Wen, 1969), 3:214–25; Dennett, *Americans in Eastern Asia*, 82–83.

89. Bryant and Sturgis to Edward Carrington, Boston, November 24, 1813, in Bryant and Sturgis (Boston) records, Baker Library Historical Collections, Harvard Business School, vol. 8, Letter Book, 1811–14, 329–31. The vessel was the *Jacob Jones*, one of the ships whose conflict with the British squadron aroused the Chinese viceroy's ire. The domestic demand for China goods during the war was so great that Stephen Girard found it profitable to ransom the *Montesquieu* after it was captured by the British forces blockading the Delaware River. Despite the $93,000 recovery cost, the ship's cargo "added a half a million dollars to his fortune" (though this latter amount is, again, probably miscounting total sales as profit). "Stephen Girard," *Hunt's Merchants' Magazine* 4, no. 4 (April 1841): 365; Downs, *Golden Ghetto*, 84, 396n66.

90. On these and related changes see chapter 3 below and Latourette, *History of Early Relations between the United States and China, 1784–1844*, 53–109; Downs, *Golden Ghetto*, 143–90; and Fichter, *So Great a Proffit*, 284–88.

91. On Perkins's role as an emissary from the Convention, see Seaburg and Paterson, *Merchant Prince of Boston*, 255–62. On the politics of the Hartford Convention, see Alison L. LaCroix, "A Singular and Awkward War: The Transatlantic Context of the Hartford Convention," *American Nineteenth Century History* 6, no. 1 (March 2005): 3–32.

Chapter Three

1. Ship's papers: Congress, April 6, 1824-April 2, 1825, Nathaniel Kinsman Papers, 1784–1882, Phillips Library, Peabody Essex Museum (Salem, MA), available through *China, America and the Pacific* (Adam Matthew Digital).

2. "Obituary Notices," Boston Commercial Gazette, November 7, 1825; Edward Gray, *William Gray, of Salem, Merchant; a Biographical Sketch, by Edward Gray; with Portraits and Other Illustrations* (Boston: Houghton Mifflin, 1914), 79; Samuel Willard Crompton, "Gray, William (1750–1825)," in *American National Biography Online*, February 2000.

3. Batavia, a colonial city populated by Chinese and European merchants, was a major opium distribution hub. Leonard Blussé, *Visible Cities: Canton, Nagasaki, and Batavia and the Coming of the Americans* (Cambridge, MA: Harvard University Press, 2008); Carl A. Trocki, *Opium, Empire and the Global Political Economy: A Study of the Asian Opium Trade*, Asia's Transformations (London: Routledge, 1999).

4. Ship's papers: Congress, April 6, 1824-April 2, 1825, Nathaniel Kinsman Papers.

5. This dynamism is missing from many histories of Americans' China commerce, which describe the period from the inaugural voyage of the *Empress of China* in 1784 to the Treaty of Nanking in 1842 as one era, that of the "Old China trade." Like the "Old South," the label implies a stability that never existed. China traders' memoirs, written after the end of the Canton system and generally nostalgic, have substantially shaped perceptions of the period. Wil-

liam C. Hunter's vivid pastiche accounts have been particularly influential: William C. Hunter, *The "Fan Kwae" at Canton before Treaty Days, 1825-1844* (London: K. Paul, Trench, 1882); and William C. Hunter, *Bits of Old China* (London: K. Paul, Trench, 1885). For an analysis of how Hunter's books became so influential, see Philip de Vargas, "Hunter's Books on the Old Canton Factories," *Yenching Journal of Social Studies* 2, no. 1 (July 1939): 93-94.

6. Economic historian Peter Temin once observed that "the Opium War was more closely connected to the American inflation than the Bank War between Jackson and Biddle." Peter Temin, *The Jacksonian Economy* (New York: Norton, 1969), 82. While the relative influence of market structures and political choices has been a running theme in the scholarship on the Jacksonian era, the juxtaposition of the Opium War and the Bank War has been less closely examined—a missed opportunity. The more recent trend has been to analyze the Panic of 1837 by placing individuals' experiences and politics rather than aggregate flows at the center of the narrative. Edward E. Baptist, "Toxic Debt, Liar Loans, Collateralized and Securitized Human Beings, and the Panic of 1837," in *Capitalism Takes Command: The Social Transformation of Nineteenth-Century America*, ed. Michael Zakim and Gary J. Kornblith (Chicago: University of Chicago Press, 2012), 69-92; Alasdair Roberts, *America's First Great Depression: Economic Crisis and Political Disorder after the Panic of 1837* (Ithaca, NY: Cornell University Press, 2012); Jessica M. Lepler, *The Many Panics of 1837: People, Politics, and the Creation of a Transatlantic Financial Crisis* (New York: Cambridge University Press, 2013). Temin's argument about silver flows has not gone wholly unchallenged, however: see Alejandra Irigoin, "The End of a Silver Era: The Consequences of the Breakdown of the Spanish Peso Standard in China and the United States, 1780s-1850s," *Journal of World History* 20, no. 2 (June 1, 2009): 207-43.

7. John Murray Forbes, *Reminiscences of John Murray Forbes, Edited by His Daughter, Sarah Forbes Hughes, in Three Volumes*, ed. Sarah Forbes Hughes (Boston: George H. Ellis, 1902), 1:245.

8. Timothy Pitkin, *A Statistical View of the Commerce of the United States of America* (New Haven, CT: Durrie and Peck, 1835), iii.

9. Peter S. Onuf, "The Political Economy of Sectionalism: Tariff Controversies and Conflicting Conceptions of World Order," in *Congress and the Emergence of Sectionalism: From the Missouri Compromise to the Age of Jackson*, ed. Paul Finkelman and Donald R. Kennon, Perspectives on the History of Congress, 1801-1877 (Athens: Ohio University Press, 2008), 47-74.

10. Outlining new principles for the tariff in 1816, Secretary of the Treasury A. J. Dallas explained that promoting neutral commerce was no longer "adapted to the present epoch" of "peace of Europe." If the United States were to prosper, other considerations—notably promoting domestic manufactures and supporting domestic consumption—claimed higher priority. Doc. No. 470, A. J. Dallas, "General Tariff of Duties" (February 13, 1816), in Walter Lowrie and Matthew St. Clair Clarke, eds., *American State Papers: Finance* (Washington, DC: Gales and Seaton, 1832), 3:87.

11. Henry Clay, "The Tariff—Duties on Teas," 8 Cong. Deb. 15 (1831). In this debate, Clay was in favor of reducing tea duties to zero; but at least one Democrat later claimed that "free tea" was a distinguishing feature of his party alone: "Had Mr. Clay been for free tea and free coffee and Mr. Polk against it, who doubts but the election of 1844 would have differently resulted?" John Wentworth and Stephen Douglass, *Free Tea, Free Coffee, Free Harbors, and Free Territory: Remarks of Mr. John Wentworth, of Illinois, Delivered in the House of Representatives, February 2, 1847, upon the Civil and Diplomatic Appropriation Bill, with His Personal Explanations, in Answer to the Attacks of the Washington Union. To Which Is Added a Portion of the Speech of His Colleague, (Mr. Douglass), Touching the Course of the Union's Reports Thereof* (Washington, DC: Blair and Rives, 1847), 2.

12. This occurred gradually. In 1816, US officials created new categories of tea imports to better differentiate "cheap" bohea teas from "luxury" varieties (souchong, hyson, imperial, gunpowder, etc.) and boosted duties on the latter. American merchants trading directly with China still received some protection—duties were still higher on teas "from any other place" (besides China) or carried in foreign vessels—but it was weaker than before for boheas. In 1830, Congress decided duties on tea could be reduced and cut rates by an average ~54 percent. The tariffs of 1832 and 1833 went even further, exempting teas from any duty at all, a policy that remained in place even when protectionist policies were renewed in the tariff of 1842. Later tariffs did impose higher rates on teas imported indirectly or in foreign vessels, but protection was weak compared with the earlier regime.

Relevant tariff acts include 1 Stat. 24, "An Act: For laying a duty on goods, wares, and merchandises imported into the United States" (July 4, 1789); 1 Stat. 180, "An Act: Making further provision for the payment of the debt of the United States" (August 10, 1790); 3 Stat. 310, "An Act: To regulate the duties on imports and tonnage" (April 27, 1816); 4 Stat. 25, "An Act: to amend the several acts imposing duties on imports" (May 22, 1824); 4 Stat. 270, "An Act: in alteration of the several acts imposing duties on imports" (May 19, 1828); 4 Stat. 403, "An Act: to reduce the duties on coffee, tea, and cocoa" (May 20, 1830); 4 Stat. 583, "An Act: to alter and amend the several acts imposing duties on imports" (July 14, 1832); 4 Stat. 629, "An Act: to modify the act of the fourteenth of July, one thousand eight hundred and thirty-two, and all other acts imposing duties on imports" (March 2, 1833); 5 Stat. 463, "An Act: relating to duties and drawbacks" (September 11, 1841); 5 Stat. 548, "An Act to provide revenue from imports, and to change and modify existing laws imposing duties and for other purposes" (August 30, 1842).

The 1832 tariff also exempted from duty Asian goods that were directly consumed or used as manufacturing inputs—rubber, dyes, spices, leathers, and other "gruff" goods. See 4 Stat. 590. Cotton goods were a more complex case. As part of the protection of domestic textile production, foreign cloth was heavily taxed under the tariffs of 1824, 1828, and 1832—but nankeens imported directly from China in US ships were still exempted, likely because this type of cloth was, like tea, similarly important for consumption.

For a narrative of how tariffs affected the China trade from 1784 to 1844, see Kenneth Scott Latourette, *The History of Early Relations between the United States and China, 1784–1844*, Transactions of the Connecticut Academy of Arts and Sciences 22 (New Haven, CT: Yale University Press, 1917), 78n138.

Merchants' interventions in tariff debates could range from formal memorials to simple letters to friendly legislators. See Doc. No. 842, "Philadelphia, citizens of, in relation to reducing and regulating the duties on teas," (January 31, 1828), in Lowrie and Clarke, *American State Papers: Finance*, 5:777–78; Bryant and Sturgis to Nathan Appleton, December 13, 1831, in Appleton Family Papers, Massachusetts Historical Society, ser. 1, subseries A, box 4, folder 14; J. and T. H. Perkins and Company to LeRoy, Bayard, and Company, May 27, 1819, in James Elliot Cabot, ed., "Extracts from Letterbooks of J. & T. H. Perkins et al.," Boston Athenaeum, available through *China, America and the Pacific* (Adam Matthew Digital) and Thomas Handasyd Perkins Papers, Massachusetts Historical Society, ser. 3, Bound Volumes, 1783–1892, reel 6; T. H. Perkins et al., "Revision of the Revenue Laws" (December 23, 1822), in Lowrie and Clarke, *American State Papers: Finance*, 4:3–5.

Congress investigated the issue of Canadian smuggling but did little to stop it. (The irony of American merchants' suffering competition from smugglers operating just outside the borders of their government's effective control is not mentioned in congressional documents.) Lowrie and Clarke, *American State Papers: Finance*, 5:279–80, 777–78.

13. Gautham Rao, *National Duties: Custom Houses and the Making of the American State*,

American Beginnings, 1500–1900 (Chicago: University of Chicago Press, 2016), 167–96. Caught by the 1825–26 credit contraction and the government's sudden interest in enforcing collections, the firms of Thomas H. Smith (New York) and Edward Thompson (Philadelphia) failed, leaving the field open for a group of Boston-based merchants to expand and consolidate their hold on the trade. Jacques M. Downs, *The Golden Ghetto: The American Commercial Community at Canton and the Shaping of American China Policy, 1784–1844* (Bethlehem, PA: Lehigh University Press, 1997), 110; Latourette, *History of Early Relations between the United States and China, 1784–1844*, 68–69; Doc. no. 736, "Trade with China," (February 6, 1826), in Lowrie and Clarke, *American State Papers: Finance*, 5:266–81; Doc. no. 752, "Frauds upon the Revenue Laws," (March 23, 1826), in Lowrie and Clarke, *American State Papers: Finance*, 5:371–477; "Letter from the Secretary of the Treasury . . . in relation to Fraud Practised, or Attempted, upon the Revenue Laws of the United States," H.R. Doc. 137, 19th Cong., 1st Sess. (March 24, 1826).

14. Daniel Peart has argued that partisan organizations mattered much less than the petitions of special interest groups did, at least for tariff legislation. This may or may not hold for the entire early republican period—but even considered as an interest group, it is still notable that the place of the China trade shifted politically after 1815, moving from having wide support to attracting broad condemnation. Daniel Peart, "Looking Beyond Parties and Elections: The Making of United States Tariff Policy during the Early 1820s," *Journal of the Early Republic* 33, no. 1 (2013): 87–108.

15. "Report on U.S. and Foreign Coins and Establishing a Mint," H.R. Doc. 111, 15th Cong., 2nd Sess. (January 26, 1819); A. Barton Hepburn, *History of Coinage and Currency in the United States and the Perennial Contest for Sound Money* (New York: Macmillan, 1903), 30–33; Sharon Ann Murphy, *Other People's Money: How Banking Worked in the Early American Republic* (Baltimore: Johns Hopkins University Press, 2017); Jesse C. Kraft, "The Circulation of Foreign Coinage: An American Response, ca. 1750–1857" (PhD diss., University of Delaware, 2019).

16. Appendix, fig. A5, "Imports of Silver to China, by Country, 1719–1833."

17. The best short account of the Panic of 1819 is Murphy, *Other People's Money*, 82–99. Other important interpretations include Murray Newton Rothbard, *The Panic of 1819: Reactions and Policies* (New York: Columbia University Press, 1962); Robert M. Blackson, "Pennsylvania Banks and the Panic of 1819: A Reinterpretation," *Journal of the Early Republic* 9, no. 3 (Fall 1989): 335–58; Clyde A. Haulman, "The Panic of 1819: America's First Great Depression," *Financial History*, no. 96 (Winter 2010): 20–24; Andrew H. Browning, *The Panic of 1819: The First Great Depression*, Kinder Institute Studies in Constitutional Democracy (Columbia: University of Missouri Press, 2019). For a recent consideration of the accuracy of the term "Panic of 1819" see Jessica Lepler, "Introduction: The Panic of 1819 by Any Other Name," *Journal of the Early Republic* 40, no. 4 (Winter 2020): 665–70. On silver shipments, see Appendix, fig. A5: "Imports of Silver to China, by Country, 1719–1833."

18. Peter Stephen Chazotte, *A New System of Banking Developed and Exemplified in a New Scheme to Establish a Merchants Bank of General Deposits, and Also in a Scheme to Establish a Grand National Bank* (Philadelphia: Author, 1815), 25; Erick Bollmann, *Plan of an Improved System of the Money-Concerns of the Union* (Philadelphia: William Fry, 1816), 29; Doc. no. 462, A. J. Dallas, "National Bank" (January 8, 1816), in Lowrie and Clarke, *American State Papers: Finance*, 3:59; Adam Seybert, *Statistical Annals* (Philadelphia: T. Dobson, 1818), 280–81; "Ginseng," *American Magazine* 1, no. 5 (October 1815): 201.

19. "Chronicle," *Niles' Weekly Register*, November 7, 1818, 175. On the importance of *Niles'* as a national newspaper of record, see Norval Neil Luxon, "*Niles' Weekly Register*," *News Magazine of the Nineteenth Century* (Baton Rouge: Louisiana State University Press, 1947). On

Hezekiah Niles's own developing opinions about banks and currency, see Robert E. Shalhope, *The Baltimore Bank Riot: Political Upheaval in Antebellum Maryland* (Urbana: University of Illinois Press, 2009), 17–22.

20. "Exportation of Specie," *Niles' Weekly Register*, December 5, 1818, 242.

21. Emphasis in original. "Exportation of Specie," *Niles' Weekly Register*, December 5, 1818, 243; "Cash—Queer Calculation," *Niles' Weekly Register,* April 17, 1819, 130.

22. Doc. no. 549, William H. Crawford, "Exportation of the Coins of the United States" (January 25, 1819), in Lowrie and Clarke, *American State Papers: Finance*, 3:393–95; Doc. no. 551, William Lowndes, "Coins, Foreign and Domestic" (January 26, 1819), in Lowrie and Clarke, *American State Papers: Finance*, 3:398–401.

23. J. and T. H. Perkins to J. J. Astor, April 18, 1816, in James Elliot Cabot, ed., "Extracts from Letterbooks of J. & T. H. Perkins et al."

24. Doc. no. 582, William H. Crawford, "Bank of the United States and Other Banks, and the Currency" (February 24, 1820), in Lowrie and Clarke, *American State Papers: Finance*, 3:496.

25. Mathew Carey, *Essays on Political Economy, or The Most Certain Means of Promoting the Wealth, Power, Resources, and Happiness of Nations Applied Particularly to the United States* (Philadelphia: Carey and Lea, 1822), 426. Carey's analysis was first published February 11, 1821. For an analysis of the American System focused on actors other than Carey, see Songho Ha, *The Rise and Fall of the American System: Nationalism and the Development of the American Economy, 1790–1837*, Financial History (London: Pickering and Chatto, 2009).

26. "The Tariff, April 1–2, 1824," in Daniel Webster, *The Papers of Daniel Webster : Speeches and Formal Writings*, ed. Charles M. Wiltse and Alan R. Berolzheimer (Hanover, NH: University Press of New England, 1986), 1:139.

27. Emphasis in original. "Extract of a letter from———, dated Boston, December 29, 1825," Doc. No. 736, "Trade with China" (February 6, 1826), in Lowrie and Clarke, *American State Papers: Finance*, 5:280. The author is identified as Thomas Handasyd Perkins on the following page. For more on Perkins's political maneuvering on behalf of his opium connections, see Michael E. Chapman, "Taking Business to the Tiger's Gate: Thomas Handasyd Perkins and the Boston-Smyrna-Canton Opium Trade of the Early Republic," *Journal of the Royal Asiatic Society Hong Kong Branch* 52 (January 1, 2012): 7–28.

28. Jane Ellen Knodell convincingly argues that while the Second Bank of the United States "fell short of the (modern) central-banker test"—monetary stability was a by-product of its activities, not its central mission—it is still quite clear from Biddle's writings that he aspired to play the role of central banker. His interest in the China trade emerged out of those aspirations. Jane Ellen Knodell, *The Second Bank of the United States: "Central" Banker in an Era of Nation-Building, 1816–1836*, Routledge Explorations in Economic History (New York: Routledge, 2017), 3. For a recent expansive consideration of Biddle's philosophy, see Jeffrey Sklansky, "The Moneylender as Magistrate: Nicholas Biddle and the Ideological Origins of Central Banking in the United States," *Theoretical Inquiries in Law* 11 (2010): 319–59; Jeffrey Sklansky, *Sovereign of the Market: The Money Question in Early America*, American Beginnings, 1500–1900 (Chicago: University of Chicago Press, 2017). Other entries in the long-running debate over whether the Second Bank of the United States or Biddle or both were central bankers include Ralph Charles Henry Catterall, *The Second Bank of the United States* (Chicago: University of Chicago Press, 1903); John Thom Holdsworth and Davis R. Dewey, *The First and Second Banks of the United States*, Publications of the National Monetary Commission (Washington, DC: Government Printing Office, 1910); Walter Buckingham Smith, *Economic Aspects of the Second Bank of the United States* (Cambridge, MA: Harvard University Press, 1953); Bray Hammond,

Banks and Politics in America, from the Revolution to the Civil War (Princeton, NJ: Princeton University Press, 1957); Jacob P. Meerman, "Nicholas Biddle on Central Banking" (PhD diss., University of Chicago, 1961); Fritz Redlich, *The Molding of American Banking: Men and Ideas*, 2 vols., 2nd ed. (New York: Johnson Reprints, 1968).

29. Nicholas Biddle to Timothy Pitkin, Philadelphia, February 4, 1835, Nicholas Biddle Papers, Manuscript Division, Library of Congress, Washington, DC, reel 20, vol. 53, 11004. Biddle's claim that 1825 was the critical year in attracting his attention to specie in the China trade is supported by contemporaneous statements he made about the inauguration of the bills. The Bank's financial records are no longer extant, but a summary of bill issuances in a previous congressional report also supports dating the bills' origins to 1825. Nicholas Biddle to Peter Paul Francis [P. P. F.] Degrand, Philadelphia, June 22, 1826, Nicholas Biddle Papers, Manuscript Division, Library of Congress, Washington, DC, reel 42, vol. 115, 170; "Report of the Committee . . . to inspect the books and examine the proceedings of the Bank of the United States," H.R. Rep. 92, 15th Cong., 2nd Sess. (January 16, 1819), 36, 57, 59.

30. Nicholas Biddle to P. P. F. Degrand, Philadelphia, June 22, 1826, Nicholas Biddle Papers, Manuscript Division, Library of Congress, Washington, DC, reel 42, vol. 115, 170; "No. 27: Form of obligation given by purchasers of bills to go circuitously," in "Bank of the United States," H.R. Rep. 460, 22nd Cong., 1st Sess. (April 30, 1832), 209.

31. The general point about bank-issued bills of exchange is developed in Albert Gallatin, *Considerations on the Currency and Banking System of the United States* (Philadelphia: Carey and Lea, 1831), 28–29. During the Bank War, Biddle had this pamphlet printed and distributed. "Investigation of Affairs and Conduct of Bank of United States," S. Doc. 17, 23rd Cong., 2nd Sess. (December 18, 1834), 323.

32. On the links between the Bank's domestic and foreign exchange businesses, see Bank of the United States, *Report of the Proceedings of the Triennial Meeting of the Stockholders of the Bank of the United States: Held according to the Thirteenth Article of the Eleventh Section of the Charter, at Philadelphia, on the First Day of September 1831* (Philadelphia, 1831), 29; Knodell, *Second Bank of the United States*, 69–98, esp. 84–85. The Bank also issued similarly structured bills intended for South American, Caribbean, and European trade, but the value of these was far lower than those issued for the "East Indies." See "No. 26: Statement of all the bills of exchange on London and Paris," in "Bank of the United States," H.R. Rep. 460, 22nd Cong., 1st Sess. (April 30, 1832), 206.

33. "Report by a Committee of Seven Appointed by the Stockholders," in Bank of the United States, *Report of the Proceedings of the Triennial Meeting of the Stockholders of the Bank of the United States*, 29.

34. Nicholas Biddle to P. P. F. Degrand, Philadelphia, April 27, 1826, Nicholas Biddle Papers, Manuscript Division, Library of Congress, Washington, DC, reel 6, vol. 14, 2826.

35. W. E. Cheong, "China Houses and the Bank of England Crisis of 1825," *Business History* 15, no. 1 (January 1973): 56–73; Knodell, *Second Bank of the United States*, 118–21. Biddle's outgoing correspondence with cashiers and other officials at BUS branch banks in the early 1820s is filled with minute instructions regarding the management and transfers of the bank's specie supplies, including managing stocks of the Spanish coin likely to be drawn out for use in the China trade. For his reactions to exigencies of 1825, in which these actions took on special importance, see Nicholas Biddle Papers, Manuscript Division, Library of Congress, Washington, DC, reel 42, vol. 114.

36. Capitalization in original: P. P. F. Degrand, "The Money-Market in the US," *Boston Weekly Report of Sales and Arrivals* (May 6, 1826), no. 367, 907. Biddle wrote to Degrand to provide the journalist with material for articles praising the BUS's operations. Nicholas Biddle to

P. P. F. Degrand, Philadelphia, April 27, 1826, in Nicholas Biddle Papers, Manuscript Division, Library of Congress, Washington, DC, reel 6, vol. 14, 2826. On Biddle's publicity efforts—and their limited efficacy—see Stephen William Campbell, "Fighting the Bank War: How Newspapers, Banks, and the Post Office Shaped Jacksonian Era Politics, 1828–1834" (PhD diss., University of California, Santa Cruz, 2013); Stephen W. Campbell, "Funding the Bank War: Nicholas Biddle and the Public Relations Campaign to Recharter the Second Bank of the U.S., 1828–1832," *American Nineteenth Century History* 17, no. 3 (September 2016): 273–99.

37. Downs, *Golden Ghetto*, 143–46.

38. On the Boston Concern, see Downs, *Golden Ghetto*, 150–62, esp. 155; John Rogers Haddad, *America's First Adventure in China: Trade, Treaties, Opium, and Salvation* (Philadelphia: Temple University Press, 2013), 31–55. Traders based in New York and Philadelphia adopted these methods later: Testimony of William Brown (February 25, 1830), *First Report from the Select Committee on the Affairs of the East India Company: China Trade*, House of Commons, Reports and Papers (London, 1830), 80; Downs, *Golden Ghetto*, 143–89.

39. J. and T. H. Perkins to John Perkins Cushing, April 28, 1805, in James Elliot Cabot, ed., "Extracts from Letterbooks of J. & T. H. Perkins et al."; Carl Seaburg and Stanley Paterson, *Merchant Prince of Boston: Colonel T. H. Perkins, 1764–1854*, Harvard Studies in Business History 26 (Cambridge, MA: Harvard University Press, 1971), 155–66, esp. 165.

40. John Perkins Cushing, "Lagniappe: 'Memo. for Mr. Forbes Respecting Canton Affairs . . . ,'" *Business History Review* 40, no. 1 (April 1, 1966): 105. On Houqua and his family firm, see John D. Wong, *Global Trade in the Nineteenth Century: The House of Houqua and the Canton System* (Cambridge: Cambridge University Press, 2016).

41. Testimony of John Argyle Maxwell (March 16, 1830), *First Report from the Select Committee on the Affairs of the East India Company*, 247; Haddad, *America's First Adventure in China*, 48–52; "Perkins and Company, Canton 1803–1827," *Bulletin of the Business Historical Society* 6, no. 2 (March 1, 1932): 1–5; Cushing, "Lagniappe: 'Memo. for Mr. Forbes Respecting Canton Affairs.'"

42. Testimony of Joshua Bates (June 10, 1830), *Select Committee of House of Lords on State of Affairs of East India Company, and Trade between Great Britain, E. Indies and China*, House of Commons Parliamentary Papers 646 (1830): 377.

43. Downs, *Golden Ghetto*, 112.

44. Michael Greenberg, *British Trade and the Opening of China, 1800–1842*, Cambridge Studies in Economic History (London: Cambridge University Press, 1951), 109–10; Dilip Kumar Basu, "Asian Merchants and Western Trade: A Comparative Study of Calcutta and Canton, 1800—1840" (PhD diss., University of California, Berkeley, 1975), 113–29.

45. Charles C. Stelle, "American Trade in Opium to China, prior to 1820," *Pacific Historical Review* 9, no. 4 (December 1, 1940): 425–44; Charles C. Stelle, "American Trade in Opium to China, 1821–39," *Pacific Historical Review* 10, no. 1 (March 1941): 57–74; Jacques M. Downs, "American Merchants and the China Opium Trade, 1800–1840," *Business History Review* 42, no. 4 (Winter 1968): 418–42; Downs, *Golden Ghetto*, 105–40; Haddad, *America's First Adventure in China*, 48–55; Seaburg and Paterson, *Merchant Prince of Boston*, 265–66.

46. Hosea Ballou Morse, *The Chronicles of the East India Company, Trading to China, 1635–1834* (Oxford: Clarendon Press, 1926), 3:72–73; Downs, *Golden Ghetto*, 116.

47. In 1823 Philip Ammidon reported that Cushing, with Houqua's assistance, was helping to set him and Samuel Russell up as a new firm to capture a share of the "India business," guaranteeing commissions and advancing funds to establish their reputation and attract new customers. Philip Ammidon to brother, December 27, 1823, Russell and Company Records, Manuscript Division, Library of Congress, Washington, DC, reel 3 (box 4); Downs, *Golden*

Ghetto, 112–18; Sibing He, "Russell and Company, 1818–1891: America's Trade and Diplomacy in Nineteenth-Century China" (PhD diss., Miami University, 1997), 54. The later merger of Perkins and Company and Russell and Company under the latter firm's name would create the largest and most dominant American China firm of the nineteenth century.

48. Jay Sexton, "The Monroe Doctrine in the Nineteenth Century," in *Outside In: The Transnational Circuitry of U.S. History*, ed. Andrew Preston and Doug Rossinow (New York: Oxford University Press, 2017), 27; Greenberg, *British Trade and the Opening of China*, 104.

49. Greenberg, *British Trade and the Opening of China*; Trocki, *Opium, Empire and the Global Political Economy*, 58, 87.

50. Man-houng Lin, *China Upside Down: Currency, Society, and Ideologies, 1808–1856*, Harvard East Asian Monographs 270 (Cambridge, MA: Harvard University Press, 2006), 72–114; Irigoin, "End of a Silver Era"; Alejandra Irigoin, "A Trojan Horse in Daoguang China? Explaining the Flows of Silver In and Out of China," in Economic History Working Papers 173/13 (London: Department of Economic History, London School of Economics and Political Science, 2013); Alejandra Irigoin, "Global Silver: Bullion or Specie? Supply and Demand in the Making of the Early Modern Global Economy," LSE Economic History Working Papers 285 (London: London School of Economics and Political Science, 2018).

51. Downs, *Golden Ghetto*, 111.

52. Downs, *Golden Ghetto*, 108–12; He, "Russell and Company, 1818–1891," 82–119.

53. Baptist, "Toxic Debt, Liar Loans, Collateralized and Securitized Human Beings, and the Panic of 1837"; Sven Beckert, "Slavery Takes Command," in *Empire of Cotton: A Global History* (New York: Knopf, 2014), 98–135.

54. Robert Bennet Forbes to Rose Smith Forbes, Canton, March 10, 1839, in Robert Bennet Forbes, *Letters from China: The Canton-Boston Correspondence of Robert Bennet Forbes, 1838–1840*, ed. Phyllis Forbes Kerr (Mystic, CT: Mystic Seaport Museum, 1996), 105.

55. W. E. Cheong, *Mandarins and Merchants: Jardine Matheson, & Co., a China Agency of the Early Nineteenth Century* (London: Curzon Press, 1979), 8.

56. On the Wabash incident: "Political Relations between the United States and China," H.R. Exec. Doc. 71, 26th Cong., 2nd Sess. (January 25, 1841), 7–9; Lo-shu Fu, trans., *A Documentary Chronicle of Sino-Western Relations, 1644–1820* (Tucson: University of Arizona Press, 1966), 1:408–13, 2:621–23; Tyler Dennett, *Americans in Eastern Asia: A Critical Study of the Policy of the United States with Reference to China, Japan, and Korea in the 19th Century* (New York: Macmillan, 1922), 119–21; Morse, *Chronicles of the East India Company, Trading to China, 1635–1834*, 3:318–21; Downs, *Golden Ghetto*, 119.

On the trial and execution of Francis Terranova, see "Political Relations between the United States and China," H.R. Exec. Doc. 71, 26th Cong., 2nd Sess. (January 25, 1841), 9–55; "M101: Despatches from U.S. Consuls in Canton, China, 1790–1906," General Records of the Department of State, RG 59, National Archives, 1964, reel 1; "Statement of Proceedings in the Matter of the American Ship *Emily* and the Seaman Francis Terranovia," in Morse, *Chronicles of the East India Company, Trading to China, 1635–1834*, 4:23–27; William J. Donahue, "The Francis Terranova Case," *Historian* 43, no. 2 (February 1, 1981): 211–24; Jacques M. Downs, "The Fateful Case of Francis Terranova: An Incident of the China Trade," *Mains'l Haul: A Journal of Pacific Maritime History* 39, no. 2 (2003): 4–13; Joseph Benjamin Askew, "Re-visiting New Territory: The Terranova Incident Re-examined," *Asian Studies Review* 28 (December 2004): 351–71.

57. Lin, *China Upside Down*.

58. Paul Arthur Van Dyke, *The Canton Trade: Life and Enterprise on the China Coast, 1700–1845* (Hong Kong: Hong Kong University Press, 2005), 135–36.

59. Using small, fast watercraft in drug smuggling operations is a common technique across time and place, from nineteenth-century Canton to 1980s Miami. Kathryn Meyer, "Fast Crabs and Cigarette Boats: A Speculative Essay," *Journal of Policy History* 3, no. 4 (October 1991): 64–88.

60. Downs, Golden Ghetto, 122, 129. On the regularity of these operations, see Jeremiah N. Reynolds, *Voyage of the United States Frigate Potomac, under the Command of Commodore John Downes, during the Circumnavigation of the Globe, in the Years 1831, 1832, 1833, and 1834: Including a Particular Account of the Engagement at Quallah-Battoo, on the Coast of Sumatra, with All the Official Documents relating to the Same* (New York: Harper, 1835), 353. The practice of using ships as floating contraband warehouses was developed most fully at Lintin, but Samuel Shaw observed a similar operation on other parts of the Pearl River during his late eighteenth-century voyages. Van Dyke, *Canton Trade*, 127; Samuel Shaw, *The Journals of Major Samuel Shaw: The First American Consul at Canton, with a Life of the Author*, ed. Josiah Quincy (Boston: Crosby and Nichols, 1847), 238–39.

61. He, "Russell and Company," 98–99.

62. Downs, *Golden Ghetto*, 128.

63. Emphasis in original. Robert Bennet Forbes, *Remarks on China and the China Trade* (Boston: Samuel N. Dickinson, 1844), 45; Downs, *Golden Ghetto*, 122, 128–29; Van Dyke, *Canton Trade*, 117–41.

64. Van Dyke, *Canton Trade*, 2.

65. Hunter, *"Fan Kwae" at Canton before Treaty Days*, 65.

66. For example, Karl Gutzlaff, a Prussian missionary, was one of the first sinologists to write extensively in English; but to support his evangelizing, he "acted as interpreter for the sale of opium" on illicit cruises up the China coast. Hunter, *"Fan Kwae" at Canton before Treaty Days*, 70.

67. Jacques M. Downs, "Fair Game: Exploitive Role-Myths and the American Opium Trade," *Pacific Historical Review* 41, no. 2 (May 1, 1972): 133–49.

68. Peter Andreas, *Smuggler Nation: How Illicit Trade Made America* (New York: Oxford University Press, 2013).

69. "Bank of the United States," *Hazard's Register of Pennsylvania* 8, no. 12 (September 17, 1831): 188.

70. "Document A.: Nicholas Biddle to A. S. Clayton, Bank of the United States, April 16, 1832," in "Bank of the United States," H.R. Rep. 460, 22nd Cong., 1st Sess. (April 30, 1832), 322.

71. "The Banks—the Currency and the Times," *Niles' Weekly Register*, April 5, 1834, 86.

72. Nicholas Biddle to Timothy Pitkin, Philadelphia, February 4, 1835, Nicholas Biddle Papers, Manuscript Division, Library of Congress, Washington, DC, reel 20, vol. 53, 11004. See also Timothy Pitkin to Nicholas Biddle, New Haven, January 6, 1835, Nicholas Biddle Papers, Manuscript Division, Library of Congress, Washington, DC, reel 19, vol. 50, 10944.

73. The Bank's interventions in the China trade have been noted by some historians, but Biddle's interpretations of his bills' effectiveness (in private letters or public reports) have more or less been taken at face value. Cf. Catterall, *Second Bank of the United States*, 112; Redlich, *Molding of American Banking*, 1:134; Smith, *Economic Aspects of the Second Bank of the United States*, 34, 89–91, 138–39, 145, 290n13; Peter Temin, "The Economic Consequences of the Bank War," *Journal of Political Economy* 76, no. 2 (March 1, 1968): 270; Downs, *Golden Ghetto*, 111–12.

74. Andrew Jackson, "Third Annual Message," December 6, 1831, in James D. Richardson, ed., *A Compilation of the Messages and Papers of the Presidents, 1789–1908* (New York: Bureau of National Literature and Art, 1909), 2:551.

75. "Bank of the United States," H.R. Rep. 460, 22nd Cong., 1st Sess. (April 30, 1832), 14–15.

76. I am indebted to Ann Daly for this insight into Clayton's wider frame of reference. For more on the "metallalist" approach, see her forthcoming work as well as David A. Martin, "Metallism, Small Notes, and Jackson's War with the B.U.S.," *Explorations in Economic History* 11, no. 3 (March 1, 1974): 227–47.

77. "Bank of the United States," 8 Cong. Deb., part 2 (1832), 2661.

78. "Bank of the United States," 8 Cong. Deb., part 2 (1832), 2655; "Report of Mr. Adams," in "Bank of the United States," H.R. Rep. 460, 22nd Cong., 1st Sess. (April 30, 1832), 402.

79. "Report of the Minority," in "Bank of the United States," H.R. Rep. 460, 22nd Cong., 1st Sess. (April 30, 1832), 313.

80. "American Trade to China," *Niles' Weekly Register*, August 9, 1828, 378–79; Condy Raguet, *A Treatise on Currency and Banking* (Philadelphia: Grigg and Elliott, 1839), 8. On declining American imports of silver into China, see Appendix, fig. A5 "Imports of silver to China, by country, 1719–1833."

81. Select Committee at Canton to Supreme Government at Calcutta, September 28, 1828, as quoted in Morse, *Chronicles of the East India Company, Trading to China, 1635–1834*, 4:179.

82. Appendix, fig. A6, "Bills of exchange in the US China trade, 1825–32."

83. "Bills of Exchange, 1835–1836," Russell and Company Records, Manuscript Division, Library of Congress, Washington, DC, reel 8, container 12.

84. Emphasis in original. Robert Bennet Forbes, *Personal Reminiscences*, 2nd ed. (Boston: Little, Brown, 1878), 149. "To guarantee our losses" refers to the superintendent's promise of the Crown's indemnification to any traders suffering property losses sustained in following the Chinese government's order to give up the opium they had imported.

85. Thomas Handasyd Perkins to Robert Bennet Forbes, Boston, February 14, 1840, in Thomas Handasyd Perkins Papers, Massachusetts Historical Society, ser. 1, Loose Papers, 1789–1853, reel 2, box 2, folder 10, part 1.

86. On the various manifestations of China in US culture, see John Rogers Haddad, *The Romance of China: Excursions to China in U.S. Culture, 1776–1876* (Gutenberg-e) (New York: Columbia University Press, 2005); John Kuo Wei Tchen, *New York before Chinatown: Orientalism and the Shaping of American Culture, 1776–1882* (Baltimore: Johns Hopkins University Press, 1999).

87. Timothy Pitkin—a moderate New England Federalist who first turned to statistics while in Congress in order to evaluate the impact of Republican foreign policy—was particularly taken with the progress of American trade with China and continued to see it as a source of both pride and profit even into the 1830s, though he also recognized how the American economy had changed. Timothy Pitkin, *A Statistical View of the Commerce of the United States of America* (Hartford, CT: Charles Hosmer, 1816); Pitkin, *Statistical View of the Commerce of the United States of America* (1835); Stephen R. Grossbart, "Pitkin, Timothy," in *American National Biography Online*, February 2000.

88. For the Chinese side of these debates—which were as little influenced by foreign thought as American debates were by Chinese—see Lin, *China Upside Down*, 147–284.

Chapter Four

1. "The Mission to China," Cong. Globe, 27th Cong., 3rd Sess., 391–92 (1843). There is also an account of the Senate debate in Benton's autobiography, Thomas Hart Benton, *Thirty Years' View, or A History of the Working of the American Government for Thirty Years, from 1820 to 1850* (New York: Appleton, 1865), 2:510–14.

2. *Senate Journal*, 27th Cong., 3rd Sess., March 3, 1843, 291–92; 5 Stat. 624, "An Act provid-

ing the means of future intercourse between the United States and the Government of China" (March 3, 1843).

3. For a well-observed statement of this perspective, see Macabe Keliher, "Anglo-American Rivalry and the Origins of U.S. China Policy," *Diplomatic History* 31, no. 2 (April 2007): 227–57.

4. "England and China," *United States Magazine and Democratic Review* 7, no. 30 (June 1840): 516; "The War with China," *American Masonic Register and Literary Companion* (Albany, NY), September 11, 1841; "The China News—Movements of England to Universal Empire," *New York Herald*, October 25, 1841; "John Quincy Adams on the China Question," *New World: A Weekly Family Journal of Popular Literature, Science, Art and News* (New York), January 1, 1842, 10; "China and Great Britain," *New-Yorker*, May 9, 1840, 123.

5. *Weekly Globe: Containing Political Discussions, Documentary Proofs, &c., for 1842* (Washington, DC: Blair and Rives, 1842), 18.

6. "The War with China," *American Masonic Register and Literary Companion* (Albany, NY), September 11, 1841.

7. The Opium War is a well-studied topic. Two superb recent histories dig expertly into sources from all sides of the conflict to detail the war's origins, its progress and politics, and its resonance in contemporary politics in China and beyond: Stephen R. Platt, *Imperial Twilight: The Opium War and the End of China's Last Golden Age* (New York: Viking, 2019); and Julia Lovell, *The Opium War: Drugs, Dreams and the Making of China* (New York: Overlook Press, 2014). Among an older body of literature, the most detailed account of the events of the war using Anglophone sources is Peter Ward Fay, *The Opium War, 1840–1842: Barbarians in the Celestial Empire in the Early Part of the Nineteenth Century and the War by Which They Forced Her Gates Ajar* (Chapel Hill: University of North Carolina Press, 1975). By contrast, James M. Polachek, *The Inner Opium War*, Harvard East Asian Monographs (Cambridge, MA: Council on East Asian Studies/Harvard University, 1992), provides an examination of the Qing response to the opium problem from Chinese sources. Other works focusing on the Chinese side of the conflict include Hsin-pao Chang, *Commissioner Lin and the Opium War*, Harvard East Asian Series (Cambridge, MA: Harvard University Press, 1964) and Arthur Waley, *The Opium War through Chinese Eyes* (Stanford, CA: Stanford University Press, 1968). For an examination of opium's crucial role in the political economy of the British Empire, see Carl A. Trocki, *Opium, Empire and the Global Political Economy: A Study of the Asian Opium Trade*, Asia's Transformations (London: Routledge, 1999). Finally, for a revisionist examination of opium use (and abuse) in China, see Frank Dikötter, Lars Laamann, and Zhou Xun, *Narcotic Culture: A History of Drugs in China* (Chicago: University of Chicago Press, 2004).

8. For a concise critique of the "tribute system" as a historical concept, see Peter C. Perdue, "The Tenacious Tributary System," *Journal of Contemporary China* 24, no. 96 (November 2, 2015): 1002–14.

9. William T. Rowe, *China's Last Empire: The Great Qing*, History of Imperial China (Cambridge, MA: Belknap Press of Harvard University Press, 2009), 172–73.

10. The scholarship on Americans' relation to the Opium War is undergoing a revision. The older literature, focused on the United States' late nineteenth-century imperial turn in Asia, largely dismissed American engagement with the Opium War as a fringe affair. Scholars who have noted American interest in the war—mainly China trade historians—have frequently argued, following Dennett, that Americans were unified in condemning the war as an illegal defense of an immoral trade, a position they attribute to the influence of American missionaries in China (whose writings are often overrepresented in the source documents used to support this conclusion, relative to how widely read they were in the period). See Tyler Dennett, *Americans in Eastern Asia: A Critical Study of the Policy of the United States with Reference to*

China, Japan, and Korea in the 19th Century (New York: Macmillan, 1922), 102. For variations on this theme see Foster Rhea Dulles, *The Old China Trade* (Boston: Houghton Mifflin, 1930); Foster Rhea Dulles, *China and America: The Story of Their Relations since 1784* (Princeton, NJ: Princeton University Press, 1946); Fay, *Opium War*; Murray A. Rubinstein, "The Northeastern Connection: American Board Missionaries and the Formation of American Opinion toward China, 1830–1860," *Bulletin of the Institute of Modern History, Academia Sinica* 9 (July 1980): 433–53; Charles C. Stelle, *Americans and the China Opium Trade in the Nineteenth Century*, Addiction in America (New York: Arno Press, 1981); Michael H. Hunt, *The Making of a Special Relationship: The United States and China to 1914* (New York: Columbia University Press, 1983); Paul A. Varg, *New England and Foreign Relations, 1789–1850* (Hanover, NH: University Press of New England, 1983); Murray A. Rubinstein, "The Wars They Wanted: American Missionaries' Use of 'The Chinese Repository' before the Opium War," *American Neptune* 48, no. 4 (1988): 271–82; Jacques M. Downs, *The Golden Ghetto: The American Commercial Community at Canton and the Shaping of American China Policy, 1784–1844* (Bethlehem, PA: Lehigh University Press, 1997); Michael C. Lazich, "American Missionaries and the Opium Trade in Nineteenth-Century China," *Journal of World History* 17, no. 2 (2006): 197–223.

More recent scholarship has revealed that Americans' public and official reactions to the Opium War were more diverse, more contested, and more deeply rooted in geopolitics—through their rivalry with Great Britain over territory, trade, and slavery—than previously understood. See Keliher, "Anglo-American Rivalry and the Origins of U.S. China Policy"; Dael A. Norwood, "Trading in Liberty: The Politics of the American China Trade, c. 1784–1862" (PhD diss., Princeton University, 2012); Gordon H. Chang, *Fateful Ties: A History of America's Preoccupation with China* (Cambridge, MA: Harvard University Press, 2015), 30–41; Alastair Su, "'The Cause of Human Freedom': John Quincy Adams and the Problem of Opium in the Age of Emancipation," *Journal of the Early Republic* 40, no. 3 (August 26, 2020): 465–96.

11. Missionary reports were not yet a major source of American information about China; like missionaries themselves, they traveled in merchant and navy vessels, and largely replicated mercantile or state perspectives.

12. "Lin, the Chinese Commissioner," *Christian Observer* (Louisville, KY), January 29, 1841, 20.

13. "The Opium Trade," *Niles' National Register*, August 17, 1839, 389. Lin's arrival at Canton also provides a fair example of the type of coverage offered by *Niles'* during the war. Unlike most other newspapers of the period, the editorial voice in the *Niles'* of this era was minimal; the once-storied protectionist paper became a copy-sheet after the death of its founder, Hezekiah Niles. However uncreative, this editorial philosophy made it "a surprisingly accurate résumé of American press opinion," a sample of "public opinion as voiced by the newspapers on public questions of the day" that no other source equals. Norval Neil Luxon, *Niles' Weekly Register, News Magazine of the Nineteenth Century* (Baton Rouge: Louisiana State University Press, 1947), 290–91.

14. "Late from China," *Niles' National Register*, September 15, 1838, 35.

15. "Foreign Articles," *Niles' National Register*, July 25, 1840, 1ff.

16. *Niles'* itself ceased publication in 1849, but the general pattern appears to hold for other periodicals too.

17. "The New Orleans Bulletin . . . ," *Southern Patriot* (Charleston, SC), March 10, 1840, 2; "The British Treaty with China," *Southern Patriot*, January 6, 1843, 1; "Mr. Adam's Lecture," *Southern Patriot*, December 3, 1841, 2.

18. "Monthly Concert," *New-York Evangelist*, June 29, 1839; "Review: Claims of Japan and Malaysia upon Christendom, . . ." *New-York Evangelist*, March 2, 1839; "Gutzlaff's Tract Opera-

tions at Macao and Vicinity," *New-York Evangelist*, August 3, 1839; "Evangelical Missions," *New-York Evangelist*, October 12, 1839; "Recent Intelligence," *New-York Evangelist*, November 2 1839; "General Intelligence: Extracts from the *Missionary Herald*," *New-York Evangelist*, December 21, 1839; "Efforts of an English Lady on a Chinese Island," *New-York Evangelist*, December 28, 1839; "The Troubles in China," *New-York Evangelist*, February 15, 1840; "From Our English Correspondent—No. 53," *New-York Evangelist*, March 21, 1840; "Missionary Gleanings: Missions of the American Board," *New-York Evangelist*, January 9, 1841; "The Monthly Concert: Missionary Gleanings," *New-York Evangelist*, June 5, 1841. For a broader exploration of the missionaries' approach to the Opium War, see Rubinstein, "Wars They Wanted."

19. The first China headline appeared on April 17, 1841. "Later from China," *New-York Tribune*, April 17, 1841; "The Chinese," *New-York Tribune*, December 30, 1842. A similar stance can be detected in the editors' decision to reprint a letter from the *Boston Daily Advertiser* by an officer serving with Commodore Kearny's squadron at Canton, which goes to great lengths to show that the irenic behavior of American officers was both more reasonable and more effective that British violence. "From China: Correspondence of the *Boston Daily Advertiser*," *New-York Tribune*, September 9, 1842.

20. Examples of news reports: "Arrival of the *Unicorn*," *New World: A Weekly Family Journal of Popular Literature, Science Art and News* (New York), June 6, 1840, 14; "From Our Own Correspondent," *New World*, October 3, 1840, 285; "England and China: Enlightened Free-booting," *Brother Jonathan* (New York) February 12, 1842, 184; John Worth Edmonds, "Origin and Progress of the War between England and China," *New World*, December 18, 1841, 388ff.; "John Quincy Adams on the China Question," *New World*, January 1, 1842, 10ff.; "England and China: Origin and History of the War," *New World*, February 19, 1842, 118ff.; "Opium Smoking in China," *Brother Jonathan*, March 26, 1842, 359; N. P. Willis, "The Poet and the Mandarin, or Le-Phi's Adventure in the Gardens of Kwonfootse, a Passage from Chinese History," *Brother Jonathan*, April 2, 1842, 390ff.; "Foreign News, Fifteen Days Later," *Brother Jonathan*, July 9, 1842, 294; "The Chinese Emperor's Express," *Brother Jonathan*, November 26, 1842, 378; "China and the Chinese," *Brother Jonathan*, January 7, 1843, 1–3; "More about the Chinese," *Brother Jonathan*, February 11, 1843, 162; "Chinese Jugglers," *Brother Jonathan*, March 4, 1843, 266.

21. "Morality: English Outrage in China," *Youth's Companion* (Boston), March 26, 1841, 183.

22. John Quincy Adams, though he knew American China traders and American missionaries personally, largely informed himself on China through his reading of British and American official documents. His critics, such as John Worth Edmonds, appear, at least in their citations, to have educated themselves similarly. See October 20, 1840, to November 22, 1841, in John Quincy Adams, *The Diaries of John Quincy Adams: A Digital Collection* (Boston: Massachusetts Historical Society, 2004), 41:132–533, http://www.masshist.org/jqadiaries (hereafter Adams, *JQA Diaries*). "England and China," *United States Magazine, and Democratic Review* (June 1840), 516ff.; John Worth Edmonds, *Origin and Progress of the War between England and China, a Lecture Delivered before the Newburgh Lyceum, Dec. 11, 1841* (New York: Newburgh Lyceum, 1841), 3.

23. On Calhoun's relationship to British power, see Bruno Gujer, "Free Trade and Slavery: Calhoun's Defense of Southern Interests against British Interference, 1811–1848" (PhD diss., University of Zürich, 1971). On slaveholders' foreign policy generally, see Matthew Karp, *This Vast Southern Empire: Slaveholders at the Helm of American Foreign Policy* (Cambridge, MA: Harvard University Press, 2016).

24. *Senate Journal*, 26th Cong., 1st Sess., March 4, 1840, 216.

25. "Speech on the Case of the Brig *Enterprise*," in John C. Calhoun, *The Papers of John C.*

Calhoun, ed. Robert Lee Meriwether, William Edwin Hemphill, and Clyde Norman Wilson (Columbia: University of South Carolina Press, 1959), 15:148–49 (hereafter Calhoun, *Calhoun Papers*). The speech was also printed in the *Congressional Globe*: "Protection of American Vessels. Speech of the Hon. J. C. Calhoun, of South Carolina, in Senate, March 13, 1840," Cong. Globe, 26th Cong., 1st Sess., App., 266–70 (March 13, 1840).

26. "Washington City, March 13, 1840," *Baltimore Sun*, March 14, 1840.

27. "Splendid and powerful" was a description of Calhoun's speech. See "From Washington," *North American and Daily Advertiser* (Philadelphia), March 16, 1840.

28. Calhoun, *Calhoun Papers*, 15:149, 154.

29. John C. Calhoun to Duff Green, Washington, April 2, 1842, in Calhoun, *Calhoun Papers*, 16:209.

30. Critiques of Britain's Asian empire were as old as the empire itself and came with a revolutionary pedigree: Thomas Paine, among others, had attacked it in the "American Crisis" as well as the "Rights of Man." Thomas Paine, "American Crisis V" and "Rights of Man, Part Second," in *The Life and Major Writings of Thomas Paine: Includes "Common Sense," "The American Crisis," "Rights of Man," "The Age of Reason" and "Agrarian Justice,"* ed. Philip Sheldon Foner (New York: Citadel Press, 1993), 118–19, 448–49.

31. "Miscellany: China," *Liberator*, November 19, 1841.

32. Calhoun's later connection to Francis Wharton, *Hunt's* primary correspondent on the Opium War and British activities in China and India, is suggestive of the war's continued relevance in American politics. Wharton was part of a group of young Northerners who sought to build a conservative alliance between Calhoun and the leaders of the Northern business community. Clyde N. Wilson, "Preface," in Calhoun, *Calhoun Papers*, 17:xiv; Francis Wharton to John C. Calhoun, Philadelphia, October 11, 1843, in Calhoun, *Calhoun Papers*, 17:500; John C. Calhoun to Francis Wharton, Fort Hill, October 23, 1843, in Calhoun, *Calhoun Papers*, 17:519–21; Francis Wharton to John C. Calhoun, Philadelphia, December 9, 1843, in Calhoun, *Calhoun Papers*, 17:597–98; John C. Calhoun to Francis Wharton, Fort Hill, December 25, 1843, in Calhoun, *Calhoun Papers*, 17:642–43; Francis Wharton to John C. Calhoun, Philadelphia, January 5, 1844, in Calhoun, *Calhoun Papers*, 17:672–73; Francis Wharton to John C. Calhoun, Philadelphia, March 8, 1844, in Calhoun, *Calhoun Papers*, 17:846–47.

33. E. W. Stoughton, "The Opium Trade—England and China," *Hunt's Merchants' Magazine* (May 1840), 391.

34. Lewis Cass to Daniel Webster, Paris, February 15, 1842, in "Correspondence in relation to the Quintuple Treaty," S. Doc. 223, 27th Cong., 3rd Sess. (February 24, 1843), 23. Much of the Cass-Webster correspondence related to the Quintuple Treaty—though not this letter—is reproduced in Daniel Webster, *The Papers of Daniel Webster: Diplomatic Papers*, ed. Kenneth E. Shewmaker, Kenneth R. Stevens, and Anita McGurn (Hanover, NH: University Press of New England, 1983), 1:710–75. For more on Cass's part in the controversy see Willard Carl Klunder, *Lewis Cass and the Politics of Moderation* (Kent, OH: Kent State University Press, 1996), 100–117.

35. October 20, 1840; October 21, 1840; October 23, 1840 ; October 29, 1840; and November 22, 1841, in Adams, *JQA Diaries*, 41:132, 133, 135, 141, and 533.

36. On the weather and the crowd, see "Hon. John Quincy Adams," *Daily Atlas* (Boston), November 24, 1841; "Hon. J. Q. Adams Lecture," *Boston Courier*, November 25, 1841, and November 22, 1841, in Adams, *JQA Diaries*, 41:533.

For "almost to suffocation," see John Quincy Adams to Louisa C. Adams, Boston, November 22–23, 1841, in *Microfilm Edition of the Adams Family Papers, Massachusetts Historical Society* (Boston: Massachusetts Historical Society, 1954), ser. 4, reel 519; also reproduced in John Quincy Adams's private letterbook, *Adams Papers Microfilm*, ser. 2, reel 154.

37. John Quincy Adams, "On the Opium War," *Proceedings of the Massachusetts Historical Society*, 3rd ser., 43 (1910): 324.

38. Adams, "On the Opium War," 314.

39. Adams, "On the Opium War," 313.

40. The *Salem Observer* made light of this uncharacteristic support of England: "Mr. Adams has formerly been almost a libeller [*sic*] of England, (in his early days,) and perhaps he may be indirectly fishing for a good word in the annals of some future English historian." *Salem (MA) Observer*, as reprinted in "J. Q. Adams," *Liberator*, December 24, 1841, 206.

41. Emphasis in original. Adams, "On the Opium War," 324.

42. Adams, "On the Opium War," 305.

43. Emphasis in original. John Quincy Adams to Richard Rush, Washington, December 30, 1842, in *Adams Papers Microfilm*, ser. 2, reel 154. A duplicate of this letter can also be found in Richard Rush, *Letters and Papers of Richard Rush*, ed. Anthony M. Brescia (Wilmington, DE: Scholarly Resources, 1980), reel 20, n. 10698.

44. Platt, *Imperial Twilight*, 330–54.

45. January 2, 1843, in Adams, *JQA Diaries*, 43:382. Although the diary entry comes years afterward, Adams is directly referring to Calhoun's resolutions of March 1840.

46. John Quincy Adams, "Lecture on the War with China," *Niles' National Register*, January 22, 1842, 326ff.; "The Old World: Letters from the London Editor . . . London, December 24th," *New World*, January 29, 1842; "Adams' Lecture on the War with China," *Chinese Repository* 11 (May 1842): 274–89. During the war, the *Chinese Repository* was published at Macao.

47. Eta, "Kentucky and the Kentuckians," *American Turf Register and Sporting Magazine* (New York, NY), August 1842, 422; John Hannam, "English Agriculture—a Glance at Its Progress and Prospectus," *American Farmer, and Spirit of the Agricultural Journals of the Day* (Baltimore), July 20, 1842, 65; "National Heads, No. 3–Chinese," *American Phrenological Journal* 4, no. 3 (March 1, 1842), 64.

48. "Hon. J. Q. Adams Lecture," *Boston Courier*, November 25, 1841; *Boston Post*, as quoted in "Mr. Adams' Lecture on China," *Pennsylvania Inquirer* (Philadelphia), November 27, 1841; "Mr. Adams on the China Question," *National Intelligencer* (Washington DC), November 30, 1841; *Salem (MA) Observer*, as reprinted in "J. Q. Adams," *Liberator*, December 24, 1841, 206.

49. "Acturus, for January . . . ," *Boston Courier*, January 6, 1842.

50. "Mr. Adams," *North American* (Philadelphia), November 27, 1841.

51. "John Quincy Adams," *Cleveland Daily Herald*, November 30, 1841.

52. "The City Article: England and China," *Arcturus* (Albany, NY), January 1842, 146, 147.

53. Dennett, *Americans in Eastern Asia*, 105–8; Dulles, *Old China Trade*, 182–83; Dulles, "China and America: The Story of Their Relations since 1784," 23–25; Downs, *Golden Ghetto*, 440n46; Hunt, *Making of a Special Relationship*, 34; Platt, *Imperial Twilight*, 435–36. There is evidence that the scholarly consensus is changing, however, to see Adams's speech as part of his antislavery campaigning. See Norwood, "Trading in Liberty"; Su, "Cause of Human Freedom."

54. King was a partner in the famously pious firm of D. W. C. Olyphant and Company, and his loud advocacy on the opium issue had made him "intensely disliked" by his peers at Canton. Downs, *Golden Ghetto*, 202.

55. C. W. King to Caleb Cushing, New York, December 29, 1840, in Caleb Cushing Papers, Manuscript Division, Library of Congress, Washington, DC, box 24, folder 3. King had met Adams and discussed Chinese affairs with him at dinner at Abbott Lawrence's house on November 10, 1840. See November 10 and December 22, 1840, in Adams, *JQA Diaries*, 41:153, 195.

56. In at least one instance, Adams's arguments appeared before he made them. The *New-York Gazette*, a year before Adams's speech, argued that "the Chinese government . . . can no

more interrupt that trade without good and sufficient cause, than it can justly demand the murder of an innocent foreigner," and it supported British reprisals for the trade's interruption. As reprinted in "England and China," *Boston Courier*, March 16, 1840.

57. E. Q. [Edmund Quincy], "The Morals of Politics," *Liberator*, December 24, 1841.

58. "England and China: Origin and History of the War," *New World*, February 19, 1842, 118–20.

59. On the China trade and US debates over banking, see chapter 3 above. On Oregon, see Francis Baylie, "Exploration of the Northwest Coast," H.R. Rep. 213, 19th Cong., 1st Sess. (May 15, 1826); republished in Caleb Cushing's "Territory of Oregon," H.R. Rep. 101, 25th Cong., 3rd Sess. (January 4, 1839). On naval visits, see David Foster Long, *Gold Braid and Foreign Relations: Diplomatic Activities of U.S. Naval Officers, 1798–1883* (Annapolis, MD: Naval Institute Press, 1988), 207–11. As part of a general policy of formalizing commercial ties, the Jackson administration had backed a small effort to establish diplomatic relations with Asian powers—but this produced no results. On Jackson's policy, see John M. Belohlavek, "The Asian Challenge: Pirates, Opiates, and New Frontiers," in *"Let the Eagle Soar!": The Foreign Policy of Andrew Jackson* (Lincoln: University of Nebraska Press, 1985), 151–77; Jonathan Goldstein, "For Gold, Glory and Knowledge: The Andrew Jackson Administration and the Orient, 1829–1837," *International Journal of Maritime History* 13, no. 2 (2001): 137–63; Andrew C. A. Jampoler, *Embassy to the Eastern Courts: America's Secret First Pivot toward Asia, 1832–37* (Annapolis, MD: Naval Institute Press, 2015).

60. "Memorial of R. B. Forbes and Others," H.R. Doc. 40, 26th Cong., 1st Sess. (January 9, 1840); *House Journal*, 26th Cong., 1st Sess., January 9, 1840, 189; and "House of Representatives, Thursday, January 9, 1840," Cong. Globe, 26th Cong., 1st Sess., 109 (January 9, 1840).

61. "Memorial of R. B. Forbes and Others," H.R. Doc. 40, 26th Cong., 1st Sess. (January 9, 1840).

62. "China Trade—Merchants of Boston and Salem, Massachusetts," H.R. Doc. 170, 26th Cong., 1st Sess. (April 9, 1840); *House Journal*, 26th Cong., 1st Sess., April 9, 1840, 781.

63. "China Trade—Merchants of Boston and Salem, Massachusetts," H.R. Doc. 170, 26th Cong., 1st Sess. (April 9, 1840). For additional documents, see *House Journal*, 26th Cong., 1st Sess., March 19, 1840, 639, and *House Journal*, 26th Cong., 1st Sess., April 3, 1840, 738. These were probably submitted to the House either directly by the same merchants who submitted petitions, or by Abbott Lawrence and Caleb Cushing, who were then corresponding with this group.

64. *House Journal*, 26th Cong., 1st Sess., February 7, 1840, 368. Cushing asserted that he had written these resolutions in a speech on March 16, 1840: "China and the United States," Cong. Globe, 26th Cong., 1st Sess. (March 16, 1840), 275. See also Claude Moore Fuess, *The Life of Caleb Cushing* (New York: Harcourt, Brace, 1923), 1:404; Dennett, *Americans in Eastern Asia*, 104.

65. *House Journal*, 26th Cong., 2nd Sess., December 15, 1840, 46–47; *House Journal*, 26th Cong., 2nd Sess., December 16, 1840, 58; December 16, 1840, in Adams, *JQA Diaries*, 41:189.

66. *House Journal*, 26th Cong., 2nd Sess., December 23, 1840, 97.

67. Cushing's February requests were split into two reports, one from the State Department delivered on February 21, 1840, and another from the Treasury, delivered at the end of the session, June 17, 1840. Everett's December request was answered by the Van Buren administration just six days later, on December 29, 1840, while Adams's more thorough query took until January 19, 1841, to arrive. "Trade with China," H.R. Doc. 119, 26th Cong., 1st Sess. (February 25, 1840); "Trade, Commerce and Navigation with China, 1821 to 1839," H.R. Doc. 248, 26th Cong., 1st Sess. (July 1, 1840); "Commerce with China," H.R. Doc. 34, 26th Cong., 2nd

Sess. (December 31, 1840); "Political Relations between the United States and China," H.R. Doc. 71, 26th Cong., 2nd Sess. (January 25, 1841).

68. George Barker Stevens, *The Life, Letters, and Journals of the Rev. and Hon. Peter Parker, M.D., Missionary, Physician, Diplomatist* (Boston, 1896), 183–94, 220–24; Edward Vose Gulick, *Peter Parker and the Opening of China*, Harvard Studies in American-East Asian Relations (Cambridge, MA: Harvard University Press, 1973), 98–99, 106–7. Parker's memorial to Webster can be found in Stevens, *Life, Letters, and Journals of Peter Parker*; Webster, *Papers of Daniel Webster: Diplomatic Papers*, 1:885–89.

69. Dennett, *Americans in Eastern Asia*, 105.

70. "Burning of Steamboat *Caroline*, and Imprisonment of McLeod," H.R. Rep. 162, 26th Cong, 2nd Sess. (February 13, 1841), 5. Adams described the report as "an inflammatory invective against the British Government." February 13, 1841, in Adams, *JQA Diaries*, 41:248.

71. Caleb Cushing, "China and the United States," Cong. Globe, 26th Cong., 1st Sess. (March 16, 1840), 275.

72. In his speech Cushing contrasted the actions of "the Americans at Canton," who "almost or quite alone, have manifested a proper respect for the laws and public rights of the Chinese empire"—by not smuggling opium—"in honorable contrast with the outrageous misconduct of the English there." Cushing, "China and the United States," Cong. Globe, 26th Cong., 1st Sess. (March 16, 1840), 275.

73. *Journal of Commerce* (New York) as reprinted in "Important from Canton," *Barre (MA) Gazette*, August 9, 1839, 2. For examples of persistence, see "Later from China," *Southern Patriot* (Charleston, SC), October 1, 1839, 2; "Summary of News," *Boston Recorder*, October 4, 1839, 149; "Weekly Record," *Boston Weekly Magazine*, October 5, 1839, 39; "The Boston Transcript . . . ," *Southern Patriot*, October 10, 1839, 2.

74. A 1792 medical thesis by a student at the University of Pennsylvania described opium's effects as akin to those of alcohol, an analogy widespread among opium traders and users too. Valentine Seaman, *An Inaugural Dissertation on Opium. Submitted to the Examination of John Ewing, S.T.P. Provost; and to the Trustees and Medical Professors of the University of Pennsylvania; for the Degree of Doctor of Medicine: On the Second Day of May, A.D. 1792, by Valentine Seaman, of New-York* (Philadelphia: Johnston and Justice, 1792), 10–11; Thomas De Quincey, *Confessions of an English Opium-Eater* (London: Taylor and Hessey, 1822); Marcus Aurin, "Chasing the Dragon: The Cultural Metamorphosis of Opium in the United States, 1825–1935," *Medical Anthropology Quarterly*, n.s. 14, no. 3 (September 2000): 414–41; Keith McMahon, *The Fall of the God of Money: Opium Smoking in Nineteenth-Century China* (Lanham, MD: Rowman and Littlefield, 2002).

75. Peter W. Snow to "their excellencies the Imperial Commissioner and Governor of the two Keang and the Governor of the two Kwang," Canton, September 23, 1839; and Peter W. Snow to John Forsyth, Canton, January 11, 1840, in "Political Relations between the United States and China," H.R. Doc. 71, 26th Cong., 2nd Sess. (January 25, 1841), 58, 69; and Dennett, *Americans in Eastern Asia*, 124n14.

76. Robert Bennet Forbes, *Remarks on China and the China Trade* (Boston: Dickinson, 1844), 44.

77. Peter Parker to Daniel Webster, Washington, January 30, 1841, in Stevens, *Life, Letters, and Journals of Peter Parker*, 187.

78. "Suggestions to the Friends of Missions," *Liberator*, March 13, 1840, 42; and "Miscellany: China," *Liberator*, November 19, 1841, 188.

79. "Commerce with China," H.R. Doc. 34, 26th Cong., 2nd Sess. (December 31, 1840). The group of merchants Stevenson refers to was almost certainly composed of the same part-

ners in Russell and Company who were behind both petitions, since Stevenson's first letter to Palmerston follows by nineteen days a letter written by John Murray Forbes (a signatory to the May petition and brother of Robert Bennet Forbes, author of the January petition) to Abbott Lawrence expressing these same concerns—more than enough time for a transatlantic steamer to get from Boston to London. See John Murray Forbes to Abbott Lawrence, Boston, May 6 and 8, 1840, in Caleb Cushing Papers, Manuscript Division, Library of Congress, Washington, DC, box 22, folder 3.

80. Martin Van Buren, "Annual Message to Congress," December 5, 1840, in James D. Richardson, ed., *A Compilation of the Messages and Papers of the Presidents, 1789–1908* (New York: Bureau of National Literature and Art, 1908), 3:618.

81. Passages in Kearny's instructions—though not the ones about opium smuggling—were taken almost verbatim from a letter sent by Wetmore to the secretary of the navy. William S. Wetmore to James K. Paulding, New York, July 22, 1840, in "M124: Miscellaneous Letters Received by the Secretary of Navy, 1801–1884," Naval Records Collection of the Office of Naval Records and Library, RG 45, National Archives, 1960, reel 174; James K. Paulding to Lawrence Kearny, Washington, November 2, 1840, in "M149: Letters Sent by the Secretary of the Navy to Officers, 1798–1868," Naval Records Collection of the Office of Naval Records and Library, RG 45, National Archives, 1950, reel 32.

82. James K. Paulding to Lawrence Kearny, Washington, November 2, 1840, in "M149: Letters to Officers," reel 32.

83. "Sandwich Islands and China. Message from the President of the United States [. . .]," H.R. Doc. 35, 27th Cong., 3rd Sess. (December 31, 1842). On Webster's probable authorship, see Daniel Webster, *The Works of Daniel Webster*, ed. Edward Everett, 9th ed. (Boston: Little, Brown, 1856), 6:463.

84. "Sandwich Islands and China. Message from the President of the United States [. . .]," H.R. Doc. 35, 27th Cong., 3rd Sess. (December 31, 1842), 2.

85. January 9, 1843, in Adams, *JQA Diaries*, 43:389; Daniel Webster, *The Letters of Daniel Webster, from Documents Owned Principally by the New Hampshire Historical Society*, ed. Claude Halstead Van Tyne (New York: McClure, Phillips, 1902), 285.

86. "Diplomatic Mission to China and Sandwich Islands," H.R. Rep. 93, 27th Cong., 3rd Sess. (January 24, 1843), 2.

87. February 21, 1843, in Adams, *JQA Diaries*, 43:432. "Intercourse with China," Cong. Globe, 27th Cong., 3rd Sess., 323–25 (1843); "Commercial Intercourse with China—Mr. Gordon" and "Commercial Intercourse with China—Mr. J. C. Clark," Cong. Globe, 27th Cong., 3rd Sess., App., 162–66, 198–202 (1843); *House Journal*, 27th Cong., 3rd Sess., February 21, 1843, 419–21.

88. Several cabinet appointments were shot down by a restive Senate; Caleb Cushing, standing as candidate for secretary of the treasury, was voted down no fewer than three times. See John M. Belohlavek, *Broken Glass: Caleb Cushing and the Shattering of the Union* (Kent, OH: Kent State University Press, 2005), 144–45. Suspicious of the president's motives, the upper chamber required that "no agent shall be sent by virtue of this act unless he shall have been appointed by and with the advice and consent of the Senate"—a directive the Tyler administration ignored completely. See "The Mission to China," Cong. Globe, 27th Cong., 3rd Sess. (1843), 391–93; 5 Stat. 624, "An Act providing the means of future intercourse between the United States and the Government of China" (March 3, 1843).

89. Cushing's reports on political, military, and commercial affairs can be found in "M92: Despatches from U.S. Ministers to China, 1843–1906," General Records of the Department of State, RG 59, National Archives, 1973, reels 2 and 3. Some of these dispatches are also repub-

lished in Caleb Cushing, *The Cushing Reports: Ambassador Caleb Cushing's Confidential Diplomatic Reports to the United States Secretary of State, 1843–1844: Mexico, Egypt, the Barbary States, India, Ceylon*, ed. Margaret Diamond Benetz (Salisbury, NC: Documentary Publications, 1976). His scientific reports can be found in the archives of the National Institute, housed at the Smithsonian: National Institute Records, Smithsonian Institution Archives, Washington, DC, boxes 1–6. For an analysis of Cushing's reports and their relation to the Treaty of Wangxia, see Kendall Johnson, *The New Middle Kingdom: China and the Early American Romance of Free Trade* (Baltimore: Johns Hopkins University Press, 2017), 170–210.

90. See, for example: Caleb Cushing to Abel P. Upshur, Secretary of State, USS *Brandywine*, December 3, 1843, no. 23, in "M92: Despatches from China," reel 2.

For a broader look at Americans' perceptions of British imperialism during this same period, see Elizabeth Kelly Gray, "'Whisper to Him the Word "India"': Trans-Atlantic Critics and American Slavery, 1830–1860," *Journal of the Early Republic* 28, no. 3 (2008): 379–406. In some ways Cushing's outlook on racial hierarchy and imperialism were the logical ends of his commitment to union with the South—a dough-faced foreign policy, in other words—but they also strongly resemble the first stage of "Anglo-Saxon" imperialist attitudes that emerged in the United States' late nineteenth-century wars in the Philippines, as described in Paul A. Kramer, "Empires, Exceptions, and Anglo-Saxons: Race and Rule between the British and United States Empires, 1880–1910," *Journal of American History* 88, no. 4 (March 1, 2002): 1315–53.

91. For early expectations, see Forbes, *Remarks on China and the China Trade*, 57, and "Diplomatic: Mr. Caleb Cushing in China," *Niles' National Register*, September 21, 1844, 35.

The negotiations are interesting in themselves, as a study of US international gamesmanship and the Qing state's response to the new world the Opium War had made. Dennett, *Americans in Eastern Asia*, 145–71; Fuess, *Life of Caleb Cushing*, 1:397–453; Downs, *Golden Ghetto*, 259–320; Belohlavek, *Broken Glass*, 150–80.

The treaty was named after the town where negotiations were conducted, just outside Macao. Alternative spellings include Wanghia, Wang-hsia, and Wang Hiya, among others. For the agreement's text, see "Treaty of Peace, Amity, and Commerce (China)," in *Treaties and Other International Agreements of the United States of America, 1776–1949*, ed. Charles I. Bevans (Washington, DC: Government Printing Office, 1968), 6:647–58.

92. Dennett, *Americans in Eastern Asia*, 170. For a long view of the consequences of the extraterritoriality clause of the treaty, see Eileen P. Scully, *Bargaining with the State from Afar: American Citizenship in Treaty Port China, 1844–1942* (New York: Columbia University Press, 2001); Teemu Ruskola, *Legal Orientalism: China, the United States, and Modern Law* (Cambridge, MA: Harvard University Press, 2013).

93. The terms of US commissioners and ambassadors to China usually overlapped, though their actual presence in China almost never did.

Chapter Five

1. "Legislative Proceedings," *North American and United States Gazette* (Philadelphia), March 4, 1848.

2. Asa Whitney, *Address of Mr. A. Whitney before the Legislature of Pennsylvania on His Project for a Railroad from Lake Michigan to the Pacific* (Harrisburg, PA: M'Kinley and Lescure, 1848), 3.

3. Whitney, *Address of Mr. A. Whitney before the Legislature of Pennsylvania on His Project for a Railroad from Lake Michigan to the Pacific*, 3, 10.

4. Whitney, *Address of Mr. A. Whitney before the Legislature of Pennsylvania on His Project for a Railroad from Lake Michigan to the Pacific*, 3, 7, 15.

5. Asa Whitney, *A Project for a Railroad to the Pacific* (New York: George W. Wood, 1849), 13.

6. Beginning in the 1820s, travelers to the center of North America had suggested that the region would become a threshold to the Far East by means of a railroad; these ideas did not (yet) attract national attention. William C. Redfield, *Sketch of the Geographical Rout [sic] of a Great Railway . . .* , 2nd ed., with additions (New York: Carvill, 1830); Caleb Atwater, *Remarks Made on a Tour to Prairie du Chien: Thence to Washington City, in 1829* (Columbus, OH: Whiting, 1831); David Haward Bain, *Empire Express: Building the First Transcontinental Railroad* (New York: Viking, 1999), 16–19.

7. For a representative example of Whitney's place in modern railroad historiography, see William G. Thomas, *The Iron Way: Railroads, the Civil War, and the Making of Modern America* (New Haven, CT: Yale University Press, 2011), 1–2, 37–38, 199. Richard White's analysis of the political economy of transcontinental railroads begins with the Civil War, but in a break with tradition, Whitney makes no appearance. The iron world Whitney's words described made possible the corroded railway politics White analyzes. Richard White, *Railroaded: The Transcontinentals and the Making of Modern America* (New York: Norton, 2011).

8. Key works include Thomas R. Hietala, *Manifest Design: Anxious Aggrandizement in Late Jacksonian America* (Ithaca, NY: Cornell University Press, 1985); Frederick Merk, *Manifest Destiny and Mission in American History: A Reinterpretation* (Cambridge, MA: Harvard University Press, 1995); Anders Stephanson, *Manifest Destiny: American Expansionism and the Empire of Right* (New York: Hill and Wang, 1995); William Earl Weeks, *Building the Continental Empire: American Expansion from the Revolution to the Civil War*, American Ways (Chicago: Ivan R. Dee, 1996); Robert E. May, *Manifest Destiny's Underworld: Filibustering in Antebellum America* (Chapel Hill: University of North Carolina Press, 2002); Amy S. Greenberg, *Manifest Manhood and the Antebellum American Empire* (New York: Cambridge University Press, 2005); Sam W. Haynes, *Unfinished Revolution: The Early American Republic in a British World* (Charlottesville: University of Virginia Press, 2010).

9. Interestingly, while China traders were generally dismissive of isthmian canals, oceanic steamers, and Perry's gunboat diplomacy, they did invest their money—and the cash of their Chinese partners—in railroads (though not transcontinentals). For a representative China trader's response to a mail steamer project, see Robert Bennet Forbes, *On the Establishment of a Line of Mail Steamers from the Western Coast of the United States, on the Pacific, to China* (Boston: Boston Journal Office, 1855). On China traders' nontrade investments, see Henrietta M. Larson, "A China Trader Turns Investor: A Biographical Chapter in American Business History," *Harvard Business Review* 12, no. 3 (April 1934): 345–58; John Lauritz Larson, *Bonds of Enterprise: John Murray Forbes and Western Development in America's Railway Age* (Cambridge, MA: Harvard University Press, 1984); John D. Wong, *Global Trade in the Nineteenth Century: The House of Houqua and the Canton System* (Cambridge: Cambridge University Press, 2016), 177–204.

10. Saturday, June 18, 1842, in Asa Whitney, "Diary of Asa Whitney, 1842–1844" (typescript), ed. Margaret Louise Brown (1930), 3, Transportation History Collection, Special Collections Research Center, University of Michigan, Ann Arbor.

11. Margaret Louise Brown, "Whitney, Asa," in *Dictionary of American Biography*, ed. Dumas Malone (New York: Scribner's, 1928); Margaret Louise Brown, "Asa Whitney: Projector of the Pacific Railroad" (PhD diss., University of Michigan, 1931), 1–18; Bain, *Empire Express*, 1–46.

12. "Article LXXI: Phrenological Character of Asa Whitney, with a Likeness," *American Phrenological Journal* 11, no. 11 (November 1, 1849): 329–33.

13. Thursday, June 23, 1842, in Whitney, "Diary of Asa Whitney, 1842–1844" (typescript), 4.

14. Quotation from Whitney, *Project for a Railroad to the Pacific*, iii. On Whitney's appearance see J. S., "Whitney's Railroad Meeting," *Philadelphia Public Ledger*, December 22, 1846, and Brown, "Whitney, Asa," 157. On his love of Napoleon, whom he called "the Greatest Man that has lived," see his account of his July 1844 visit to St. Helena: July 12, 1844, in Whitney, "Diary of Asa Whitney, 1842–1844" (typescript)," 60–65.

15. "Asa Whitney," in New York, Passenger Lists, 1820–1957, *Ancestry.com* (Provo, UT: Ancestry.com Operations, 2010).

16. Though his arguments were published in many places, Whitney's efforts reached their fullest expression in his 1849 pamphlet, Whitney, *Project for a Railroad to the Pacific*. The best account of his publicity efforts remains Margaret Louise Brown, "Asa Whitney and His Pacific Railroad Publicity Campaign," *Mississippi Valley Historical Review* 20, no. 2 (September 1933): 209–24.

17. Whitney, *Project for a Railroad to the Pacific*, 6–12.

18. Whitney, *Project for a Railroad to the Pacific*, iv.

19. The disturbance was caused by a group of "National Land Reformers" (members of New York's "anti-rent" party) who objected to what they thought was his plan to grant land to a corporation. "A Public Meeting," *New-York Daily Tribune*, January 4, 1847; "The Great Railroad to the Pacific," *New-York Daily Tribune*, January 5, 1847; "City News: Tuesday—The Great Rail-Road Meeting," *New-York Spectator*, January 9, 1847; and Brown, "Asa Whitney and His Pacific Railroad Publicity Campaign," 215–16.

20. Emphasis in original. "Memorial of Thomas Allen and others, and Committee of Convention of States at St. Louis, for National Railroad and Electric Telegraph from Mississippi River to Pacific Ocean," S. Rep. 194, 31st Cong., 1st Sess. (September 12, 1850), 2. On the constitutionalism of Whitney's plan, see John Lauritz Larson, *Internal Improvement: National Public Works and the Promise of Popular Government in the Early United States* (Chapel Hill: University of North Carolina Press, 2001), 246.

21. Whitney, *Project for a Railroad to the Pacific*, 30, 35, 38–40. The scope of Whitney's vision is similar to that of his contemporary Elihu Burritt. Margot Minardi, "'Centripetal Attraction' in a Centrifugal World: The Pacifist Vision of Elihu Burritt," *Early American Studies: An Interdisciplinary Journal* 11, no. 1 (2013): 176–91.

22. Whitney, *Project for a Railroad to the Pacific*, 13–33.

23. Whitney, *Project for a Railroad to the Pacific*, 13.

24. Whitney, *Project for a Railroad to the Pacific*, 14, 38.

25. Whitney, *Project for a Railroad to the Pacific*, 40.

26. *House Journal*, 28th Cong., 2nd Sess., January 28, 1845, 283; *Senate Journal*, 28th Cong., 2nd Sess., January 28, 1845, 114; "Railroad from Lake Michigan to the Pacific. Memorial of Asa Whitney, of New York City, relative to the construction of a railroad from Lake Michigan to the Pacific Ocean," H.R. Doc. 72, 28th Cong., 2nd Sess. (January 28, 1845); "Memorial of Asa Whitney, of the City of New York, praying a grant of land, to enable him to construct a railroad from Lake Michigan to the Pacific Ocean," S. Doc. 69, 28th Cong., 2nd Sess. (January 28, 1845); Asa Whitney, *To the People of the United States* (n.p., 1845).

27. On Whitney's publicity efforts, see Nelson H. Loomis, "Asa Whitney: Father of Pacific Railroads," *Proceedings of the Mississippi Valley Historical Association* 6 (1913): 166–75; Robert Spencer Cotterill, "Early Agitation for a Pacific Railroad, 1845–1850," *Mississippi Valley Historical Review* 5, no. 4 (March 1, 1919): 396–414; Brown, "Asa Whitney and His Pacific Railroad Publicity Campaign"; Bain, *Empire Express*, 13–46; H. Craig Miner, *A Most Magnificent Machine: America Adopts the Railroad, 1825–1862* (Lawrence: University Press of Kansas, 2010), 226–38.

28. "Phrenological Character of Asa Whitney."

29. Eighteen states out of the thirty then in the Union endorsed his plan. Whitney, *Project for a Railroad to the Pacific*, 89–107.

30. In 1856 the Democratic and Republican parties both endorsed plans to build a transcontinental road, a commitment continued in subsequent elections. The Whig Party and the American Party did not, and then also failed nationally; the causal link is left as an exercise for the reader. Gerhard Peters and John T. Woolley, "The American Presidency Project," http://www.presidency.ucsb.edu, accessed March 6, 2021.

31. Lucien Bonaparte Chase, *History of the Polk Administration* (New York: Putnam, 1850), 289; *The Democratic Party and Its Fruits* (Washington, DC: National and Jackson Democratic Association Committee, 1848), 6, as quoted in Norman A. Graebner, *Empire on the Pacific: A Study in American Continental Expansion* (New York: Ronald Press, 1955), 226.

32. Quotation from editor's preface to Matthew Fontaine Maury, "Art. II—A Rail Road from the Atlantic to the Pacific," *Western Journal* 1, no. 7 (July 1848): 351. See also "Art. I.—The Natural Laws of Commerce," *Western Journal* 1, no. 4 (April 1848): 173–78.

33. "Humbugs of the Day," *New York Herald*, October 10, 1845; "Whitney's Pacific Railway," *American Railway Times* (Boston), June 20, 1850.

34. "Resolutions of the Legislature of Kentucky, relative to Mr. Asa Whitney's plan of a railroad from Lake Michigan to the Pacific Ocean," H.R. Misc. Doc. 55, 30th Cong., 1st Sess. (March 22, 1848).

35. "Chamber of Commerce and Whitney's Railroad Project," *Hunt's Merchants' Magazine and Commercial Review* 21, no. 4 (October 1, 1849): 417, 416. See also "Resolutions of the Chamber of Commerce of New York, in Favor of Whitney's Plan for a Railroad from Lake Michigan to the Pacific," S. Misc. Doc. 3, 31st Cong., 1st Sess. (August 7, 1849).

36. "Whitney's Railroad Meeting," *Philadelphia Public Ledger*, December 22, 1846.

37. H. Craig Miner, *A Most Magnificent Machine: America Adopts the Railroad, 1825–1862* (Lawrence: University Press of Kansas, 2010), 232.

38. George Wilkes, *Project of a National Railroad from the Atlantic to the Pacific Ocean for the Purpose of Obtaining a Short Route to Oregon and the Indies*, 2nd ed. (New York: Author, 1845), 6.

39. J. D. B. De Bow, "Additional Remarks by the Editor on the Projected Southern and Northern Routes across the Continent to the Pacific," *De Bow's Review: Agricultural, Commercial, Industrial Progress and Resources* 3, no. 6 (June 1847): 485. Contrary to De Bow's implication, Whitney never argued that he was the first to propose a transcontinental road; he merely claimed that his plan was the best means of accomplishing it.

40. Quotation from "China and Great Britain," *New-Yorker*, May 9, 1840, 123.

41. On the American treaties and the rights of US citizens in China, see Tyler Dennett, *Americans in Eastern Asia: A Critical Study of the Policy of the United States with Reference to China, Japan, and Korea in the 19th Century* (New York: Macmillan, 1922), 91–194; Eileen P. Scully, *Bargaining with the State from Afar: American Citizenship in Treaty Port China, 1844–1942* (New York: Columbia University Press, 2001). The classic text on the origins and early years of the treaty port system is John King Fairbank, *Trade and Diplomacy on the China Coast: The Opening of the Treaty Ports, 1842–1854*, 2 vols. (Cambridge, MA: Harvard University Press, 1964).

42. On this new establishment and its consequences, see Dennett, *Americans in Eastern Asia*, 175–94; Eldon Griffin, *Clippers and Consuls: American Consular and Commercial Relations with Eastern Asia, 1845–1860* (Ann Arbor, MI: Edwards Brothers, 1938); Curtis T. Henson, *Commissioners and Commodores: The East India Squadron and American Diplomacy*

in China (Tuscaloosa: University of Alabama Press, 1982); Scully, *Bargaining with the State from Afar.*

43. [Breese Report], "The Committee on Public Lands, to whom were referred a memorial of sundry citizens of Indiana, praying construction of national railroad from the Mississippi to Columbia river, and the memorial of Asa Whitney, proposing to construct railroad from Lake Michigan to Pacific ocean, report," S. Doc. 466, 29th Cong., 1st Sess. (July 31, 1846), 13–23, 27–51.

44. For a survey of a few, see Charles Vevier, "American Continentalism: An Idea of Expansion, 1845–1910," *American Historical Review* 65, no. 2 (January 1, 1960): 323–35.

45. Cotterill, "Early Agitation for a Pacific Railroad," 413. A more recent economic historian argues that transcontinental railroads could pay their own way, given the right conditions— and local traffic: Xavier H. Duran, "Was the First Transcontinental Railroad Expected to Be Profitable?: Evidence from Entrepreneur's [*sic*] Declared Expectations, an Empirical Entry Decision Model, and Ex-Post Information" (PhD diss., London School of Economics, 2010); Xavier H. Duran, "The First U.S. Transcontinental Railroad: Expected Profits and Government Intervention," *Journal of Economic History* 73, no. 1 (2013): 177–200.

46. "Railroad to the Pacific," Cong. Globe, 30th Cong., 1st Sess. (July 29, 1848), 1011. Benton later proposed his own project for a national railroad: Thomas Hart Benton, "National Central Highway from the Mississippi River to the Pacific Ocean," Cong. Globe, 30th Cong., 2nd Sess. (February 7, 1849), 470–74; "Highway to the Pacific," Cong. Globe, 31st Cong., 2nd Sess. (December 16, 1850), 56–58; Thomas Hart Benton, *Discourse of Mr. Benton, of Missouri: Before the Boston Mercantile Library Association . . .* (Washington, DC: Towers, 1854).

47. The series originally appeared in the *St. Louis Enquirer* in fall 1819 under the heading "Commerce with Asia" and was reprinted in 1844 as part of a campaign pamphlet published by the St. Louis County delegates to the state Democratic convention. "Commerce with Asia," *St. Louis Enquirer*, September 25, 29, October 2, 6, 13, 27, November 3, 17, 1819; Thomas Hart Benton, *Selections of Editorial Articles from the "St. Louis Enquirer" on the Subject of Oregon and Texas, as Originally Published in That Paper in the Years 1818–1819 . . .* (St. Louis: Missourian Office, 1844). The pamphlet is rare but is available on microfilm: Yale Collection of Western Americana and Newberry Library, *Western Americana: Frontier History of the Trans-Mississippi West, 1550–1900* (New Haven, CT: Research Publications, 1977), reel 50, no. 475. Previous scholars have generally cited the 1844 pamphlet; here I have cited the *St. Louis Enquirer* columns when possible because they are now more readily accessible through online databases than the microfilm.

48. For other accounts of Benton's plans, see Henry Nash Smith, *Virgin Land: The American West as Symbol and Myth* (Cambridge, MA: Harvard University Press, 1950), 19–34; Graebner, *Empire on the Pacific*; Richard Warner Van Alstyne, *The Rising American Empire* (New York: Oxford University Press, 1960); J. Valerie Fifer, "Transcontinental: The Political Word," *Geographical Journal* 144, no. 3 (November 1978): 438–49.

49. For a sensitive reading of the essays focusing on Benton as a Missouri booster, see John D. Morton, "'This Magnificent New World': Thomas Hart Benton's Westward Vision Reconsidered," *Missouri Historical Review* 90, no. 3 (April 1996): 284–308. For details on Benton's proposed route, see "Commerce with Asia," *St. Louis Enquirer*, October 6, 1819, and Benton, *Selections*, 25. For context on the debate over expansion Benton was responding to in 1819, see Reginald Horsman, "The Dimensions of an 'Empire for Liberty': Expansion and Republicanism, 1775–1825," *Journal of the Early Republic* 9, no. 1 (Spring 1989): 1–20; Peter J. Kastor, "'What Are the Advantages of the Acquisition?': Inventing Expansion in the Early American Republic," *American Quarterly* 60, no. 4 (2008): 1003–35.

50. From this perspective Benton was a "Jackson Man with Feet of Clay" twice over— once in the way Charles Sellers suggested, but also by modeling his geopolitics on the system

Clay championed. Charles Grier Sellers, "Jackson Men with Feet of Clay," *American Histori-cal Review* 62, no. 3 (April 1957): 537–51. On Clay's rather different ideas about how to expand the American system internationally, see Stephen Meardon, "Henry C. Carey's 'Zone Theory' and American Sectional Conflict," *Journal of the History of Economic Thought* 37, no. 2 (June 2015): 305–20.

51. Benton, *Selections*, 23. The emphasis Benton placed on this myth of Jeffersonian origins increased over time. See "Commerce with Asia," *St. Louis Enquirer*, November 17, 1819; Thomas Hart Benton, *Thirty Years' View, or A History of the Working of the American Government for Thirty Years, from 1820 to 1850* (New York: Appleton, 1865), 1:14; Jessie Benton Frémont, "Bio-graphical Sketch of Senator Benton, In Connection with Western Expansion," in John Charles Frémont, *Memoirs of My Life* (Chicago: Belford, Clarke, 1887), 8–17; Smith, *Virgin Land*, 22–23. Benton was overstating his case: it was not Jefferson who had argued in such terms, but his associates from the China-trade-interested city of Philadelphia, Tench Coxe and Albert Gallatin. See "Principles of the Plan for making an Appian Way or National Portage to unite the extensive inland Navigation of the western Lakes with an Atlantic Sea Port in the most eligible & direct Route," in Tench Coxe, Papers of Tench Coxe, in the *Coxe Family Papers at the Historical Society of Pennsylvania*, Microfilm Publications of the Historical Society of Penn-sylvania (Philadelphia: Historical Society of Pennsylvania, 1977), ser. 1, Volumes and Printed Materials, reel 29, 741–73; Albert Gallatin, *Report of the Secretary of the Treasury, on the Subject of Public Roads and Canals: Made in Pursuance of a Resolution of the Senate, of March 2, 1807* (Washington, DC: Senate, 1808).

In his younger days he credited Henry Marie Brackenridge's book *Views of Louisiana* for inspiring his support for efforts to "open an intercourse with China, Japan, and the In-dian archipelago" overland. Thomas Hart Benton to Henry Marie Brackenridge, Washington City, January 30, 1821, LB #92, box 1, folder 31, Henry Marie Brackenridge and Family Papers, 1816–1889, Darlington Collection, Archives and Special Collections, University of Pittsburgh Library System, https://digital.library.pitt.edu/islandora/object/pitt:31735051658072; Henry Marie Brackenridge, *Views of Louisiana: Together with a Journal of a Voyage Up the Missouri River, in 1811* (Pittsburgh: Cramer, Spear and Eichbaum, 1814). I am indebted to John Craig Hammond for highlighting Benton's crediting of Brackenridge.

52. "Commerce with Asia," *St. Louis Enquirer*, October 13, 1819. It's possible that "Old Bul-lion" Benton's belief that the China trade was a "hard money" business contributed to his opposition to the Cushing mission; a simple commodity exchange business needed no dip-lomatic support.

53. Emphasis in original. "Commerce with Asia," *St. Louis Enquirer*, September 25, 1819.

54. Ryan Schuessler, "Benton Statue Will Gleam Again," *St. Louis Beacon*, July 13, 2011; Jes-sie Benton Frémont, "Biographical Sketch of Senator Benton, In Connection with Western Expansion," 16.

55. "Occupation of the Oregon," Reg. Deb., 18th Cong., 2nd Sess. (March 1, 1825), App., 711–12.

56. President Monroe had considered including a statement of this "principle of separate republics" in his annual message of 1824, but he was opposed by the committed expansionists in his cabinet—especially John Quincy Adams and John C. Calhoun. Bradford Perkins, *Cre-ation of a Republican Empire, 1776–1865*, Cambridge History of American Foreign Relations 1 (New York: Cambridge University Press, 1993), 173.

57. "Railroad from Lake Michigan to the Pacific. Memorial of Asa Whitney, of New York City, relative to the construction of a railroad from Lake Michigan to the Pacific Ocean," H.R. Doc. 72, 28th Cong., 2nd Sess. (January 28, 1845), 1.

58. "Consolidation" may have been one of his proposal's problems. A term used frequently

in resolutions supporting Whitney's plan was also a critical one for anxious slaveholders, who feared what centralization would do to their control of local law and enslaved property. Frank Towers, "The Threat of Consolidation: States' Rights and American Discourses of Nation and Empire in the Nineteenth Century," *Journal of the Civil War Era* 9, no. 4 (December 5, 2019): 612–32.

59. Benton, *Selections*, 3.

60. For example: "Speech of Hon. Thos. P. Akers, of Missouri, in the House of Representatives," Cong. Globe, 34th Cong., 3rd Sess. (January 14, 1857), App., 153–54. Ironically, Benton had opposed the US mission to China. "The Mission to China," Cong. Globe, 27th Cong., 3rd Sess. (March 3, 1843), 391–92; Benton, *Thirty Years' View*, 2:510–14.

61. The Pacific Railroad Act finally passed in 1862. 12 Stat. 489, "An Act: To aid in the construction of a railroad and telegraph line from the Missouri River to the Pacific Ocean" (July 1, 1862); Bain, *Empire Express*, 104–18.

62. Several bills were based on Whitney's plan; none made it out of the chambers into which they were first reported. See H.R. 468, 30th Cong. (1848); S. 297, 30th Cong. (1849); H.R. 156, 31st Cong. (1850); S. 333, 31st Cong. (1850); H.R. 186, 32nd Cong. (1852)

63. Asa Whitney, *Plan for a Direct Communication between the Great Centres of the Populations of Europe and Asia: Read before the Royal Geographic Society of London on the 9th of June, 1851* (London: Clowes, 1851); Bain, *Empire Express*, 45–46.

64. "Pacific Railroad," Cong. Globe, 37th Cong., 2nd Sess. (April 18, 1862), 1727; Brown, "Asa Whitney and His Pacific Railroad Publicity Campaign," 223; Bain, *Empire Express*, 46.

65. For example, when two large meetings of rail promoters convened in St. Louis and then in Memphis in late 1849, they failed to make any progress, instead only producing new fodder for conspiracy theories and press wars. Albert Pike, *National Plan of an Atlantic and Pacific Rail Road: And Remarks of Albert Pike, Made Thereon, at Memphis, November, 1849*, 4th ed. (Little Rock, AK: Gazette and Democrat, 1849); Cotterill, "Early Agitation for a Pacific Railroad."

66. 10 Stat. 219, "An Act: Making appropriations for the support of the army, for the year ending, the thirtieth of June, in the year eighteen hundred and fifty-four" (March 3, 1853).

67. Frank Heywood Hodder, "The Railroad Background of the Kansas-Nebraska Act," *Mississippi Valley Historical Review* 12, no. 1 (June 1, 1925): 3–22; Jere W. Roberson, "The South and the Pacific Railroad, 1845–1855," *Western Historical Quarterly* 5, no. 2 (April 1, 1974): 163–86.

68. Walker Brooke, "Railroad to the Pacific," Cong. Globe, 32nd Cong., 2nd Sess. (January 17, 1853), 315; William M. Gwin, "Memoirs of Hon. William M. Gwin (Continued)," ed. William Henry Ellison, *California Historical Society Quarterly* 19, no. 2 (June 1940): 175.

69. Some of the US Army Corps of Engineers' reports analyzed potential routes in terms of the access they could provide to Asian markets, just as Whitney had done. Spencer Fullerton Baird et al., *Reports of Explorations and Surveys, to Ascertain the Most Practicable and Economical Route for a Railroad from the Mississippi River to the Pacific Ocean* (Washington, DC: Tucker, 1855), 1:14, 130.

70. The same platform also maintained the same anti-internal improvement plank that had been the party's standard since 1840. "Democratic Party Platform of 1856," June 2, 1856, in Peters and Woolley, "American Presidency Project."

71. James Buchanan, "First Annual Message," December 8, 1857, in James D. Richardson, ed., *A Compilation of the Messages and Papers of the Presidents, 1789–1908* (New York: Bureau of National Literature and Art, 1908), 5:457; James Buchanan, "Second Annual Message," December 6, 1858, in Richardson, *A Compilation of the Messages and Papers of the Presidents*, 5:527. The interior quotation marks in the first quotation are references to article 4, section 4 of the Constitution. For other recommendations to Congress, see Richardson, *Compilation of the Messages and Papers of the Presidents*, 5:572–73, 650.

72. For Republicans emphasizing "military necessity" arguments, see William H. Seward, "Pacific Railroad," Cong. Globe, 35th Cong., 2nd Sess. (December 22, 1859), 158; "Pacific Railroad," H.R. Rep. 428, 36th Cong., 1st Sess. (April 13, 1860).

73. Putatively continent-crossing, at least. As Richard White points out, these roads "did not really span the continent" but more often began at the Missouri River. White, *Railroaded,* xxi.

74. Fifer, "Transcontinental," 438.

75. Fifer, "Transcontinental"; "Trans-Continental, adj. and n.," in *Oxford English Dictionary* (New York: Oxford University Press, January 2020).

76. "Monthly Record of Current Events," *Harper's New Monthly Magazine* 6, no. 34 (March 1853): 550. For the 1853 dating, see Fifer, "Transcontinental"; *OED,* "Trans-continental, adj. and n."

77. "Route to the East Indies," *Weekly Ohio Statesman* (Columbus), November 5, 1845; emphasis in the original. This is the earliest incidence of the term I could find using archival resources and textual databases available as of November 2013. Databases consulted for this search include Chronicling America (Library of Congress); America's Historical Newspapers (Readex, Newsbank, Inc.); America's Historical Imprints (Readex, Newsbank, Inc.); U.S. Congressional Serial Set (Readex, Newsbank, Inc.); Nineteenth Century U.S. Newspapers (Gale/CENGAGE Learning); Nineteenth Century Collections Online (Gale/CENGAGE Learning); American Periodicals (Proquest); Hein Online Congressional; Proquest Congressional; A Century of Lawmaking for a New Nation (Library of Congress); Making of America (University of Michigan); Making of America (Cornell University); JSTOR.org; The Making of Modern Law: Legal Treatises 1800–1926 (Gale/CENGAGE Learning); Sabin Americana, 1500–1926 (Gale/CENGAGE Learning); The Making of the Modern World: Goldsmiths' Library of Economic Literature and the Kress Library (Gale/CENGAGE Learning); HathiTrust Digital Library; Google Books; and the Internet Archive.

78. John L. O'Sullivan, "Annexation," *United States Magazine and Democratic Review* 17, no. 85 (July/August 1845): 9.

79. William Earl Weeks, *Dimensions of the Early American Empire, 1754–1865,* vol. 1 of *The New Cambridge History of American Foreign Relations* (New York: Cambridge University Press, 2013), 150.

Chapter Six

1. Humphrey Marshall to Edward Everett, Macao, March 8, 1853, no. 9, in "M92: Despatches from U.S. Ministers to China, 1843–1906," General Records of the Department of State, RG 59, National Archives, 1973, reel 9. Also reprinted in "Correspondence with the late Commissioner to China," H.R. Exec. Doc. 123, 33rd Cong., 1st Sess. (July 19, 1854), 78–82. For an examination of Marshall's time in China, see Kenneth Wesley Rea, "Humphrey Marshall's Commissionership to China, 1852–1854" (PhD diss., University of Colorado at Boulder, 1970).

2. Humphrey Marshall to Edward Everett, Macao, March 8, 1853, no. 9, in "M92: Despatches from China," reel 9.

3. Humphrey Marshall to Edward Everett, Macao, March 8, 1853, no. 9, in "M92: Despatches from China," reel 9.

4. Matthew Karp, *This Vast Southern Empire: Slaveholders at the Helm of American Foreign Policy* (Cambridge, MA: Harvard University Press, 2016).

5. For more on this early "Gladstone coolies" project, see Hugh Tinker, *A New System of Slavery: The Export of Indian Labour Overseas, 1830–1920* (London: Oxford University Press, 1974).

6. On the etymology of the word "coolie," see Moon-Ho Jung, "Coolie," in *Keywords for American Cultural Studies*, ed. Bruce Burgett and Glenn Hendler (New York: New York University Press, 2007), 64–66; "Coolie, n.," in *OED Online* (Oxford University Press, March 2012). For works that summarize the history of indentured Asian labor in the Americas see Edward Bartlett Rugemer, *The Problem of Emancipation: The Caribbean Roots of the American Civil War* (Baton Rouge: Louisiana State University Press, 2008), 260–64; Evelyn Hu-DeHart, "La Trata Amarilla: The 'Yellow Trade' and the Middle Passage, 1847–1884," in *Many Middle Passages: Forced Migration and the Making of the Modern World*, ed. Emma Christopher, Cassandra Pybus, and Marcus Rediker (Berkeley: University of California Press, 2007), 166–83; Jung, *Coolies and Cane*; Moon-Ho Jung, "Outlawing 'Coolies': Race, Nation, and Empire in the Age of Emancipation," *American Quarterly* 57, no. 3 (2005): 677–701. On Americans' specialization in the trade, see David Northrup, *Indentured Labor in the Age of Imperialism, 1834–1922* (Cambridge: Cambridge University Press, 1995), 156–60.

7. Adam McKeown, "Global Migration, 1846–1940," *Journal of World History* 15, no. 2 (June 1, 2004): 158–59.

8. Elizabeth Kelly Gray, "'Whisper to Him the Word "India"': Trans-Atlantic Critics and American Slavery, 1830–1860," *Journal of the Early Republic* 28, no. 3 (2008): 379–406.

9. Quotation from arch-proslavery apologist and fervent opponent of the coolie trade J. D. B. De Bow's 1848 study of West Indian labor: *"Liberate your West India slaves; force them* [other slave territories], *as you can, to liberate theirs, and you can have the monopoly of the world!"* Editor, "The West India Islands," *De Bow's Review* 5/6 (May/June 1848), 488. (Emphasis in original.) For a similar account, see "Gov. Hammond's Letters on Slavery.—No. 3," *De Bow's Review* 8 (February 1850), 128–29. Democratic Party organs were quick to reproduce this rhetoric as well: "Slaves and Slavery," *United States Magazine and Democratic Review* 19, no. 100 (October 1846): 243–54. Hammond and De Bow's positions tracked closely those of thinkers like John C. Calhoun, who argued in an 1840 letter to an associate that Britain aimed at "control of the commerce of the world, by controlling the labour, which produces the articles by which it is principally put in motion." John C. Calhoun to Duff Green, Washington, April 2, 1840, in John C Calhoun, *The Papers of John C. Calhoun*, ed. Robert Lee Meriwether, William Edwin Hemphill, and Clyde Norman Wilson (Columbia: University of South Carolina Press, 1959), 16:209.

10. "The Territorial Question. Speech of Mr. Hunter, of Virginia, in Senate, March 25, 1850," Cong. Globe, 31st Cong., 1st Sess., App., 380 (March 25, 1850). For similar see "The Oregon Bill. Speech of Mr. D. Wallace, of South Carolina, in the House of Representatives, July 26, 1848," Cong. Globe, 30th Cong., 1st Sess., App., 956 (July 26, 1848). While California was technically a "free state" in its laws, the state's politicians were often proslavery advocates, and various forms of bondage were actively practiced within its borders. Stacey L. Smith, *Freedom's Frontier: California and the Struggle over Unfree Labor, Emancipation, and Reconstruction* (Chapel Hill: University of North Carolina Press, 2013).

11. The first shipment of Chinese workers arrived in Havana in June 1847, but it took some time for American observers to notice and become concerned. Hu-DeHart, "Trata Amarilla," 167.

12. "Orientals in America," *New York Times*, April 15, 1852; "Cotton, Cane and the Coolies," *New York Times*, May 3, 1852; "Labor in Cuba," *New York Times*, December 10, 1852.

13. "Cuban Annexation: Speech of Hon. J. R. Giddings, of Ohio, In the House of Representatives, December 14, 1852," Cong. Globe, 32nd Cong., 2nd Sess., App., 40 (December 14, 1852). The speech was also published separately. Joshua R. Giddings, *Speech of Hon. J. R. Giddings, of Ohio, on Cuban Annexation: Delivered in the House of Representatives, December 14, 1852* (United States: s.n., 1852). On Giddings's eventful congressional career, including detailed ac-

counts of some of the other instances when he baited his proslavery colleagues to the point of violent confrontation, see James Brewer Stewart, *Joshua R. Giddings and the Tactics of Radical Politics* (Cleveland, OH: Press of Case Western Reserve University, 1970).

14. "The Ostend Conference," H.R. Exec. Doc. 93, 33rd Cong., 2nd Sess. (March 3, 1855), 128; C. Stanley Urban, "The Africanization of Cuba Scare, 1853–1855," *Hispanic American Historical Review* 37, no. 1 (1957): 29.

15. William H. Robertson to William L. Marcy, Havana, August 6, 1855, and September 3, 1855, in "Slave and Coolie Trade," S. Exec. Doc. 99, 34th Cong., 1st Sess. (August 5, 1856), 3–4. On Soulé, see J. Preston Moore, "Pierre Soulé: Southern Expansionist and Promoter," *Journal of Southern History* 21, no. 2 (May 1955): 203–23. On the long history of fears of foreign-led slave conspiracies, see Jason T. Sharples, "Discovering Slave Conspiracies: New Fears of Rebellion and Old Paradigms of Plotting in Seventeenth-Century Barbados," *American Historical Review* 120, no. 3 (June 1, 2015): 811–43; Jason T. Sharples, *The World That Fear Made: Slave Revolts and Conspiracy Scares in Early America* (Philadelphia: University of Pennsylvania Press, 2020).

16. As reprinted in "Emancipation in Cuba: Correspondence of the Journal of Commerce," *New York Times*, April 24, 1855.

17. Sigma, "Coolees, No. XIV," *Boston Evening Transcript*, June 9, 1856.

18. This distinction was maintained by planters in other parts of the world, though for different reasons. The Cuban government office charged with regulating coolie traffic was the Comisión de población blanca (White Population Commission), a subagency of the Junta de fomento y colonización (Development and Settlement Board). This classification advertised the fiction that the laborers bonded to fungible eight-year contracts were treated as "free" (white) immigrants—and so did not fall under any anti–slave trading statutes or treaties. Hu-DeHart, "Trata Amarilla," 171.

19. "The Tariff—Mr. Taylor," Cong. Globe, 34th Cong., 3rd Sess., App., 256 (February 5, 1857).

20. "British Policy in Central America and Cuba," Cong. Globe, 34th Cong., 3rd Sess., App., 178 (February 5, 1857). For similar accounts, see "Arrest of Walker," Cong. Globe, 35th Cong., 1st Sess., 1977 (May 5, 1858).

21. "Making Appropriations to Facilitate the Acquisition of the Island of Cuba, by Negotiation," S. Rep 351, 35th Cong., 2nd Sess. (January 24, 1859), 15.

22. "The Coolie Trade," *De Bow's Review* 22 (July 1857), 31.

23. Emphasis in original. G. W. P., "Chincha Islands . . ." *Littell's Living Age* 4, no. 506 (January 28, 1854): 214. Peck's report was first published in the *New York Times* and later formed part of his book on his travels. George Washington Peck, *Melbourne, and the Chincha Islands; with Sketches of Lima, and a Voyage round the World* (New York: Scribner, 1854). On the guano trade, see Edward D. Melillo, "The First Green Revolution: Debt Peonage and the Making of the Nitrogen Fertilizer Trade, 1840–1930," *American Historical Review* 117, no. 4 (October 1, 2012): 1028–60.

24. On the *Waverly*, see "The Coolie Trade—Wholesale Massacre," *Albany Evening Journal*, January 21, 1856; "The Coolie Trade—Wholesale Massacre," *Boston Daily Atlas*, January 21, 1856; "Coolees, No. X," *Boston Evening Transcript*, May 26, 1856; "Slave and Coolie Trade," S. Exec. Doc. 99, 34th Cong., 1st Sess. (August 5, 1856), 6–11, 97–99; Jung, "Outlawing 'Coolies,'" 686.

25. Parker informed the American mercantile community in China that those who chose to persist in the coolie trade would forfeit their right to US protection, rendering "themselves liable to the heavy penalties" imposed by the Chinese government—including, potentially, death. However, the withdrawal of US protection meant very little in practice. The US military

presence in China was slight compared with other powers', and subsequent commissioners to China did not follow through on Parker's threats. For Parker's proclamation, see "Public Notice," in S. Exec. Doc. 22, 35th Cong., 2nd Sess. (December 21, 1858), 625–26. On conditions as Parker reported them, see "Extract from a Private Letter," Macao, April 6, 1856, in Peter Parker to William L. Marcy, Macao, April 10, 1856, No. 9, attachment E, in "M92: Despatches from China," reel 13. Reproduced in ". . . Correspondence of Messrs. McLane and Parker, late commissioners to China," S. Exec. Doc. 22, 35th Cong., 2nd Sess. (December 21, 1858), 773. On the reception it received, see "From China," *Boston Daily Advertiser*, March 25, 1856; "The Coolie Trade," *Boston Daily Atlas*, March 25, 1856; "Dr. Parker . . . ," *Daily Picayune* (New Orleans), April 2, 1856; "The Peruvian Slave Trade," *Liberator*, April 4, 1856; "Summary of News," *Boston Investigator*, April 16, 1856; "We Have Received, . . ." *New York Times*, April 17, 1856; "The Following Paragraph . . . ," *New York Times*, April 21, 1856; "The Coolies," *Boston Evening Transcript*, April 22, 1856; "The Kansas Evidence Arrived at Washington—Government on the Coolie Trade," *Boston Evening Transcript*, May 20, 1856; "Foo-Chow-Foo Correspondence," *New York Herald*, June 1, 1856.

26. On Sampson and Tappan see "The News," *New York Herald*, May 2, 1856; Sampson and Tappan to Peter Parker, Boston, January 24, 1857, in "Correspondence of Messrs. McLane and Parker, late commissioners to China," S. Exec. Doc. 22, 35th Cong., 2nd Sess. (December 21, 1858), 1128–29; Boston Board of Trade, *Report of the Committee Appointed by the Government of the "Board of Trade," to Take into Consideration the Communication of Messrs. Sampson and Tappan, Dated April 24th, 1856* (Boston: J. H. Eastburn, 1856). The firm's involvement in the trade, and their half-competent attempts to evade public knowledge of their business, were the subject of a long and merciless series of columns by Lucius M. Sargent, writing under the pseudonym "Sigma" for the *Boston Evening Transcript*. Sargent was probably at least partly motivated by a personal dislike of the firm's partners, but his columns were no less devastating or popular for that. In the course of destroying Sampson and Tappan's reputation, and that of their business partners Lomer and Company, he helped chisel in stone the infamy of the American coolie trade. See "The Coolie Trade," *Boston Evening Transcript*, April 16, 1856; "Coolees, No. II," *BET*, April 19, 1856; "Coolees, No. III," *BET*, April 21, 1856; "Coolees, No. IV," *BET*, April 25, 1856; "Coolees, No. V," *BET*, April 29, 1856, 29; "Coolees, No. VI," *BET*, May 2, 1856; "Coolees, No. VII," *BET*, May 6, 1856; "Coolees, No. VIII," *BET*, May 9, 1856; "Coolees, No. IX," *BET*, May 23, 1856; "Coolees, No. X," *BET*, May 26, 1856; "Coolees, No. XI," *BET*, May 30, 1856; "Coolees, No. XII," *BET*, June 2, 1856; "Coolees, No. XIII," *BET*, June 5, 1856; "Coolees, No. XIV," *BET*, June 9, 1856; "Coolees, No. XV," *BET*, June 25, 1856; "Coolees, No. XVI," *BET*, June 27, 1856; Coolees, No. XVII," *BET*, June 30, 1856; "Coolees, No. XVIII," *BET*, July 5, 1856; "Coolees, No. XIX," *BET*, July 8, 1856; "Coolees, No. XX," *BET*, July 11, 1856; "Coolees, No. XXI," *BET*, July 15, 1856; "Coolees, No. XXII," *BET*, July 18, 1856; "Coolees, No. XXIII," *BET*, July 24, 1856; "Coolees, No. XXIV," *BET*, July 28, 1856; "Coolees, No. XXV," *BET*, August 31, 1856; "Coolees, No. XXVI," *BET*, August 6, 1856; "Coolees, No. XXVII," *BET*, August 11, 1856; "Coolees, No. XXVIII," *BET*, August 13, 1856; "Coolees, No. XXIX," *BET*, August 18, 1856; "Coolees, No. XXX," *BET*, August 25, 1856; "Coolees, No. XXXI," *BET*, September 1, 1856; "Coolees, No. XXXII," *BET*, September 3, 1856; "Coolees. No. XXXIII," *BET*, September 9, 1856; "Coolees, No. XXXIV," *BET*, September 15, 1856; "Coolees, No. XXXV," *BET*, September 22, 1856; "Coolees, No. XXXVI," *BET*, September 25, 1856; "Coolees, No. XXXVII," *BET*, September 27, 1856; "Coolees, No. XXXVIII," *BET*, October 1, 1856; "Coolees, No. XXXIX," *BET*, October 3, 1856.

On Sigma, see Rossiter Johnson and John Howard Brown, eds., "Sargent, Lucius Manlius," in *The Twentieth Century Biographical Dictionary of Notable Americans . . .* (Boston: Biographical Society, 1904); John H. Sheppard, "Reminiscences of Lucius Manlius Sargent,"

New-England Historical and Genealogical Register and Antiquarian Journal 25, no. 3 (July 1871): 209–21.

27. Apart from a few gullible or guilt-ridden shipmasters, Parker's posturing was ignored by American merchants on the China coast, when it was not mocked outright; his public notice was known among the wags in the American mercantile community as "St. Peter's First Epistle to the Coolies." See "Foo-Chow-Foo Correspondence," *New York Herald*, June 1, 1856.

28. Emphasis in original. Sigma, "Coolees, No. XXV," *Boston Evening Transcript*, July 31, 1856. According to the *Transcript*, the advertisement appeared in the January 28, 1856, edition of *El Heraldo de Lima*, but I have not been able to confirm this.

29. On slave ship design, see Marcus Rediker, *The Slave Ship : A Human History* (New York: Viking, 2007), 41–72.

30. Edgar Holden, "A Chapter on the Coolie Trade," *Harper's New Monthly Magazine* 29, no. 169 (June 1864): 1–11. The captain of the Sampson and Tappan ship *Indiaman* described a similar feature in his vessel. See Capt. Duncan McCallum to Messrs. Sampson and Tappan, October 20, 1855, as quoted in Sigma, "Coolees, No. XVIII," *Boston Evening Transcript*, July 5, 1856.

31. For contemporary reaction see "The Coolie Trade," *Merchants' Magazine and Commercial Review* 42 (June 1, 1860), 763ff. For more on mutinies and mortality rates, see table 17: "Ships Carrying Chinese Emigrants on Which Mutinies Occurred, 1847–1874," in Arnold Joseph Meagher, "The Introduction of Chinese Laborers to Latin America: The 'Coolie Trade,' 1847–1874" (PhD diss., University of California, Davis, 1975), 185A; "Table A.5, Mortality on Ocean Voyages in the Nineteenth Century" and "Table A.6, Changing Mortality Patterns in the Nineteenth Century," in Northrup, *Indentured Labor in the Age of Imperialism, 1834–1922*, 163, 164; John McDonald and Ralph Shlomowitz, "Mortality on Chinese and Indian Voyages to the West Indies and South America, 1847–1874," *Social and Economic Studies* 41, no. 2 (June 1, 1992): 203–40.

32. "The White Slave Trade," *New York Journal of Commerce*, April 5, 1856.

33. "Satan Rebuking Sin," *New-York Daily Tribune*, April 8, 1856; "The 'Cooly' Business," *Liberator*, May 23, 1856.

34. "Satan Rebuking Sin," *New-York Daily Tribune*, April 8, 1856.

35. "Coolie Slave Trade," *Liberator*, April 18, 1856.

36. "Coolie Slave Trade," *Liberator*, April 18, 1856.

37. Reprinted, with attribution, as "The 'Cooly' Business," *Liberator*, May 23, 1856.

38. *House Journal*, 34th Cong., 1st Sess., April 7, 1856, 796; *Senate Journal*, 34th Cong., 1st Sess., April 17, 1856, 260–61; *Senate Journal*, 34th Cong., 1st Sess., April 24, 1856, 277–78; "Coolie Trade," Cong. Globe, 34th Cong., 1st Sess., 1012 (April 24, 1856).

39. In the House, the resolutions were proposed by Kentucky representative and former China commissioner Humphrey Marshall and New York representative Benjamin Pringle; in the Senate Louisiana Judah Benjamin and Massachusetts's Charles Sumner proposed investigations. All identified as members of their respective states' "Opposition" parties, at least at the time (Benjamin was soon to ally himself with the Democrats under the leadership of John Slidell). The only Democrat to contribute anything to official inquiries into the coolie trade was Senator Henry Wilson, a Massachusetts Free Soiler, who presented a petition from a constituent urging prohibition of the trade; it was referred to the Committee on Commerce, pursuant to Sumner's earlier resolution. After Sumner's caning, Wilson alluded to the coolie trade in a rambling speech memorializing his colleague. See *Senate Journal*, 34th Cong., 1st Sess., April 30, 1856, 291; "Kansas Affair," Cong. Globe, 34th Cong., 1st Sess., 1403 (June 13, 1856).

40. "Slave and Coolie Trade," H.R. Exec. Doc. 105, 34th Cong., 1st Sess. (May 19, 1856); "Slave and Coolie Trade," S. Exec. Doc. 99, 34th Cong., 1st Sess. (August 5, 1856). The Senate

report, delivered three months after the House report, was the same document with a few minor additions. Later reports on American diplomacy in China, part of regular congressional oversight, solidified the narrative that had taken root in 1856. E.g., see "Correspondence of Messrs. McLane and Parker, late commissioners to China," S. Exec. Doc. 22, 35th Cong., 2nd Sess. (December 21, 1858), and "Correspondence and Dispatches of the Ministers to China," S. Exec. Doc. 30, 36th Cong., 1st Sess. (March 13, 1860).

41. Oolong, "For the Journal of Commerce," *New York Journal of Commerce*, April 11, 1856, emphasis in the original; Robert Bennet Forbes to William L. Marcy, Washington, April 19, 1854, in Forbes Family Papers, Massachusetts Historical Society, ser. 2, Robert Bennet Forbes Papers, 1768–1889, reel 12, number 4, folder 10.

42. See, for example, "Commerce in Coolies," *New York Times*, April 12, 1856.

43. "The Coolie Trade," *Boston Daily Atlas*, March 25, 1856; "The Slave Trade in a New Form," *Boston Daily Atlas*, April 8, 1856; "Coolie Emigrants," *Boston Daily Atlas*, April 10, 1856; "Coolie Emigration," *Boston Daily Atlas*, April 12, 1856; "The Coolie Emigration," *Boston Daily Atlas*, April 17, 1856; "Coolie Emigration and the Slave Trade," *Boston Daily Atlas*, August 6, 1856; "Horrors of the Coolie Trade," *Boston Daily Atlas*, October 27, 1856; "Coolies Landed in Havana," *Boston Daily Atlas*, December 5, 1856.

44. "From China," *Boston Evening Transcript*, August 12, 1856; Russell and Company to Messrs. JM Forbes and Company, Hong Kong, July 3, 1860, in Forbes Family Business Records, Baker Library Historical Collections, Harvard Business School, box 3, folder 35.

45. On later commissioners' efforts, see William Bradford Reed to Lewis Cass, Macao, January 13, 1858, no. 1, in "M92: Despatches from China," reel 16; John E. Ward to Lewis Cass, Macao, January 24, 1860, no. 1, in "M92: Despatches from China," reel 19; and "Correspondence and Dispatches of the Ministers to China," S. Exec. Doc. 30, 36th Cong., 1st Sess. (March 13, 1860), 204–6.

46. On Reed's request and the attorney general's denial, see J. S. Black to Lewis Cass, Washington, March 11, 1859, in "M179: Miscellaneous Letters of the Department of State, 1789–1906," General Records of the Department of State, RG 59, National Archives, 1963, reel 168. On Trescot and Russell's fight, see "The Slave and Coolie Trade," *New York Times*, August 20, 1860. See also "African Slave Trade," H.R. Exec. Doc. 7, 36th Cong., 2nd Sess. (December 5, 1860), 441–43, 446–48, 455–57.

47. Samuel Wells Williams, "The Journal of S. Wells Williams, LL.D.," ed. Frederick Wells Williams, *Journal of the North China Branch of the Royal Asiatic Society* 42 (1911): 221.

48. Frank Walcott Hutt, ed., *A History of Bristol County, Massachusetts* (New York: Lewis Historical Publishing, 1924), 1:35–36.

49. Thomas Dawes Eliot, "Coolie Trade," H.R. Rep. 443, 36th Cong., 1st Sess. (April 16, 1860), 24.

50. Thomas Dawes Eliot, "Coolie Trade," H.R. Rep. 443, 36th Cong., 1st Sess. (April 16, 1860), 15. On the procedural objections of Henry Cornelius Burnett (D-KY), Lawrence O'Bryan Branch (D-NC), and John Henninger Reagan (D-TX), see Cong. Globe, 36th Cong. 1st Sess., 1441, 1492, 1557, 1574 (1860).

51. For Eliot's request, see *House Journal*, 37th Congress, 1st Sess., July 13, 1861, 78. The report was delivered on December 23, 1861, and Eliot's bill passed on January 15, 1862: *House Journal*, 37th Cong., 2nd Sess., December 23, 1861, 124–25; *House Journal*, 37th Cong., 2nd Sess., January 15, 1862, 185.

52. H.R. 109, 37th Cong. (1862).

53. "The Cooly Trade," Cong. Globe, 37th Cong., 2nd Sess., 555–56 (June 30, 1862).

54. 12 Stat. 340, "An Act to prohibit the 'Coolie Trade'" by American Citizens in American

Vessels" (February 19, 1862). For more on the bill's path in Congress, see Jung, *Coolies and Cane*, 36–38.

55. For more on the capabilities of the consular service, see Charles Stuart Kennedy, *The American Consul: A History of the United States Consular Service, 1776–1914* (New York: Greenwood Press, 1990); Eileen P. Scully, *Bargaining with the State from Afar: American Citizenship in Treaty Port China, 1844–1942* (New York: Columbia University Press, 2001); Nicole M. Phelps, "One Service, Three Systems, Many Empires: The U.S. Consular Service and the Growth of U.S. Global Power, 1789–1924," in *Crossing Empires: Taking U.S. History into Transimperial Terrain*, ed. Kristin L. Hoganson and Jay Sexton (Durham, NC: Duke University Press, 2020), 135–58.

56. Consul Goulding to Secretary of State Hamilton Fish, November 19, 1869, Hong Kong, in Jules Davids, ed., *The Coolie Trade and Outrages against the Chinese*, vol. 12, American Diplomatic and Public Papers: The United States and China, ser. 2, The United States, China, and Imperial Rivalries (Wilmington, DE: Scholarly Resources, 1979), 72–76; J. Ross Browne to Secretary of State Hamilton Fish, August 23, 1869, San Francisco, CA, in Davids, *American Diplomatic and Public Papers*, 1979, 12:66–71.

57. Cong. Globe, 41st Cong., 2nd Sess., 5121–24 (1870).

58. Cong. Globe, 41st Cong., 2nd Sess., 5125 (1870).

59. Cong. Globe, 41st Cong., 2nd Sess., 5125 (1870). On Stewart's bill, see S. 973, 41st Cong., 2nd Sess. (1870), "A Bill to Prohibit Contracts for Servile Labor."

60. Cong. Globe, 41st Cong., 2nd Sess., 5150 (1870).

61. 16 Stat. 256 § 7, "An Act to Amend the Naturalization Laws and to Punish Crimes against the Same, and for Other Purposes" (July 14, 1870). For an extended legislative history of the Naturalization Act and subsequent anti-Chinese legislation, see the very thorough Martin Gold, *Forbidden Citizens: Chinese Exclusion and the U.S. Congress; A Legislative History* (Alexandria, VA: TheCapital.Net, 2012), esp. 1–32.

62. Charles I. Bevans, ed., *Treaties and Other International Agreements of the United States of America, 1776–1949* (Washington DC: Government Printing Office, 1968), 6:682–83.

63. 1 Rev. Stat. 378–79 (1875).

64. 18 Stat. 477, "An Act supplementary to the acts in relation to immigration" (March 3, 1875). For an examination of the Page Law's import, see George Anthony Peffer, *If They Don't Bring Their Women Here: Chinese Female Immigration before Exclusion* (Urbana: University of Illinois Press, 1999).

65. John Murray Forbes to Thomas Dawes Eliot, Boston, April 1860 (typescript), Forbes Family Business Records, Baker Library Historical Collections, Harvard Business School, box 1, folder 14.

66. On Forbes's relationship with Marshall, see John Murray Forbes to Paul S. Forbes, Milton, December 5, 1858, in John Murray Forbes, Letters of J. M. Forbes, 1843–1867 (typescript), Historical Collections, Baker Library, Harvard Business School, 1936. On his proposed plantation, see John Murray Forbes, *Letters and Recollections of John Murray Forbes*, ed. Sarah Forbes Hughes (Boston: Houghton, Mifflin, 1899), 1:147–48; John Murray Forbes to J. Hamilton Cowper, Boston, September 18, 1856, in John Murray Forbes and Sarah Forbes Hughes, *Letters (Supplementary) of John Murray Forbes* (Boston: George H. Ellis, 1905), 1:165–67. The St. Johns River area of Florida, the proposed site of Forbes's plantation, was an area popular with New Englanders after the war as well. See Philip J. Pauly, *Fruits and Plains: The Horticultural Transformation of America* (Cambridge, MA: Harvard University Press, 2007), 95–229. On Forbes's career as a railroad investor, see John Lauritz Larson, *Bonds of Enterprise: John Murray Forbes and Western Development in America's Railway Age* (Cambridge, MA: Harvard University Press, 1984).

Chapter Seven

1. *House Journal*, 40th Cong., 2nd Sess., June 9, 1868, 823. There was some dispute as to Burlingame's precise rank within the embassy, as well as the content of his instructions—the result of rumors spread by the foreign residents in China who opposed the embassy's policy—but when he was welcomed by Western courts, Burlingame was recognized as head of the mission, minister plenipotentiary and envoy extraordinary. "The Presentation of the Chinese Embassy to the President," *National Intelligencer*, June 6, 1868; *Foreign Relations of the United States [FRUS]* (Washington, DC: Government Printing Office, n.d.), 1868–69, 1:601–4; Knight Biggerstaff, "A Translation of Anson Burlingame's Instructions from the Chinese Foreign Office," *Far Eastern Quarterly* 1, no. 3 (May 1, 1942): 277–79; Martin Robert Ring, "Anson Burlingame, S. Wells Williams and China, 1861–1870, a Great Era in Chinese-American Relations" (PhD diss., Tulane University, 1972), 231.

2. For an admiring look at Burlingame's oratory, see James G. Blaine, "Mr. Burlingame as an Orator," *Atlantic Monthly* 26, no. 157 (November 1870): 629–32. The *Daily Alta California*'s Boston correspondent had less flattering views, at least on Burlingame's career before his China posting: "It is the general belief here that Burlingame has grown very much intellectually since he went to China; he used to be regarded a smart, gassy man, without any depth." "Letter from Boston," *Daily Alta California*, July 15, 1868. For other assessments of Burlingame's skills, see Frederick Wells Williams, *Anson Burlingame and the First Chinese Mission to Foreign Powers* (New York: Scribner's, 1912); David L. Anderson, "'Fair Diplomatic Action': Anson Burlingame and the Cooperative Policy in China," in *Imperialism and Idealism: American Diplomats in China, 1861–1898* (Bloomington: Indiana University Press, 1985), 1–15; John Rogers Haddad, "Cooperation: Burlingame and the Reinvention of Sino-American Relations," in *America's First Adventure in China: Trade, Treaties, Opium, and Salvation* (Philadelphia: Temple University Press, 2013), 208–30.

3. "Hon. Charles Sumner's Speech," in Boston City Council, *Reception and Entertainment of the Chinese Embassy, by the City of Boston, 1868* (Boston: Mudge, 1868), 35.

4. Immanuel C. Y. Hsu, "Late Ch'ing Foreign Relations, 1866–1905," in *The Cambridge History of China*, ed. John K. Fairbank and Kwang-Ching Liu (Cambridge: Cambridge University Press, 1980), 11:70–141. On attitudinal change, see Williams, *Anson Burlingame*, 250. On the continuity of this ambiguity in US-China relations, see Tyler Dennett, *Americans in Eastern Asia: A Critical Study of the Policy of the United States with Reference to China, Japan, and Korea in the 19th Century* (New York: Macmillan, 1922); David L. Anderson, *Imperialism and Idealism: American Diplomats in China, 1861–1898* (Bloomington: Indiana University Press, 1985).

5. It is less of a problem from the perspective of scholarship on China; Burlingame's mission, while not seen as a major milestone, is understood as in keeping with the general program of the Tongzhi Restoration. Hsu, "Late Ch'ing Foreign Relations, 1866–1905," 74–75.

6. Hosea Ballou Morse, *The International Relations of the Chinese Empire*, 3 vols. (London: Longmans, Green, 1910); Williams, *Anson Burlingame*; Dennett, *Americans in Eastern Asia*; Michael H. Hunt, *The Making of a Special Relationship: The United States and China to 1914* (New York: Columbia University Press, 1983); Anderson, *Imperialism and Idealism*; David M. Pletcher, *The Diplomacy of Involvement: American Economic Expansion across the Pacific, 1784–1900* (Columbia: University of Missouri Press, 2001); John Schrecker, "'For the Equality of Men and for the Equality of Nations': Anson Burlingame and China's First Embassy to the United States, 1868," *Journal of American-East Asian Relations* 17, no. 1 (March 1, 2010): 9–34; Walter LaFeber, *The American Search for Opportunity, 1865–1913*, vol. 2 of *The New Cambridge History of American Foreign Relations* (Cambridge: Cambridge University Press, 2013).

7. Charles J. McClain Jr., "The Chinese Struggle for Civil Rights in Nineteenth Century America: The First Phase, 1850–1870," *California Law Review* 72, no. 4 (July 1, 1984): 529–68; Earl M. Maltz, "The Federal Government and the Problem of Chinese Rights in the Era of the Fourteenth Amendment," *Harvard Journal of Law and Public Policy* 17, no. 1 (Winter 1994): 223–52; Charles J. McClain, "Tortuous Path, Elusive Goal: The Asian Quest for American Citizenship," *Asian Law Journal* 2 (1995): 33; Bernadette Meyler, "The Gestation of Birthright Citizenship, 1868–1898: States' Rights, the Law of Nations, and Mutual Consent," *Georgetown Immigration Law Journal* 15 (2000): 519–62; Kerry Abrams, "Polygamy, Prostitution, and the Federalization of Immigration Law," *Columbia Law Review* 105, no. 3 (April 1, 2005): 641–716.

8. *House Journal*, 40th Cong., 2nd Sess., June 9, 1868, 823; "Speech of Hon. N. P. Banks," Boston City Council, *Reception and Entertainment of the Chinese Embassy, by the City of Boston, 1868*, 56. Some variation of this cliché was repeated in virtually every speech, article, headline, or diplomatic correspondence related to the Burlingame mission. It is slightly less common in sources dealing with other official interactions between the United States and China.

9. The Taiping Civil War killed an estimated twenty to thirty million people; the American Civil War's butcher's bill has most recently been revised upward to 750,000. Tobie S. Meyer-Fong, *What Remains: Coming to Terms with Civil War in 19th Century China* (Stanford: Stanford University Press, 2013), 1; J. David Hacker, "A Census-Based Count of the Civil War Dead," *Civil War History* 57, no. 4 (2011): 307–48. For a well-told narrative that interweaves the fortunes of these two wars—though with a primary focus on China—see Stephen R. Platt, *Autumn in the Heavenly Kingdom: China, the West, and the Epic Story of the Taiping Civil War*, Kindle ed. (New York: Knopf, 2012).

10. For a survey of different schools of thought on the Tongzhi Restoration, see "Restoration," in William T. Rowe, *China's Last Empire: The Great Qing*, History of Imperial China (Cambridge, MA: Belknap Press of Harvard University Press, 2009), 201–30. The classic examination of the restoration as an attempted reconstruction of the Qing central state is Mary Clabaugh Wright, *The Last Stand of Chinese Conservatism: The T'ung-Chih Restoration, 1862–1874*, Stanford Studies in History, Economics, and Political Science 13 (Stanford, CA: Stanford University Press, 1957). On Reconstruction as an "unfinished revolution," see, of course, Eric Foner, *Reconstruction: America's Unfinished Revolution, 1863–1877*, New American Nation Series (New York: Harper and Row, 1988).

11. While the scholarship on China has situated Burlingame's mission within this moment of potential, for the most part the American historiography has not, though there are exceptions: Schrecker, "For the Equality of Men and for the Equality of Nations," 20–21.

12. Ulysses S. Grant, "First Annual Message," December 6, 1869, in Gerhard Peters and John T. Woolley, "The American Presidency Project," http://www.presidency.ucsb.edu, accessed March 6, 2021.

13. *Banquet to His Excellency Anson Burlingame: And His Associates of the Chinese Embassy, by the Citizens of New York, on Tuesday, June 23, 1868* (New York: Sun Book and Job Printing House, 1868), 15; "Mr. Burlingame's Mission in Europe," *North China Herald and Supreme Court and Consular Gazette*, February 22, 1870, 135.

14. Williams, *Anson Burlingame*, 3–14; Anderson, *Imperialism and Idealism*, 18–19.

15. Williams, *Anson Burlingame*, 13–14; Anderson, *Imperialism and Idealism*, 18–19. On the political pressure, see Abraham Lincoln to William H. Seward, Monday, March 18, 1861, in *Abraham Lincoln Papers at the Library of Congress*, Manuscript Division (Washington, DC: American Memory Project, 2000), http://memory.loc.gov/ammem/alhtml/malhome.html. This pattern of authoritarian states' reacting coldly to the ascension of Republicans to power in the United States was widespread—among major empires, only China and Russia reacted

favorably to the Lincoln administration. Don H. Doyle, *The Cause of All Nations: An International History of the American Civil War* (New York: Basic Books, 2014).

16. A "young man" just shy of his forty-first birthday. Anson Burlingame to William H. Seward, Marseille, September 10, 1861, no. 1, in "M92: Despatches from U.S. Ministers to China, 1843–1906," General Records of the Department of State, RG 59, National Archives, 1973, reel 21.

17. Anson Burlingame to William H. Seward, Hong Kong, November 1, 1861, no. 2, in "M92: Despatches from China," reel 21; Anderson, *Imperialism and Idealism*, 32; Cassius Clay to William H. Seward, St. Petersburg, December 13, 1867, *FRUS*, 1868–69, 1:461.

18. William H. Seward to Anson Burlingame, Washington, March 6, 1862, *FRUS*, 1862, 1:839.

19. Platt, *Autumn in the Heavenly Kingdom*, 95.

20. William H. Seward to Anson Burlingame, Washington, March 6, 1862, *FRUS*, 1862, 1:839.

21. Anson Burlingame to William H. Seward, Shanghai, June 17, 1862, no. 17, in "M92: Despatches from China," reel 21.

22. Anson Burlingame to William H. Seward, Peking, June 20, 1863, *FRUS*, 1863, 2:937–41.

23. Jennifer M. Rudolph, *Negotiated Power in Late Imperial China: The Zongli Yamen and the Politics of Reform*, Cornell East Asia Series 137 (Ithaca, NY: East Asia Program, Cornell University, 2008).

24. Enclosure A: Anson Burlingame to Consul General George F. Seward, Peking, June 15, 1864, enclosed in Burlingame to William H. Seward Peking, June 18, 1864, *FRUS*, 1864, 3:429–30. George F. Seward, nephew to the secretary of state, was an ambitious consul general; he later served as the US minister to China.

25. Anson Burlingame to William H. Seward, New York, February 28, 1865, no. 117, in "M92: Despatches from China," reel 24.

26. William H. Seward to Anson Burlingame, Washington, September 9, 1863, *FRUS*, 1863, 2:960–61.

27. Prince Gong was formerly romanized as "Prince Kung."

28. John Rogers Haddad, *America's First Adventure in China: Trade, Treaties, Opium, and Salvation* (Philadelphia: Temple University Press, 2013), 214; Anderson, *Imperialism and Idealism*, 25.

29. Circular: Acting Secretary of State to Anson Burlingame, Washington, August 28, 1861, in "M77: Diplomatic Instructions of the Department of State, 1801–1906," General Records of the Department of State, RG 59, National Archives, 1965, reel 38; Anson Burlingame to William H. Seward, Hong Kong, November 30, 1861, no. 4, in "M92: Despatches from China," reel 21.

30. Anson Burlingame to William H. Seward, Peking, December 23, 1863, in "M92: Despatches from China," reel 22; Anson Burlingame to William H. Seward, Peking, June 3, 1864, *FRUS*, 1864, 3:400ff.

31. Anson Burlingame to William H. Seward, Peking, November 7, 1863, and Anson Burlingame to William H. Seward, Peking, November 26, 1863, *FRUS*, 1864, 3:343–46, 349; Anderson, *Imperialism and Idealism*, 30–32; Haddad, *America's First Adventure in China*, 217–18.

32. Anson Burlingame to William H. Seward, Peking, March 17, 1864, *FRUS*, 1864, 3:375–76; William H. Seward to Anson Burlingame, Washington, June 11, 1864, *FRUS*, 1864, 3:425–26; Williams, *Anson Burlingame*, 48–50.

This was reciprocated; early in his tenure, Chinese authorities sought assurances that American shipyards would not supply the Taiping with steamships, which Burlingame duly conveyed. Anson Burlingame to William H. Seward, Hong Kong, November 30, 1861, no. 4, in

"M92: Despatches from China," reel 21; William H. Seward to Anson Burlingame, Washington, February 4, 1862, no. 6, in "M77: Diplomatic Instructions," reel 38.

33. Anson Burlingame to William H. Seward, Hong Kong, November 30, 1861, no. 4, in "M92: Despatches from China," reel 21; William H. Seward to Anson Burlingame, Washington, February 4, 1862, no. 6, in "M77: Diplomatic Instructions," reel 38.

34. *FRUS*, 1864, 3:438–49; 1865–66, 2:458–60.

35. Anson Burlingame to William H. Seward, Peking, June 20, 1863, *FRUS*, 1863, 2:940.

36. Samuel Wells Williams to Robert Stanton Williams, Tremont Temple, August 24, 1868, in S. Wells Williams, Samuel Wells Williams Family Papers, 1809–1983, Manuscripts and Archives, Yale University Library, reel 4.

37. Anson Burlingame to William H. Seward, Peking, April 10, 1867, *FRUS*, 1867–68, 1:472–73.

38. Anson Burlingame to William H. Seward, Peking, April 10, 1867, *FRUS*, 1867–68, 1:472–73.

39. As Martin Ring notes, this was the second time Chinese officials had asked favors of Burlingame on the eve of a departure; the first was to secure his help in solving the Osborne fleet fiasco. Ring, "Anson Burlingame, S. Wells Williams and China, 1861–1870," 110, 167–74, 214–18. Burlingame's wife, Jane, reported the appointment as a surprise to their eldest son. Jane Burlingame to Edward (Ned) Burlingame, Peking, November 23, 1867, Anson Burlingame and Edward L. Burlingame Family Papers, Manuscript Division, Library of Congress, Washington, DC, box 3.

40. *FRUS*, 1868–69, 1:493–500; Biggerstaff, "Translation of Anson Burlingame's Instructions from the Chinese Foreign Office"; Morse, *International Relations of the Chinese Empire*, 2:185–93. Burlingame did not report any intention to negotiate a treaty to either the State Department or public audiences until after visiting Washington in June 1868.

41. Technically, Burlingame's rank was 1B, which was adjusted to the highest possible rank (1A) after his death as a mark of respect. Ring, "Anson Burlingame, S. Wells Williams and China, 1861–1870," 231; Frederick F. Low to Hamilton Fish, Peking, May 19, 1870, no. 6, in "M92: Despatches from China," reel 29.

42. The most thorough explanation of Burlingame's suite is found in Knight Biggerstaff, "The Official Chinese Attitude toward the Burlingame Mission," *American Historical Review* 41, no. 4 (July 1, 1936): 686–87. See also "The Presentation of the Chinese Embassy to the President," *National Intelligencer*, June 6, 1868; *FRUS*, 1868–69, 1:601–3; Biggerstaff, "Translation of Anson Burlingame's Instructions from the Chinese Foreign Office." On the bard, see "Tientsin," *North-China Herald*, December 14, 1867, 410.

43. Schrecker, in addition to being one of the few historians to analyze Burlingame's mission as influenced by the partisan political context of 1868, also notes that "Burlingame had tactical diplomatic goals for the treaty"—to set a precedent for his negotiations in Europe and "bolster the position of his allies in the Zongli Yamen." Schrecker, "For the Equality of Men and for the Equality of Nations," 27. These were goals that worked within the Republicans' Reconstruction program for the United States as well.

44. Biggerstaff, "Official Chinese Attitude toward the Burlingame Mission," 693–94.

45. Williams, *Anson Burlingame*, 117–18.

46. "Local Intelligence: Grand Dinner to the Chinese Embassy," *Daily Alta California*, Wednesday, April 29, 1868, 1.

47. Anson Burlingame to William H. Seward, San Francisco, April 30, 1868; New York, May 22, 1868; New York, May 23, 1868, "M98: Notes from the Chinese Legation in the United States to the Department of State, 1868–1906," General Records of the Department of State, RG 59, National Archives, 1965, reel 1.

48. "The Presentation of the Chinese Embassy to the President," *National Intelligencer* (Washington, DC), June 6, 1868; *FRUS*, 1868-69, 1:603-4; Williams, *Anson Burlingame*, 128-30.

49. Williams, Anson Burlingame, 129; William H. Seward and Frederick William Seward, *William H. Seward: An Autobiography from 1801 to 1834, with a Memoir of His Life, and Selections from His Letters* (New York: Derby and Miller, 1891), 3:381; William H. Seward, *The Works of William H. Seward*, ed. George E. Baker (Boston: Houghton Mifflin, 1884), 5:587n1.

50. "The Presentation of the Chinese Embassy to the President," *National Intelligencer* (Washington, DC), June 6, 1868; *FRUS*, 1868-69, 1:603-4; Williams, *Anson Burlingame*, 128-30.

51. For a fuller exploration of Seward's vision for empire, see Ernest N. Paolino, *The Foundations of the American Empire: William Henry Seward and U.S. Foreign Policy* (Ithaca, NY: Cornell University Press, 1973), esp. 145-63.

52. "Circular (August 8, 1862)," *FRUS*, 1862, 192.

53. John Sherman, "Establishment of a Bureau of Immigration," S. Rep. 15, 38th Cong., 1st Sess. (February 18, 1864); 13 Stat. 385, "An Act to Encourage Immigration (July 4, 1864).

54. Patricia Cloud and David W. Galenson, "Chinese Immigration and Contract Labor in the Late Nineteenth Century," *Explorations in Economic History* 24, no. 1 (January 1987): 24-25.

55. "Treaty with China, July 28, 1868: Additional Articles to the Treaty between the United States and China, of June 18, 1858," in *Treaties and Other International Agreements of the United States of America, 1776-1949*, ed. Charles I. Bevans (Washington DC: Government Printing Office, 1968), 6:680-84. For additional analyses of the treaty's articles, see Schrecker, "For the Equality of Men and for the Equality of Nations," 26-30; Ring, "Anson Burlingame, S. Wells Williams and China, 1861-1870," 252-57. On negotiations at Auburn, see William Henry Seward, *The Works of William H. Seward*, ed. George E. Baker (Boston: Houghton, Mifflin, 1884), 5:29.

56. Bevans, *Treaties and Other International Agreements of the United States of America, 1776-1949*, 6:680-84.

57. "Editorial Selections: The New American Treaty with China," *North-China Herald*, September 11, 1868, 439.

58. Interestingly, even J. Ross Browne, the antitreaty (and Californian) US minister to China, did not believe Chinese migrants to the United States were trafficked as coolies. Nevertheless, in recommending that the government pass new laws to prevent the coolie traffic more generally, he chose to ignore the fact that the Burlingame Treaty had already bound the United States to do so a year earlier. J. Ross Browne to Hamilton Fish, San Francisco, August 23, 1869, in "M92: Despatches from China," reel 27.

59. Mark Twain, "The Treaty with China: Its Provisions Explained," *New-York Tribune*, August 4, 1868, 2. Twain and Burlingame had first met in the Sandwich Islands in 1866, when Twain was working as a correspondent for the *Sacramento Union* and Burlingame passed through on a return journey to China after a term of leave. See Schrecker, "For the Equality of Men and for the Equality of Nations," 31; Hsin-yun Ou, "Mark Twain, Anson Burlingame, Joseph Hopkins Twichell, and the Chinese," *ARIEL: A Review of International English Literature* 42, no. 2 (April 2011): 49; Samuel Clemens to Edward Burlingame, Hartford, October 7, 1868, in Mark Twain, *Mark Twain's Letters: 1835-1910*, ed. Edgar Marquess Branch et al., Mark Twain Papers (Berkeley: University of California Press, 1988), 2:261.

60. Mark Twain, "The Treaty with China: Its Provisions Explained," *New-York Tribune*, August 4, 1868, 2.

61. 15 Stat. 223-24, "An Act concerning the Rights of American Citizens in Foreign States" (July 27, 1868). The first draft of the law was initially opposed by radical Republicans afraid that it would empower a president they already distrusted with new powers to declare war.

62. Negotiated by the former Jacksonian operative and Massachusetts historian George Bancroft, the Prussian treaty was the first of several dozen bilateral agreements the United States entered into to regulate naturalization protocols. "Naturalization Treaty with the North German Confederation," in Bevans, *Treaties and Other International Agreements of the United States of America, 1776–1949*, 8:70–73.

63. For an example of how congressional debate on these issues proceeded, see "Rights of American Citizens Abroad," House, January 30, 1868, Cong. Globe, 40th Cong., 2nd Sess., 865ff.

64. For examples of such attempts see, for example, "Immigration of Chinese, etc.," House, December 12, 1867, Cong. Globe, 40th Cong., 2nd Sess., part 1, 163; Benjamin Markley Boyer, "President's Annual Message," House, December 17, 1867, Cong. Globe, 40th Cong., 2nd Sess., part 1, 237; James A. Johnson, "Immigration of Chinese," House, January 29, 1868, Cong. Globe, 40th Cong., 2nd Sess., part 1, 837–38; James A. Johnson, "Personal Explanations, " House, February 7, 1868, Cong. Globe, 40th Cong., 2nd Sess., part 2, 1045; James A. Johnson, "Impeachment of the President," February 24, 1868, Cong. Globe, 40th Cong., 2nd Sess., part 2, 1382; Senate, July 22, 1868, Cong. Globe, 40th Cong., 2nd Sess., part 5, 4332.

Illustrating the mental division between goods and people, even the most virulently anti-Chinese representative in the 40th Congress, California's James A. Johnson, regarded the construction of the transcontinental railroad as crucial to capturing Asian trade and thus securing American union ("it will make us through all time one nation") and world hegemony ("The trade of China and Japan ours [sic], it will do for us what it has done for England"). Johnson, "Central Branch Union Pacific Railroad," House, March 16, 1868, Cong. Globe, 40th Cong., 2nd Sess., part 2, 1889.

65. *Senate Exec. Journal*, 40th Cong., 2nd Sess., July 24, 1868, 355–56.

66. Beginning with 1 Stat. 103, "An Act to establish an uniform Rule of Naturalization" (March 26, 1790).

67. The Senate met in executive session, so there are no records of debate about the amendment; but in subsequent debates, various parties with knowledge of the debate introduce this idea into the record. Charles Sumner, who had shepherded the treaty through the Senate to a unanimous vote and consistently championed color-blind definitions of citizenship privileges, preferred to recall that the limitation was not made in opposition to race or country of origin, but rather to clarify the issue with China's most favored nation status; it seems this understanding was not shared by his colleagues. See Doolittle, "Suffrage Constitutional Amendment," Senate, February 8, 1869, Cong. Globe, 40th Cong., 3rd Sess., 1011; "Naturalization Law," House, June 9, 1870, Cong. Globe, 41st Cong., 2nd Sess., 4275; "Political Disabilities," Senate, February 9, 1872, Cong. Globe, 42nd Cong., 2nd Sess., 910–11. For an extended legislative history of the Naturalization Act and subsequent anti-Chinese legislation, see Martin Gold, *Forbidden Citizens: Chinese Exclusion and the U.S. Congress; A Legislative History* (Alexandria, VA: TheCapital.Net, 2012), esp. 1–32.

68. Mark Twain, "The Treaty with China: Its Provisions Explained," *New-York Tribune*, Tuesday, August 4, 1868, 1.

69. S. Wells Williams to William H. Seward, Peking, July 1868, *FRUS*, 1868–69, 1:518.

70. William H. Seward to J. Ross Browne, September 7, 1868, Washington, *FRUS*, 1868–69, 1:572; William H. Seward to J. Ross Browne, September 8, Washington, *FRUS*, 1868–69, 1:573.

71. Daniel Cleveland to J. Ross Browne, July 21, 1868, enclosure in J. Ross Brown to William H. Seward, San Francisco July 24, 1868, *FRUS*, 1868–69, 1:541.

72. "Our North Pacific States," August 1869, in Seward, *Works of William H. Seward*, 5:578.

73. *Reception and Entertainment of the Chinese Embassy, by the City of Boston, 1868*, 27.

74. Emphasis in original. *Banquet to His Excellency Anson Burlingame*, 18.

75. John Murray Forbes's support for more radical Republican policies was something of an exception—his views were closer to Burlingame's (steps toward racial equality and openness would promote economic prosperity) than to those of the men who took over Russell and Company once he had retired from the China trade. Eric Foner, *Reconstruction: America's Unfinished Revolution, 1863–1877*, updated edition (New York: Harper Perennial Modern Classics, 2014), 234n12; John Murray Forbes and Sarah Forbes Hughes, *Letters (Supplementary) of John Murray Forbes* (Boston: George H. Ellis, 1905), 3:25–26, 43–46.

76. *North-China Herald and Market Report*, December 14, 1867, 408. For an analysis of the paper's status among other newspapers in China, see Frank H. H. King and Prescott Clarke, *A Research Guide to China-Coast Newspapers, 1822–1911*, Harvard East Asian Monographs 18 (Cambridge, MA: East Asian Research Center, Harvard University, 1965), 28–29, 78–81.

77. "The Chinese Embassy," *North-China Herald and Market Report*, December 24, 1867, 421; "The Chinese Embassy," *North-China Herald and Market Report*, February 19, 1868, 77.

78. "The Address of the Citizens of the United States, Resident in Shanghai . . . ," *Supreme Court and Consular Gazette*, July 24, 1869, 50.

79. *Banquet to His Excellency Anson Burlingame*, 15, 17.

80. "The Chinese Embassy," *North-China Herald*, September 5, 1868, 427; "The China Mission," *North-China Herald*, September 19, 1868, 45. Unlike many American commentators (and historians since), the *North-China Herald* did not harp on Burlingame's claim that China invited Christian missionaries "to plant the shining cross on every hill and in every valley." *Banquet to His Excellency Anson Burlingame*, 17. Dennett, *Americans in Eastern Asia*, 384; Schrecker, "For the Equality of Men and for the Equality of Nations," 24.

81. "Slightly Mixed," *North-China Herald*, October 1, 1868, 116–18.

82. "The Burlingame Mission," *North-China Herald*, November 10, 1868, 539; "Salt," *North-China Herald and Supreme Court and Consular Gazette*, February 22, 1870; "Imports—Sundries," *North-China Herald*, March 15, 1870, 192; "Home Views on China," *North-China Herald*, March 1, 1870, 146.

83. "Editorial Selections: The New American Treaty with China," *North-China Herald*, September 11, 1868, 439. The *North-China Herald* was particularly unimpressed with the articles granting China the right to appoint consuls, and it found the article governing the right to free migration "ludicrous."

84. Anderson, *Imperialism and Idealism*, 54–61; J. Ross Browne, "Under the Dragon's Footstool: Second Paper—Arrival at Pekin," *Overland Monthly* 6, no. 3 (March 1871): 233–43; J. Ross Browne and Lina Fergusson Browne, *J. Ross Browne; His Letters, Journals, and Writings* (Albuquerque: University of New Mexico Press, 1969).

85. Anderson, *Imperialism and Idealism*, 49.

86. Quotations: "The Address of the Citizens of the United States, Resident in Shanghai . . ." *Supreme Court and Consular Gazette*, July 24, 1869, 50. Full statements: "The Address of the Citizens of the United States, Resident in Shanghai . . . ," "The Address of the British Community of Shanghai," and "Mr. Browne's Reply," in *The Supreme Court and Consular Gazette*, July 24, 1869, 50–55. Manuscript copies of the original petitions (complete with signatures from the memorialists) can be found as enclosures in J. Ross Browne to Hamilton Fish, San Francisco, August 21, 1869, in "M92: Despatches from China," reel 27.

87. "The Address of the Citizens of the United States, Resident in Shanghai . . ."; "The Address of the British Community of Shanghai"; and "Mr. Browne's Reply," in *Supreme Court and Consular Gazette*, July 24, 1869, 50–55.

88. "Our Chinese Diplomacy—Mr. Browne Botches It," *New York Herald*, August 29, 1869,

6; "J. Ross Browne's Departure from China: His Great Mistake," *New York Herald*, August 29, 1869, 8. For examples of the *Herald*'s reports' being dissected in Shanghai, see "News of the Week," *North-China Herald*, February 16, 1869, 68; "News of the Week," *North-China Herald*, February 20, 1869, 77; "News of the Week," *North-China Herald*, July 10, 1869.

89. "Telegrams," *New York Times*, August 26, 1869, 1; "Telegrams," *New York Times*, August 30, 1869, 1; "The Treaty Concluded . . . ," *New York Times*, August 30, 1869, 4; "Telegrams," *New York Times*, August 31, 1869, 1.

90. "Gunboat Diplomacy," *New York Times*, September 4, 1869, 4.

91. Schrecker, "For the Equality of Men and for the Equality of Nations."

92. *Reception and Entertainment of the Chinese Embassy, by the City of Boston, 1868*, 29.

93. Anson Burlingame to Samuel Wells Williams, Paris, March 27, 1869, Samuel Wells Williams Papers, Manuscripts and Archives, Yale University Library, ser. 1, reel 4, folder 129, frame 01741. NB: This letter is misfiled with letters from March 1867.

94. "Mr. Burlingame's Mission in Europe," *North China Herald and Supreme Court and Consular Gazette*, February 22, 1870; for a similar sentiment, see "The Chinese Question: From the Springfield Republican," *National Anti-Slavery Standard*, December 4, 1869.

95. James A. Johnson, "Reconstruction—Rights of Citizens," February 8, 1868, Cong. Globe, 40th Cong., 2nd Sess., part 2, 1067. Johnson's comments were made before the treaty was contemplated, but they reflect the general intertwining of anti-Chinese, anti-Radical Reconstruction, and anti-Black sentiment.

96. *Senate Exec. Journal*, 40th Cong., 2nd Sess., July 24, 1868, 355–56; *New York Herald*, July 25, 26, 1868; *New York Sun*, July 27, 1868. Later, Senator Garrett Davis (D-KY) would claim he voted against it. See "Contracts for Servile Labor," Senate, July 8, 1870, Cong. Globe, 41st Cong., 2nd Sess., 5385; Andrew Gyory, *Closing the Gate: Race, Politics, and the Chinese Exclusion Act* (Chapel Hill: University of North Carolina Press, 1998), 27–28, 272n23.

97. William H. Seward to Anson Burlingame, State Department, September 15, 1868, Anson Burlingame and Edward L. Burlingame Family Papers, Manuscript Division, Library of Congress, Washington, DC, box 1.

98. "Departure of the Chinese Embassy for England," *New York Herald*, September 9, 1868, 6.

99. Hamilton Fish to George Bancroft, Washington, August 31, 1869, enclosure in Hamilton Fish to Frederick F. Low, Washington, December 3, 1869, *FRUS*, 1870–71, 304–7.

100. Anson Burlingame to Samuel Wells Williams, Paris, August 13, 1869, Samuel Wells Williams Family Papers, Manuscripts and Archives, Yale University Library, ser. 1, reel 4, box 4, folder 140.

101. Ulysses S. Grant, *The Papers of Ulysses S. Grant*, ed. John Y. Simon (Carbondale: Southern Illinois University Press, 1967), 19:523; Hamilton Fish to Frederick F. Low, Washington, December 3, 1869, *FRUS*, 1870–71, 303; Hamilton Fish to George M. Robeson, Secretary of the Navy, Washington, April 4, 1870, *FRUS*, 1870–71, 332.

102. Ulysses S. Grant, "First Annual Message," December 6, 1869, in Peters and Woolley, "American Presidency Project."

103. Anson Burlingame to Samuel Wells Williams, Berlin, January 23, 1870, Samuel Wells Williams Family Papers, Manuscripts and Archives, Yale University Library, ser. 1, reel 4, folder 140. On the letter itself, Williams left a note that it was the "Last & the best letter which he wrote to me—About 2 mon[th]s before his decease."

104. A. G. Curtin to Hamilton Fish, St. Petersburg, February 23, 1870, no. 24, and A. G. Curtin to Hamilton Fish, St. Petersburg, February 28, 1870, no. 25, in *American Relations with China*, ed. Jules Davids, American Diplomatic and Public Papers, the United States and China,

ser. 2, The United States, China, and Imperial Rivalries, 1861–1893, 1 (Wilmington, DE: Scholarly Resources, 1979), 187, 188.

105. Biggerstaff, "Official Chinese Attitude toward the Burlingame Mission," 701. Visiting China as part of a world tour in his retirement, William H. Seward encountered Burlingame's fellow commissioners, Zhigang and Sun Jiagu, in Shanghai in mid- October 1870, just as they were on the final leg of their return journey to Beijing. William Henry Seward, *William H. Seward's Travels around the World*, ed. Olive Risley Seward (New York: Appleton, 1873), 100.

106. George Bancroft to Hamilton Fish, American Legation, Berlin, March 3, 1870, Anson Burlingame and Edward L. Burlingame Family Papers, Manuscript Division, Library of Congress, Washington, DC, box 2.

107. Committee of Arrangements of the City Council of Boston, *A Memorial of Anson Burlingame Late Envoy Extra-ordinary and Minister Plenipotentiary from the Chinese Empire to the Treaty Powers* (Boston: Council, 1870); Haddad, *America's First Adventure in China*, 227.

108. Frederick F. Low to Hamilton Fish, Peking, May 19, 1870, no. 6, in "M92: Despatches from China," reel 29.

109. Seward, *William H. Seward's Travels around the World*, 169.

110. *Reception and Entertainment of the Chinese Embassy, by the City of Boston, 1868*, 24–29.

111. Frederick W. Seward to Frederick Wells Williams, June 14, 1911, reprinted in Williams, *Anson Burlingame*, 145.

112. Williams, *Anson Burlingame*, 118. Williams's use of "yellow peril" was anachronistic, belonging to the time in which he wrote—after Japan's geopolitical rise—rather than the time he described.

113. LaFeber, *American Search for Opportunity, 1865–1913*, 1, 17–18.

Chapter Eight

1. Frederick Ferdinand Low to Hamilton Fish, Peking, January 10, 1871, in *Foreign Relations of the United States* [*FRUS*] (Washington, DC: Government Printing Office, n.d.), 1871–72, 77–87. On Low's early career, see David L. Anderson, *Imperialism and Idealism: American Diplomats in China, 1861–1898* (Bloomington: Indiana University Press, 1985), 66–68.

2. Frederick Ferdinand Low to Hamilton Fish, Peking, January 10, 1871, *FRUS*, 1871–72, 85.

3. John Sherman and Edwin D. Morgan, "Bills, Reports, and Memorials on International Coinage," S. Rep. 117, 40th Cong., 2nd Sess. (June 9, 1868), 11.

4. Denby died suddenly from a heart attack after giving a speech in 1904; his book was published the following year. It was likely based on his public lectures. "Col. Charles Denby Dead," *New York Times*, January 14, 1904, 9; Charles Denby, *China and Her People: Being the Observations, Reminiscences, and Conclusions of an American Diplomat*, 2 vols., Travel Lovers' Library (Boston: Page, 1905).

5. Denby, *China and Her People*, 2:43.

6. Denby, *China and Her People*, 2:108.

7. Denby, *China and Her People*, 2:111, 107, 113.

8. For an elaboration of the way border policing has served as a mechanism for state formation in the United States, see Peter Andreas, *Smuggler Nation: How Illicit Trade Made America* (New York: Oxford University Press, 2013), as well as Andrew Wender Cohen, "Smuggling, Globalization, and America's Outward State, 1870–1909," *Journal of American History* 97, no. 2 (September 1, 2010): 371–98.

Key works on immigration restriction and the administrative state include Kunal Madhukar Parker, *Making Foreigners: Immigration and Citizenship Law in America, 1600–2000* (New

York: Cambridge University Press, 2015); Andrew Gyory, *Closing the Gate: Race, Politics, and the Chinese Exclusion Act* (Chapel Hill: University of North Carolina Press, 1998); Hidetaka Hirota, *Expelling the Poor: Atlantic Seaboard States and the Nineteenth-Century Origins of American Immigration Policy* (New York: Oxford University Press, 2017); Anna O. Law, *The Immigration Battle in American Courts* (New York: Cambridge University Press, 2010); Moon-Ho Jung, "Outlawing 'Coolies': Race, Nation, and Empire in the Age of Emancipation," *American Quarterly* 57, no. 3 (September 1, 2005): 677–701; Moon-Ho Jung, *Coolies and Cane: Race, Labor, and Sugar in the Age of Emancipation* (Baltimore: Johns Hopkins University Press, 2006); Rosanne Currarino, *The Labor Question in America: Economic Democracy in the Gilded Age*, The Working Class in American History (Urbana: University of Illinois Press, 2011). The tariff is less well covered in recent scholarship, though it is attracting more interest, particularly among scholars who see it as an important link between debates about race, empire, and labor. See April Merleaux, "The Political Culture of Sugar Tariffs: Immigration, Race, and Empire, 1898–1930," *International Labor and Working-Class History* 81 (March 2012): 28–48; April Merleaux, *Sugar and Civilization: American Empire and the Cultural Politics of Sweetness* (Chapel Hill: University of North Carolina Press, 2015); Marc-William Palen, *The "Conspiracy" of Free Trade: The Anglo-American Struggle over Empire and Economic Globalization, 1846–1896* (New York: Cambridge University Press, 2016); Douglas A. Irwin, *Clashing over Commerce: A History of U.S. Trade Policy* (Chicago: University of Chicago Press, 2017).

9. Thomas J. McCormick, *China Market: America's Quest for Informal Empire, 1893–1901* (Chicago: Quadrangle Books, 1967); Charles S. Campbell, *Special Business Interests and the Open Door Policy* (New Haven, CT: Yale University Press, 1951); Walter LaFeber, *The New Empire: An Interpretation of American Expansion, 1860–1898* (Ithaca, NY: Cornell University Press, 1963); James J. Lorence, "Organized Business and the Myth of the China Market : The American Asiatic Association, 1898–1937," *Transactions of the American Philosophical Society*, n.s., 71, no. 4 (1981).

Most scholars of US-China relations reasonably see the 1890s as a turning point: either as the culmination of long-standing "Open Door" proclivities or as the beginning of a new aggressively imperial formulation. Tyler Dennett, *Americans in Eastern Asia: A Critical Study of the Policy of the United States with Reference to China, Japan, and Korea in the 19th Century* (New York: Macmillan, 1922); Walter LaFeber, *The American Search for Opportunity, 1865–1913*, vol. 2 of *The New Cambridge History of American Foreign Relations* (Cambridge: Cambridge University Press, 2013); Michael H. Hunt, *The Making of a Special Relationship: The United States and China to 1914* (New York: Columbia University Press, 1983); Warren I. Cohen, *America's Response to China: A History of Sino-American Relations*, 4th ed. (New York: Columbia University Press, 2000); Dong Wang, *The United States and China : A History from the Eighteenth Century to the Present* (Lanham, MD: Rowman and Littlefield, 2013).

10. For an insider's survey of the tea trade just after this bubble popped, see *Six Essays on the Trade of Shanghai: Reprinted from "The Celestial Empire"* (Shanghai: Gazette Office, 1874), 11–39.

11. Appendix, fig. A7: "U.S.-China trade, by value, 1821–1901"; fig. A8, "Total U.S.-China trade (imports plus exports) as a percentage of total U.S. foreign trade (imports plus exports), 1821–1901; Susan B. Carter et al., eds., *Historical Statistics of the United States: Millennial Edition Online* (New York: Cambridge University Press, 2006), Ca208–212.

12. Although absolute numbers of firms and population increased, declines relative to other foreigners were not reversed before the twentieth century. Chong Su See, *The Foreign Trade of China* (New York: Faculty of Political Science of Columbia University, New York; China Society of America, 1919), 395; Chinese Maritime Customs Service, *Reports on Trade at the Treaty*

Ports, 16 vols. (Shanghai: Statistical Department of the Inspectorate General of Customs, 1864); Chinese Maritime Customs Service, *Returns of Trade and Trade Reports*, 80 vols. (Shanghai: Statistical Department of the Inspectorate General of Customs, 1882).

13. Appendix, fig. A9, "U.S. trade in China as a share of China's total foreign trade, 1865–1900."

14. These figures led economist Peter Schran to declare that in this period "the China trade remained a marginal affair in United States perspective, and the U.S. trade did not amount to much more from the Chinese point of view." Peter Schran, "The Minor Significance of Commercial Relations between the United States and China, 1850–1931," in *America's China Trade in Historical Perspective: The Chinese and American Performance*, ed. Ernest R. May and John King Fairbank, Harvard Studies in American-East Asian Relations (Cambridge, MA: Harvard University Press, 1986), 237.

15. Stephen Chapman Lockwood, *Augustine Heard and Company, 1858–1862: American Merchants in China*, Harvard East Asian Monographs (Cambridge, MA: East Asian Research Center, Harvard University, 1971); Jacques M. Downs, *The Golden Ghetto: The American Commercial Community at Canton and the Shaping of American China Policy, 1784–1844* (Bethlehem, PA: Lehigh University Press, 1997); Sibing He, "Russell and Company, 1818–1891: America's Trade and Diplomacy in Nineteenth-Century China" (PhD diss., Miami University, 1997).

16. Russell and Company, as always, being the most famous in this regard. John Russell Young, "New Life in China," *North American Review* 153, no. 419 (October 1891): 421.

17. *Six Essays on the Trade of Shanghai*, 5.

18. "Suspension of Russell & Co.," *New York Times*, June 5, 1891, 2.

19. Jay Sexton, "American Steam in the Mid-Nineteenth Century Pacific: The Case of Pacific Mail," *Journal of Pacific and American Studies*, 2020, 5–22.

20. Thomas Knox, "John Comprador," *Harper's New Monthly Magazine*, August 1878, 431–32.

21. On British firms underselling US firms at public auctions in New York—and the threat of native Chinese firms expanding to do the same—see "China," in *Commercial Relations of the United States with Foreign Countries* [*CRUS*] (Washington, DC: Government Printing Office, n.d.), 1882–83, 2:651–52.

22. On firms' attempts to diversify, see Lockwood, *Augustine Heard and Company*; He, "Russell and Company." On the steamer business specifically, see Edward Kenneth Haviland, "American Steam Navigation in China, 1845–1878, part 1," *American Neptune* 16, no. 3 (June 1956): 157–79; Haviland, "American Steam Navigation in China, part 2," *American Neptune* 16, no. 4 (October 1956): 243–69; Haviland, "American Steam Navigation in China, part 3," *American Neptune* 17, no. 1 (January 1957): 38–74; Haviland, "American Steam Navigation in China, part 4," *American Neptune* 17, no. 2 (April 1957): 134–51; Haviland, "American Steam Navigation in China, part 5," *American Neptune* 17, no. 3 (July 1957): 212–30; Haviland, "American Steam Navigation in China, part 6," *American Neptune* 17, no. 4 (October 1957): 298–314; Haviland, "American Steam Navigation in China, part 7," *American Neptune* 18, no. 1 (January 1958): 59–85; Haviland, "American Steam Navigation in China, part 8," *American Neptune* 49, no. 1 (January 1989): 21–28; Kwang-Ching Liu, "Financing a Steam-Navigation Company in China, 1861–62," *Business History Review* 28, no. 2 (June 1, 1954): 154–81; Kwang-Ching Liu, "Steamship Enterprise in Nineteenth-Century China," *Journal of Asian Studies* 18, no. 4 (August 1, 1959): 435–55; Kwang-Ching Liu, *Anglo-American Steamship Rivalry in China, 1862–1874*, Harvard East Asian Studies 8 (Cambridge, MA: Harvard University Press, 1962).

23. "Notes by Warren Delano II on U.S. Sea Trade, 1877," in Frederic A. Delano Papers, 1812–1959, FDR Presidential Library and Museum, ser. 6, box 27.

24. John Murray Forbes, *Reminiscences of John Murray Forbes, edited by His Daughter, Sarah Forbes Hughes, in Three Volumes*, ed. Sarah Forbes Hughes (Boston: George H. Ellis, 1902), 3:275; John Lauritz Larson, *Bonds of Enterprise: John Murray Forbes and Western Development in America's Railway Age* (Cambridge, MA: Harvard University Press, 1984).

25. Hunt, *Making of a Special Relationship*, 144.

26. Mira Wilkins, "The Impacts of American Multinational Enterprise on American–Chinese Economic Relations, 1786–1949," in *America's China Trade in Historical Perspective: The Chinese and American Performance*, ed. Ernest R. May and John King Fairbank, Harvard Studies in American–East Asian Relations (Cambridge, MA : Harvard University Press, 1986), 259–88; Pletcher, *Diplomacy of Involvement*, 134–52.

27. Lockwood, *Augustine Heard and Company*, 103–14; Wilkins, "Impacts of American Multinational Enterprise on American–Chinese Economic Relations," 272–88; Pletcher, *Diplomacy of Involvement*, 97–152. The steepest decline in both US firms and US personnel in China occurred from 1873 to 1881. Chinese Maritime Customs Service, *Reports on Trade at the Treaty Ports*; Chinese Maritime Customs Service, *Returns of Trade and Trade Reports*; See *Foreign Trade of China*, 299, 395.

28. Eric Rauchway, *Blessed among Nations: How the World Made America* (New York: Hill and Wang, 2006).

29. Walter T. K. Nugent, *Money and American Society, 1865–1880* (New York: Free Press, 1968); Michael O'Malley, *Face Value: The Entwined Histories of Money and Race in America* (Chicago: University of Chicago Press, 2012); Nicolas Barreyre, *Gold and Freedom: The Political Economy of Reconstruction*, trans. Arthur Goldhammer (Charlottesville: University of Virginia Press, 2015).

30. James A. Garfield, "The Currency Conflict," *Atlantic Monthly* 37, no. 220 (February 1876): 235.

31. "Report and Accompanying Documents of the United States Monetary Commission Organized under Joint Resolution of August 15, 1876," S. Rep. 703, 44th Cong., 2nd Sess. (March 2, 1877), 1:109–10.

32. Nugent, *Money and American Society*, 91–258; Samuel DeCanio, *Democracy and the Origins of the American Regulatory State* (New Haven, CT: Yale University Press, 2015), 92–120.

33. Henry Richard Linderman and John Torrey, "The Production of Gold and Silver," *Bankers' Magazine*, ser. 3, 7, no. 9 (March 1873): 710, 712. The trade dollar literature is of a mature vintage, though newly revived by DeCanio's discoveries about the origins of the Coinage Act and a renewed interest among economic historians and historians of capitalism in specie flows and the politics of money. Porter Garnett, "The History of the Trade Dollar," *American Economic Review* 7, no. 1 (March 1917): 91–97; M. C. Waltersdorf, "The American Trade Dollar," *Social Science* 8, no. 1 (1933): 17–23; John Craf, "The American Trade Dollar," *Social Studies* 54, no. 6 (September 1963): 226–27; John M. Willem, *The United States Trade Dollar: America's Only Unwanted, Unhonored Coin* (Racine, WI: Whitman, 1959); David J. St. Clair, "American Trade Dollars in Nineteenth-Century China," in *Pacific Centuries: Pacific and Pacific Rim History since the Sixteenth Century*, ed. Dennis Owen Flynn, Lionel Frost, and A. J. H. Latham, Routledge Explorations in Economic History 12 (New York: Routledge, 1999), 152–70; Samuel DeCanio, "Populism, Paranoia, and the Politics of Free Silver," *Studies in American Political Development* 25, no. 1 (April 2011): 1–26; DeCanio, *Democracy and the Origins of the American Regulatory State*; Alejandra Irigoin, "A Trojan Horse in Daoguang China? Explaining the Flows of Silver in and out of China," Economic History Working Papers 173/13 (London: London School of Economics and Political Science, 2013); Alejandra Irigoin, "Global Silver: Bullion or Specie? Supply and Demand in the Making of the Early Modern Global Economy,"

LSE Economic History Working Papers 285 (London: London School of Economics and Political Science, 2018).

34. "Banking facilities between the United States and China," H.R. Exec. Doc. 159, 42nd Cong., 3rd Sess. (January 25, 1873), 1–4. Bailey's report is dated October 10, 1872. His argument was later mirrored in the majority report in "Report and Accompanying Documents of the United States Monetary Commission Organized under Joint Resolution of August 15, 1876," S. Rep. 703, 44th Cong., 2nd Sess. (March 2, 1877), 1:116.

35. Edward Cunningham, "Correspondence: Improved Banking Facilities between the United States and China," *Nation* 16, no. 403 (March 20, 1873): 195–96.

36. On Grant's confusion, see DeCanio, *Democracy and the Origins of the American Regulatory State*, 115. At 420 grains troy and 900 fine (90 percent pure; i.e., 378 grains of pure silver), the coin contained more pure silver than the "standard" US silver dollar (412.5 grains troy, 900 fine, for 371.25 grains of silver), and a hair more than Spanish or Mexican dollars (317 grains at 902 fine, or 377.25 grains of silver). This was by design: its creators thought this "added value" would mean the coin "would take the place of the Mexican dollar in the immense trade of the East." George Sewall Boutwell, *Reminiscences of Sixty Years in Public Affairs* (New York: McClure, Phillips, 1902), 2:155.

37. 17 Stat. 424, "An Act Revising and Amending the Laws relative to the Mints, Assay Offices, and Coinage of the United States" (February 12, 1873); Willem, *United States Trade Dollar*, 70–71.

38. St. Clair, "American Trade Dollars in Nineteenth-Century China," 152–53.

39. David Bailey, Hong-Kong, January 16, 1877, *CRUS*, 1876, 207.

40. George F. Seward to Hamilton Fish, Hong Kong, February 29, 1876, *FRUS*, 1876, 45.

41. St. Clair, "American Trade Dollars in Nineteenth-Century China," 152.

42. John Fiske and James Grant Wilson, *Appletons' Cyclopaedia of American Biography* (New York: Appleton, 1887), 5:164. Despite a century of scoffing from prominent historians and economists, political scientist Samuel DeCanio has conclusively demonstrated that the Populists were *right* in claiming that the Coinage Act was the result of a conspiracy—though they got some of the details wrong. It was not eastern bankers bribing Treasury officials and congressmen, but rather California banker and Comstock lode mine owner William C. Ralston funding the effort; and the purpose was not simply deflation to improve bond returns or the resumption of specie payments, but rather the elimination of a glut in silver. DeCanio, "Populism, Paranoia, and the Politics of Free Silver"; DeCanio, *Democracy and the Origins of the American Regulatory State*, 92–120.

43. Willem, *United States Trade Dollar*, 134–35.

44. Emphasis in original. Gordon H. Chang, "China and the Pursuit of America's Destiny: Nineteenth-Century Imagining and Why Immigration Restriction Took So Long," *Journal of Asian American Studies* 15, no. 2 (2012): 146. The short answer, well covered by the scholarship on immigration and US foreign relations (including Chang's own work) is that the Supreme Court and presidents from Hayes to Arthur interpreted US treaties with China as binding commitments that superseded state or federal legislation completely restricting or excluding Chinese migrants.

45. The literature on Chinese exclusion—and immigration restriction more generally—is deep and growing. For a compact summary of the origins of the "federal immigration order," including Chinese exclusion, see Parker, *Making Foreigners*, 116–47. Gyory offers a through and well-observed narrative analysis of the political history behind the "first" Chinese Exclusion Act: Gyory, *Closing the Gate*. Beth Lew-Williams has argued, provocatively, that the authors of the 1882 act intended it to be a more moderate diplomatic-controlled "restriction," and that it

became the basis of "exclusion" only once its measures failed: Beth Lew-Williams, "Before Re-striction Became Exclusion: America's Experiment in Diplomatic Immigration Control," *Pacific Historical Review* 83, no. 1 (February 2014): 24–56; Beth Lew-Williams, *The Chinese Must Go: Violence, Exclusion, and the Making of the Alien in America* (Cambridge, MA: Harvard University Press, 2018). This assertion is contradicted somewhat by a growing body of litera-ture that finds the origins of *federal* immigration bureaucracies and restriction techniques in existing *state-level* practices, not international diplomacy: Hirota, *Expelling the Poor*; Anna O. Law, "Lunatics, Idiots, Paupers, and Negro Seamen—Immigration Federalism and the Early American State," *Studies in American Political Development* 28, no. 2 (October 2014): 107–28; Brendan O'Malley, "Protecting the Stranger: The Origins of U.S. Immigration Regulation in Nineteenth-Century New York" (PhD diss., City University of New York, 2015). Other key works include Mary Roberts Coolidge, *Chinese Immigration* (New York: Henry Holt, 1909); Stuart Creighton Miller, *The Unwelcome Immigrant: The American Image of the Chinese, 1785–1882* (Berkeley: University of California Press, 1969); Erika Lee, *At America's Gates: Chinese Immigration during the Exclusion Era, 1882–1943* (Chapel Hill: University of North Carolina Press, 2003); Mae M. Ngai, *Impossible Subjects: Illegal Aliens and the Making of Modern America* (Princeton, NJ: Princeton University Press, 2004); Stacey L. Smith, *Freedom's Frontier: California and the Struggle over Unfree Labor, Emancipation, and Reconstruction* (Chapel Hill: University of North Carolina Press, 2013).

46. "Hon. William H. Seward," *New York Times*, February 25, 1871, 2.

47. For a detailed analysis of another powerful expositor of this perspective, the Califor-nian economist Alexander Del Mar, see Kashia Arnold, "Alexander Del Mar: Free Trade and the Chinese Question," *Southern California Quarterly* 94, no. 3 (September 1, 2012): 304–45.

48. These were all very common terms that litter records of congressional debate as well as other publications in the period. For one particularly pungent example, see Rep. Wil-liam Mungen, "The Heathen Chinese," Cong. Globe, 41st Cong., 3rd Sess. (January 7, 1871), 351–60.

49. Jung, "Outlawing 'Coolies.'"

50. Marshall Jewell to Hamilton Fish, St. Petersburg, December 31, 1873, *FRUS*, 1874–75, 807–808; Hamilton Fish to Robert Schenck, Washington, February 4, 1874, *FRUS*, 1874–75, 494; Edward Thornton to Hamilton Fish, Washington, October 28, 1874, *FRUS*, 1874–75, 573; Richard Beardsley to Hamilton Fish, Cairo, September 16, 1873, *FRUS*, 1874–75, 1170–72.

51. Frederick F. Low to Hamilton Fish, Harbor of Nagasaki, May 13, 1871, and Samuel Wells Williams to Hamilton Fish, Peking, July 26, 1871, *FRUS*, 1871–72, 112–15, 149–51; Samuel Wells Williams to Hamilton Fish, Peking, November 6, 1873, *FRUS*, 1874–75, 202–6.

52. "New Attempt to Send Chinese to Peru," *Overland China Mail*, January 17, 1878, as re-printed in The *Anti-slavery Reporter*, ser. 3, May 14, 1878, 49.

53. "A Wide-Reaching Failure," *New York Times*, December 8, 1878, 5; "Olyphant & Co's Failure," *New York Times*, December 9, 1878; "Olyphant & Co., of China," *NYT*, March 5, 1879, 8. The affair is also thoroughly covered in *FRUS*, 1877–78 and 1878–79; and *CRUS*, 1878 and 1879.

54. Samuel Wells Williams to Hamilton Fish, Peking, November 30, 1873, *FRUS*, 1874–75, 220.

55. "Banking facilities between the United States and China," H.R. Exec. Doc. 159, 42nd Cong., 3rd Sess. (January 25, 1873), 1–4; David H. Bailey to JC Bancroft Davis, Hong Kong, Sep-tember 9, 1873, and September 12, 1873 in "M108: Despatches from U.S. Consuls in Hong Kong, 1844–1906," General Records of the Department of State, RG 59, National Archives, 1965, reel 9.

56. David H. Bailey to JC Bancroft Davis, Hong Kong, April 25, 1871, *FRUS*, 1871–72, 207–10.

57. John S. Mosby to Frederick W. Seward, Hong Kong, September 22, 1879, in "The Consul-

ate at Hong Kong," H.R. Exec. Doc. 20, 46th Cong., 2nd Sess. (January 12, 1880), 17, 21. Frederick W. Seward's handpicked investigator, a State Department employee reassigned from Japan, estimated that Bailey pocketed a mere $11,000 in fraudulently collected fees. While scholarly assessments on Bailey have varied, I am inclined to agree with Mary Roberts Coolidge, who argued that Bailey's reports were "a mosaic of falsehood and misrepresentation" and an effort to "cover up mal-administration in office by an appearance of zeal." Coolidge, *Chinese Immigration*, 50. Cf. Gyory, *Closing the Gate*, 63, 280n7.

58. See, for example, "Report of the Joint Special Committee to Investigate Chinese Immigration," S. Rep. 689, 44th Cong., 2nd Sess. (February 27, 1877). Even as investigations into Bailey's fraud were being published by Congress, his reports on how Chinese migration paths were "inbred" with "slavery" and "concubinage" were republished again, by congressional resolution: "Expatriation and Slavery in China," H.R. Exec. Doc. 60, 46th Cong., 2nd Sess. (March 12, 1880).

59. Interview of Frederick F. Low, in Aaron Augustus Sargent, "Report of the Joint Special Committee to Investigate Chinese Immigration," S. Rep. 689, 44th Cong., 2nd Sess. (February 27, 1877), 65–92; George F. Seward to Hamilton Fish, Peking, July 1, 1875, enclosing "sixteen inquiries from the senatorial Chinese investigating committee of California answered by Dr. Williams of the American legation of China," *FRUS*, 1876, 61–70; Frederick Wells Williams, *The Life and Letters of Samuel Wells Williams, LL.D., Missionary, Diplomatist, Sinologue* (New York: G. P. Putnam's, 1889), 427–31; George F. Seward, *Chinese Immigration, in Its Social and Economical Aspects* (New York: Scribner's, 1881).

60. Ulysses S. Grant, "Sixth Annual Message," December 7, 1874, in James D. Richardson, ed., *A Compilation of the Messages and Papers of the Presidents, 1789–1908* (New York: Bureau of National Literature and Art, 1908), 7:288. The Page Act is typically considered primarily in its antiprostitution aspects, but it addresses a broader range of activities: 18 Stat. 477, "An Act supplementary to the acts in relation to immigration" (March 3, 1875).

61. Democratic Party Platforms, 1876, 1880, in Gerhard Peters and John T. Woolley, "The American Presidency Project," https://www.presidency.ucsb.edu/people/other/democratic-party-platforms; Republican Party Platforms, 1876, 1880, in Peters and Woolley, "The American Presidency Project," https://www.presidency.ucsb.edu/people/other/republican-party-platforms, accessed August 15, 2019.

62. Sen. James Blaine, "Chinese Immigration," Cong. Rec., 45th Cong., 3rd Sess. (February 14, 1879), 1303.

63. "Chinese Immigration: Letter from Senator Blaine," *New York* Tribune, February 24, 1879, 5. For a detailed analysis of this debate and its importance as a turning point in Chinese exclusion from a regional issue to a nationally salient political issue, see Gyory, *Closing the Gate*, 136–168.

64. Rutherford B. Hayes, "Veto Message," March 1, 1870, in Richardson, *Compilation of the Messages and Papers of the Presidents*, 7:518.

65. In his memoir, Angell says he told Hayes and Secretary of State Evarts he would refuse to serve if "direct and formal prohibition of Chinese immigration was desired." Reassured that it was not exclusion the administration wanted, but restriction, he continued. Evarts was likely most interested in heading off pressure from exclusionists in an election year. James Burrill Angell, *The Reminiscences of James Burrill Angell* (New York: Longmans, Green, 1912), 131; Anderson, *Imperialism and Idealism*, 118–26; Yucheng Qin, *The Diplomacy of Nationalism: The Six Companies and China's Policy toward Exclusion* (Honolulu: University of Hawai'i Press, 2009), 109–13.

66. Charles I. Bevans, ed., *Treaties and Other International Agreements of the United States of America, 1776–1949* (Washington DC: Government Printing Office, 1968), 6:685–87.

67. Bevans, *Treaties and Other International Agreements of the United States of America*, 7:688–90.

68. "Republican Party Platform of 1880" and "1880 Democratic Party Platform," in Peters and Woolley, "American Presidency Project."

69. 22 Stat. 58, "An Act to Execute Certain Treaty Stipulations relating to Chinese" (May 6, 1882). On the naming distinction, see Lew-Williams, *Chinese Must Go*, 8.

70. 22 Stat. 214, chap. 376, "An Act to Regulate Immigration" (August 3, 1882). Paralleling the way the Chinese Restriction Act made the anti-Chinese regulations of Pacific states into national policy, the Immigration Act federalized Atlantic state regulations barring impoverished or diseased immigrants. Hirota, *Expelling the Poor*.

71. Lew-Williams, "Before Restriction Became Exclusion"; Lee, *At America's Gates*; Pletcher, *Diplomacy of Involvement*, 307–8.

72. LaFeber and McCormick, members of the Wisconsin school, trace the origins of this shift in thought to the 1870s but agree with Parrini and Sklar that the moment when it became consensus governing US policy was in the mid-1890s—after the Panic of 1893 and subsequent recovery of US exports seemed to demonstrate its explanatory power. Carl P. Parrini and Martin J. Sklar, "New Thinking about the Market, 1896–1904: Some American Economists on Investment and the Theory of Surplus Capital," *Journal of Economic History* 43, no. 3 (1983): 559–78; McCormick, *China Market*; LaFeber, *New Empire*.

73. Chester Arthur, "Third Annual Message," December 4, 1883, in Richardson, *Compilation of the Messages and Papers of the Presidents*, 8:175; John Russell Young to Frederick T. Frelinghuysen, Peking, October 18, 1882, *FRUS*, 1883, 129–41; Pletcher, *Diplomacy of Involvement*, 145.

74. Francis P. Knight, New-Chwang, September 30, 1873, in *CRUS*, 1874, 251.

75. *CRUS*, 1898, 1:21.

76. John Goodnow, Shanghai, December 2, 1898, in *CRUS*, 1898, 1:980.

77. John Russell Young, "New Life in China," *North American Review* 153 (1891): 421.

78. Julian Ralph, "Special Correspondence from the East: American Helplessness in China," *Harper's Weekly*, December 1, 1894, 1143.

79. "Autobiography: Book I" and "Autobiography: Book II," in Charles Alexander Tomes Papers, 1886–1951, Massachusetts Historical Society, Boston, box 5.

80. Augustine Heard Jr., "Old China and New" (typescript) (1894), 38, 42–43, 46, in Heard Family Business Records, Historical Collections, Baker Library, Harvard Business School, vol. FP-4, folder GQ-2–2.

81. "Address of Joseph C. Hendrix, President of the American Bankers' Association," in *Proceedings of the Twenty-Fourth Annual Convention of the American Bankers' Association, Held at Denver, Colorado* (New York: American Bankers' Association, 1898), 8–9.

82. The American merchant marine, decimated by the Civil War, did not begin to recover until the establishment of a "new" overseas empire after the 1898 war. Rodney P. Carlisle, *Rough Waters: Sovereignty and the American Merchant Flag* (Annapolis, MD: Naval Institute Press, 2017), 39–50, 75–77; Susan B. Carter et al., eds., *Historical Statistics of the United States: Millennial Edition Online* (New York: Cambridge University Press, 2006), Df594–605.

Appendix

1. "Of the three chief sources of statistics on the American trade, none is complete or wholly reliable." Jacques M. Downs, *The Golden Ghetto: The American Commercial Community at Canton and the Shaping of American China Policy, 1784–1844* (Bethlehem, PA: Lehigh University Press, 1997), 349.

2. Differences in calendar systems, exchange rates, units of measurement, and prices in different ports all make comparison difficult across series—even within one organization. For example, while the US customshouse year and the Canton tea trading season both ignored Gregorian niceties, they ended at different points of the calendar year, making precise comparisons within a particular year impossible.

3. Paul Lamartine Yates, *Forty Years of Foreign Trade: A Statistical Handbook with Special Reference to Primary Products and Under-developed Countries* (London: Allen and Unwin, 1959), 27.

Index

Page numbers in italics refer to figures.

"An Act to Prohibit the 'Coolie Trade' by
American Citizens in American Vessels,"
127; American role in trade, 121, 127, 130;
China traders' defense of, 124–25; Chincha Islands and, 120; Chinese citizenship issue, 128–29; coercion of workers,
122; congressional role, 125–27, 243n39;
Forbes's failed Florida plantation and,
130, 245n66; human trafficking and, 169–
70, 259n48; middle passage comparison, 116, 120–22, 125–26, 131; mutinies on
ships, 121–22; slavery and, 113–14, 116–17;
slave trade and, 116, 120–22; Southern opposition, 117–19; treatment of, 115, 170–71
India: American traders' access to, 38, 44;
exports, 25–26; opium, 16, 54, 61–62, 63,
66, 75; trade, 42–43, 58
Indiaman (ship), 243n30
Indus (ship), 208n32
Ingraham, Joseph, 196n20
Izard, Ralph, 28

jackal diplomacy, 104
Jackson, Andrew, 51, 68, 73
Jacob Jones (ship), 214n87, 214n89
Jardine, Matheson and Company, 65–66, 70
Jay, John, 19, 22, 35–38, 42
Jay Treaty (1794), 40, 62, 206nn8–9, 209n50;
Article 13 of, 38, 206n12; criticism of,
42–43; Jeffersonian Republicans and, 36;
Washington's view of, 37
Jefferson, Thomas, and Jefferson admin-
istration, 35–36, 38–41, 44–50, 63, 106,
199n21, 204n72
Jeffersonian Republicans: China trade and,
35–37, 40, 42–43, 50, 55; Jay Treaty and,
37–38; "merchant-Republicans," 37, 51,
207n18; proponents of agriculture, 39
Jenks, Jeremiah, 175
Johnson, Andrew, 144, 152, 154
Johnson, James A., 251n64, 253n95
Jones, William, 40

Kansas-Nebraska Act (1854), 109
Kearny, Lawrence, 91, 231n81
King, C. W., 85, 228nn54–55
King, Rufus, 20
Kinsman, Nathaniel, 53–54

Knox, John Jay, 165
Knox, Thomas, 162
Kossuth, Louis, 137–38

LaFeber, Walter, 261n72
Lawrence, Abbott, 87, 228n55, 229n63
Lee, Arthur, 29
Lee, Richard Henry, 20, 28, 198n12, 202n61
Leopard (ship), 45
Lewis, Meriwether, 40, 207n26
Lewis and Clark expedition, 40, 206n40
Liberator (newspaper), 82, 85–86, 91, 123
Lincoln, Abraham, and Lincoln administra-
tion, 127, 138, 145, 151, 247n15
Lincoln, Levi, 87
Linderman, Henry R., 165–66, 168
Lintin system, 66–67, 222n60
Lin Zexu, 75, 77, 79, 87, 91, 225n13
Low, Frederick F., 153, 157–59, 172

Macao, 6, 79, 93, 113, 171; Canton system
and, 2–3
Maclay, William, 28–30, 201n52
Madison, James, and Madison administra-
tion, 40; British and, 41–42, 45; China
trade and, 50–51; East India Company
(British) and, 43–44; idea of China, 36,
39; luxuries, 35; slavery issue, 24; on tariffs, 22–23, 27, 29, 201n41, 201n48
Magee, James, 7–8, 195n6
manufacturing and manufactured goods:
British, 39; in China, 50, 162, 176; domestic, 101, 137, 158, 164, 176; exports to
China, 176–77, 261n72
Marshall, Humphrey, 113–14, 117, 121, 130,
243n39
McCormick, Thomas, 159, 261n72
McDuffie, George, 69
McKeown, Adam, 115
Mitchill, Samuel L., 47
monetary policy, 12, 56, 58–60, 68–69, 71,
75, 159, 164, 165, 175–76
money: China trade, and export, 30–31, 56–
58; China traders, blamed for specie scarcity, 57–58; Comstock lode and, 165, 168,
258n42; gold standard, 164–66, 168, 172;
"Money Question," 164; silver glut and,
165–68; Spanish silver dollars (pesos), 8,